TEACHING SOCIAL STUDIES IN THE ELEMENTARY SCHOOL
The Basics for Citizenship

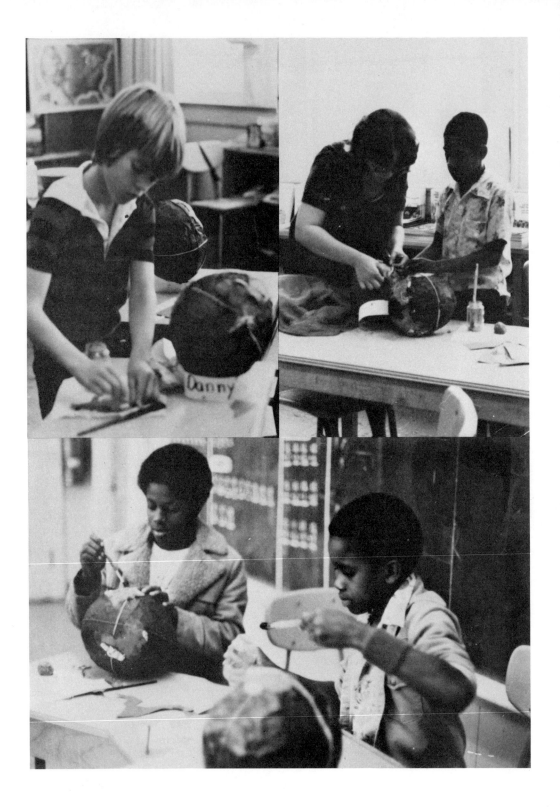

TEACHING SOCIAL STUDIES IN THE ELEMENTARY SCHOOL
The Basics for Citizenship

THEODORE KALTSOUNIS

University of Washington, Seattle

PRENTICE-HALL, INC., Englewood Cliffs, New Jersey 07632

Library of Congress Cataloging in Publication Data

KALTSOUNIS, THEODORE.
   Teaching social studies in the elementary school.

   Includes index.
   1. Social sciences—Study and teaching (Elementary)
I. Title.
LB1584.K295   372.8'3'044   78–17190
ISBN 0–13–895631–6

in my father's memory

Photographs on page ii
courtesy of Stanley Elementary School, Tacoma School District, Tacoma, Washington.
Photographs on pages 3, 47, 67, 81, 97, 111, 126, 143, 156, 177, 187, 213, 239,
247, 266, 273, 294, 325, 342, 349, and cover
courtesy of the Public Information Office, Seattle Public Schools, Seattle, Washington.
Photographs on pages 27, 301, and 311 by Kay Franks,
courtesy of the Information Department, Tacoma School District, Tacoma, Washington.
Photograph on page 37 by Mary Wilbert Smith,
courtesy of the Information Department, Tacoma School District, Tacoma, Washington.

© 1979 by PRENTICE-HALL, INC., Englewood Cliffs, New Jersey 07632

Printed in the United States of America

10 9 8 7 6 5 4 3 2 1

Prentice-Hall International, Inc., *London*
Prentice-Hall of Australia Pty. Limited, *Sydney*
Prentice-Hall of Canada, Ltd., *Toronto*
Prentice-Hall of India Private Limited, *New Delhi*
Prentice-Hall of Japan, Inc., *Tokyo*
Prentice-Hall of Southeast Asia Pte. Ltd., *Singapore*
Whitehall Books Limited, *Wellington, New Zealand*

CONTENTS

v

ACCOUNTABILITY AND THE SOCIAL STUDIES *26*

Planning and Teaching Social Studies

A SOCIAL STUDIES CURRICULUM FOR DECISION MAKING *46*

DEVELOPING CONCEPTS AND GENERALIZATIONS THROUGH INQUIRY *80*

DEALING WITH ISSUES, VALUES, AND THE VALUING PROCESS   *110*

**THE UNIT PLAN AND THE LESSON PLAN:
BRIDGING THE OLD AND THE NEW**   *142*

Instructional Resources for Social Studies

COMMUNITY RESOURCES AND CURRENT EVENTS 246

MAPS, GLOBES, AND OTHER AUDIOVISUAL AIDS 272

Special Considerations in Social Studies

GUIDELINES TO TEACHERS, ADMINISTRATORS, AND PARENTS *348*

PREFACE

This book is for practicing and prospective elementary school teachers alike. Because social studies is in a period of transition, both kinds of teacher need help bridging the gap between the so-called traditional social studies and the new, or "the new-new," social studies that emerged from the curriculum movement of the 1960s. Prospective teachers must learn to teach social studies in a way that is probably much different from how they themselves were taught, and teachers on the job must accommodate their ways of teaching social studies to new trends. In neither case is the task easy.

Of the many social studies textbooks for teachers and future teachers published in the last 15 years, most fall into one of two categories: Either they present social studies in the traditional manner, adding sections or chapters in which the new trends are simply described; or they completely neglect the traditional social studies and ask the teachers to implement programs that are totally foreign to them. In other words, the first set of books does little more than whet teachers' appetites for the new trends, whereas the second set overwhelms teachers and tends to lead many of them away from social studies. They become dissatisfied with what they have, but they feel fearful or inadequate to try one of the new programs.

This book is intended to help teachers move gradually from the old to the new social studies. It does not reject the traditional social studies but tries to transform it by incorporating the new trends: The traditional position is briefly described, then the reader is guided toward the changes. Recommended adjustments and new directions are given clear justifications. The two main features of the new social studies—conceptualization and the valuing process—are not treated merely as separate sections but permeate the entire book, influencing every component of the proposed social studies program.

The book is practical because it addresses a series of basic questions that a teacher must answer before being able to teach social studies effectively. These questions, in the order in which the chapters deal with them, are:

1. What is social studies supposed to accomplish in the elementary school and how could accountability be achieved in the various levels?
2. What should be the general area of study for each grade; for my own grade?
3. What should be the five or six unit topics that can provide a comprehensive treatment of the area of study designated for my grade?
4. What are the basic elements that could provide the basic content for each topic?
5. What is the best way to teach or deal with each one of these elements?
6. How do I relate what the children learn with their personal lives and value systems?
7. How can I develop a comprehensive plan for effectively teaching a particular topic?
8. How do I evaluate both pupil progress and the effectiveness of my program?
9. What do I do with the textbooks and how do I use other commercially available materials?
10. Where do I go for additional resources to enrich learning experiences?
11. How is social studies taught in alternative schools and programs?
12. How can I improve myself as a social studies teacher?
13. How can my school help me do well in social studies?
14. What can I do to recruit the help of parents in teaching social studies?

Chapters 1 and 2 respond to the first question by explaining why each student must develop the qualities needed to cope with mounting social conflict. Chief among these qualities are decision-making abilities. These involve the individual's knowledge as well as values.

Responding to questions 2, 3, and 4, Chapter 3 advises teachers to adhere to the traditional areas of study—family, community, city, region, nation, world. No better framework has been found. But the topics in each area must allow for its comprehensive treatment and should accommodate basic issues, especially contemporary ones. Concepts, generalizations, and issues are recommended as the structural elements of topic content, giving substance to social studies and also contributing toward developing dynamic citizens. Such content helps children (1) acquire basic knowledge about human relationships, and (2) become involved in, and develop skills useful to, coping with these human relationships.

Both chapters 4 and 5 respond to questions 5 and 6. Chapter 4 proffers the inquiry approach as the most effective method to teach concepts, generalizations, and thinking skills; Chapter 5 presents the valuing process as a model for dealing with issues and values.

In response to question 7, Chapter 6 explains how the traditional unit plan is modified to allow the teaching of concepts, generalizations, and issues through inquiry and the valuing process.

Responding to question 8, on evaluation, Chapter 7 explains why evaluation is an integral part of instruction. Diagnostic, formative, and summative evaluation of pupil progress are examined. Criteria are also provided for evaluating social studies programs.

As implied in questions 9 and 10, a variety of resources are needed to make inquiry and the valuing process work. Chapters 8 through 11 are addressed to these resources and their most effective uses.

Question 11 does not concern all teachers equally. But more and more teachers are experimenting with alternative programs. Chapter 12 deals specifically with social studies in nongraded and open school situations, in early childhood education, in schools dominated by certain ethnic or racial groups, and in programs for gifted and for physically and mentally handicapped children.

Finally, Chapter 13 is addressed to teacher self-improvement and to the kind of support and cooperation the teacher needs from the school administrator and the parents if a social studies program is to be successful.

The 13 chapters are organized in four interrelated parts. Part I (Chapters 1 and 2) examines the goals of social studies. Part II (Chapters 3–7) deals with planning and teaching social studies. Part III (Chapters 8–11) describes instructional resources and their use. Part IV (Chapters 12 and 13) deals with such special considerations as social studies for alternative schools and guidelines for teachers, administrators, and parents.

The book's format is mainly expository, with many illustrations and suggested activities to support or clarify definitions of concepts, processes, and practices. It presents the basic information about teaching social studies in the elementary school but does not dictate how this information should be imparted to students. To do so would stifle the imagination and resourcefulness of instructors, who would rather design their own method of teaching the contents of the book. However, an instructor's manual is available for those who desire specific instructions on at least one way of using the book.

It should be emphasized from the outset that teaching social studies is not a well-established process. Many questions remain unresolved, and the value of many practices has yet to be established. Thus, this book may appear at times to offer more answers than there in fact are. But there is no other way to help the practitioner. For example, it is not enough for teachers to know the advantages and disadvantages of the various models of valuing; they need a plan of action based on these models. Such plans of action are provided throughout the book without any claim that they are the best or the only ones that could be implemented.

Because, again, social studies is in transition, it is natural that there be some confusion among those teaching it. It is hoped that this book will clear up the confusion and provide a direction for a program that can make a difference—a program that can inspire both the prospective and the practicing teacher to accept change and strive for further improvement.

Goals and Objectives
of Social Studies

OBJECTIVES

Studying this chapter will enable the reader to:

1. recognize that because social studies contributes to the individual's survival and well-being, it is considered to be one of the basic subjects.
2. identify the purpose of social studies as the ability to understand and cope with human relationships.
3. justify the ability to make decisions as the ultimate objective of social studies.
4. distinguish between two types of decision making, and identify their various components and logical steps.
5. realize that the shift toward decision making necessitates dealing with values as well as with knowledge, and providing opportunities for active participation in the social arena.
6. identify both the differences and the similarities between decision making and problem solving.
7. become familiar with two major approaches to values and value conflicts and with the implications of these approaches for decision making.
8. be convinced that a social studies program based on decision making promotes a dynamic, participatory citizenship that reflects the finest of the American cultural imperatives.

WHY SHOULD SOCIAL STUDIES BE TAUGHT IN THE ELEMENTARY SCHOOL?

This is a critical period for American education. Innovations on all fronts, the civil rights movement, and national economic problems having shaken the educational equilibrium, it is no longer clear who controls the schools or what function they should serve. A report developed by the National Committee for Citizens in Education suggests that "The public has lost control of the public schools. . . . Lacking a clearly defined controlling force, education appears to be left at the mercy of numerous pressure groups, including ethnic groups, school board members, citizen advisory boards, and even the courts." [1] Throughout the nation the schools' organizational patterns, educational goals, and instructional practices have been questioned. "A new rebellion is breaking out in U.S. schools," it was stated recently in *U.S. News and World Report*.[2] State legislatures and even the U.S. Congress have been drawn into this increasingly widespread and diversely motivated debate. As the debate intensifies, the public withholds financial support from the schools, further lowering professional morale, weakening determination, and raising apprehensions about the future.

Following a period of excitement during the 1960s, social studies is in a difficult position, having become an issue in the educational debate. Not only are newly developed programs under attack, but confusion prevails regarding the essential function of social studies. The public and professionals alike are asking many questions. Does social studies imply the accumulation of knowledge that can rapidly become outdated, or should it seek to develop in individuals those personal powers (such as a positive self-concept) necessary to help them function in today's complex society? Should social studies teach conformity to the established social and political order ("my government—good or bad"), or should it expose children to societal problems and help them to critically evaluate government policies and actions, enabling them to someday contribute toward the solution of those problems and the formulation of policies? Should elementary school children spend most of their time accumulating knowledge which they may apply later or should they be provided with as many opportunities as possible to begin to develop their thinking skills? How early should children begin applying whatever knowledge they have or acquire as they grow? Should children be helped to explore their value systems so that they can become aware of what forces them to make whatever decisions they make, or should values be left entirely to the home and other agencies? Should controversies be addressed in the elementary school, or should young children be led to believe that all is well with our society and the world?

Answers to these and many more such questions are very difficult to come by in a diverse society like ours. The frustration they evoke combines with the mounting costs of education to impel the public toward rejecting new trends and demanding a return to the so-called basics—"the three Rs": reading, writing, and arithmetic. This tendency is already manifesting itself in the implementation of increasingly limited programs: Many elementary schools now pay little attention to social studies and science; and for some time music, art, and physical education have been thought superfluous and their systematic development is constantly diminishing.

But are the three Rs indeed the only basics? By way of answer we must first define "basic." A reasonable definition is at hand, and, humans being social animals, we apply it to the biological and cultural realms alike: A basic is, in the biological realm, anything that is a prerequisite to survival, and is, in the cultural realm, anything that is a prerequisite to the skills or activities useful or necessary to a society or its members. In the cultural realm reading skills are obviously essential to persons engaged in nearly any activity characteristic of a society like ours—whether it be filling a purchase order, interpreting a statute, or properly using an electric coffee maker. The utility of writing skills is the logical converse (anything to be read must first have been written), and the need to manipulate numbers is nearly as prevalent. Moreover, reading and writing, being activities inseparable from the literature of a culture, can be a source of personal enrichment. (Of course, cultural basics can affect our physical survival, both directly and indirectly: A person unable to read or to count might suffer serious harm through failure to understand a road sign or by taking more than the prescribed quantity of a drug; many if not most jobs and careers are closed to persons not proficient in the three Rs.)

Granted, then, that the three Rs are basics. But are they by our definition the only basics? It can be well argued that some individual needs are even more basic than reading, writing, and arithmetic. In our complex society survival quite often means being able to cope with one's self or to get along with others. About 50,000 persons in the United States die in automobile accidents each year not because they cannot read the road signs but because, lacking self-control, they behave in ways that cause accidents. Loneliness often directs people toward suicide. Problems of life make some desperate to the point that they harm themselves or others. Our mental institutions and prisons are filled to capacity. The fact is that people need a strong self-concept and the skills necessary to get along with themselves and others long before they need to learn how to read and write. Perhaps, indeed, children are better able to learn how to read, write, and manipulate numbers if they have developed the personal powers that help them accept themselves and successfully deal with others.

It can be forcibly argued, as it is in this book, that education must serve certain needs more basic than those served by the three Rs. The process of socialization must be guided with respect to two elements that, although analytically separable, are virtually inseparable in their effect on the person: learning the skills of interaction, and developing a proper self-concept. In the context of formal education, social studies is the domain most pertinent to these needs. Thus, although the value of the three Rs is not to be discounted, teaching them exclusively and neglecting social studies would appear to be an error detrimental to children. Children need opportunities to experience success. They need to understand themselves, their potential as human beings, and their relationships with others. They need enriching experiences that demonstrate the value of such skills as reading, writing, and arithmetic. It is interesting that although most schools concentrate on the traditional basic skills—the three Rs—they do not always appear to be very effective in developing these skills. Could it be that the more-basic processes of developing a proper self-concept and learning to socialize are not sufficiently emphasized to maximize effective learning of the three Rs?

The thesis of this chapter is that social studies is as important as, if not more important than, any other subject in the elementary school, and should be taught throughout the elementary school years as well as before and after them. The notion of the general purpose of social studies provided in the preceding paragraphs will now be further elaborated.

THE GENERAL PURPOSE OF SOCIAL STUDIES

Overall Purpose of Education and Social Studies

In view of the recent debate over social studies, it is not unusual to hear teachers and especially laypersons ask: What is social studies all about? To answer this question effectively one must first examine the purpose of education in general toward which social studies is aiming.

There are many definitions of education, each reflecting a philosophical orientation, but most can be categorized as either "traditional" or "progressive." Representing the traditional point of view, Mortimer Smith of the Council for Basic Education advocates that "education as carried on in schools must deal primarily with the intellectual training, with making young people literate in the essential fields of knowledge, with transmitting the heritage and culture of the race." [3] Although Mr. Smith acknowledges other purposes of education, such as "the social adjustment of the individual child, . . . his physical welfare, the development of his personality, and his vocational competence," these are not priority items for the school. He would rather have the family and other educational agencies deal with these aspects of education.

Theodore Brameld, a progressivist, asserts that the educative process "centers in the necessity for all kinds of human groups to learn how to transmit and how to modify the patterns, the habits and practices, the traditions and skills, that have accumulated as these organized groups have formed themselves in cultures." [4] Progressive education does not deny the importance of knowledge and intellectual training, but it also strives to make children more effective participants in the life of their society and, to the extent possible, more effective influences on the constant, pervasive changes in society. To knowledge, progressive education adds relevance. Harold Shane equates relevance with survival. "A relevant education, an education for survival," he says, "is one which introduces children and youth to participation in the tasks that they and adults confront together in the real world. . . ." [5]

The most influential proponent of progressive education was John Dewey. His theory and overall purpose of education, here explained briefly, will serve as the framework within which to place the purpose of social studies. Dewey defined education as the process of bringing newborn children into the life of the society in which they are born. [6] According to this definition newborns are outside their society because they lack the knowledge and skills necessary to participate in it. When societies were simple, the newborn were not very far from participation. The people around them were able to teach the needed knowledge and skills, by what is now called informal education.

For millennia all education was informal. But as changes in societies accelerated, social structures, resources, and relationships became more complex. The newborn were pushed farther and farther away from the life of their society, until informal education was no longer enough to confer full membership in the society. There was too much knowledge to be acquired and too many skills to be developed. Formal education became necessary. "Without such formal education," wrote Dewey, "it is not possible to transmit all the resources and achievement of a complex society." [7]

Education, therefore, derives its direction from the nature of society and the environment in which it exists and, as Shane points out, it becomes relevant. It provides young people with whatever knowledge is valued by society and assists them to develop those skills necessary for life, or survival, in that society. This does not necessarily mean conformity, of course. If a society values change, education should prepare young people to initiate change.

The purpose of education having been described, its content should be easy to prescribe: Simply identify the knowledge that ought to be transmitted and define the skills that must be developed. That is exactly what happened when societies were stable and change was rare and took minor forms. Children had to learn certain things about the physical environment; they had to learn the symbols used by society to store knowledge and to communicate ideas and feelings; they had to learn the nature of the society's institutions, its customs and proprieties. During recent times, however, changes have been so rapid and so significant that a prescriptive curriculum can become outdated before children finish school. Education must take this fact into consideration. The value of this fundamental premise of today's education will become more evident as the purpose of social studies is defined.

Social studies deals with that portion of education that has to do with human relationships. Science deals with the physical environment; music and art deal with individual esthetic expression; reading and language arts deal with the skills of communication through language; while mathematics deals with number relationships. Most human relationships take one or more of the following forms: person to person, person to group, group to group, person to institution, group to institution, and institution to institution. (With the recent emphasis on self-concept, one might add the relationship of person to self.)

Children have much to learn about human relationships. They must learn, for example, that person to person contacts are the universal fiber of every society. They must learn that people differ in many ways and that, in our society at least, every individual has the right to be different. Children must learn about the variety of formal and informal groups in society and the various functions these groups serve. They need to know the nature of our society's basic institutions, beginning with the family and ending with such large organizations as the federal government and the United Nations. Figures 1–1 and 1–2 show the overall purposes of education and the role of social studies, respectively.

Societal Conditions and Social Studies

If education is the process that assists individuals to become full participating members of a changing society, knowledge alone about the various forms of human relationships is not enough. Individuals must also develop the necessary skills and some basic values and dispositions that will govern their relationships with other people. These skills and affective elements must begin to be developed as early as possible. Children need to develop skill, for example, to participate in orderly group discussions. They should learn how to cast a ballot, how to read a map, or how to approach the various institutions in ways most effective for their purposes. They should know, for instance, how to apply for a job or how to open a bank

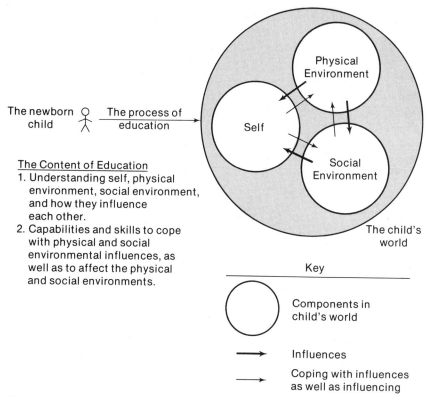

The newborn child

The process of education

The Content of Education
1. Understanding self, physical environment, social environment, and how they influence each other.
2. Capabilities and skills to cope with physical and social environmental influences, as well as to affect the physical and social environments.

The child's world

Key

Components in child's world

Influences

Coping with influences as well as influencing

Figure 1–1
The Overall Purpose of Education

account. They should know their rights as well as their responsibilities as members of a family. Children should learn to value human dignity and to respect all individuals regardless of race, color, sex, occupation, religion, ethnic origin, or place of residence.

It was implied earlier that the purpose of education changes as the society changes—with respect to its resources, its achievements, its store of knowledge. How does social change affect the purpose of social studies? Social studies is probably more affected than any other subject taught in school. This is especially true due to the tremendous changes that have taken place in human relationships during the last few years. Since World War II, throughout the world as well as throughout American society, change has assumed unprecedented proportions. The two superpowers, the United States and the Soviet Union, have for some time controlled the destiny of practically every nation in the world. The emergence of the Third World and the rise of the People's Republic of China to world prominence have shifted the balance of power. While the threat of atomic warfare has always been a foremost concern in the minds of world leaders, the threat

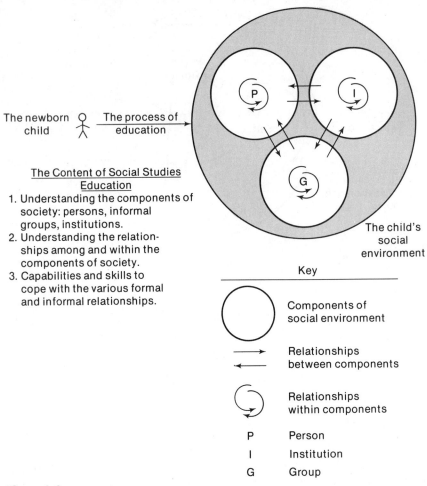

The newborn child | The process of education

The child's social environment

The Content of Social Studies Education

1. Understanding the components of society: persons, informal groups, institutions.
2. Understanding the relationships among and within the components of society.
3. Capabilities and skills to cope with the various formal and informal relationships.

Key

◯ Components of social environment

→ ← Relationships between components

↻ Relationships within components

P   Person
I   Institution
G   Group

Figure 1–2
The Overall Purpose of Social Studies

of another oil boycott by the oil-producing countries has become worrisome. While worldwide the production of food has increased, world population has increased in still-greater proportion, and there is not enough food for everyone to eat.

In this country the awakening minority groups have shaken the social equilibrium and altered perceptions of society. The civil rights movement has shown everyone that for a long time as a society we spoke one way and believed and behaved another. The black, red, brown, and yellow minorities, and women as well, angered by past and present injustices done to them, have forcefully demanded their rightful positions within the social structure. Although we have far to go, we have finally begun to recognize the pluralistic nature of our society. At the same time, the relationships

10

among management, labor, and the government have become very complex. City life has become problematic, and the federal and state governments play a larger role in the everyday affairs of citizens. Crime is rising everywhere. Our relationships with the rest of the world are rather touchy and our elected officials have difficulty deciding whether we should concentrate on domestic problems or seek to sustain our country's leadership role among the Western nations and the world.

All these changes have caused the common core of social values to diminish and have considerably increased the conflict in human relationships. With such a rapid pace of change during the last few decades, no one knows what the nature of society will be in the very near future. One thing is certain, however: Change will continue, confronting the individual with conflict and with new situations. Each person will need knowledge, skills, and the personal powers necessary to understand and adjust to change and to resolve conflict. In a world in flux such as ours, the person most capable of making sound decisions, when faced with conflict situations of any kind, is the one best equipped to cope with human relationships and to succeed in life. It is for this reason that the most recent trend in social studies has been to recognize enhanced decision-making capability as its ultimate purpose. It must be stated again, however, that the emphasis on decision making does not mean a disregard for knowledge and the variety of social and academic skills that comprised the purpose of social studies in the past. As will be demonstrated in the next section, sound decision making is impossible without knowledge and the skills necessary to acquire and apply knowledge.

THE VIABILITY OF DECISION MAKING

From Moralistic Social Studies to Decision Making

It was during the late 1960s and the '70s that decision making became a central focus in social studies. A brief sketch of the history of social studies education will trace its emergence.

Throughout nearly the entire colonial period of this nation's history, social studies was not taught as a separate subject. One reason is that what was to become the United States was then a collection of colonies, and no cohesive content of American history and society had developed yet that would comprise the domain of social studies. Whatever historical information was considered important was presented through the readers, which were mostly historical in content. The first social studies book, a geography written by Jedidiah Morse, was published in 1784. Other geographies and histories followed. Most of these books were moralistic and what we now call ethnocentric: Christian countries were better than non-Christian countries; the Western world was better than the non-Western world; and most books having been written by New Englanders, New England was treated more favorably than other parts of the country, especially the South. The first writers were Protestants and were scornful of Catholics. Once Catholics started writing books, they repaid the Protestants in kind. It was not at all unusual for such books to condemn smoking, drinking, and similar "evils." [8]

Beginning in 1892, the National Education Association, soon followed by the National Society for the Study of Education, attempted to shape the content and presentation of social studies. Their various committees and publications recommended a scope and sequence that became dominant throughout the years. The curriculum, which consisted mainly of history, geography, and civics, was determined chiefly by a scientific approach. Through the initiative of such educators as Harold Rugg, social studies attempted to be responsive to the needs of society by becoming more utilitarian.

However, social studies came to be dominated by the descriptive approach, and remained so until the late 1950s–early '60s. Social studies books described the physical characteristics of countries—borders, rivers, mountains, climate, products, exports, imports, etc.—processes such as how a bill becomes law, and events such as battles. But as colonial empires subsided and many newly independent countries came into existence, knowledge proliferated and social studies became increasingly difficult to cover. Children were studying facts that they retained only for examinations, and no longer. The descriptive approach coupled with expository presentation made social studies an unpopular subject. It was time for change.

The 1960s were exciting years for social studies. The civil rights movement brought increasing attention and a growing sense of urgency to questions of discrimination and human rights. By the mid-1960s the U.S. Congress, the president, and various federal agencies were giving much attention to such issues. And to make an impact in this area, Congress allocated a considerable amount of money to improve the teaching of social studies in the schools. Lacking a theoretical basis for improving their subject, social studies people turned to science and mathematics experts and adopted the conceptual approach to curriculum improvement.

The conceptual approach is a method of organizing facts around basic understandings. The following is an illustration from science. For a long time science education programs dealt with the description and operation of various machines. The number of machines kept increasing, however, and it was difficult to include them all in the program. Finally, science education experts recognized that most of the machines operate on the basis of very few scientific principles, and they developed programs to teach these principles and to provide opportunities to apply the principles to learn how the various machines work. For instance, if a student understands the combustion engine, it should not be difficult for him to figure out how various models of cars work; all are basically the same. Social studies experts decided to imitate the science experts and started developing programs based on the conceptual approach. For example, instead of teaching the South American countries one by one, social studies teachers can organize their common characteristics into a few basic understandings about South America. One such understanding could be the following: During recent history the military displays a tendency to interfere in the governmental affairs of South American countries.

The conceptual approach appealed to those who had complained about the deficiencies of the descriptive program. As the approach spread quickly, college professors of social sciences were pleased, because children were now learning what they considered to be the "hard stuff." Indeed, the college professors became instrumental in developing the conceptual programs: For any topic they determined the basic understandings; social studies education people would then design the ways to teach these understandings. During the 1960s nearly all publishers revised their social studies programs to reflect the conceptual approach. (This approach will be further discussed in subsequent chapters.)

There is no question that the conceptual approach, or the "new social studies," added to the respectability of social studies, generated excitement, and raised many hopes. However, implementation of the new programs revealed some points of concern. Although conceptual programs proved to be good for college-bound students, many other students found them too difficult and, in content, removed from their concerns. Many educators felt that although the social sciences are valuable sources of knowledge, social studies, especially in the elementary school, ought to familiarize students with principles and skills that are immediately practical in the society. Not all students will go to college, but all will have to function in society. For example, not all students can, or should, systematically study political science, but they all need to know how government affects them and how they can influence government.

Contemporary society is not the neatest place to live in: Human relationships are plagued by prejudice, narrow interests, alienation, lack of compassion, hypocrisy and self-deception, and disregard for human dignity and human rights. Society's problems are significant, and in a democracy social responsibility is ultimately the individual's. Thus, children need not only to acquire knowledge directed to an understanding of these problems; they also must develop the requisite skills for resolving them. During the late 1960s, then, social studies education moved, not away from the conceptual approach but through it, toward teaching decision making. The new social studies became the "new-new" social studies.

The Nature of Decision Making

Decision making requires no single skill but a broad array of capabilities. Sound decisions require knowledge. Ill-informed decisions are impulsive decisions, and are not the characteristic of an educated person. Some decisions can in fact be made on the basis of knowledge alone: Once we have the knowledge, our decision has virtually been made for us. For example, from past experience we know what is the best location for a school: in a place centrally located to the population it will serve and free of such hazards as ponds, dumps, and the like. Not all decisions, however, are dictated by knowledge alone. For example, what is the best way to stop the rise of crime? If knowledge were enough, society would have arrived at a workable solution to this problem. Instead, none of many proposed solutions appears workable or satisfactory to everyone.

There are, then, two types of decisions: those for which knowledge is enough, and those for which it is not enough. Human relationships abound with decisions of the second type. To make such decisions, individuals rely as much as possible on knowledge, but must ultimately resort to their value systems. Because value systems vary among individuals and among groups, so do decisions. For example, as a remedy to the rising crime rate a person with a conservative value system might favor severe punishment of criminals, whereas a person with a more liberal set of values might favor rehabilitation of the criminal.

Decisions, whether based on knowledge alone or on knowledge and values combined, can be made effectively only after a number of related skills have been developed. The skills applicable to knowledge, often called critical thinking skills, involve inquiry; as enumerated by Dewey, they include discovering a problem, gathering and analyzing information, forming and testing hypotheses, and reaching conclusions.[9] The skills, on the other hand, applicable to values are subsumed under the valuing process. Values develop in many ways and contexts: They develop gradually or as a result of emotionally meaningful experiences; they develop in school as well as outside the school. The valuing process can also make individuals aware of their own values. Through value clarification, exploration of feelings, value assessment, and conflict resolution, individuals can identify and project their values, and can also modify them or develop new ones.

The following is an illustration of how inquiry and valuing can affect making a decision that involves both knowledge and values. An elementary school youngster—a sixth grader—was approached by a teenager who tried to persuade him to try marijuana. Though the teenager was persuasive, the youngster was reluctant, because he had just seen a film about the hazards of taking drugs. He decided to think it over. As he walked away he wondered who was right, the film or the teenager. In the school library he read many of the materials set aside in a special section, "Know More about Drugs." He also looked into some magazines that adults usually read and raised many questions with his teacher. All of this was inquiry.

From what this child read and heard, he was convinced that in general drugs are bad. The evidence on marijuana, however, was not that convincing. A number of articles concluded that marijuana is hazardous; others, especially those in the adult magazines, said that marijuana is no worse than the cigarettes his father smokes or the liquor both of his parents drink. The knowledge he accumulated through his inquiry was not enough to help him make up his mind. His dilemma remained: Should he or should he not accept the teenager's offer?

Finally he asked himself some questions that touched upon his values. What if he smoked marijuana? Will he eventually get into the habit and take other drugs that he knows are bad? He definitely did not want that to happen. What if his parents found out? He knows they are dead set against marijuana. Is it worth it to disobey his parents? What will other sixth graders think if they find out that he refused to take marijuana? Will they think he "chickened out" or will they think he was brave? In all these questions the sixth grader examined his inner world to find out what was important to him and what was not. He wanted to determine what he was sacrificing and what he was gaining by accepting or rejecting the teenager's offer. Raising such questions and weighing the consequences of alternative actions involved the youngster in the valuing process. Out of this process a decision would emerge that would strengthen some values and probably weaken others.

Once knowledge has been gathered through inquiry and feelings and values have been explored, through the valuing process, the next step is the decision. From the alternatives each person chooses the course of action that feels most comfortable. The person then justifies this decision according to how well its consequences agree with both the information available and the person's value system. Needless to say, decisions that involve values are more difficult and more controversial than those that involve knowledge alone, such decisions being virtually dictated by the facts.

The final step in decision making is action. Without action, a decision made on the basis of knowledge alone is merely an intellectual exercise. On the other hand, if a choice must be made among controversial alternatives, the anticipation of action will influence which decision is made. Figure 1–3 shows the two types of decision making in diagrammatic form.

There is in fact a term for the decision-making process when it omits the final step, action. As taught and practiced in the schools it is called problem solving.

Figure 1–3
Two Types of Decision Making

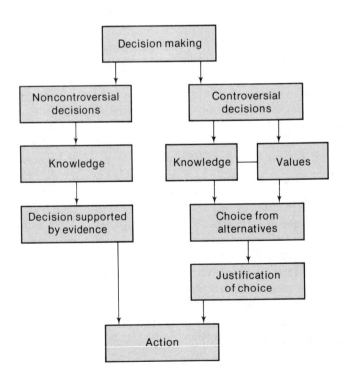

Problem Solving and Decision Making

Decision making and problem solving are similar processes, the main differences being that problem solving, at least as applied in schools, stops short of action and has usually avoided controversy by avoiding, or skirting, value-laden issues. Problem solving deals with questions that can be resolved with evidence alone; the individual has only to substantiate by the facts that a solution is correct. The steps of problem solving are identical to the critical thinking employed in the process of inquiry:

1. Initial stage, in which the person becomes aware of a problem requiring a solution.
2. Data gathering, in which the person becomes familiar with the problem and seeks information for solution.
3. Hypothesis formation, in which the person formulates tentative solutions.
4. Hypothesis testing, in which solutions are tested.
5. Reaching conclusions, in which the solution that is proven correct by the facts is chosen.

But what of the problems for which information alone cannot produce a clear solution? For such problems the person's value system becomes instrumental, which means controversy is invited. For this reason the schools had avoided value-laden issues in the past. To deal with controversial problems the decision-making approach was developed. But this approach not only addresses controversy, it also, by definition, requires action. In problem solving, students were asked to verbalize solutions but were not expected to carry them out. The recent ascendency of decision making in the schools should not, however, be used to discredit problem solving. Each is an important process: Decision making can demonstrate the complexity of problems, the crucial role that values play, and the need for action; problem solving, by contrast, enables teachers and students to concentrate on the pure lineaments of the inquiry process, which, after all, is integral to decision making as well. Moreover, a program based solely on controversy might appear to be too exclusively negative. A good social studies program, then, should include both problem solving and decision making.

Moral Education and Decision Making

Moral education is here broadly defined as that part of education that is concerned with the nature of values and with their application in making decisions. As such, moral education is very much related to decision making, and is a crucial aspect of contemporary social studies, insofar as such programs deal with value-related situations. The area of moral education has not yet been crystallized. There are differing points of view as to how values influence decision making. We shall now examine the two currently most prominent approaches.

THE RATHS, HARMIN, AND SIMON APPROACH   Louis E. Raths, Merrill Harmin, and Sidney B. Simon assert that most difficulties in making decisions are caused by unclarified value systems: "Persons with unclear values lack direction for their lives, lack criteria for choosing what to do with their time, their energy, their very being." [10] A process of value clarification should therefore assist children to make sound decisions in their everyday lives. As their values become clarified children will become more purposeful and productive, sharper critical thinkers, and better able to relate with each other.

Rather than advocating any particular set of values, Raths, Harmin, and Simon see values as general guides to behavior that grow out of each person's experiences. "Persons have experiences; they grow and learn. Out of experiences may come certain general guides to behavior. These guides tend to give direction to life and may be called values. Our values show what we tend to do with our limited time and energy." [11] In making sound decisions, therefore, individuals need to clarify their values, but these values need not conform to any predetermined framework: "Whatever values one obtains should work as effectively as possible to relate one to his world in a satisfying and intelligent way." [12]

Raths, Harmin, and Simon propose a model, called the valuing process, to be used to clarify existing values, to develop new ones, or to make decisions. The model consists of seven steps:

CHOOSING	(1)	freely
	(2)	from alternatives
	(3)	after thoughtful consideration of the consequences of each alternative
PRIZING	(4)	cherishing, being happy with the choice
	(5)	willing to affirm the choice publicly
ACTING	(6)	doing something with the choice
	(7)	repeatedly, in some pattern of life [13]

According to Raths, Harmin, and Simon, any decision that fits the model is a sound decision. Moreover, any values that result from use of the model are acceptable even if the values of two or more individuals conflict. Consistency of values among individuals would require a structured system of values, or universal values. Because Raths, Harmin, and Simon, claiming that their approach is value-free, do not advocate a structured value system, they have been criticized. John S. Stewart, for example, pointed out that the process of value clarification deals with *what* individuals value, but not with *why* they do so.[14] In Lawrence Kohlberg's approach it is "why" that is more important.

THE KOHLBERG COGNITIVE-DEVELOPMENTAL APPROACH   Lawrence Kohlberg has developed a cognitive-developmental approach to moral education. As do most contemporary approaches to moral education, Kohlberg's approach concentrates on the method the individual applies to make decisions in conflict situations. Kohlberg asserts that persons in conflict situations are concerned about the following 10 "universal moral values or issues," as he calls them: punishment, property, roles and concerns of affection, roles and concerns of authority, law, life, liberty, distributive justice, truth, and sex. "A moral choice," he writes, "involves choosing between two (or more) of these values as they *conflict* in concrete situations of choice." [15]

Reasoning is a key element, according to Kohlberg, in the making of moral choices. The individual chooses one of two or more conflicting values on the basis of a number of reasons that are hierarchically arranged as the six stages of moral reasoning. They range from the attempt to avoid punishment (the lowest stage in the hierarchy) to a strong desire to uphold what the individual considers high ethical principles that apply to all people (the highest stage in the hierarchy). Kohlberg believes that an individual can be educated to move from the lowest to the highest stages of moral reasoning. In simplified form the six stages are as follows:

Stage 1:   Individuals make decisions that are dictated by blind obedience to authority or a desire to avoid punishment. Example: Children decide to tell the truth because they know they will be punished if caught doing otherwise.

Stage 2:   Individuals make decisions on the basis of what satisfies their own needs. Sometimes they will make decisions that help others if they expect something in return. Example: A child decides to share crayons with another child because it is the only way to use that child's soccer ball during recess.

Stage 3:   Individuals make decisions that would please others and earn their approval. Example: Children who would rather play than do homework nevertheless decide to do their homework in order to please their parents and earn praise from them.

Stage 4:   Individuals decide to behave in a certain way because they feel it is their duty to do so in order to show respect for authority and demonstrate obedience to the rules. Example: Though it rains hard and there are no cars in sight, a child waits for the light to change to green before crossing.

Stage 5:   Individuals decide to act according to a system of rules because they agree that the rules are good and know that almost everyone around them approves of them. However, individuals reserve the right to work to change the rules if they think they no longer serve a good purpose. Example: All children in a particular class

for a long time thought that it was a good rule to take off their
hats while in the classroom. Some children joined the class whose
subculture valued the wearing of a hat at all times. A child
decides to work to change the rule and make optional the wearing
of a hat in the classroom.

Stage 6: Individuals make decisions on the basis of what they consider to
be high ethical principles that appear to them to be consistent
with each other and valid at all times and in all situations and
places. They represent justice in terms of reciprocity, equality,
and human rights. It is the application of the golden rule. Example:
Children decide not to steal something because they do not
want anyone to steal their own things. They also realize that
others would not like to have their own things stolen.[16]

In defining Kohlberg's concept of a moral dilemma, Ronald Galbraith and Thomas Jones pointed out that "a good moral dilemma should
have three characteristics. It should present a real conflict for the central
character; it should include a number of moral issues for consideration;
and it should generate differences of opinion among students about the
appropriate response to the situation." [17] Thus, what Kohlberg calls a moral
dilemma resembles those social studies decision-making situations that cannot be resolved without reference to the individual's value system; in both
cases the individual is faced with a number of alternatives and whatever
decision is made is justified by the individual's value system. Kohlberg
simply asserts that each individual's value system fits some stage of the
hierarchy. It is the function of the school to assist children to move toward
higher stages and, therefore, toward higher qualities of values.

Implications of the Two Approaches
for Decision Making

It is obvious that both approaches—that of Raths, Harmin, and Simon
and that of Kohlberg—deal with the task of choosing among alternatives
in situations involving conflict. Both are concerned with the individual's
ability to distinguish between right and wrong. Furthermore, both approaches assert that the quality of the individual's decisions—and consequently the quality of the person's behavior—rests on the values applied.
So far the two approaches are in agreement, and agree also with the decision-making skills needed in social studies. Ultimately, however, the two
approaches differ, as do their implications for social studies. Should decisions in social studies be made (as the value-clarification approach advocates) on the basis of clarified values, regardless of what they are? Or
should decisions be made on the basis of predetermined values that are
considered to be of higher quality as reflected in Kohlberg's stages of moral
reasoning?

Value clarification is clearly a useful method to be applied in the class-room, as Kohlberg agrees: "Like value clarification, the cognitive-developmental approach to moral education stresses open or socratic peer discussion of value dilemmas." [18] However, value clarification in the schools cannot be completely value-free, because society—any society—can survive only if its core of common values is sustained. The Raths, Harmin, and Simon approach to moral education must therefore be modified in practice to include assessment and clarification of those values and value-laden situations that involve the fundamental principles of our society. These principles, intended to protect everyone's human rights, are expressed in our Declaration of Independence, the U.S. Constitution, and the Bill of Rights.

Kohlberg's cognitive-developmental approach is not without its critics, who find fault with his hierarchical arrangement of stages, with his method of classifying people in these stages, or with how individuals are thought to move from one stage to the next. There is no question, however, that the requirements of "good citizenship" in our society coincide with Kohlberg's fifth and sixth stages of cognitive development. Children should be provided with opportunities to discuss these principles and, through value clarification, find out how much they agree or disagree with them and analyze why.

Teachers and school districts may choose to experiment with either of the two approaches but to adopt either exclusively and system wide might be a mistake. Neither has been developed or tested to justify such a step. Rather, guided by the objectives of social studies, teachers should take from each whatever appears useful in encouraging children to make decisions that promote the common good.

Cultural Imperatives, Citizenship, and Decision Making

For more than 10 years a method of assessing educational outcomes has been sought. This effort, presently carried out by the National Assessment of Educational Progress (NAEP), was originally supported by the Carnegie Corporation and is now under the auspices of the Education Commission of the States, an organization set up by 47 states and territories to deal with educational efforts and problems.

Before educational performance can be assessed, the objectives of education must be stated. Social studies objectives were divided into two categories: those for citizenship and those for social studies—although social studies experts usually perceive social studies and citizenship objectives as being linked. However, as Jean Fair wrote, "the two sets of NAEP objectives can be viewed as complementary and in some respects overlapping." [19]

Following are the broad citizenship and social studies objectives as developed by the NAEP project:

CITIZENSHIP OBJECTIVES

I.   Show concern for the well-being and dignity of others.
II. Support just law and the rights of all individuals.
III. Know the main structure and functions of their governments.
IV. Participate in democratic civic improvement.
V.   Understand important world, national, and local civic problems.
VI. Approach civic decisions rationally.
VII. Help and respect their own families.

SOCIAL STUDIES OBJECTIVES—13-YEAR-OLDS

I.   Develop a knowledge base for understanding the relationships between human beings and their social and physical environment.
II. Develop an understanding of the origins and interrelationships of beliefs, values, and behavior patterns.
III. Develop the competencies to acquire, organize, and evaluate information for purposes of solving problems and clarifying issues.
IV. Develop the human relations skills necessary to communicate and work with others.
V.   Develop a positive self-concept, build self-esteem, and move toward self-actualization.
VI. Develop and demonstrate a commitment to the right of self-determination for all human beings and a willingness to take rational action in support of means for securing and preserving human rights.[20]

That the two sets of objectives overlap is obvious, as it is that the NAEP citizenship and social studies objectives reflect the fundamental values of the American heritage: knowledge, the dignity of the individual, equality for all, the rule of reason in making decisions, and the development of democratic skills and attitudes through active involvement in the everyday life of society.

As in any social system, practice often falls short of the ideal. The greater the difference between the two, the larger the corrective role that the individual must take. Today, not only the quality but indeed the survival of our way of life depend on a strong and true commitment by our citizens to freedom and justice for all. They must understand and accept differences among themselves and reason together to resolve problems; they must know how to judge situations by the facts, to avoid the traps of demagogy and excessive emotionalism.

Citizenship and social studies objectives, therefore, reflect the need to perpetuate the cultural imperatives if our system is to survive. Decision making also reflects the cultural imperatives: It values knowledge and the rational process; it values the careful examination of values; its ultimate objective is the just resolution of problems or conflicts, with equal respect for individual dignity and the general welfare. Citizenship education, the cultural imperatives, and decision making all require the individual's active rational involvement. One may say that a social studies program oriented toward decision making is a truly patriotic program.

SUMMARY

This chapter discusses the importance of social studies in the elementary school in view of the current emphasis on the basic skills—those skills needed for survival in today's world. It is argued that, with respect to survival, the knowledge and skills provided by contemporary social studies are just as basic as, if not more basic than, the three Rs.

The purpose of social studies is defined within the context of the overall purpose of education, which is to provide the knowledge and skills needed to cope with given physical and social environments. Social studies concentrates on those bodies of knowledge and those skills needed to cope with the social environment and with human relationships. Because human relationships today are characterized by conflict and the need to choose among alternatives, the main goal of social studies is to develop the individual's ability to make decisions.

Decision making implies the use of reasoning, which in turn requires knowledge. Some decisions can be made on the basis of knowledge alone, but most require use of the individual's value system. Because knowledge and the individual's values are so basic in decision making, social studies attempts to provide learners with those skills needed to acquire and use knowledge, to assess social values, and to clarify their own values.

The final step in decision making is action. Social studies students are given opportunities to carry out their individual decisions. Thus, social studies deals not only with the concepts and generalizations of a particular topic, but with its relevant issues of action as well. It is through such issues that the learner is given challenging situations in which to practice decision making.

Social studies, then, is viewed as a way to good citizenship. Good citizenship is perceived not as conformity, but as effective participation in the affairs of society. It is a dynamic citizenship that reflects our fundamental cultural imperatives. Failure to develop good citizenship could be devastating for the individual and the society alike.

ACTIVITIES

1. Design a simple questionnaire and survey a number of adults to assess their satisfaction with public education. What are some of their complaints? What are their stands on the controversial questions listed at the beginning of the chapter?

2. Search in the literature for a definition of basic education and identify its components. Notice and discuss the differences between this definition and the one provided in this chapter.
3. Reflect on a major decision you have made in your life and outline the steps you followed. Compare the steps you took in your decision making with those in the model in Figure 1–3. What similarities do you notice? What differences, and why?
4. Prepare a list of the major problems in our society. Discuss these problems in class and identify things the children may be able to do to contribute to their solution.
5. Ask your instructor for a mixed list of questions, some of which can be resolved with available data alone and some that cannot be, and separate them.
6. List the characteristics of a "good American." Have a class discussion on whether a social studies program based on decision making can develop these characteristics.

NOTES

1. "The Public Has Lost Control—Who Shall Govern the Schools?" *Phi Delta Kappan,* 56 (January 1975), 375.
2. "Parents vs. Educators: Battle Over What's Taught in Schools," *U.S. News and World Report,* July 19, 1976, 38–39.
3. Mortimer Smith, "Fundamental Differences Do Exist," in Paul Woodring and John Scanlon, eds., *American Education Today* (New York: McGraw-Hill, 1963), p. 28.
4. Theodore Brameld, *Education as Power* (New York: Holt, Rinehart & Winston, 1965), p. 12.
5. Harold G. Shane, "The Rediscovery of Purpose in Education," in Theodore W. Hipple, ed., *Crucial Issues in Contemporary Education* (Pacific Palisades, Calif.: Goodyear, 1973), p. 12.
6. John Dewey, *Democracy and Education* (New York: Macmillan, 1916), p. 3.
7. Ibid., p. 9.
8. John Nietz, *Old Textbooks* (Pittsburgh: University of Pittsburgh Press, 1961).
9. John Dewey, *Democracy and Education.*
10. Louis E. Raths, Merrill Harmin, and Sidney B. Simon, *Values and Teaching* (Columbus, Ohio: Charles E. Merrill, 1966), p. 12.
11. Ibid., p. 27.
12. Ibid., p. 28.
13. Ibid., p. 30.
14. John S. Stewart, "Clarifying Values Clarification: A Critique," *Phi Delta Kappan,* 56 (June 1975), 684.
15. Lawrence Kohlberg, "The Cognitive-Developmental Approach to Moral Education," *Phi Delta Kappan,* 56 (June 1975), 672.
16. Adapted from Lawrence Kohlberg and Elliot Turiel, "Moral Development and Moral Education," in G. Lesser, ed., *Psychology and Educational Practice* (Chicago: Scott, Foresman, 1971), pp. 415–16.
17. Ronald E. Galbraith and Thomas M. Jones, "Teaching Strategies for Moral Dilemmas," *Social Education,* 39 (January 1975), 16–22.

18. Lawrence Kohlberg, "The Cognitive-Developmental Approach to Moral Education," p. 673.

19. Jean Fair, "What Is National Assessment and What Does It Say to Us?" *Social Education*, 38 (May 1974), 400.

20. Jean Fair, ed., *National Assessment and Social Studies Education* (Washington, D.C.: National Council for the Social Studies, 1975), pp. 101–3.

OBJECTIVES

Studying this chapter will enable the reader to:

1. define the term "accountability" as used in educational circles today and articulate the arguments for and against accountability.
2. accept accountability as a desirable trend and recognize the role that the instructional objectives play in accountability.
3. recognize that accountability is difficult in social studies because many objectives cannot be reduced to behaviors that can be developed through intervention of a short duration.
4. accept and practice the idea of behavioral objectives, but not at the sacrifice of important long-range objectives.
5. classify behavioral or instructional objectives into five different types and distinguish between content and process objectives.
6. value content as well as process objectives and acquire skill in developing such objectives.
7. list in a logical sequence the steps by which a school faculty or committee may develop sound instructional objectives for a particular school.

ACCOUNTABILITY
AND THE SOCIAL STUDIES

Accountability has become a household word in today's educational circles. It means that an enterprise (teaching, in this case) is judged on the basis of the quality of its product (in this case, the student). Despite the inherent problems in implementing accountability, the concept appeals to friends as well as critics of education. As Myron Lieberman states, "the underlying issue is not whether to have accountability, but what kind of accountability will prevail."[1] Stephen Barro summarizes the trends that brought accountability to the forefront:

1. the new federally stimulated emphasis on evaluation of school systems and their programs;
2. the growing tendencies to look at educational enterprises in terms of cost effectiveness;
3. increasing concentration on education for the disadvantaged as a priority area of responsibility for the schools; and
4. the movement to make school systems more directly responsive to their clientele and communities, either by establishing decentralized community control or by introducing consumer choice through a voucher scheme.[2]

Irving Morrissett sees the reasons for accountability from a somewhat different perspective:

Despite the innovations and the spending, there is a widespread feeling that education is still dismally short of our hopes and requirements. Our youth are generally unenthusiastic about their schools and are plagued by doubts and confusion concerning careers, values, and both domestic and international society.[3]

Accountability takes place at two levels of different scope. The narrower of the two concentrates on the teacher's responsibility: Is the task for which the teacher was hired being performed? The broader scope of accountability applies to the totality of the school, the district, or the state system of education: Is each performing according to predetermined objectives? Accountability at the teacher level is controversial, and teachers' organizations oppose it.

It stresses the output of the teacher in terms of pupil achievement, but it does not account for the multitude of variables found in any teaching situation. . . . No allowances are made for pupil ability, parental education, or the wealth of the school district, all of which influence the success of the teaching.[4]

Furthermore, accountability of the teacher often leads to the undesirable practice of teaching to the test. The broader concept of accountability seems less controversial, less threatening, and consequently more desirable.

In the context of social studies, accountability presents a number of more specific problems. The concept assumes that educational objectives can be reduced to measurable, quantifiable behaviors. However, the extent to which this can be done varies from one subject to another. Measurement is no problem, for instance, in such subjects as reading and arithmetic; the skills involved can be easily defined and ordered in a sequence. There are few such skills in social studies, but social studies usually goes beyond this. Loyalty to one's country, for instance, cannot be taught and measured as spelling or the multiplication tables are.

Pressures for accountability force teachers and schools to concentrate on those subjects they can measure and to neglect those they cannot. (This pressure is perhaps one of the main reasons why the elementary schools place so much emphasis on the three Rs.) "But to say that for a particular child it is more desirable in a particular year," argues Donald Robinson, "to seek to improve his measurable reading skills than to strengthen his self-concept and his ability to relate to others is open to question. . . ."[5]

Yet the problems posed by accountability are no excuse to shun the issue. All educators must pay attention to what they do and try to assess their effectiveness. If the function of social studies teachers is to help children understand and cope with human relationships, how successful are we in this endeavor? Some claim that if social studies had not been taught at all during the last 50 years, society might be better off today. The trend of accountability, however controversial, steers us in the right direction. Says Robinson:

> The debate over accountability and its several manifestations—performance contracting, merit salaries, the voucher plan, etc.—is bound to help many schoolmen think more precisely about what their goals are, how they can be achieved, and how we can measure ourselves about the degree to which they have been achieved.[6]

How can Robinson's advice be followed in social studies? This chapter will attempt to answer this question.

NEED FOR CLARITY IN INSTRUCTIONAL OBJECTIVES

"Instructional objectives" is a very precise term but one that must be explicitly understood if clearly defined objectives are to be formulated. Instructional objectives are not to be confused with the educational goals of a school system, the broad goals of a subject, teacher objectives, or a list of content specifics. Broad educational objectives (for example, "To make children sensitive to the needs of other people") are too general to provide direction for instruction, as are the goals of a particular subject. Teacher objectives (for example, "To list on the board the causes of the American Revolution" or "To teach the causes of the American Revolution") are tasks the teacher intends to perform and are not addressed directly to changes in the learner's behavior. Lists of content specifics are not objectives at all. What, then, are instructional objectives?

Unlike broad educational goals, instructional objectives are specific. Their attainment (or lack of it) can be determined through the student's behavior, sometimes immediately and sometimes only after much time has passed. Instructional objectives manifest themselves in some kind of activity of the student, whereas teacher objectives or lists of content specifics do not necessarily involve the learner. Examples of instructional objectives are:

1. The learner will be able to state three causes of the American Revolution.
2. A learner attempting to resolve a social problem will tend to consider more than one solution.
3. A child making a decision is able to give at least two specific reasons to justify the choice.
4. The child will be able to give at least two reasons why most large cities are near waterways.

The difference between instructional objectives and other types of objectives should be clear. Yet instruction in social studies has generally suffered in the past from reliance on broad, often vague objectives. The value of instructional objectives, with their specificity and clarity, cannot be overstated. As Cecil Clark points out, instructional objectives usually produce the following desirable results:

1. The teacher will have a method by which to measure at least partially, important objectives not measured in the past.
2. The teacher and the student will have greater visible evidence that the objectives have been achieved.
3. The student will experience considerably more freedom in achieving an objective.
4. The student will feel greater focus and direction on what is important, on what to study for, and on what he will be evaluated [on].
5. In the long run, both the teacher and the student will save time and energy.
6. The student will participate more in his own instruction.
7. The teacher will feel greater security with this more direct evidence of "teaching effectiveness." [7]

BEHAVIORAL OBJECTIVES IN SOCIAL STUDIES

The best-known advocate of behavioral objectives is Robert F. Mager, whose ideas appeared, in 1962, in *Preparing Instructional Objectives.*[8] According to Mager, a behavioral objective "describes a desired state in the learner. We . . . know that we have successfully achieved our objective when the learner can demonstrate his arrival at this state."[9]

How a behavioral objective is stated makes a difference. Most important is that the intent of the writer of the objective—the desired outcome—be clearly stated. In Mager's experience the best way to state objectives clearly is to follow three steps:

> First, identify the terminal behavior by name; we can specify the kind of behavior which will be accepted as evidence that the learner has achieved the objective.
>
> Second, try to further define the desired behavior by describing the important conditions under which the behavior will be expected to occur.
>
> Third, specify the criteria of acceptable performance by describing how well the learner must perform to be considered acceptable.[10]

For example, a behavioral objective on wheat growing, stated according to Mager's specifications, would read as follows:

> Given a map of the United States showing the various climatic patterns throughout the country, the learner will be able to name at least three states which are among the major producers of wheat.

The terminal behavior in this objective is: "to identify by name . . . wheat producing states." The conditions under which the behavior is expected to occur are: "When a map of the United States showing the various climatic conditions is given to the learner." The criterion of acceptable performance is "to name at least three states which are among the major producers of wheat."

Behavioral objectives and instructional objectives are virtually identical. Yet many teachers and other professionals give behavioral objectives a more precise meaning than they give to instructional objectives. Behavioral objectives are perceived to deal with the trivial, to the neglect of important instructional opportunities. As Benjamin Cox observed, for example, "Critics Eisner and Haberman believe that only the simplest of aspects of instruction are readily stated in behavioral terms. The dynamics of classroom interaction are much too complex and reflect too many affective considerations to be predicted by specific behavioral objectives."[11]

The emphasis on behavioral objectives emerged as a movement and it appears to have been a valid development. It provided clearer objectives than ever before, gave direction to instruction, and made evaluation operational. But behavioral objectives can be, and have been, carried to extremes, which can have a restrictive effect. To avoid such restrictiveness, objectives must be divided into two categories, short range and long range. Short-range objectives are specific and their achievement can be determined in specific situations immediately after instruction. (Two examples are: (1) After this lesson students will be able to identify which articles in last Sunday's paper represent factual reporting and which ones represent opinions. (2) After this lesson the children will be able to list five ways of showing sensitivity to a newcomer in the neighborhood.)

Long-range objectives, although they cannot be measured immediately after instruction, are equally important, because they often represent more than can be achieved through a series of precise behavioral objectives. For example, showing sensitivity toward new neighbors takes much more than relevant knowledge or specific skills. This objective cannot usually be achieved quickly. Eventually, however, the child's behavior might give evidence that the objective has been achieved or at least has been approached. Short-range objectives are what Benjamin Bloom, J. Thomas Hastings, and George Madaus call formative objectives; long-range objectives are called summative objectives.[12] A good social studies program should include both types of objective, to avoid the pitfalls that critics attribute to short-range objectives.

Whether objectives are short- or long-range, and precisely or imprecisely measurable, they should be so stated that the expected outcome is not in doubt. Ambiguous terms should be avoided. The left column below lists typical ambiguous terms, the right column lists more precise terms for expected outcomes.

TO BE AVOIDED	PREFERABLE
To know	To describe
To appreciate	To list
To show an interest in	To define
To comprehend	To distinguish
To become aware of	To outline
To learn	To clarify one's feelings
To be able to make decisions	To give examples of
To understand	To paraphrase
To become sensitive to	To predict
To demonstrate belief in	To recognize
To show concern for	To put into one's own words
To show commitment in	To compare
To think critically	To contrast
To evaluate the logical consistency of	To choose
To evaluate the adequacy of	To justify
To accept	To complete

The utility of behavioral objectives in social studies is beyond question, for such objectives reduce the vagueness that prevailed in the past. However, behavioral objectives should not be allowed to trivialize social studies by dwelling only on what can be immediately observed and measured. Nor do behavioral objectives always have to be written in the formal way advocated by Mager, above. As Mager himself wrote:

> But though each of these items might help an objective to be more specific, it will not be necessary to include all three in each objective. The object is to write objectives that communicate; the characteristics described above are merely offered as guides to help you to know when you have done so. You do not work on an objective until it demonstrates the above characteristics; rather, you work on it until it clearly communicates one of your intended educational outcomes—and you write as many statements as are needed to describe all your intended outcomes.[13]

TYPES OF INSTRUCTIONAL OBJECTIVES

Traditional social studies, directed as it was to transmitting knowledge, stressed only objectives that tended to increase the student's knowledge. Social studies today, however, must be adapted to a world in which change and conflict are ever present. As we have seen, coping with change and conflict requires more than knowledge alone; also needed is the ability to make decisions and act upon them with full knowledge of their consequences. To do so requires in turn the ability to clarify personal values and make lasting commitments. Furthermore, getting along with other people requires certain socially acceptable skills and behaviors.

Thus it is that decision making is now the ultimate goal in social studies. Accordingly there are ancillary social studies objectives—five in number: (1) knowledge; (2) social values; (3) intellectual or critical thinking skills; (4) value clarification; and (5) social skills. Each of these objectives can be classified into one of two categories: content and process. Knowledge objectives and social values objectives are content objectives. The first represent the body of knowledge considered worth transmitting. Social values objectives represent the kinds of commitments the society wants its youth to develop. These are expressed in the Declaration of Independence, the Constitution, and the Bill of Rights. Is social studies, then, a form of indoctrination? No. But students are made to confront our system's traditional, core values. Such values are usually presented as concrete issues for students to assess; they may accept, modify, or even reject those values. Values objectives are a more recent emphasis, following a period of emphasis on the value-free valuing method, which was not concerned with the development of any specific set of values.

Intellectual skills, value-clarification skills, and social skills are processes. Intellectual skills are those used in acquiring and applying knowledge. In social studies three ways of classifying intellectual skills are most commonly used: that of Benjamin Bloom [14] and his associates, that of J. P. Guilford,[15] and that of Hilda Taba.[16] In all three schemata, skills are arrayed in a hierarchy from simplest to the most complex.

Bloom et al. posit six major categories of skills: (1) knowledge, (2) comprehension, (3) application, (4) analysis, (5) synthesis, and (6) evaluation. *Knowledge* includes such behaviors as recalling specific facts, terminology, events, and relationships. *Comprehension* implies the ability to translate one form of communication into another. *Application* means the ability to apply what has been learned to new problem situations. *Analysis* implies the ability to discover the parts and the principles of organization of a communication or subject. *Synthesis* (of a higher mental level) implies the ability to compose the parts of a communication into a whole. *Evaluation* (which demands yet more intellectual involvement) refers to the ability to make judgments by internal and external criteria.

In his theory of mental operations, Guilford identifies five basic skills (again arranged hierarchically from least intellectually involved to most): (1) *cognition*—familiarization or acquaintance with facts and ideas; (2) *memory*—committing to memory specific pieces of information; (3) *convergent thinking*—developing the "right attitude" or establishing behavioral norms; (4) *divergent thinking*—demonstrating creativity and ability to project; and (5) *evaluation*—defined as in Bloom's taxonomy.

Taba proposes three categories of skills, or "cognitive tasks." The first task is concept formation: "Concepts are formed as students respond to questions which require them: (1) to enumerate items; (2) to find a basis for grouping items that are familiar in some respect; (3) to identify the common characteristics of items in a group; (4) to label the groups; and (5) to subsume items that they have enumerated under those labels." [17] The second cognitive task consists of interpreting, inferring, and generalizing. The third task is using known principles and facts to explain unfamiliar phenomena or to predict consequences from known conditions.

The most comprehensive approach to the skills of value clarification, and the one most popular with teachers, is by Louis Raths, Merrill Harmin, and Sidney Simon.[18] As seen in Chapter 1, first the children are given opportunities to make free choices after they have considered all possible alternatives and their consequences. Second, the children are allowed to feel and express pride in their choices. Third, the children act repeatedly on their choices. Through this approach children discover, analyze, and place their values in a hierarchy, all on their own. At the same time, they develop new values.

Finally, there are the social skills. Jack Fraenkel lists the following: (1) planning with others, (2) participating in research projects, (3) participating productively in group discussions, (4) responding courteously to the questions of others, (5) leading group discussions, (6) acting responsibly, and (7) helping others.[19]

There has been much debate whether content objectives or process objectives are more important. Both types of objective are equally important, and neither should dominate the curriculum. Knowledge without skills to apply it is atrophic; learning skills without knowledge would exist in a vacuum.

Balanced use of content and process objectives is best assured by beginning with content and determining how it can be applied to develop the process objectives. For example, assume that a second grade teacher is preparing a unit entitled "Communities Work Together" (a commonplace unit in the second grade as will be seen in Chapter 3). A suggested guiding generalization for developing this unit is: "Communities cooperate to solve common problems or to meet common needs." Generalizations, as well as issues, contain the content to be learned; from them the process objectives can be drawn. As will be seen in Chapters 4 and 6, the types of activities designed for learning the content objectives either favor or thwart the process objectives. The matrix in Figure 2-1 is one model for combining content and process objectives.

Listed in the left-hand column are usually the basic understandings, or generalizations, and issues that reflect the realities of the social world with respect to the unit of study. Arrayed across the top of the matrix are the process skills—in the example shown, Guilford's five mental operations and two value-clarification skills suggested by Raths, Harmin, and Simon. Teachers can be as selective as they want to be in choosing among the totality of skills, but they should be aware that teachers tend to emphasize knowledge and the lower levels of intellectual involvement.[20] Hence they should always try to include the following: (1) higher-level intellectual skills, (2) value-clarification opportunities, and (3) social skills.

The next step in combining objectives is to design a specific instructional objective for each box in the matrix, as illustrated in the model with the statements a–g. That is, for each generalization or issue, there will be an instructional objective that separately involves each process objective. With this method, neither content nor process is favored over the other.

STEPS IN DETERMINING INSTRUCTIONAL OBJECTIVES

Only the teacher of a given class can determine its instructional objectives. But, because social studies, unlike, say, science or mathematics, is not precisely structured, all teachers in a school need to cooperatively determine the instructional objectives for each grade level. Such cooperation

Content: \ Processes:	Cognition	Memory	Convergent thinking	Divergent thinking	Evaluation	Choosing freely	After considering alternatives	...etc.
Communities cooperate to solve common problems or to meet common needs.	a	b	c	d	e	f	g	
Improve communication and transportation . . .								
etc.								

a. The children have a general awareness that people in a community work together to provide for their needs.
b. The children memorize five different ways in which people in the community work together to provide for common needs.
c. In designing a new community children apply known ways of interdependence.
d. In designing a new community children formulate new ways of interdependence among community members.
e. The children can assess how well the various parts of a community relate to and depend on each other.
f. The children individually choose freely whether they would like to live in a community with maximum interdependence (city) or with minimum interdependence (farm).
g. The children individually list three positive and three negative consequences of life in a community with minimum interdependence.

Figure 2–1
Model for Designing Combined Content and Process Objectives

prevents the overlapping and repetition that can disturb children and make them lose interest in the subject. If a school district wishes to set district-wide instructional objectives, a committee should be formed that represents all grade levels.

The teachers of a school or a district committee could apply the following steps in determining social studies instructional objectives:

1. Read as many articles and other materials as possible on the goals of education and the goals of social studies in particular. The first two chapters of this book could be a good beginning.
2. Have several meetings to discuss what is read. Establish a common understanding of the trends, issues, and terminology involved. More important, make sure you understand the rationale behind each new movement or possible direction.
3. Request from state officials and study any state education objectives available. (Most general education objectives sound more like social studies

objectives than anything else. Unfortunately, most of these encompassing and humane goals are neglected in the school by arbitrary administrative decisions which lead to narrow practices.) For example, the State Board of Education of the state of Washington adopted, in 1972, the following objectives after systematic input from all levels and directions of the people of the state:

a. As a result of the process of education, all students should have the basic skills and knowledge necessary to seek information, to present ideas, to listen to and interact with others, and to use judgment and imagination in perceiving and resolving problems.

b. As a result of the process of education, all students should understand the elements of their physical and emotional well-being.

c. As a result of the process of education, all students should know the basic principles of the American democratic heritage.

d. As a result of the process of education, all students should appreciate the wonders of the natural world, human achievements and failures, dreams and capabilities.

e. As a result of the process of education, all students should classify their basic values and develop a commitment to act upon these values within the framework of their rights and responsibilities as participants in the democratic process.

f. As a result of the process of education, all students should interact with people of different cultures, races, generations and life styles with significant rapport.

g. As a result of the process of education, all students should participate in social, political, economic and family activities with the confidence that their actions make a difference.

      h. As a result of the process of education, all students should be prepared for their next career steps.

      i. As a result of the process of education, all students should use leisure time in positive and satisfying ways.

      j. As a result of the process of education, all students should be committed to life-long learning and personal growth.[21]

4. From the background developed thus far, design about 6 to 12 goals for the entire K–12 social studies program of your school or district. For example, having followed this approach, and reflecting the general goals of education stated above, a group of teachers from a number of small districts in the state of Washington developed, under my direction, the following social studies program goals:

      a. The students will develop basic understanding about human relationships manifested in the forms of person to person, person to group, group to group, person to institution, group to institution and institution to institution contacts and dealings.

      b. The students will develop an understanding of the way in which beliefs, values and behavior patterns develop and how they are interrelated in a variety of settings and situations ranging from such small groups as the family to very large entities such as nations and a variety of associations of nations.

      c. The students will understand basic problems and conflicting values in the various forms of human relationships and they will develop skills that would enable them to deal with such problems and conflicts rationally.

      d. The students will develop a curiosity for social phenomena as well as appropriate skills to seek information and use it to explain and influence these phenomena.

      e. The students will understand how events of the past have influenced the shape of today's forms of human relationships and they will learn to use past experience as a viable method to attempt to solve current societal problems.

      f. The students will develop a basic commitment to the dignity of the individual and the democratic process. They will be able to implement the democratic process in their relationships with others. Emphasis will be placed on respect for law and the rights of all individuals as well as on the fulfillment of civic responsibility.

      g. The students will become aware of their potential as human beings and as members of their group. This, along with the increase of their knowledge and the development of academic and social skills, will enable them to develop a positive self-concept and will facilitate the growth of their social identity.

5. Study contemporary society to the extent possible and have discussions on the current social realities. These realities should be reflected in the program if social studies is to prepare children to succeed in life and, more particularly, in human relations.

6. Using the process suggested in the next chapter of this book, develop a scope and sequence for each grade. Make sure the topics reflect all social sciences and behavioral sciences—are your topics considered important by social and behavioral scientists? Also, make sure that the topics can

        bring out significant contemporary issues and conflicts. These provide opportunities for the students to engage in decision making.

7. Continuing with the process suggested in the next chapter, develop or adopt from social science sources about half a dozen generalizations and half a dozen issues for each topic. Make sure they collectively treat each topic comprehensively and deal with contemporary society.

8. Diagnose students' developmental levels and make sure you know what those at each level already studied, and know. Consider also what children at a particular level are capable of learning.

9. Using the process suggested in Chapters 4 and 5, reduce the generalizations and issues to instructional objectives. Make sure these objectives include (a) knowledge, (b) social values, (c) intellectual skills at all levels, (d) value-clarification skills, and (e) social skills. Also make sure the instructional objectives are as specific as possible to allow for adequate evaluation.

(Most of the steps outlined above are demonstrated in detail throughout the next four chapters, but especially in Chapter 6, which deals with the unit plan.) To show how the steps described above come to fruition in the classroom, let us use the fourth grade topic, "The Earth Satisfies Our Needs." From the scope and sequence discussed in Chapter 3, the following generalizations and issues can be selected as the backbone of the unit and the source of instructional objectives:

GENERALIZATIONS

1. The earth's resources are used in multiple ways to satisfy people's needs.
2. Humans continuously develop new methods to improve the fertility of the soil in order to increase productivity.
3. Humans constantly seek to satisfy their needs for food, clothing, and shelter, and their other wants; in so doing, they attempt to adapt and exploit the earth.
4. Each culture tends to view its physical habitat differently. A society's value system, goals, organization, and level of technology determine which elements of the land are prized and utilized.
5. Soils are altered by nature and by people.

ISSUES

1. How can we conserve the earth's resources?
2. How could the world achieve an even distribution of essential resources to better satisfy the needs of the various people around the world?
3. Should some nations be forced to change their techniques of agriculture to increase the land's productivity?

These five generalizations and three issues yield, for a normal, heterogeneous fourth grade class, the following instructional objectives as classified into the five types discussed earlier:

1. Knowledge. The children will demonstrate their knowledge of the topic by:
   a. listing at least five different natural resources that people use to satisfy their needs.
   b. explaining how our lives and the well-being of our nation depend upon the resources we get from the earth.
   c. discussing fertilizer and new farming methods that increase productivity.
   d. listing certain countries in which productivity lags because of traditional farming methods.
   e. describing at least five ways in which humans have changed, adapted, or exploited the earth to satisfy their needs.
   f. giving examples of how technology has made some resources more valuable than others.
   g. describing at least five ways in which humans abuse the earth to satisfy their needs.
   h. distinguishing between renewable and nonrenewable natural resources.
   i. discussing some ways in which the government assists in the wise use of natural resources.
   j. using a map or globe to show how the earth's resources are unequally distributed.

2. Social values. The children will value:
   a. efforts to conserve resources and commit themselves to that end by becoming involved in conservation efforts.
   b. the role of the government in conservation by supporting it.

3. Intellectual skills. The children will be able to:
   a. analyze present circumstances to identify trends.
   b. read and develop simple graphs.
   c. suggest alternative solutions to social issues.
   d. predict the consequences of alternative solutions.
   e. develop plans of action for reducing or eliminating social problems.
   f. justify their plans of action by showing how the consequences accord with or improve the common good.

4. Value-clarification skills. The children will be able to:
   a. articulate their feelings concerning the abuse of the earth's resources.
   b. express and clarify their feelings about how this nation's food surplus and the excess resources of other nations ought to be used to meet the need for them around the world.
   c. express their feelings about the need for world cooperation in resolving the problems created by the uneven distribution of resources.
   d. demonstrate pride (if they wish) in our nation's capability to produce large quantities of food as well as in their individual efforts to conserve resources.
   e. express their feeling concerning the role of government in the conservation of resources.

   5. Social skills. The children will be able to:
       a. work together in planning activities.
       b. listen carefully to the views of other children even though they
           might not agree with them.
       c. carry out social action plans without offending, or while being
           considerate of, other people.

SUMMARY

The arguments for and against accountability are briefly discussed in this chapter.
In general, accountability has had positive effects; it prompts educators to sharpen
and clarify their educational goals and to elevate teaching from a routine practice to
a thoughtful design for the achievement of predetermined specific objectives.

The emphasis on behavioral objectives has been one approach to accountability.
Many feel, however, that behavioral objectives over-stress specificity, trivializing
instruction at the expense of long-range objectives. Like other subjects, social studies
includes both short-range and long-range objectives, and behavioral objectives can be
accommodated to both types.

To avoid confusion, in this book the term "instructional objectives" is used
instead of "behavioral objectives" in the context of the classroom. For social studies,
five types of instructional objectives are identified: (a) knowledge, (b) social values,
(c) intellectual skills, (d) value-clarification skills, and (e) social skills. The first two
types are content objectives, the latter three are process objectives.

The following steps are recommended in the development of instructional objectives for social studies:

   1. Study the goals of education in general.
   2. Discuss the goals of education with colleagues and identify trends.
   3. Study the goals of education within the state.
   4. From the above, design about a dozen goals for the entire K–12 social
       studies program.
   5. Study contemporary society and identify social realities.
   6. Develop a scope and sequence for each grade that reflects both the
       educational goals and the social realities.
   7. Develop or adopt from social science sources generalizations and issues
       for each topic.
   8. Diagnose the students' developmental level and needs.
   9. From the generalizations and issues, develop specific instructional
       objectives of all five types that suit the students' level.

ACTIVITIES

   1. From a mixed list of objectives, distinguish between the vague and the specific.
   2. Take a general objective such as "The children will develop sensitivity toward the
       needs and problems of other people," and reduce it to more specific instructional
       objectives. Classify these instructional objectives into the five different types.

3. From a list of instructional objectives containing the five types, separate content and process objectives.

4. Obtain state or national statements of educational objectives. Analyze them to identify those that fall within the domain of human relationships. (Most educational objectives fall within that domain.) Observe practice in local schools and determine whether practice reflects the emphasis placed on human relationships by the state and national objectives.

5. Analyze the stated objectives of commercially available units or the objectives of textbooks to assess the quality of the instructional objectives. Are they specific? Do they include short- as well as long-range objectives? Do they include content as well as process objectives? Do they include high-level intellectual skills? Do they provide opportunities for the children to clarify their values?

6. Ask a curriculum supervisor, or anyone responsible for curriculum development, to describe the actual process used in determining instructional objectives. How close is this process to the steps recommended in the chapter?

NOTES

1. Myron Lieberman, "An Overview of Accountability," *Phi Delta Kappan,* 52 (December 1970), 195.

2. Stephen M. Barro, "An Approach to Developing Accountability Measures for the Public Schools," *Phi Delta Kappan,* 52 (December 1970), 196.

3. Irving Morrissett, "Accountability, Needs Assessment, and Social Studies," *Social Education,* 37 (April 1973), 271–72.

4. Bob L. Taylor, "Implications of the National Assessment Model for Curriculum Development and Accountability," *Social Education,* 38 (May 1974), 407.

5. Donald W. Robinson, "Accountability for Whom? for What?" *Phi Delta Kappan,* 52 (December 1970), 193.

6. Ibid.

7. D. Cecil Clark, *Using Instructional Objectives in Teaching* (Glenview, Ill.: Scott, Foresman, 1972), p. 27.

8. Robert F. Mager, *Preparing Instructional Objectives* (Belmont, Calif.: Fearon, 1962).

9. Ibid., p. 10.

10. Ibid., p. 12.

11. C. Benjamin Cox, "Behavior as Objective in Education," *Social Education,* 35 (May 1971), 440.

12. Benjamin S. Bloom, J. Thomas Hastings, and George F. Madaus, *Handbook on Formative and Summative Evaluation of Student Learning* (New York: McGraw-Hill, 1971), p. 30.

13. Robert F. Mager, *Preparing Instructional Objectives,* p. 12.

14. Benjamin S. Bloom et al., *Taxonomy of Education Objectives, Handbook I: Cognitive Domain* (New York: David McKay, 1956).

15. J. P. Guilford, "Three Faces of Intellect," *The American Psychologist,* 14 (August 1959), pp. 469–79.

16. Hilda Taba, *Teacher's Handbook for Elementary Social Studies* (Reading, Mass.: Addison-Wesley, 1967).

17. Ibid., p. 92.
18. Louis Raths et al., *Values and Teaching* (Columbus, Ohio: Charles E. Merrill, 1966).
19. Jack R. Fraenkel, *Helping Students Think and Value* (Englewood Cliffs, N.J.: Prentice-Hall, 1973), pp. 167–68.
20. John V. Godbold, "Oral Questioning Practices of Teachers in Social Studies Classes," in June R. Chapin, ed., *Social Studies Dissertations 1969–1973.* Social Science Education Consortium Publication No. 168, Boulder, Colo., 1974, p. 100.
21. *What Are Schools For?* (Olympia: Washington State Board of Education, 1972).

Planning and Teaching
Social Studies

OBJECTIVES

Studying this chapter will enable the reader to:

1. become familiar with the deficiencies of both the descriptive social studies curriculum and the conceptual social studies programs of the '60s.
2. define and show commitment to a dynamic social studies curriculum based on decision making and leading toward participation in society.
3. realize the importance of both knowledge and values in the dynamic curriculum.
4. articulate and use several basic criteria in the development of a scope and sequence for a dynamic program.
5. realize that a dynamic program can be developed without completely abandoning existing programs.
6. realize that concepts, generalizations, and issues can support a sound social studies program.
7. be assured that knowledge derived from the social and behavioral sciences remains important in a dynamic social studies program.
8. derive concepts, generalizations, and issues from social science and behavioral science sources.

A SOCIAL STUDIES CURRICULUM
FOR DECISION MAKING

The curriculum is the means by which a school is to achieve its objectives. If the objectives are the blueprint for a house, the curriculum is the building material. No school or teacher can achieve worthwhile objectives without a sound and appropriate curriculum.

During the last few decades the school curriculum has been in ferment. In practically every subject several attempts have been made to eliminate obvious curricular deficiencies. But as yet no general satisfaction has been forthcoming. A recent Gallup Poll revealed that one of the 10 major problems confronting the public schools remains poor curriculum.[1]

This chapter describes the changing social studies curriculum and the difficulties it presents for the teacher, and proposes trends and curriculum-development procedures for realizing the objectives presented in the previous chapters. It must be emphasized, however, that no one program can serve as a model for all programs. Instead a way of thinking is outlined by which teachers, individually or collectively, can develop a sound social studies program.

In Chapter 1 the successive stages of social studies approaches were enumerated; first was the moralistic approach, next the descriptive, then the conceptual approach. This approach is now being supplanted by the decision-making approach. No transition from one approach to the next has been clear-cut or widely accepted; while the forerunners in the field are excited by the promise of the decision-making approach, the most progressive textbook series are still dominated by the conceptual approach. Moreover most teachers and many textbook series continue to use the descriptive approach, which, being familiar and simple to teach, yields a strong sense of security. Thus, before developing a program oriented to decision making, it is perhaps to the point to briefly investigate the shortcomings of the descriptive and conceptual approaches, respectively.

DEFICIENCIES OF THE DESCRIPTIVE CURRICULUM

A major deficiency of the descriptive curriculum is that, in practice at least, it lacks a basic structure. Most users of this approach choose their topics according to personal likes and dislikes rather than by reference to a basic philosophical framework. Facts and events are taught in isolation rather than being marshaled as evidence for the formulation of basic under-standings.

Lacking sound criteria for the selection of content, descriptive cur-ricula can deteriorate into collections of trivia. They are noted also for a manifest anti-intellectualism in practice. Bruce Joyce has written:

> When I take a Professor of Non-Education into a second grade classroom where children are drawing pictures of their Community Helper, the Friendly Mailman, I want to hide under the table in the science corner. Whatever the causes, the charge of anti-intellectualism seems to me to have some merit. Many textbooks and many teachers begin with what the child is familiar with, in accordance with the expanding horizons approach, but they leave him right there, rather than leading him to a more sophisticated level of understanding.[2]

Anti-intellectualism has another source in the descriptive curriculum: the absence of opportunities to apply knowledge. A descriptive program is primarily directed to providing knowledge. It undervalues intellectual abili-ties and ignores the essential role of activity in the development of intel-lectual skills: If students are to learn, they need opportunities to organize their newly acquired knowledge, to apply it to new situations. William Rader has written: "Most of the information presented in the textbooks is descriptive rather than analytical, and the books do not give students an opportunity to review critically the information presented or to apply the techniques and concepts of social sciences."[3]

Most publishers have made a sincere effort to update their texts, but too often old editions of descriptive textbooks remain in use. These edi-tions contain material that is outdated when it is not outright fantasy. Some units on the Netherlands, for example, still give the impression that every-one walks around in wooden shoes. Most such books say little or nothing about Holland's membership in the European Common Market or the North Atlantic Treaty Organization.

Moreover, old textbooks and related materials reflect old biases. (This deficiency continues even in some current texts, because publishers, moti-vated by profit, often submit to the various pressure groups in the market.) Many children today live with only one parent. Yet in the traditional social studies textbooks every child lives with both parents. Few children are fortunate enough to live in Cape Cod colonial-style homes, but all children in the old books do. Only recently have social studies books acknowledged that our society includes blacks, American Indians, the more recent immi-grants, Asian-Americans, chicanos, and other minorities; women were al-ways presented in stereotypic roles. Our society was depicted as being white, mainly of Northern European stock, and blessed with affluence and happiness. There were no problems, and therefore no need to develop in children a desire to improve society or the skills with which to do so.

The descriptive approach is in fact without merit. As shown in Chapter 1, it made social studies a dull subject and allowed no opportunities for children to develop into capable and useful citizens. As I have said elsewhere,

> Whether the course was about the local state or a foreign country, the children were mostly memorizing the names of rivers, mountains and cities, or they were making lists of imports and exports. Soon after they had passed an examination, youngsters in most cases were forgetting everything. If there was anything left in their minds, it was usually a bitter taste for social studies as a subject.[4]

THE SHORTCOMINGS OF THE CONCEPTUAL CURRICULUM

The conceptual curriculum was developed during the 1960s as a corrective to the deficiencies of the descriptive curriculum. It was an attempt to rid social studies of trivia and biases and enable children to begin thinking as social scientists do.

The principle that guided the conceptual approach in the development of the curriculum was the structure of knowledge as defined by social scientists. From the influence of the psychologist Jerome Bruner, it came to be believed that the study of any topic ought to be based upon the structural elements—that is, the *concepts* and *generalizations*—borrowed from relevant social science disciplines. A concept groups particular objects, events, processes, or ideas according to their common characteristics; mountain, democratic government, religion, and assembly line are examples of concepts. A generalization is a statement of a relationship between two or more concepts that has broad applicability. The statements "When the demand for housing increases, rent increases," and "Communication is basic to the existence of culture and groups," are examples of generalizations. Concepts and generalizations are discussed later in this chapter.

Social scientists dominated curriculum development during the 1960s. They dictated what concepts and generalizations were to be taught in each topic, and social studies education specialists and teachers designed the appropriate learning activities. Social sciences (*not* social studies), concepts, inquiry, and data were prominent terms in the titles as well as the texts of the new books—for example, *Concepts and Inquiry* (Allyn and Bacon); *The Social Sciences: Concepts and Values* (Harcourt Brace Jovanovich); the *Taba Program in Social Science* (Addison-Wesley); and *Holt Databank System* (Holt, Rinehart and Winston). In the 1960s, as Glenys Unruh writes, "an important contribution of the era of curriculum development was the wider collaboration of scholars and teachers in the creation of curriculum guides and materials which interrupted an earlier cycle of mediocrity in curriculum development."[5]

Thus, concepts and generalizations were becoming the ultimate objective of social studies education. Children were learning the language of the social scientists, and curriculum developers felt they had found the way to overcome the teachers' inadequacies and put substance in social studies. Inquiry was projected as the most effective way to teach.

Despite these developments and the excitement they generated, the conceptual approach had serious shortcomings. It generated a curriculum that was too academic, and too middle-class, for much of the youth. As such, it was rejected by various minorities. The conceptual programs teach a few cursory facts about subcultures, but not all of them are designed to be *used* by all subcultures as a way of improving human relations through understanding. "If the new social studies [another name for the conceptual approach] or any successive movements for rational reform are to have the impact they deserve," wrote Hazel Hertsberg, "they must be modified to take account of a factor largely neglected: the subculture of students themselves." [6]

At a time when young people were demonstrating a grave concern about major social crises, the conceptual curriculum was concerned only with what can be substantiated or proven. It disregarded sharp value conflicts in human relationships and ignored popular demands that education be made relevant and meaningful. Unruh states:

> Preoccupation of the curriculum developers with curriculum structure and new teaching styles left them somewhat unprepared for the shock of the "crisis" writings near the close of the decade that suddenly attracted wide audiences not previously accustomed to reading about schools. . . . Social issues gained center stage in the educational community, and equality of educational opportunity, relevance, accountability, and school community responsibility became major concerns.[7]

Some felt that the conceptual programs, meant to solidify the content of social studies, overemphasized the social sciences at the expense of important humanistic elements. If the focus of social studies is the development of the child, there was probably too much emphasis on inquiry as a formal process, on concepts, and on generalizations from the social sciences. "The social studies classroom," Richard Whittmore states, "should be . . . a place where the rational and the romantic can exist side by side as equally valid categories of understandings, where the two cultures of science and art find common ground." [8]

John Jarolimek points up the shortcomings of the conceptual curriculum by raising a number of questions that apparently were overlooked by the curriculum reformers of the '60s:

> 1. How can social studies programs be made more meaningful, more highly individualized, and, most important, more *personal* for learners?

2. How can the in-school social studies program be related to the out-of-school lives of pupils?
3. How can the concepts and content of the social sciences, history, and humanities be *used* to provide pupils with insights about the world in which they live?
4. How can social studies programs realistically and truthfully depict the diversity of racial, ethnic, and national backgrounds of the people of this country?
5. How can social studies education become a vital force in combating the evils of racism that flow through the bloodstream of this society?
6. How can social studies programs help pupils build values consistent with the democratic traditions of this society?
7. How can social studies programs help pupils build skills that will enable them to learn how to learn and keep on learning about their social world for a lifetime?
8. How can the social studies program help the learner become a more effective decision maker?
9. How can the social studies program help learners grasp the reality of our international involvements—socially, economically, militarily? [9]

THE DYNAMIC SOCIAL STUDIES CURRICULUM

The curriculum is dynamic when it leads to action. Neither the descriptive nor the conceptual curriculum is dynamic, because one requires only that the learners acquire a body of information; the other requires only that the learners understand concepts and generalizations. The only skills valued are those needed to acquire knowledge.

The central focus of the dynamic curriculum is the student's performance in human relationships. Knowledge is important—but not for its own sake, rather, to help students participate in the life of society. For example, whether racism, a long-standing problem in our society, can be reduced in the future depends on the future behavior of individuals. The more a class learns about this problem, the more the students are likely to feel that they, as individuals, should do something about it. Their choice of a course of action is usually dictated by their knowledge of the problem. The more they know about racism, the more numerous the alternative courses of action are likely to be—and, more important, the more likely are they to choose the proper action.

Because it uses knowledge as a means to an end, the dynamic curriculum is selective in its approach to knowledge. Children's needs and the features of their social environment are the basic criteria by which knowledge is selected. Studying the history of racism as a worldwide phenomenon is not the same as studying it to learn how to cope with it here and now. The former kind of study is subject-centered, the latter is student-centered. Knowledge selection that is student-centered makes the curriculum "relevant," which the descriptive and conceptual curricula were not.

But, again, knowledge is often not enough in itself to guide learners toward proper action. Particularly in human relationships, often no one course of action is the self-evidently correct one. The individuals' values play complicating roles. The more individuals examine their own values and acknowledge the values of others around them, the greater the likelihood of sound decisions. In the dynamic curriculum, then, students' value systems are as important as knowledge of the social environment and its problems.

The dynamic curriculum is behavior oriented, and behavior implies a context of norms. If individuals act on their own values, the well-being of society must rest on a consensus of values. In our society the framework for social action has always been a common core of values reflected in the Declaration of Independence, the Constitution, and the Bill of Rights. Such values have of late come under attack, chiefly because of the historical disparity between our expressions of adherence to them and our actual practice, which long denied freedom and equal opportunity to large numbers of people. But does this abuse discredit those values, or does it, rather, say more about human weakness and fallibility of behavior?

However, the schools should not indoctrinate students to these values. Instead, the curriculum should provide ample opportunities to study these values and, by reasoning, assess their validity. Only through such a process can a core of values be created that permits sound decision making and effective social action.

DEVELOPING A DYNAMIC CURRICULUM

A dynamic program must meet the following conditions: (1) Curriculum content is (a) drawn from the social sciences and (b) related to the learners and their social context; (2) knowledge is not an end in itself, but a means to assisting learners, concerned members of society, to determine courses of action to improve society and their place in it; (3) because acting implies norms, social values become a part of the curriculum; (4) such values are assessed by the children for possible voluntary, not involuntary, acceptance; (5) finally, children are given skills to acquire knowledge and values and to apply them in making decisions.

Developing such a curriculum does not require that the traditional social studies framework be completely abandoned. To do so would alienate teachers trained and experienced in descriptive and conceptual curricula. How, then, is a dynamic curriculum developed?

The Scope and Sequence

Once the objectives have been set, the scope and sequence are next developed. Nationwide surveys during the 1950s and early '60s by Frank Hodgson,[10] Ralph Preston,[11] Richard Burns and Alexander Frazier,[12] D. L.

Barnes,[13] and Fay Adams [14] reveal that the traditional social studies curriculum was similar across the nation. In the primary grades it consisted of home, school, community helpers, pets, farm life, communication, transportation, food, clothing, shelter, and American Indians; in the fourth grade, climate studies of the world's regions; in the fifth grade, the history and geography of the United States (sometimes Canada and Latin America, as well); and in the sixth grade, the rest of the world, with emphasis on Europe.

The conceptual curriculum did not drastically change the traditional descriptive framework. In the primary grades it simply systematized the study of the family and the community. It also placed more emphasis on the study of individuals and their potential in working with other people. For the most part, community studies were concentrated in the second grade, and the city became the major topic for study in the third grade— apparently because the majority of the population was moving to the cities. The fourth grade still dealt with regions, but now instead of from the physical geographer's point of view it was from the cultural geographer's. Some conceptual programs dealt with the local state in the fourth grade; the scope of the fifth and sixth grades remained the same.

Some new programs effected drastic changes in their scope and sequence, but with no stated justification. In the first grade, for example, the Allyn and Bacon program introduced study of U.S. leaders instead of the traditional study of the family.

The conceptual programs introduced one distinct difference from the descriptive, especially in the primary grades: fewer themes in each grade. For example, in the first grade the traditional descriptive program dealt with the following themes: our families, home, schools, work and play, pets, the farm, and holidays. Most conceptual programs concentrated mainly on the family and the school, the social entities most immediate in the child's environment.

The chart below shows how the traditional descriptive and the conceptual programs differ in scope and sequence, as well as how various conceptual programs differ one from another.[15] The conceptual programs included are those based on the three major social studies projects of the '60s that completed a K–6 or 1–6 program early in that decade: the Minnesota Social Studies Curriculum Program, developed by Edith West at the University of Minnesota; the Greater Cleveland Social Science Program, developed by the Educational Research Council of Greater Cleveland; and the Taba Curriculum Development Project, developed by the late Hilda Taba.

The more recent emphasis on decision making has changed little from the scope and sequence of the conceptual programs. The framework has remained about the same, the major changes being the new importance of

Grade	Traditional Program	Minnesota Program	Greater Cleveland Program	Taba Program
K	Home School	The earth as the home of man A world of many people Our global earth A home of varied resources Man changes the earth	Learning about our world Children in other lands	
1	Our families, home, and school Work and play Pets Farm Holidays	Families around the world Hopi family Chippewa family Quechua family Japanese family	Learning about our country Explorers and discoverers: Balboa, Byrd, Columbus, Cook, Cousteau, DeSoto, Glenn, and others	Our school School plant, friends, school workers, transportation, activities, composition Family living structure, composition, work, income, values, transportation
2	Helpers in the community The post office, fireman, dairy, bakery, grocery store	Families around the world Boston family in early eighteenth century Soviet family in urban Moscow Hausa family in Nigeria Kibbutz family in Israel Urban family in Paris	Communities at home and abroad Our community The aborigines of Central Australia The Eskimos of Barrow, Alaska An historical community (Williamsburg, Va.) A military community (Fort Bragg, N.C.) An apple-growing community (Yakima, Wash.) A forest-products community (Crossett, Ark.) A steelmaking community (Pittsburgh, Pa.) A rural community (Webster City, Iowa)	Services in the supermarket Construction workers and materials, utilities, suppliers, store workers Services in our community Business, government, other community workers

Grade	Traditional Program	Minnesota Program	Greater Cleveland Program	Taba Program
3	The town or local community Food, clothing, shelter, communication, transportation, Indians, pioneers	Communities around the world Rural and urban communities An American frontier community Paris community Manus community	The making of Anglo-America The metropolitan community (historical study of an imaginary city) Cleveland: A metropolitan community Boston and Brockton: a metropolitan community	Nonliterate of Africa People of the hot dry lands The boat people of Hong Kong The people of Switzerland
4	Our state Type regions Contrasting communities in the U.S. Exploration and pioneer days	Our own community A community in the Soviet Union A Trobriand Island community Indian village south of Himalayas	The story of agriculture The story of industry India: a society in transition	California An interdisciplinary treatment of California at the present time
5	United States— past and present Western Hemisphere	The United States of America Overview Sequent occupance Local area Representative cities Canada Overview Case studies of regions Latin America Overview Sequent occupance Buenos Aires Cuzco etc.	Human Adventure Part I—Ancient Civilization Part II—Four World Views (China, India, Israel, Greece) Part III—The classical world of Greece and Rome Part IV—Medieval Civilization The Middle East	Anglo-America The dynamic character of America through the study of history, her people, and social, political, and economic conditions today

Grade	Traditional Program	Minnesota Program	Greater Cleveland	Taba Program
6	Old World Western Hemisphere Eastern Hemisphere	Indian America Colonization of North America Revolutionary America Westward expansion Civil War and reconstruction	Part V—Rise of Modern Civilization in the West Part VI—New World and Eurasian Cultures Part VII—Empires and Revolutions Part VIII—The Coming of World Civilization Latin America	Latin America Generalizations such as the following are developed: Civilizations change when they meet a new culture. The types of people a country has give a nation its unique features. Change in one important aspect of a country's way of life usually brings about other changes, etc.

issues, and use of the humanities as well as the social sciences as sources. One current social studies program, randomly selected, that collates conceptual and decision-making programs has the following scope and sequence: [16]

LEVEL K—ME

1. Me
2. My family
3. My school
4. My community
5. My tools

LEVEL 1—THINGS WE DO

1. Me and you
2. People
3. Living with others
4. Using space

LEVEL 2—THE WORLD AROUND US

1. Learning about the world
2. Feeling about the world
3. Communicating about the world
4. Thinking about the world
5. Depending on the world
6. Acting on the world

LEVEL 3—WHO ARE WE?

1. What is Earth?
2. What is a human being?
3. What are groups?
4. Who am I?
   Building map skills

LEVEL 4—PLANET EARTH

1. You and your environment
2. Culture and human needs
3. Living in the air–ocean
4. The water around you
5. The land you live on
6. You in the life system
7. The energy you use

8. Looking beyond earth
   Building map skills

LEVEL 5—THE UNITED STATES

1. The United States—people and places
2. The United States—our natural environment
3. Culture in the United States
4. The United States in the global community
5. The beginning of the United States
6. The United States grows and changes
7. The modern United States
8. The United States in today's world
   Building map skills
   Atlas

LEVEL 6—THE WAY PEOPLE LIVE

1. What makes you a human being?
2. How and why are human beings alike and different?
3. How does culture vary and change?
4. Our urbanized earth
   Building map skills
   Atlas

The above program does not present the world simply as something to be studied. It places students in the world and helps them understand their place in it and the active roles they can play in it. Students are given opportunities not only to gain knowledge but also to feel and act.

How Does a Teacher Adopt a Scope and Sequence?

There are three ways in which teachers, alone or in concert within a school, can adopt a scope and sequence. One is to allow a textbook series to determine what should be taught and in what order. Although the simplest solution, it is not necessarily the most appropriate. Each school is a unique situation, and each class is a group of children with special characteristics and needs, which no textbook series can exactly meet. Moreover, any book in a series has been developed for the average child in a class, but in any class many children (or sometimes the entire class) are above or below average. In such cases, areas of study and unit topics must be accommodated to the children's environment and experiences.

A second way to arrive at a scope and sequence is for the teachers to develop their own. This is the best way, but it is difficult, especially for small districts. Teachers must have considerable knowledge and must incur endless hours of work and employ many resources; they must have a good library and the involvement of social scientists and other consultants.

The third, most practical, and most used way falls between the first two. Through a variety of textbook series, curriculum guides, and other sources, teachers familiarize themselves with what is recommended for teaching in each grade. With respect to the first, second, and fifth grades, there is nationwide near unanimity; family is the area of study for the first grade, the community for the second grade, and the United States and its neighbors for the fifth grade.

Some third grade programs continue with community studies, others introduce early American history, and still others deal with the relationships of people and the earth. But the most common area of study for the third grade is the urban scene and its advantages and disadvantages. There is also general agreement in the fourth grade; most textbooks deal with regions and the relationships between people and the land. Many districts, however, are legally required to teach about the local state in the fourth grade. Quite often, as a compromise, the state is studied as part of a larger U.S. region (the Southwest, for example). In the sixth grade, the world continues to be studied, but the scope is extended beyond the Old World and the Western Hemisphere. Some sixth grade programs now study a society or the development of a civilization, usually Western civilization; common themes are "Man and Society," "The Human Adventure," and the like, and, more recently, themes dealing with the world's major problems.

A complete elementary school program provides a curriculum for the kindergarten as well. But not all available programs include the kindergarten. Kindergarten curricula vary in scope and sequence. Some deal with the school, the seasons, and major holidays, others with elements from the first and second grade programs, namely the family and the community. A recent theme of study in kindergarten is the individual. Kindergarteners study themselves as individuals and are made aware of their potential for growth. They also study themselves as members of groups such as their class, their family, or any other informal group to which they might belong.

The following areas of study perhaps provide the framework for the curriculum:

Kindergarten:	Me and Others
First Grade:	My Family and Other Families
Second Grade:	My Community and Other Communities
Third Grade:	Movement Toward and Around the Cities
Fourth Grade:	People Need the Earth
Fifth Grade:	The Development of Our Society
Sixth Grade:	The Interaction of World Cultures

The suggested areas of study approximate those of most programs, from which there is no strong reason to depart. Instead of changing the areas of study, the new programs change what is taught in each area. First, each area of study must be flexible enough to allow for treatment of local concerns; second, any framework must allow for the study of contemporary society (although not, of course, to the neglect of the past). The above framework meets both of these criteria. By adhering to the common areas of study, teachers can use the variety of existing learning resources developed for these areas at approximately the suggested grade or developmental levels. For example, much material on the United States has been written at approximately the fifth grade level.

Once the areas of study have been assigned, the unit topics must be assigned within each of the seven areas of study. Usually there are four to six topics in each level. Four basic criteria should guide the selection of unit topics in a dynamic curriculum:

1. Topics should reflect content that is considered important by social scientists. Teachers should therefore study some good social science books on particular areas of study. What do anthropologists or sociologists, for instance, consider important to cover in a book on the family? College textbooks used in courses that deal with the seven recommended areas of study are probably the best books to survey.

2. Topics should provide for a comprehensive treatment of the various areas of study. Sometimes it is necessary to combine chapter titles proposed by social scientists into broader units. Whether combining or selecting from recommended chapters or sections to arrive at topics, teachers should avoid dealing with only the past, or the present, or with only one aspect of an area of study. For example, all types of family life in our society should be dealt with, not just, say, the middle class.

3. Topics should allow for consideration of the local scene. The study of regions, for instance, should include the local region. (Unless a unified thematic approach is used, the local region should be studied first, to enable the children to use their experiences in the learning process.)

4. Topics should address important contemporary issues. This is the crucial criterion for the dynamic curriculum, because only by dealing with issues can students develop the skills they need to resolve conflict and contribute toward the improvement of society. There can be no action, the mark of a dynamic curriculum, unless study of topics leads to consideration of issues.

I suggest the following unit topics for the seven areas of study:

Grade Level: Kindergarten
Area of Study: Me and Others
Unit Topics: 1. Things I Can Do
                  2. Things I Know

3. The Way I Feel
4. Me and My Family
5. Me and My Friends
6. When I Grow Up

Grade Level: First
Area of Study: My Family and Other Families
Unit Topics: 1. Families All Over
                 2. Families Are Different
                 3. Families Have Needs
                 4. Families Have Rules
                 5. Families Change

Grade Level: Second
Area of Study: My Community and Other Communities
Unit Topics: 1. The Local Community
                 2. Communities a Long Time Ago
                 3. Communities Are Different
                 4. Communities Work Together
                 5. Communities Change

Grade Level: Third
Area of Study: People Move In and Around the Cities
Unit Topics: 1. Cities Attract People
                 2. The Suburbs Are Getting Bigger
                 3. Cities Are Different
                 4. The Mayor's Difficult Job
                 5. The History of Big Cities

Grade Level: Fourth
Area of Study: People Need the Earth
Unit Topics: 1. People and the Land Long Ago:
                    The Indian vs. "The White Man"
                 2. The Earth Satisfies Our Needs
                 3. The Earth Is Abused
                 4. Regions of the Earth
                 5. Our Region and State

Grade Level: Fifth
Area of Study: The Development of Our Nation
Unit Topics: 1. The Making of Our Nation
                 2. The Effects of Industrialization and Immigration
                 3. People and Institutions in Our Society
                 4. Our Nation and the World
                 5. Do We Practice What We Believe?

Grade Level:	Sixth
Area of Study:	The Interaction of World Cultures
Unit Topics:	1. Early Civilizations: Far East and Middle East
	2. Early Civilizations: Greece and Rome
	3. People in the World Today: Major Cultures
	4. Forces that Divide the World
	5. Forces that Unite the World

The Content of Each Topic

Content is valuable both for its own sake and for developing abilities and social skills. The conceptual and decision-making (the dynamic) approaches have both helped to provide a sound content in social studies —the conceptual approach by supplying a structure of concepts and generalizations; the decision-making approach by adding issues to the study of each topic. This section presents the procedures that can be used to formulate concepts, generalizations, and issues.

CONCEPTS AND GENERALIZATIONS   Concepts, remember, are words or phrases that denote groups of objects, events, processes, or ideas with common characteristics; generalizations are statements of relationship between two or more concepts that have broad applicability. These definitions, although widely accepted, are often a source of confusion as to the difference between them. The problem is that concepts and generalizations are developed by similar processes.

To enable youngsters to form a generalization, we make them aware of the broad application of the relationship it represents; we bring to their attention as many instances of application as possible. If, for example, we want students to understand the generalization that "poverty breeds crime," we bring to their awareness as many poverty situations as possible and demonstrate that in each situation crime is high. The children themselves then conclude that the observed relationship between poverty and crime is a generalization. In other words, the children discover the generalization by putting together specific instances.

Forming concepts involves a similar process of generalizing. Youngsters faced with an object, event, process, or idea must decide in what category to classify it and give it a name. Youngsters confronted with the political system (a process distributing and using power) of a foreign country put together a number of specifics—how leaders assume and exercise power, the extent to which the people control the government, and how decisions are made. From these specifics, the child reaches the conclusion that this foreign country's political system is a democracy, a dictatorship, or whatever. In other words, from a number of specific characteristics, the child generalizes about the system and classifies it accordingly.

Both concepts and generalizations are classified in a variety of ways. Concepts are usually classified into concrete, or tangible, and abstract, or intangible. The concept "mountain," for example, refers to something concrete—one can see it, touch it, walk on it. On the other hand, concepts such as cooperation, tolerance, democracy, and the like are intangible; they cannot be experienced through the senses. Intangible concepts are the more difficult to teach, and most concepts in social studies are of this type.

Some concepts are broader than others. I remember a few years ago watching television with my three-year-old daughter when a tiger appeared on the screen. Sophia jumped with excitement, saying, "Daddy, Daddy, there is a cat." I replied, "No, Sophia, that is a tiger." But Sophia was right; what she saw was a cat. The concept "tiger" is a narrower one denoting only one portion of cats, but Sophia was not familiar with the specific characteristics that set the tiger apart from other cats. It took a trip to the zoo to convince Sophia of the difference between the broad concept of cat and the narrower one of tiger. Sophia could have also used the still-broader word "animal" to identify what she saw.

Roy Price has identified the major concepts from the social sciences and allied disciplines that appear to be most appropriate for an elementary and secondary program in social studies: (a) substantive concepts: sovereignty of nation, conflict, the industrialization-urbanization syndrome, secularization, compromise and adjustment, comparative advantage, power, morality and choice, input and output, scarcity, saving, the modified market economy, habitat and its significance, culture, institution, social control, social change, interaction; and (b) value concepts: dignity of human kind, empathy, government by consent of the governed, loyalty, and freedom and equality.[17]

Generalizations can be classified as weak or strong, according to their balance of confirming versus disconfirming instances. Suppose we randomly select 100 localities around the world to check the strength of the generalization, "Rent increases with the increase of the demand for housing." If in all of these places rent increased as housing demand increased, the generalization is strong. The fewer the confirming cases, the weaker the generalization and the higher the probability that it is wrong.

Like concepts, generalizations can be broad or narrow. "Change has been a universal condition of human society" is a very broad generalization; it applies to the entire world and all times. On the other hand, some generalizations are true only for one area or period of time. "The geographic features of the midwestern United States influence that region's economy and way of life" is a generalization limited to the stated region. Generalizations should be specific to the topic. The more a generalization applies directly to only the one topic, the better the direction it provides for the topic's content.

THE ISSUES   No study area or unit topic lacks issues. To omit them is to teach only half way. But what are social issues? Anna Ochoa and Gary Manson define social issues by their origin: "Social issues arise when the goals, the structures, and the processes of communities or societies combine or conflict in ways that threaten the survival, the well-being, or the progress of the group or its members." [18] For instance, the school board of a community, faced with financial problems and declining enrollment, decides to close down two elementary schools. But doing so would threaten the well-being of the neighborhoods around those two schools. A sharp issue arises in the community: Should the two elementary schools be closed?

Issues can also be conflicts concerning friendship, loyalty, honesty, and the like. What is fundamental to issues in the social studies context is that they be controversial. They are posed as questions that cannot be answered by appeal to evidence alone. Values and philosophical positions must be employed. Thus, to any issue there is no one possible answer but many. All issues are questions, but not all questions are issues. The question, "What is the best way to eliminate crime?" for example, is an issue, because there is no agreement on the answer. But the question, "What are the effects of crime?" can be answered factually by those who study crime, and therefore is not an issue.

Social studies education textbooks have long discussed whether or not controversial issues should be taught. Most social studies educators have favored doing so, but only with inherently controversial topics, such as communism or racism. But *all* topics contain some kind of controversy, just as all topics contain concepts and generalizations. Controversial issues should therefore be continuously taught in social studies. Not teaching them deprives students of opportunities to engage in decision making and social action. For example, during study of the family in the first grade, it is as easy to deal with controversy as it is in teaching about communism. Children might be asked, "What is the best way for each one of us to demonstrate responsibility in family life?" Some children are expected to do things at home whereas others are not; some have opportunities to think about this question whereas others do not. What is appropriate in this situation and how can this be decided the best way?

Anytime children consider an issue, they add to their knowledge. (For example, before deciding what they should do to reduce crime, they must learn the dimensions of the problem and what is now being done about it.) But what issues most contribute to the classroom is the development of a way of thinking in resolving conflict situations. This will be discussed in more detail in Chapter 5.

What are the best issues to include in the curriculum? Keeping in mind the following three criteria can be helpful:

1. Choose enduring issues. Some issues are temporary, while others remain with us for a long time. The latter are more appropriate.
2. Choose issues that are relevant to the contemporary scene. They are best for generating action.
3. Make sure the issues are open-ended and are stated in a way that suggests as many alternative solutions as possible. For instance, "Is busing the best way to resolve school segregation?" is not as open-ended and as comprehensive as "What is the best way to eliminate school segregation?"

The following six controversial issues were selected for thorough treatment in the 1975 yearbook of the National Council for the Social Studies:

1. Should traditional sex modes and values be changed?
2. Should the study of death be a necessary preparation for living?
3. Should the majority rule?
4. Should integration be a society goal?
5. Should we believe that our planet is in peril?
6. Should the nation-state give way to some form of world organization? [19]

Concepts, generalizations, and issues, then, are the backbone of the social studies curriculum. (The method of teaching them is developed in Chapters 4 and 5.) It must be emphasized that the change from the conceptual to the dynamic curriculum has not diminished the importance of the social science disciplines in determining the curriculum. Concepts and generalizations remain essential to understanding society and its problems, and enduring issues remain essential to promoting rational action.

The Role of the Disciplines in Determining the Curriculum

Social scientists can be an important source not only of social studies unit topics, as we have seen, but of concepts, generalizations, and issues as well. Only thus can trivia and bias be avoided. Concepts, generalizations, and issues are the structure of social science disciplines; Joseph Schwab states:

. . . the structures of the disciplines are twice important to education. First, they are necessary to teachers and educators: they must be taken into account as we plan curriculum and prepare our teaching materials; otherwise, our plans are likely to miscarry and our materials, to mismatch. Second, they are necessary in some part and degree within the curriculum as elements of what we teach. Otherwise, there will be failure of learning or gross mislearning by our students.[20]

In the last 15 years a number of publications were issued that are helpful to the teacher or the curriculum developer in search of input from the disciplines. Among them are:

1. Bernard Berelson and Gary A. Steiner, *Human Behavior: An Inventory of Scientific Findings* (New York: Harcourt Brace Jovanovich, 1964). Lists concepts and generalizations and supporting evidence. They are organized around topics usually taught in the elementary school.

2. John U. Michaelis and A. Montgomery Johnston, eds., *The Social Sciences: Foundations of the Social Studies* (Boston: Allyn and Bacon, 1965). Presents generalizations from the various social science disciplines.

3. Raymond H. Muessig and Vincent R. Rogers, eds., *Social Science Seminar Series,* six volumes (Columbus, Ohio: Charles E. Merrill Publishing Co., 1965). Each volume deals with the structure, methods, and basic generalizations of one social science discipline.

4. Irving Morrissett, ed., *Concepts and Structure in the New Social Science Curricula* (West Lafayette, Ind.: Social Science Education Consortium, 1966). Deals with concepts and structure of knowledge and procedures of organizing a curriculum around concepts and the relationships among concepts, processes, and values.

5. William E. Lenchtenburg, *A Troubled Feast—American Society Since 1945* (Boston: Little, Brown, 1973). Deals with the most persistent social ills of American society.

A SAMPLE CURRICULUM

To provide a complete curriculum for the elementary school is beyond the scope of this book. Moreover, to do so would be to proffer a procrustean bed: Every curriculum must be made to suit the children for whom it is intended and the characteristics and peculiarities of their social environment. Nevertheless, the scope and sequence suggested earlier can be expanded upon; under each topic, two or three generalizations and at least one issue are suggested—as *samples only*. Concepts are not listed, because they are implicit in the generalizations and issues. Teachers may adopt these suggestions and add their own, or they may reject them and create their own list. Teachers need not copy generalizations and issues verbatim from social science sources; they may put them in their own words or construct their own, as long as they reflect basic understandings supported by evidence. The generalizations that follow have been constructed by me, mainly from evidence presented in the five social science sources listed above.

GRADE LEVEL: Kindergarten
AREA OF STUDY: Me and Others

Unit Topic 1:   Things I Can Do

Generalizations:

    a.   Humans can do more things than animals.

    b.   People learn how to do things and as they grow they learn how to do more things and do them better.

Issues:

    a. Should we all be good in everything?

Unit Topic 2:   Things I Know

Generalizations:

    a.   People learn from their experiences.

    b.   Reading and the use of other symbols assist people to learn.

Issues:

    a.   Should everyone learn how to read?

Unit Topic 3:   The Way I Feel

Generalizations:

    a.   People have some things that make them feel good and some things that make them feel bad.

    b.   People and things around affect people's feelings.

Issues:

    a.   Should we let others know how we feel?

Unit Topic 4:   Me and My Family

Generalizations:
- a.   People need families to meet their needs.
- b.   No two families are alike.

Issues:
- a.   Should children help with family chores?

Unit Topic 5:   Me and My Friends

Generalizations:
- a.   Most people like to have friends.
- b.   People share and do things with their friends.

Issues:
- a.   Should we dislike someone who cannot or does not want to be our friend?
- b.   What is the best way to treat a friend?

Unit Topic 6:   When I Grow Up

Generalizations:
- a.   Most grown-ups have a job to do.
- b.   People need to learn how to do their jobs.

Issues:
- a.   What would you like to be when you grow up?
- b.   How should we choose what to do when we grow up?

GRADE LEVEL: First
AREA OF STUDY: My Family and Other Families

Unit Topic 1:   Families All Over

Generalizations:
- a.   The family and the institution of marriage are universal phenomena.
- b.   The large majority of adults in all societies are married.

Issues:
- a.   Should people get married or stay single?

Unit Topic 2:   Families Are Different

Generalizations:
- a.   Societies have customary but different ways of treating distant family members such as grandparents, uncles, aunts, cousins, and others.
- b.   While in some societies the kinship line follows a matrilineal or patrilineal organization, in our society the kinship line follows a bilateral organizational pattern.

Issues:

    a.   Which form of family is better, the nuclear or the extended family?

    b.   What is the best way to take care of our elderly?

Unit Topic 3:   Families Have Needs

Generalizations:

    a.   Families work in different ways to provide for their physical needs.

    b.   Family members need and get affection and love from each other.

Issues:

    a.   Should children receive pay for doing chores around the house?

Unit Topic 4:   Families Have Rules

Generalizations:

    a.   Because family members come into frequent contact with one another, they tend to share values and norms.

    b.   The family strongly influences the behavior of its members by setting and/or enforcing standards for proper behavior by its members.

Issues:

    a.   Who should make the family rules?

Unit Topic 5:   Families Change

Generalizations:

    a.   When members of the family move from one area to another, from one socioeconomic level to another, from one occupation to another, or from one religion to another, the family changes.

    b.   The life style of the family changes when both parents work outside the home.

Issues:

    a.   Should mothers work outside the home?

    b.   Should fathers stay home and care for the family while mothers work outside the home?

GRADE LEVEL: Second
AREA OF STUDY: My Community and Other Communities

Unit Topic 1:   The Local Community—Seattle, Washington

Generalizations:

    a.   Seattle's geographic location makes it an important trade center.

    b.   The Northwest Indian culture is quite evident in the Seattle area.

Issues:

    a. Should the charm of old landmarks such as the public market be sacrificed in the name of progress?

Unit Topic 2: Communities of Long Ago

Generalizations:

    a. Communities of long ago produced their own food and almost everything else they needed.

    b. Communities in the past developed around places where people found work—trading communities, mining communities, and others.

Issues:

    a. Was community life in the "good old days" better than it is in today's communities?

    b. Should people live in the community in which they were born or should they move out and live in any community they want?

Unit Topic 3: Communities Are Different

Generalizations:

    a. The style of life varies between urban and rural communities.

    b. The style of life varies between U.S. communities and communities in other parts of the world.

Issues:

    a. Which style of community life is better?

Unit Topic 4: Communities Work Together

Generalizations:

    a. Improved communication and transportation increased the interdependence of communities.

    b. Communities cooperate to solve common problems or to meet common needs.

Issues:

    a. Is life in our communities overdependent on resources from other communities?

Unit Topic 5: Communities Change

Generalizations:

    a. The population shift to urban areas caused some communities to grow larger while others grew smaller.

    b. Migration brings about cultural diffusion between groups and cultural diversity within groups.

Issues:

    a. What should our attitude be toward change?

GRADE LEVEL: Third
AREA OF STUDY: People Move In and Around the Cities

Unit Topic 1: Cities Attract People

Generalizations:
    a.   Industrialization brought a sharp increase in urbanization.
    b.   Movement from rural to urban areas occurs particularly among
        the young, because there are more opportunities for
        them in the cities.
Issues:
    a.   Should young people stay on the farm?

Unit Topic 2: The Suburbs Are Getting Bigger

Generalizations:
    a.   The proportion of lower-status groups decreases as one
        moves from the center of the city to the periphery. Some
        people move to the suburbs for prestige.
    b.   Some people move to the suburbs to avoid crime and
        congestion usually found within the cities.
Issues:
    a.   Should people working in the city be expected to live
        in the city?

Unit Topic 3: Cities Are Different

Generalizations:
    a.   Some cities were developed and exist mainly to provide
        specific central-service functions such as government.
    b.   The main function of cities developed at ports or railroad
        junctions is commercial.
Issues:
    a.   Should cities with a narrow function diversify?

Unit Topic 4: The Mayor's Complicated Job

Generalizations:
    a.   As the upper classes move toward the suburbs, cities collect
        fewer taxes to cope with city problems.
    b.   City governments work to meet the needs of a diverse
        population with diverse needs.
Issues:
    a.   Should people who work in the city but live in the
        suburbs pay city taxes?
    b.   How could the cities provide for equal educational
        opportunity?

Unit Topic 5:   The History of Big Cities

Generalizations:

a.   Most big cities developed at junctions of important
     transportation routes or by ports.

b.   The industrial revolution and immigration affected the growth
     of the big cities in the United States.

Issues:

a.   Should cities be allowed to grow indefinitely?

GRADE LEVEL: Fourth
AREA OF STUDY: People Need the Earth

Unit Topic 1:   People and the Land Long Ago: American Indians vs. "The White Man"

Generalizations:

a.   The Indians respected land and its natural resources; they lived
     in harmony with their surroundings rather than changing them.

b.   White settlers drastically changed their environment to meet
     their needs.

Issues:

a.   Should "the white man" have adopted the Indian philosophy
     toward nature?

Unit Topic 2:   The Earth Satisfies Our Needs

Generalizations:

a.   The earth's resources are used in multiple ways to
     satisfy people's needs.

b.   Humans continuously develop new methods to improve the
     fertility of the soil to increase productivity.

Issues:

a.   How can we conserve the earth's resources?

Unit Topic 3:   The Earth Is Abused

Generalizations:

a.   Human beings' technological ability to change the
     environment has increased.

b.   For a long time humans exploited and consumed the earth's
     natural resources without giving due consideration to the
     limitations of supply.

Issues:

a.   What laws meant to protect the environment are or could be justified?

Unit Topic 4: Regions of the Earth

Generalizations:

    a. The way people live in any place in the world depends on their values, abilities, and needs as well as on the natural environment and resources of the region.

    b. The need for goods and services in a region fosters trade and interdependence.

Issues:

    a. How can the various regions cooperate more effectively?

Unit Topic 5: Our Region and State

Generalizations:

    a. The Northwest region of the United States includes mountains, rivers, valleys, and an irregular coastline that contribute to a diversified economy and way of life.

    b. The Northwest region attracted many immigrants from similar climatic and occupational areas.

Issues:

    a. Should the Northwest share its abundant natural resources with other regions?

GRADE LEVEL: Fifth
AREA OF STUDY: The Development of Our Nation

Unit Topic 1: The Making of Our Nation

Generalizations:

    a. As a result of the British victories over the French in 1763, Anglo-Saxon institutions became dominant in North America.

    b. The direction and flow of North American settlement was influenced by the geographical features of the continent.

Issues:

    a. Were the settlers justified in displacing the Indians?

    b. Is revolution justified for people who feel oppressed?

Unit Topic 2: The Effects of Industrialization and Immigration

Generalizations:

    a. The Industrial Revolution gradually transformed the United States from a rural, agricultural society to an urban one.

    b. The immigrants of the nineteenth century played a significant role in the industrial development of the United States.

Issues:

    a. Should the United States continue an open policy on immigration?

Unit Topic 3: People and Institutions in Our Society

Generalizations:

a. People of all races, religions, and cultures contributed to the
U.S. cultural heritage.

b. In a democracy, government is by right an institution made
by the people for the people; the sole source of authority
is the people.

Issues:

a. What can be done to insure equal rights for all?

Unit Topic 4: Our Nation and the World

Generalizations:

a. The foreign policy of the United States has been characterized
by an effort to contain the spread of communist influence
in the world.

b. Isolationists and internationalists have attempted to influence
what role the United States plays in the world.

Issues:

a. Should the United States use its food surplus as a
diplomatic weapon with other countries?

Unit Topic 5: Do We Practice What We Believe?

Generalizations:

a. Most people in the United States believe that the recognition
of human rights and the dignity of the individual are basic
to personal relationships and the conduct of government.

b. The history of the United States has been characterized by
the practice of racial discrimination.

Issues:

a. How can racial discrimination be reduced in U.S. communities?

b. Are the values implied in the Declaration of Independence, the
Constitution, and the Bill of Rights still valid?

GRADE LEVEL: Sixth
AREA OF STUDY: The Interaction of World Cultures

Unit Topic 1: Early Civilization: Far East and Middle East

Generalizations:

a. Remarkable civilizations developed more than 3000 years ago
along the Indus, Yellow, and Nile rivers.

b. Conflicts among groups of people and migrations of people were
characteristic of the early history of the Far East and
Middle East.

Issues:

    a. How would our lives be different if they were influenced by the philosophies of the early civilizations of the Far East?

Unit Topic 2:   Early Civilization: Greece and Rome

Generalizations:

    a. The foundations for our way of life were laid in ancient Greece and Rome.

    b. Rome conquered Greece, but respected and preserved the superior culture of the Greeks.

Issues:

    a. Should the American people continue to base their way of life only on the ancient Western cultures?

Unit Topic 3:   People in the World Today: Major Cultures

Generalizations:

    a. People having lived in isolation during the past developed certain assumptions about life that vary from society to society.

    b. Humankind evolved from isolated, self-sufficient communities to an interdependent world and brought about more trade, more migration, and more diffusion of ideas and practices.

Issues:

    a. Is there a culture that is better than the others?

Unit Topic 4:   Forces That Divide the World

Generalizations:

    a. While in the past people were divided by geographic features, ideology is the main divisive factor today.

    b. Race has been a major divisive factor in the world.

Issues:

    a. What can be done to reduce the causes of conflict around the world?

Unit Topic 5:   Forces That Unite the World

Generalizations:

    a. People tend to unite on the basis of a common way of life.

    b. The nations of the world established the United Nations to facilitate international cooperation.

Issues:

    a. How can the United Nations become more effective?

    b. Should we cooperate with nations that disregard human rights?

THE CURRICULUM AND THE SPECIAL EMPHASES

In recent years several special emphases have claimed a place in the elementary school curriculum; most important among them have been career education, consumer education, law-related education, environmental education, and sex education. Moreover, in some schools such areas as sensitivity toward other people, ethnic studies, minorities and women, energy education, future education, values clarification, and the concept of humanism in social studies have been added to the ongoing social studies program.

Teachers and administrators have had difficulty finding room for these special emphases. Yet all are important—but they should be a part of the regular, ongoing social studies program. If unit topics in fact reflect the social realities, they invite generalizations and issues that address the various special emphases. A quick review of the curriculum suggested in this chapter should substantiate this point of view. For every area of special emphasis listed above, generalizations and issues can be found. Related to career education, for example, the program offers such generalizations and issues as the following, to list just a few:

1. Most grown-ups have a job to do.
2. What would you like to be when you grow up?
3. How should you choose what to do when you grow up?
4. Families work in different ways to meet their physical needs.
5. Humans continuously develop new methods to improve the fertility of the soil to increase productivity.
6. The Northwest region attacted many immigrants from similar climatic and occupational areas.

No social studies program that neglects the special emphases is a good program.

THE NEXT STEP

Concepts, generalizations, and issues, then, are the backbone of the social studies program; organized around carefully selected topics, they form a framework that reflects the social realities as well as the social and behavioral sciences. However, this framework should be viewed not as a body of knowledge to be presented to students but instead as a source of specific social studies instructional objectives—both content and process. Among these objectives (discussed in Chapter 2) are: (a) knowledge, (b) social values, (c) intellectual skills, (d) value-clarification skills, and (e) social skills. The methods of formulating these objectives and realizing them in teaching are discussed in the next two chapters.

SUMMARY

The function of social studies should be to develop dynamic citizens—concerned, knowledgeable citizens capable of participating in and contributing to the affairs of society rather than blindly and passively conforming to it. To accomplish this objective, social studies needs an appropriate curriculum. Because dynamic citizenship develops through involvement and practice, the procedures and curriculum recommended in this chapter allow for them.

Neither the descriptive nor the conceptual curriculum can develop citizenship traits, because each is concerned only with knowledge, be it as facts or concepts and generalizations. The dynamic curriculum values knowledge, not as an end in itself but as a means of making decisions. To provide opportunities for decision making, the dynamic curriculum adds issues to generalizations and concepts.

A dynamic curriculum does not require that the traditional scope and sequence be abandoned. The area of study for each grade could be close to the traditional, but the topics should be comprehensive and should bring out contemporary issues.

No particular scope and sequence can be considered the best. Published programs display as many variations as similarities. A sample scope and sequence is provided in this chapter, but a teacher or group of teachers might do better to develop their own.

The next step is to develop half a dozen generalizations and half a dozen issues for each topic. These are the backbone of the program and the background for the more specific instructional objectives. Translating generalizations and issues into instructional objectives and developing these objectives are explored in the next two chapters.

ACTIVITIES

1. Secure old social studies textbooks and evaluate each to identify deficiencies. Report the findings and discuss.

2. Compare recent and older textbooks to determine differences in treatment of social problems and controversial issues.

3. Ask your instructor for a random list of unit topics and classify them in grade levels that reflect the traditional scope and sequence.

4. Survey the teachers in a local school to determine the area of study and the unit topics studied in each grade. Individual students may also examine different current textbooks to determine the scope and sequence of each.

5. Using the data from the preceding activity and the appropriate criteria from the chapter, develop a scope and sequence of your own that satisfies your interests and local conditions. Students may be divided into groups and each group may work on one grade level. This activity could be the beginning for a continuous activity leading to the development of a localized program.

6. Take a random list of concepts, generalizations, and issues and separate them.

7. View a film and identify three basic concepts, three generalizations, and three issues basic to its content.

8. From a unit in the sample curriculum in this chapter, individually develop more generalizations and issues. The same activity could be done with the topics developed through activity 5.

NOTES

1. George H. Gallup, "Sixth Annual Gallup Poll of Public Attitudes Toward Education," *Phi Delta Kappan,* 56 (September 1974), 20.

2. Bruce R. Joyce, "The Primary Grades: A Review of Textbook Materials," in C. Benjamin Cox and Byron G. Massialas, eds., *Social Studies in the United States: A Critical Appraisal* (New York: Harcourt Brace Jovanovich, 1967), p. 27.

3. William D. Rader, "The Intermediate Grades: Should Children Answer Their Own Questions?" in Cox and Massialas, eds., *Social Studies,* p. 43.

4. Theodore Kaltsounis, "Cognitive Power Through the Social Studies: Upper Grades," *Educational Leadership,* 27 (April 1970), 665.

5. Glenys G. Unruh, "Beyond Sputnik," *Educational Leadership,* 30 (April 1973), 588.

6. Hazel W. Hertzberg, "The New Culture: Some Implications for Teacher Training Programs," *Social Education,* 34 (March 1970), 272.

7. Glenys Unruh, "Beyond Sputnik," p. 589.

8. Richard Whitemore, "By Inquiry Alone?" *Social Education,* 34 (March 1970), 283.

9. John Jarolimek, "In Pursuit of the Elusive New Social Studies," *Educational Leadership,* 30 (April 1973), 598–99. Reprinted with the permission of the Association of Supervision and Curriculum Development.

10. Frank M. Hodgson, "Trends in Social Studies in the Elementary Schools," *School and Society,* 80 (September 18, 1954), 85–87.

11. Ralph C. Preston, *Teaching Social Studies in the Elementary School,* rev. ed. (New York: Holt, Rinehart & Winston, 1962), p. 22.

12. Richard R. Burns and Alexander Frazier, "A Survey of Elementary School Social Studies Programs," *Social Education,* 21 (May 1957), 202–4.

13. D. L. Barnes, "What Are We Teaching in Social Studies and Sciences?" *Education,* 81 (October 1960), 121–23.

14. Fay Adams, *Curriculum Content and Basic Materials in the Social Studies* (Los Angeles: University of Southern California, 1962).

15. Celia Stendler Lavatelli, Walter J. Moore, and Theodore Kaltsounis, *Elementary School Curriculum* (New York: Holt, Rinehart & Winston, 1972), pp. 144–47.

16. Lee F. Anderson, general ed., *Windows of the World, The Houghton Social Studies Program* (Boston: Houghton Mifflin, 1976).

17. Roy A. Price, "Syracuse University—Social Science Concepts and Workways as the Basics for Curriculum Revision," *Social Education,* 29 (April 1965), 218–20.

18. Anna Ochoa and Gary A. Manson, "Social Issues, Social Action, and the Social Studies," in John Jarolimek and Huber M. Walsh, eds., *Readings for Social Studies in Elementary Education,* 3rd ed. (New York: Macmillan, 1974), p. 437.

19. Raymond H. Muessig, ed., *Controversial Issues in the Classroom: A Contemporary Perspective,* 45th Yearbook of the National Council for the Social Studies (Washington, D.C.: National Council for the Social Studies, 1975).

20. Joseph J. Schwab, "The Concept of the Structure of a Discipline," in Louis J. Hebert and William Murphy, eds., *Structure in the Social Studies* (Washington, D.C.: National Council for the Social Studies, 1968), p. 44.

Studying this chapter will enable the reader to:

1. be convinced that through proper instruction children can begin at an early age to develop generalizations.
2. reduce generalizations to all five types of instructional objectives: knowledge, social values, intellectual skills, value-clarification skills, and social skills.
3. define and accept inquiry as the most appropriate method of acquiring knowledge and developing intellectual or thinking skills.
4. perceive inquiry as a broad method of reflective teaching and learning that involves inductive and deductive thinking as well as exposition.
5. describe various models of inquiry.
6. appreciate the importance of questions in inquiry and in the formation of concepts and generalizations.
7. design questions that will promote high-level thinking abilities.
8. design teaching plans based on generalizations that will assist children to understand the generalizations as well as develop intellectual and other types of skills.
9. realize that in education, generalizations serve as means and not as ends. Children develop them to understand and cope with the world in which they live.

DEVELOPING CONCEPTS
AND GENERALIZATIONS
THROUGH INQUIRY

Some claim that elementary school students should concentrate only on facts, that they are not yet ready for the higher-level thinking that concepts and generalizations involve. Thinking, they claim, cannot be done in a vacuum; children must first acquire the facts and then learn how to think about them later. This is the basic defense of the descriptive approach to social studies.

There are two main reasons why conceptualization has been eschewed. First is the erroneous assumption (implied, never stated) that children do not start to learn until they begin formal education. In fact, children have been learning for their previous six years. For example, when children try a variety of ways to reach the cookie jar high up in the cupboard, they are thinking. When, watching television, they conclude "that man is a bad guy; he shoots people," they are thinking. Children are neither empty of knowledge nor totally incapable of thinking when they enter the elementary grades.

The second main reason for not teaching children conceptualization is the impression that, according to Piaget's stages of cognitive development, thinking is associated only with the last stage, formal operations, which usually begins to develop around the fifth or sixth grade level. This impression is of course totally false. Children engage in thinking even at the sensory-motor stage, the lowest of the four stages—although it is true that certain limitations in thinking ability characterize the lower stages.

Celia Lavatelli, one of Piaget's students, asserts that the sensory-motor stage children are able to apply "mental invention." [1] When given a closed box, children try different ways to open it; they are capable of thinking of a solution to the problem and trying it. Beginning at age four, children are able to make judgments, if the context is concrete. Most kindergarten children might have difficulty with multiple classifications, but they can classify things on the basis of one criterion; they can also begin to arrange things in a series. It is not unusual to find preschool programs that would include such objectives related to thinking as those recommended by Shirley Moore and Sally Kilmer:

> Group familiar objects, people, and events into appropriate categories, using both broad general classes (such as "animals") and smaller subclasses (such as "dogs").

Notice how things are alike or different.
Notice the separate parts of objects; combine parts into wholes.
Associate one experience with another.[2]

Piaget's concrete operational stage begins at about the age of seven. By that time most children are able to think in the abstract. They are able, for instance, to go back to the origin of a decision and trace the steps in making it. They can also think of solutions to a problem and put them to test, though at the early stages children tend to think of testing one solution at a time. Finally, by age eleven most children are capable of formal operations and of engaging in hypothetico-deductive reasoning, one of the most advanced forms of thinking.

Thus, children can think quite early, although, again, their thinking processes are quite restricted at the early stages. The solution, however, is not to neglect their thinking but to design for each developmental level special ways to help them develop their thinking. The implications of Piaget's theories should not be to forego thinking, but to make possible the development of thinking in an orderly fashion. As Lavatelli summarized:

Piaget's theory of the development of logical intelligence is helpful. . . .
He postulates age-related changes in thinking processes. Teachers of young children (up to about seven years of age) can anticipate learning difficulties because the child's thinking tends to be egocentric and perceptually-oriented, and then modify their teaching accordingly. With the seven- to eleven-year-old learner, teachers will find that taking into account Piaget's model of concrete-operational thought will facilitate learning processes. And at the fifth- and sixth-grade levels teachers need to be alert to ways to assist development of hypothetico-deductive reasoning.[3]

RESEARCH FINDINGS ON THE ABILITY OF YOUNG CHILDREN TO CONCEPTUALIZE

The emergence of conceptualization in the social studies curriculum, in the early 1960s, generated much research to determine whether or not elementary school children can engage in the appropriate kind of thinking. The findings were conclusive: Yes, they can, provided instruction at the lower levels is based on concrete objects and experiences, and that the generalizations reflect simple relationships involving few variables.

Bernard Spodek attempted to determine how well kindergarten children can begin to grasp history and geography concepts.[4] His intentions were not to enable young children to fully develop the concepts, but to begin with an understanding of simple forms and, through a spiral curriculum, move into more complex forms of the concepts taught. Spodek's experiment demonstrated that this method works. Gloria Camarota found that primary grade children successfully dealt with the concepts involved in films and filmstrips designed for intermediate grades.[5] Vincent Rogers and Dorothy Layton experimented with first and third grade children to find out how well they could classify pictures to arrive at concepts.[6] Their findings indicated that first and third grade children did not differ in their ability to conceptualize. Rogers and Layton reported that one-third of both groups demonstrated an ability to conceptualize at a high level of abstraction.

Mary Rusnak conducted a three-year study teaching important social studies skills and concepts.[7] She found that first graders could develop and use advanced social studies concepts and relationships. She also identified limitations (some of which appear to parallel those described by Piaget) in teaching concepts and generalizations to young children:

> (1) Since the first graders cannot read the social studies material, great use was made of other materials—pictures, field trips, films, etc.; (2) the need for simplicity was pointed up by the fact that first graders could not deal with more than two facts or activities simultaneously; (3) the fact that activities had to be divided into 15-minute periods indicated the need for brevity; (4) the children depend on close guidance from the teacher in order to understand what they are doing and why.[8]

Finally, there is the well-known work of Lawrence Senesh, an economist, who taught basic economic concepts to first graders.[9] Senesh was successful mainly because he used the children's everyday experiences to convey an understanding of concepts and generalizations. He thoroughly studied the life of a first grader; finding out, for example, that the children made gingerbread before Christmas, he used that activity to teach the concepts of division of labor and the assembly line. He divided the class into two groups, organizing one in an assembly line and having those in the other make gingerbread individually. The children in the assembly line performed small tasks, all coordinated to come up with the final product. From this experience the children developed a simple understanding of the concepts of division of labor and the assembly line.

REDUCTION OF GENERALIZATIONS TO INSTRUCTIONAL OBJECTIVES

As discussed in the previous chapter, the backbone of the contemporary social studies curriculum consists of generalizations (and their constituent concepts) and issues. Within the dynamic approach, they provide a sound knowledge base, and they prevent the social studies content from becoming superficial, as it was in the past. In this chapter teachers will learn appropriate procedures for developing and using generalizations, and their constituent concepts, to achieve social studies objectives. Issues will be considered in Chapter 5.

Developing generalizations requires systematic planning. The first step is to reduce generalizations to instructional objectives. This step is necessary because generalizations are usually articulated at the adult level. For example, in Chapter 3 one of the second grade units presents the generalization: "Migration develops cultural diversity within groups and cultural diffusion between groups." This generalization, difficult even for upper grade elementary school students, is likely to be far beyond the grasp of second grade students. However, with appropriate help, young children can begin to understand the relationships implicit in it. To accomplish this goal one must reduce the generalization to its component parts and sequence them according to the children's abilities and experiences.

The first step in perceiving a relationship is to understand its parts— the concepts. The concepts in the sample generalization are "migration," "cultural diversity," "cultural diffusion," and "groups"—difficult concepts all, especially the first three. If they are to be understood by children, they must be further reduced to small relationships and pertinent specifics. For instance, the concept "migration" could be thus reduced:

1. People move from one place to another.
2. There are different reasons for which people move.
3. It is easier to move now than it was a hundred years ago.
4. The Mormons moved west to avoid persecution.
5. Some workers move constantly from place to place to find work.
6. The Spanish moved north and came in contact with the Navajos.

By the same procedure, the concept "cultural diversity" can also be reduced:

1. Various ethnic groups eat different foods.
2. The various churches celebrate major holidays differently.
3. Communities in our country are made up of a variety of subcultural groups.
4. Modern means of communication and transportation facilitate the mixing of ways of life.

Likewise, the concept "cultural diffusion":

1. People often try foods usually eaten by other ethnic groups.
2. Every cultural group has something to offer to enrich our lives.
3. People moving into a new town adopt some of the ways of life of the people living in that town.

The concept "groups" might be easier because children usually experience group activities every day in school. It might be necessary, however, to expand on their understanding of the concept to include such entities as communities, nations united in some way, ethnic groups, and many others. In other words, children need to learn that there are small and large groups and that there are reasons why groups hold together.

The same process of reduction demonstrated on concepts can be applied to the relationships in a generalization. Our difficult sample generalization can be reduced to smaller, more visible relationships that are implicit:

1. When two groups of people live next to each other they exchange ways of life without even realizing it.
2. The more a group borrows ways of life from other groups, the more its own way of life changes.
3. The more people travel and come in contact with groups having different ways of life, the more they change their way of life.

This list—although by no means exhaustive of all specific learnings that could be derived from the generalization—and the lists of concepts above appear to be enough to enable elementary school students to understand the generalization and its concepts.

The next task is to sequence these specifics and distribute them to the various developmental levels of children. Knowledge of child development and of the children's experiential backgrounds now comes in handy. For example, kindergarteners may understand that "people move from one place to another" simply by discovering how many of them were born in different places. They may also be reminded that they occasionally eat different national foods, and thus learn that "various ethnic groups eat different foods." But some specific relationships, such as "modern means of communication and transportation facilitate the mixing of ways of life," or "The more a group borrows ways of life from other groups, the more its own way of life changes," must be deferred to a much later stage of development. It must be emphasized that there is no one ideal sequence for given specifics. General knowledge about children, and the insights of Piaget and others, may give rise to suggested sequences, but the final judge of what is best is the teacher. Objectives for a typical second grade are provided in a later section of the chapter.

Helping Children Reach Instructional Objectives

There are two ways of teaching: the expository and the inquiry modes. Either mode can be used to guide children toward instructional objectives. Before we decide which method is more appropriate, each will be briefly discussed.

"In the context of teaching," say John Jarolimek and Clifford Foster, "exposition has to do with the teacher's providing facts, ideas and other essential information to the learner." [10] The teacher is the main source of information, prescribes what is to be learned, and directs learning. Learners are expected to follow directions and meet whatever requirements are established. There is little self-direction by the learners. During the ascendency of the descriptive approach, prior to the 1960s, social studies textbooks were expository. They presented information, questions to be answered, and assignments to be done. Learning resources were used simply to provide input.

On the other hand, according to Jarolimek and Foster, "to *inquire* means that one is carrying on an investigation." [11] In an inquiry-oriented classroom the teacher's role is to manipulate the environment to create appropriate problems and stimulate questions and investigations among students. Instead of being the main source of information for the children the teacher guides them in finding the information for themselves and in addressing it to their questions. Inquiry is a child-centered mode of teaching.

The expository mode requires mainly deductive reasoning; the inquiry mode, mainly inductive. Deductive thinking proceeds from the general to the particular; inductive, from the particular to the general. Using the deductive approach, a teacher states a generalization and then presents as many supporting instances as seem necessary. For instance, the teacher may write on the board the social science generalization: "Among those arrested, persons from a lower socioeconomic level have a greater chance of being convicted than do persons from a higher socioeconomic level." Then the teacher proves this by presenting actual records of arrests and convictions from many places around the country. The data confirm the generalization.

The inductive approach starts from the opposite direction: The teacher brings in records of arrests and convictions during a period of time from the local community (or, if that community is small, from a nearby community) and asks the children to examine them, then, by means of recorded addresses, to group those arrested according to neighborhood of residence. From their knowledge of the community or from some other source, they can identify those residing in poor neighborhoods and those in prosperous neighborhoods. A chart like the one below may then be drawn.

Type of Neighborhood	Number of Persons Arrested	Percentage of Persons Convicted
Poor neighborhoods		
Prosperous neighborhoods		

If the community is typical, it will be noticeable that a higher percentage of those convicted comes from poor neighborhoods than from prosperous neighborhoods. The children then, by themselves or under the teacher's probing, may raise the question, in so many words: Is this observed relationship true in all communities? The teacher helps the children prepare similar charts for other communities, comparison of which makes them realize the truth of the generalization.

The deductive and inductive approaches can also be applied to teach more specific relationships derived from broad generalizations. For example, from the generalization "Migration develops cultural diversity within groups and cultural diffusion between groups" comes the more specific "Communities in our country are made up of a variety of subcultural groups." The teacher may state this and then try to prove it, or may instead first make students aware of the subcultures in the local community and other communities. Many ways can be used: guest speakers, field trips in various parts of the community, use of the telephone book to identify ethnic restaurants, and the like.

Expository teaching, then, is basically deductive; inquiry is basically inductive—but not entirely. Inquiry sometimes needs deductive thinking and even exposition. Hypotheses, for example, cannot be proved without deduction. Thus, although inductive and deductive thinking are distinct, expository teaching and inquiry teaching are not always so. Inquiry is a broad concept that encompasses many skills and approaches, as will now be seen in some detail.

VARIOUS MODELS OF THE INQUIRY METHOD

Since the early 1960s much has been written about inquiry. Although some seem to believe this method of teaching and thinking is a new discovery, it is in fact as old as Socrates. Good teachers have always used it and professional educators have always valued many of its elements.

Edwin Fenton defines inquiry as two linked, sequential processes—hypothesis formation and hypothesis testing—involving the following steps:

1. Recognizing a problem from data
2. Formulating hypotheses
   a. Asking analytical questions
   b. Stating hypotheses
   c. Remaining aware of the tentative nature of hypotheses
3. Recognizing the logical implications of hypotheses
4. Gathering data
   a. Deciding what data will be needed
   b. Selecting or rejecting sources

5. Analyzing, evaluating, and interpreting data
    a. Selecting relevant data
    b. Evaluating sources
        (1) Determining the frame of reference of an author
        (2) Determining the accuracy of statements of fact
    c. Interpreting the data
6. Evaluating the hypothesis in light of the data
    a. Modifying the hypothesis in light of the data
        (1) Rejecting a logical implication unsupported by data
        (2) Restating the hypothesis
    b. Stating a generalization [12]

Jack Nelson simplifies the same steps:

1. Identifying and defining issues
2. Hypothesis developing
3. Evidence gathering and evaluation
4. Hypothesis testing
5. Drawing tentative conclusions [13]

Essential to inquiry is forming hypotheses, which implies a problem that can be resolved through information. Inquiry, of course, is not used only to solve social problems; it is also used to generate knowledge. As Charlotte Crabtree points out, inquiry

> may arise from problems and conflicts in the social world. . . . Inquiries may also be conducted specifically for purposes of generating knowledge, verifying a knowledge claim, criticizing value assumptions, or resolving observed discrepancies between earlier found knowledge (or theory structures) and some new information, evidence or insight, challenging the old.[14]

This knowledge-generating function of inquiry is the focal point of this chapter; the form of inquiry that arises from social conflicts is the subject of the next chapter.

The everyday lives of few children expose them to the problems that promote systematic knowledge-generating inquiries. The teacher must create these problems for children by manipulating the classroom environment, by raising appropriate questions, or by doing both. If, for example, students are meant to learn that "communities in our country are made up of a variety of subcultural groups," several things could lead them to raise such questions as: "Where did the people in our community come from? How do people in our community worship? Why do all people in the community not go to the same church? Why is there a German district, or an Italian district, or a Greek district, or an Oriental district in our community?

Are most communities around the country like ours, made up of many cultural groups?" All these questions imply hypotheses that must be tested by collecting and analyzing data. By testing these hypotheses, the children learn that indeed "communities in our country are made up of a variety of subcultural groups." This generalization is in turn the basis for developing the broader, or higher-level, generalization that "migration develops cultural diversity within groups and cultural diffusion between groups."

The reader should be cautioned: Inquiry need not always be orderly and mechanical. Simply out of natural curiosity children may be gathering data before a particular problem arises. Moreover, information gathered for one problem may suggest other problems. The point is that the teachers know the skills of inquiry and make sure to involve students in all of them in a natural way.

Inquiry and Intellectual Skills

Thus far inquiry has been presented as a means of acquiring knowledge and of examining values, with special reference to resolving social problems and conflicts. However, developing the inquiry skills is itself an important social studies objective. Because the school offers only a fraction of the knowledge needed throughout a person's life, children must become independent learners, which means they must become skillful in inquiry. Some experts believe, indeed, that it is more valuable for the student to acquire such skills in school than to acquire knowledge there.

Inquiry involves not one skill but many, which we shall call intellectual skills, although they are known also as cognitive skills or abilities. Fenton believes that 12 abilities are fundamental to inquiry:

1. Grasping the meaning of a statement.
2. Judging whether there is ambiguity in a line of reasoning.
3. Judging whether certain statements contradict each other.
4. Judging whether a conclusion follows necessarily.
5. Judging whether a statement is specific enough.
6. Judging whether a statement is actually the application of a certain principle.
7. Judging whether an observation statement is reliable.
8. Judging whether an inductive conclusion is warranted.
9. Judging whether the problem has been identified.
10. Judging whether something is an assumption.
11. Judging whether a definition is adequate.
12. Judging whether a statement made by an alleged authority is acceptable.[15]

Benjamin Bloom has been a prime mover in promoting the intellectual abilities as educational objectives; with his associates at the University of Chicago, he published the classic *Taxonomy of Educational Objectives, Handbook I: Cognitive Domain.* As we saw in Chapter 2, Bloom et al. array six categories of abilities hierarchically from simplest to most complex. Each category is composed of several more specific abilities:

KNOWLEDGE: The ability to

---

    a. recall specifics
    b. recall ways and means of dealing with specifics
    c. recall the universals and abstractions of a particular field of knowledge

COMPREHENSION: The ability to

---

    a. translate or paraphrase accurately
    b. interpret, explain, or summarize a communication or a situation
    c. extrapolate trends and tendencies from given data

APPLICATION: The ability to

---

    a. use general and abstract ideas in concrete situations
    b. use rules of procedure in specific situations

ANALYSIS: The ability to

---

    a. identify the elements of a communication or situation
    b. identify the relationships between the various elements
    c. identify the organizational elements of a communication or a particular situation

SYNTHESIS: The ability to

---

    a. put elements together to produce or create a unique communication or situation
    b. produce a plan or propose a set of operations
    c. develop a theory or a set of abstract relations to explain particular data or phenomena

EVALUATION: The ability to

---

    a. judge the value of a communication in terms of its logic, consistency, and other such internal evidence
    b. judge material with reference to external criteria that one selects or remembers.[16]

J. P. Guilford's five mental operations, also discussed in Chapter 2, involve a similar pattern of abilities.[17] Although cognition, memory, and convergent thinking were the abilities heavily stressed by the school in the past, divergent thinking and evaluation were neglected until recently. These latter two abilities resemble what Bloom et al. call synthesis and evaluation.

In the early 1960s, Paul Torrance attempted to find out the extent to which teachers were developing the abilities of divergent thinking and evaluation.[18] He asked 390 elementary teachers throughout Minnesota to identify a unit they taught in social studies and list their three most important objectives with respect to it. The objectives, classified on the basis of Guilford's five operations, gave disappointing results: Of 1070 objectives submitted by the teachers only nine were related to divergent thinking and only five to evaluation. Have things improved since the early 1960s? Most knowledgeable observers say not enough, but each teacher must be the judge.

The third model of thinking abilities briefly discussed in Chapter 2 is one developed by Hilda Taba exclusively for social studies.[19] Taba identifies three cognitive tasks: (1) concept formation, (2) interpretation of data, and (3) application of principles. Each task involves several abilities, some easily observable overt behaviors, others covert mental operations:

TASK 1: CONCEPT FORMATION—the ability to

1. enumerate and list items
2. differentiate on the basis of some criterion
3. group items
4. identify common properties or characteristics
5. label and categorize items
6. determine the hierarchical order of items

TASK II: INTERPRETATION OF DATA—the ability to

1. identify the main points in a communication using the ability of differentiating
2. explain items of identified information
3. relate points to each other, determining cause and effect relationships
4. go beyond what is given and make inferences
5. find implications
6. extrapolate

TASK III: APPLICATION OF PRINCIPLES—the ability to

1. predict consequences
2. explain unfamiliar phenomena
3. formulate hypotheses
4. analyze the nature of a problem or a situation
5. retrieve relevant knowledge
6. determine the causal links leading to prediction or hypothesis
7. explain and support predictions and hypotheses
8. verify predictions through the use of logical principles or factual knowledge

For the elementary schools of Contra Costa County, in California, Taba developed a complete social studies program that implemented her model of thinking.[20] The program's main objective was to help children develop concepts and generalizations. This program, eventually revised and published nationally by Addison-Wesley Publishing Company, has made Taba's model of thinking the most influential model in elementary school practice, especially with reference to concept formation. For example, it is not unusual to walk into elementary school classrooms and find children making lists of what they saw on a field trip or what impressed them after hearing or reading a particular story. The children are then divided into groups to classify the listed items by whatever criteria appear to make sense to them. The children then propose labels (words or phrases) to fit each classification.

It should be emphasized that all models posit higher as well as lower levels of thinking abilities. Research findings, alas, show that teaching practice tends to stay with the lower abilities.[21] Yet, children cannot use inquiry effectively to gain knowledge or to make sound decisions unless they develop those higher-level abilities.

Inquiry, Reflective Thinking, and Exposition

In practice, as was said earlier, exposition and inquiry are not mutually exclusive. Inquiry, being a broad approach to teaching, invariably includes exposition and deductive thinking. During the early stages of the conceptual approach, the inquiry method was thought to properly involve only inductive thinking; the two were synonymous. Because deductive thinking was associated with exposition, proponents of inquiry excluded it as well as exposition. It soon became clear, however, that deductive thinking is involved in the inquiry approach. But it was restored with inquiry presented under the guise of a new word: "reflective" thinking, an apparent borrowing from John Dewey, who had written about reflective thinking more than 40 years ago.[22]

Massialas and Cox's inquiry model has also been called the reflective model.[23] It can be shown in diagrammatic form:

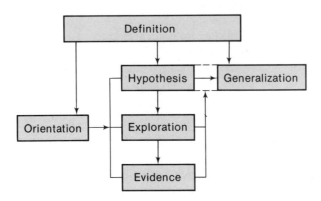

The first step, *orientation*, resembles what in other models is called identification of the problem. As in most inquiry models, the second step is the formation of hypotheses. During these first two steps, thinking is inductive. The next steps, *exploration* and *evidencing*, test the validity of the hypothesis or hypotheses. Most exploration and evidencing is by deductive thinking. About exploration, Massialas and Cox state: "Whereas orientation and hypothesizing tend to be inductive in nature, this phase tends to be deductive. The hypothesis is more carefully explicated in terms of logical deductions and implications, and assumptions and premises." [24] The final step in this reflective model is reaching a *generalization* or verifying a hypothesis. As the depiction of the Massialas and Cox model shows, *definition* plays a role, but as a pervasive element rather than as a separate step: "The task of defining is really not to be isolated in the process inasmuch as meaning and definition are constant elements in all phases of reflective inquiry." [25]

Inquiry, then, like reflective thinking, starts with problems or questions that lead to hypotheses, or "educated guesses" as to solutions or answers, which must then be verified. Children need much information to clarify their problems and to verify their solutions. Although they can be guided to acquire most of this information by themselves, there is no reason why the teacher cannot provide some of it by the expository method. In fact, it can be desirable as a way of speeding up thinking, for the inquiry or reflective approach puts less stress on the gathering of information than on how that information is used to reach conclusions. More exposition in the inquiry approach might eliminate some criticisms directed against inquiry. Particularly, it saves time and eliminates the monotony usually created by constantly asking the children to search for everything.

We can now illustrate how the inquiry or reflective model can be implemented in the classroom. Say a first grade class is studying about the family, and the teacher wants the children to learn that there are many family life styles. The teacher could tell this to the children, but they would soon forget it—as they do much of what they learn through exposition. Instead, the teacher uses the inquiry approach.

One day the teacher places pictures of different types of housing on the bulletin board—small houses, big houses, large apartment buildings, triplexes, farm houses, and the like. Directing attention to the display, the teacher leads a discussion on how life might differ from one type of house to the next. Children are encouraged to give personal experiences. With this experience as a background, the teacher asks, "In what other ways are our families different?" (the problem). With the teacher's help, the children make some suggestions (hypotheses). The children might now be paired to talk to each other about their families and identify at least one difference between them. When pulled together, the suggestions give rise to more hypotheses.

From the children's suggestions, the teacher prepares a simple questionnaire to which they respond with their parents' help. (A brief accompanying note to the parents states the purpose of the activity, to avoid any misunderstanding.) Among the questions are: "How many people are in your family? Does your family have pets? Do you have grandparents living with your family? Do both of your parents work? What is your favorite family food?" Such questions direct the children to collect information with which to test their hypotheses.

To ready the data for use, the teacher prepares forms for recording them. Each question has its own form, on its own sheet of paper, to prevent any confusion from a single, complex chart. For example:

Your Name	Do you have grandparents living with your family?	
	Yes	No

All charts are displayed around the room; from their data the children verify differences in family styles; they test their hypotheses. The hypotheses can be further tested, and the learning strengthened when the students later study family life in other parts of the world.

THE ROLE OF QUESTIONS IN INQUIRY
AND CONCEPTUALIZATION

Conceptualization and inquiry are closely related; the steps of inquiry guide the process of conceptualization. Each step of inquiry requires a number of intellectual skills. Questions are instrumental not only in the inquiry method but in developing and using intellectual skills as well.

The first step in inquiry is to identify a problem. The problem could involve resolving a conflict (such as "What can be done to reduce crime in our communities?") or could involve formulating a concept or a generalization (for example, "What kinds of people make up our communities?" or "In what other ways are our families different?"). Once the problem, always stated as a question, is clarified, the learner formulates hypotheses. The first substep in forming hypotheses is "asking analytical questions." [26] Hypotheses are tested mainly by raising appropriate questions.

Questions are therefore fundamental to inquiry. Indeed, some inquiry models have relied entirely on questions raised by the teacher and the learners. Richard Suchman argues that "inquiry is an attitude toward learning and a philosophy of education. The central values are the open mind and the autonomous probing of the learner." [27] Suchman's inquiry method is to present children with a new phenomenon and ask them to raise probing questions if they cannot explain it. To each question the teacher responds *yes* or *no*, generating more questions by the children until they can explain the phenomenon.

Questions are also important in developing specific intellectual skills. As we have seen, models of intellectual skills are hierarchically arranged, and questions have been developed to fit each level of skill. For example, Hilda Taba, for each of her three cognitive tasks, recommends the following eliciting questions: [28]

I. Concept formation
   What did you see? hear? note?
   What belongs together? On what criterion?
   How would you call these groups? What belongs under what?

II. Interpretation of data
   What did you note? see? find? Why did so-and-so happen?
   What does this mean? What picture does it create in your mind?
   What would you conclude?

III. Application of principles
   What would happen if . . . ? What idea might account for . . . ?
   Why do you think this would happen?
   What would it take for so-and-so to be true or probably true?
   Or not true?

96

James Gallagher's and Mary Aschner's work formulates questions based on Guilford's mental operations—for example: [29]

1. Cognitive-memory questions—They call for facts.
   a. What is the largest city in . . . ?
   b. Name the ABC countries of South America.
   c. What is the name for . . . ?
      Who is . . . ?
      Where is the . . . ?
      Describe. . . .
      What is a . . . ?

2. Convergent questions—They call for integration of given or remembered data and require some reasoning.
   a. What is there about the location of . . . that accounts for its importance?
   b. In what ways are these two countries alike?
   c. Why is abundant rainfall important to . . . economy?
      Explain how this could happen.
      Tell us why you think so.
      Give reasons for such a judgment.
      How did you reach that conclusion?
      Why is it called . . . ?
      What conclusion have you reached?

3. Divergent questions—They call for creativity and imagination.
   a. How might the lives of people in . . . be different if the city were located in the torrid zone?
   b. What might happen on the earth if the sun did not "come up" one morning?
   c. What might happen if suddenly all the electric power were shut off for a week?
      What would happen if . . . ?
      How many ways can you . . . ?
      Give me all the reasons you can think of. . . .
      Present as many possible solutions to our problems as you can.
      Give me all the synonyms you can think of for. . . .
4. Evaluation questions—They deal with matters of judgment, value, and choice.
   a. Would you prefer to be a North American cowboy or a South American gaucho?
   b. Would you prefer to live in a city or on a farm? Why?
   c. What do you think is the best means of transportation to travel from . . . to . . . ?
   d. What is the most important . . . ?
      Name the two most influential causes . . . .
      What are the chances that . . . ?
      Give an estimate of . . . .
      In your judgment, what is the best course of action?
      What do you think of my choice?

Gary Manson and Ambrose Clegg developed questions to suit Bloom's six categories of knowledge and abilities: [30]

1. Knowledge
   What did the book say about . . . ?
   Define . . . .
   List the three . . . .
   Who invented . . . ?
2. Comprehension
   Explain the . . . .
   What can you conclude?
   State in your own words . . . .
   What does the picture mean?
   If it rains, then what?
   What reasons or evidence . . . ?
3. Application
   If you know A and B, how could you determine C?
   What other possible reasons . . . ?
   What might they do with . . . ?
   What do you suppose would happen if . . . ?

4. Analysis

What was the author's purpose, bias, or prejudice?

What must you know for that to be true?

Does that follow?

Which are facts and which are opinions?

5. Synthesis

If no one else knew, how could you find out?

Can you develop a new way?

Make up . . . .

What could you do if . . . ?

6. Evaluation

Which policy will result in the greatest good for the greatest number?

For what reason could you favor . . . ?

Which of the books would you consider of greater value?

Evaluate that idea in terms of cost and community acceptance.

(Morris Sanders and Francis Hunkins have also designed sets of questions that operationalize Bloom's categories.[31])

The questions above are presented in some detail to stress their dual importance; they are needed equally in developing concepts and generalizations and intellectual skills. Development of higher-level skills and abilities requires the use of higher-level questions, but, as Hunkins points out, "research evidences that teachers and pupils have not been asking powerful questions." [32] There is no justification for this habit. If the school is to develop children's personal powers to enable them to resolve their conflicts and control their destinies, teachers must educate children to be able to ask, and answer, probing questions. Lower-level questions help children gain knowledge, but to be meaningful knowledge must be applied; higher-level questions help children to do so.

But questions do not ask themselves: Skill is needed to properly and effectively articulate them. Jack Morgan and Joan Schreiber suggest the following guidelines: [33]

1. Precise wording—Students should never be puzzled about what is being asked.

2. Appropriate timing—Questions should provide continuity to the discussion topic. . . .

3. Clarity of purpose—Formulate questions in accordance with purpose. . . .

4 Individualizing questions—Length and difficulty of questions depend on the nature of the learner. . . .

5. Directing questions—Direct the question to the entire class, pause to allow comprehension, and then call on the student who is to respond.

6. Eliciting student response—To encourage wide participation ask questions of students who do not ordinarily respond.

7. Encouraging student questions—Encourage students to ask questions of each other. . . .

8. Exploring incomplete answers—Incomplete answers should be further pursued until understanding is obtained.
9. Stimulating creative thought—Students need to think creatively, independently, and reach their own conclusions.

Morgan and Schreiber also suggest that the following question-asking practices be avoided:

1. Avoid asking questions requiring a "yes" or "no" answer.
2. Avoid directing most of your questions to the bright students or class volunteers.
3. Avoid asking leading questions.
4. Avoid playing a guessing game with the students.
5. Avoid asking questions about unimportant facts or issues.

GENERALIZATIONS AS MEANS RATHER THAN ENDS

Generalizations have been treated thus far as if they were ends in themselves rather than a means toward such broader social studies objectives as decision making and citizenship. The argument so far could be summarized thus:

1. Generalizations are reduced to specific knowledge objectives—those facts and relationships needed to understand the generalizations.
2. The inquiry mode of teaching is the best for achieving knowledge objectives. Inquiry begins with inductive thinking, but also applies deductive thinking during hypothesis testing. Exposition can sometimes be used to gain information during inquiry. An advantage of the inquiry mode of teaching is that, by involving the learner in the learning process, it makes learning more permanent. At the same time, the inquiry process allows development of intellectual skills, which enable the learner to become an independent developer of concepts and generalizations.
3. Finally, the value of questions and questioning strategies is related not only to development of concepts and generalizations but also to the intellectual skills involved in inquiry.

But children must be able to use concepts and generalizations as means toward other ends. In Chapter 2, social studies instructional objectives were enumerated: (1) knowledge, (2) values, (3) intellectual skills, (4) value-clarification skills, and (5) social skills. All five are essential to decision makers and effective members of society. Although the process outlined above assists in the development of knowledge and intellectual skills objectives, it neglects the other three. So also did teaching practice in the 1960s. In this section it will be seen how generalizations can be used to develop values, value-clarification skills, and social-skills objectives. Before doing so, it should be noted that generalizations are in fact inherently better suited to knowledge and intellectual skills objectives, and less well suited to values and value-clarification skills objectives, which are better approached through issues. Generalizations and issues are equally appropriate for developing social skills. (Strategies for dealing with issues will be presented in Chapter 5.)

The generalization used earlier, "Migration develops cultural diversity within groups and cultural diffusion between groups," when addressed to social realities and the children's level of ability, yields for discussion in the classroom the following social values:

1. Respect for differences among people.
2. Appreciation for the contributions of many cultural groups in the development of our way of life.
3. A willingness to accept and promote intergroup relations.

All three are part of the so-called American creed, but are fallen short of in practice. The children ought to be given an opportunity to consider these professed values and, by the rational process, decide whether or not they should accept them. Following acceptance (provided that is what happened) they should be expected to act accordingly.

In considering these social values, the children can examine and clarify their own values and behavior—for example, with respect to the following:

1. The extent to which they individually respect differences in other people.
2. The extent to which their actions are consistent with their own beliefs.
3. The extent to which they appreciate the contributions of all cultural groups to the development of our way of life.
4. The extent to which they approve of and promote intergroup relations.

Finally, a number of new or further refined old social skills may also emanate from a generalization. For example, from "Migration develops cultural diversity within groups and cultural diffusion between groups" might come:

1. The children will be courteous to newcomers in class or in town.
2. The children will further develop their skill to cooperate with others through involvement in learning projects.

Generalizations, then, need not be taught as ends in themselves; they can address all types of social studies instructional objectives, although, again, they yield ground to issues with respect to some instructional objectives.

LEARNING ACTIVITIES FOR CONCEPTS
AND GENERALIZATIONS

Having discussed reducing generalizations to instructional objectives and the superiority of inquiry for developing concepts and generalizations, let us now formulate a complete plan of instructional objectives for the development of a generalization.

Throughout this chapter have appeared several instructional objectives based on the generalization "Migration develops cultural diversity within groups and cultural diffusion between groups." This generalization was recommended for a second grade unit. Let us assume that the appropriate objectives for the second grade are:

A. Knowledge—The children will know that:
   1. People move from one place to another.
   2. There are different reasons why people move.
   3. Different ethnic groups eat different foods.
   4. People often try foods usually eaten by other ethnic groups.
   5. Every cultural group has something to offer to enrich our lives.
B. Social values—The children will value:
   1. Differences among people.
C. Intellectual skills—The children will be able to:
   1. Prepare lists of food items eaten by various ethnic groups.
   2. Analyze their home menus for a week and identify any foods from other ethnic groups eaten by their families.
D. Value-clarification skills—The children will be able to:
   1. Determine the extent to which each of them respects differences in other people.
E. Social skills—The children will be able to:
   1. Be courteous to newcomers in their class.
   2. Further develop their skill to cooperate with their classmates.

The first two categories of objectives—knowledge and social values—are content objectives, remember; the other three are process objectives. The teacher's primary instructional target is the content objectives. The process objectives develop as the content objectives are being realized. For example, for the children to learn the content objective, "People often try foods usually eaten by other ethnic groups," they must do an activity that involves analysis. In so doing they not only learn the content but increase their ability to analyze as well. Content and analysis are not taught separately but are combined.

Properly designed questions lead to appropriate activities. These questions are based directly on the content objectives—and usually are simply translations from the declarative form of the instructional objectives. For example, "Why do people move from one place to another?" is based on the instructional objective "The children will know that there are different reasons for which people move." All content objectives should be converted into questions. Otherwise, there will be no activities directed toward the development of those objectives that were not converted. Each question may be followed by as many activities as seem necessary for an adequate response. For example, the question quoted earlier in this paragraph may be followed by these activities:

1. The teacher will contact a couple of parents who have moved to the community or who are about to move away from the community to come to class and give reasons for their move.
2. Children will be stimulated to think of other reasons that might cause people to move. They may think of relatives who live away from the community and recall any particular reasons for their living away.

The design of activities is crucial, because they determine whether the process objectives are achieved. The teacher must make sure that the activities reflect all predetermined process objectives. Questions and activities are further discussed in Chapter 6.

Following is a complete sample plan for teaching the generalization used extensively in this chapter:

Grade Level:	Second
Characteristics of	
Children in Class:	Average heterogeneous group
Area of Study:	My Community and Other Communities
Unit Topic:	Communities Change
Generalization:	Migration develops cultural diversity within groups and cultural diffusion between groups.

INSTRUCTIONAL OBJECTIVES:

Content Objectives

    a. Knowledge—The children will know that:
1. People move from one place to another.
2. There are different reasons why people move.
3. Various ethnic groups eat different foods.
4. People often try foods usually eaten by other ethnic groups.
5. Every cultural group has something to offer to enrich our lives.

    b. Social values—The children will value:
1. Differences among people.

Process Objectives

    c. Intellectual skills—The children will be able to:
1. Prepare lists of food items eaten by various ethnic groups.
2. Analyze their home menus for a week and identify any foods from other ethnic groups eaten by their families.

d. Value-clarification skills—The children will be able to:
  1. Determine the extent to which each of them individually respects differences in other people.
e. Social skills—The children will be able to:
  1. Be courteous to newcomers in their class.
  2. Further develop their skill to cooperate with their classmates.

QUESTIONS (derived from content objectives)	LEARNING ACTIVITIES (reflecting the process objectives)
A. Were all the people in our community born here?	1. Ask children to indicate how many of them were born in the community and how many came from other places.
	2. Have children find out how many of their parents were born in the community and how many came from other communities.
B. Why do people move from one place to another?	1. Have a couple of parents who have moved to the community or who are about to move away from the community come to the class and give reasons for their move.
	2. Stimulate the children to think of other reasons why people might move. You might have them think of relatives who live away from the community and recall any particular reasons for their living away.
C. How different are the foods we eat and why?	1. Ask children to prepare a list of as many foods as they remember eating during the week.
	2. Compare the lists to identify differences in the menus.
	3. Bring into class some obviously ethnic food (the kind of food will depend on what is the most visible ethnic group in the community), and discuss its ethnic origin. Ask children if they know of other ethnic foods.
	4. In the yellow pages of a phone book, identify with the class various ethnic restaurants in the community.
D. Who eats in the ethnic restaurants?	1. After the above activities and with the children's assistance, make a list of as many ethnic foods as possible.
	2. Ask the children to individually name their favorite foods from the list. Ask each child whether the food mentioned comes from the same ethnic group to which the child belongs.
	3. Give the children a chance to talk about their experiences eating in different ethnic restaurants.

E. How would our community be without the various ethnic restaurants?	1. Ask the children to speculate and describe how they would feel if they had to eat the same food every day.
	2. Give them an opportunity to express how they would feel if they could not find their favorite ethnic food in the community.
	3. Prepare an ethnic dish (of the most visible ethnic group in your community) and have the children taste it. Use the expository method to tell them how and when this group moved into the community. Indicate that if these people had not joined their community they wouldn't even know that a dish like that existed.
F. What other groups of people are in our community and what new things have they brought to the community?	1. Prepare a list of the various cultural groups in your community, such as blacks, Jews, Italians, Germans, etc.
	2. Show sound filmstrips, such as "Minorities Have Made America Great" (Prentice-Hall Media), and discuss the contributions of each ethnic group. (Of the 12 groups presented in the filmstrip series, select those represented in your community.)
	3. In the prepared list of cultural groups in your community, place next to each group at least one contribution they have made to the heritage of the United States.

The questions provide the link between the objectives and the activities and assure that each activity is designed to achieve a specific purpose. Activities without an objective in mind should be avoided even if they are interesting and entertaining.

Activities represent the plan of action for achieving the objectives. All other parts of the plan, including the stated questions, usually stay in the background and are there mainly to assist the teacher. The activities are what involve the children in inquiry, and as such must accommodate limitations in the children's abilities. Thus, because the sample plan is for the second grade, most of the activities revolve around the children's own experiences. In more advanced levels, however, activities can draw on other environments farther away from the children in time and space. Also, more reading can be assigned to older children.

It is obvious from the sample plan that the generalization is not expected to be fully realized in the second grade. Second graders can comprehend some of its simple local applications but not in history and in other parts of the world. In later grades, however, as they learn about movements of people in other times and places, they will develop a more profound understanding of the generalization. A curriculum that attempts to develop basic concepts and generalizations by drawing first from the child's immediate environment and then from progressively more remote fields of experience is called a *spiral curriculum*.

The overall plan follows a logical structure, the parts of which depend on each other. The plan starts with a broad area of study that is reduced to a number of unit topics. Each topic is reduced to generalizations and issues. Generalizations (also the issues) become the source for content and process objectives. The content objectives are converted into basic questions which, in turn, give rise to specific learning activities. In developing the plan one moves from the general to the particular; in implementing the plan one moves from the particular (the activities) to the general.

SUMMARY

The purpose of social studies is to develop the powers the individual needs to cope with human relationships. Life in today's society requires knowledge of social phenomena, knowledge of and commitment to social values, intellectual skills, ability to clarify one's own values, and a number of social skills. These life requirements constitute the specific objectives of social studies.

To arrive at the most worthwhile of these objectives, unit topics are selected that reflect social realities and illuminate contemporary issues. Several basic generalizations and issues are selected for each topic. These generalizations and issues, the values they reflect or activate, and the method used to develop them become the sources for the specific social studies objectives. Social realities and the children's backgrounds and abilities influence each step.

This chapter deals with reducing generalizations to specific objectives—content and process. The content objectives are then converted to basic questions, from which, in turn, learning activities are designed to provide responses to the questions and, in so doing, reach the content objectives.

The mode of teaching is inquiry, which uses questioning strategies and activities that involve the children in exploring data, forming hypotheses, and reaching conclusions. Through these strategies and activities, children are helped to their intellectual abilities. Questioning strategies and activities also provide opportunities for clarifying values and for developing social skills. The quality of questions and activities determines development of the process objectives.

Generalizations are not always developed fully when introduced. As children's experiences expand, so does their understanding of particular generalizations.

ACTIVITIES

1. Observe a young child for a period of time and describe ways used to solve problems encountered.
2. Each student should review a research study that attempts to test children's ability to think. Discuss these studies.

3. Take a generalization from the social or behavioral sciences and indicate what children in the first grade might be able to learn that could help them to eventually understand the generalization. Do the same for sixth grade children. What differences do you notice? Be sure you include items that reflect all five types of instructional objectives.

4. Indicate what children may do to reach each objective developed in the preceding activity.

5. Take a random list of questions from all levels and classify them by using one of the models of thinking provided in the chapter.

6. Assume that you have made an exploratory visit to a place in the local community where you plan to take your class. Describe the place and design a set of questions to which the children should respond in order to develop higher levels of thinking.

7. Each student should take a generalization and develop a complete teaching plan as illustrated in the chapter. Students may coordinate their generalizations along particular unit topics and develop plans that they can share. Such plans can be used to teach complete units, or sometimes complete programs.

8. Every time you take a course in a social science or behavioral science, ask yourself: "What are the basic generalizations derived from this subject?" If they are not clear in your mind, inform the instructor of the utility of the generalizations in curriculum development, and ask that such generalizations be articulated.

NOTES

1. Celia S. Lavatelli, Walter J. Moore, and Theodore Kaltsounis, *Elementary School Curriculum* (New York: Holt, Rinehart & Winston, 1972), p. 60.

2. Shirley G. Moore and Sally Kilmer, *Contemporary Preschool Education: A Program for Young Children* (New York: John Wiley, 1973), p. 38.

3. Lavatelli, Moore, and Kaltsounis, *Elementary School Curriculum,* p. 60.

4. Bernard Spodek, "Developing Social Studies Concepts in the Kindergarten," *Social Education,* 27 (May 1963), 253–56.

5. G. Camarota, "New Emphases in Social Studies for the Primary Grades," *Social Education,* 27 (February 1963), 77–80.

6. Vincent Rogers and Dorothy E. Layton, "An Exploratory Study of Primary Grade Children's Ability to Conceptualize Based upon Content Drawn from Selected Social Studies Topics." Master's thesis, University of Minnesota, 1963.

7. M. Rusnak, "Introducing Social Studies in the First Grade," *Social Education,* 25 (October 1961), 291–92.

8. Sylvia E. Harrison and Robert J. Solomon, "Review of Research in the Teaching of Social Studies: 1960–1963," *Social Education,* 24 (May 1964), 277–92.

9. Lawrence Senesh, "The Pattern of the Economic Curriculum," *Social Education,* 32 (January 1968), 47–50, 59.

10. John Jarolimek and Clifford D. Foster, *Teaching and Learning in the Elementary School* (New York: Macmillan, 1976), p. 94.

11. Ibid., p. 99.

12. Edwin Fenton, "Structure and Inquiry," in Louis J. Hebert and William Murphy, eds., *Structure in the Social Studies* (Washington, D.C.: National Council for the Social Studies, 1968), pp. 80–81.

13. Jack L. Nelson, *Teaching Elementary Social Studies Through Inquiry* (Highland Park, N.J.: Dreier Educational Services, 1970).

14. Charlotte Crabtree, "Supporting Reflective Thinking in the Classroom," in Jean Fair and Fannie P. Shaftel, eds., *Effective Thinking in the Social Studies.* 37th Yearbook of the National Council for the Social Studies (Washington, D.C.: National Council for the Social Studies, 1967), p. 81.

15. Fenton, "Structure and Inquiry," p. 79.

16. Benjamin S. Bloom et. al., *Taxonomy of Educational Objectives, Handbook I: Cognitive Domain* (New York: David McKay, 1956), pp. 201–7.

17. J. P. Guilford, "Three Faces of Intellect," *The American Psychologist,* 14 (August 1959), 469–79.

18. Paul E. Torrance and Janet Ross, *Improving Social Studies Education in Minnesota* (Minneapolis: Bureau of Educational Research at the University of Minnesota, 1961). Mimeographed.

19. Hilda Taba, *Teachers' Handbook for Elementary Social Studies* (Reading, Mass.: Addison-Wesley, 1967), p. 92.

20. Hilda Taba and James Hills, *Teacher Handbook for Contra Costa Social Studies, Grades 1–6* (Hayward, Calif.: Rapid Printers and Lithographers, 1965).

21. Joan E. Schreiber, "Teacher's Question-Asking Techniques in Social Studies," *Dissertation Abstracts,* 28 (August 1967), 523-A; John C. Youngers, "A Descriptive Study of the Cognitive Emphases Expressed in 'Man: A Course of Study,'" in June R. Chapin, ed., *Social Studies Dissertations: 1969–1973* (Boulder, Colo.: ERIC Clearinghouse for Social Studies/Social Science Education, 1974), p. 114; Theodore W. Parsons and Fannie R. Shaftel, "Thinking and Inquiry: Some Critical Issues," in Jean Fair and Fannie R. Shaftel, eds., *Effective Thinking in the Social Studies.* 37th Yearbook of the National Council for the Social Studies (Washington, D.C.: NCSS, 1967), p. 130; Paul E. Torrance and Janet Ross, *Improving Social Studies.*

22. John Dewey, *How to Think* (Boston: D. C. Heath, 1933), pp. 106–16.

23. Byron G. Massialas and C. Benjamin Cox, "A Reflective Model," in Rodney F. Allen, John V. Fleckenstein, and Peter M. Lyon, eds., *Inquiry in the Social Studies* (Washington, D.C.: National Council for the Social Studies, 1968), pp. 70–73.

24. Ibid., p. 72.

25. Ibid., p. 72.

26. Fenton, "Structure and Inquiry," p. 80.

27. J. Richard Suchman, "Learning Through Inquiry," in Rodney F. Allen, John V. Fleckenstein, and Peter M. Lyon, eds., *Inquiry in the Social Studies* (Washington, D.C.: National Council for the Social Studies, 1968), p. 57.

28. Hilda Taba and James Hills, *Teacher Handbook,* pp. 85, 94, 102.

29. James J. Gallagher and Mary Jane Aschner, "A Preliminary Report on Analysis of Classroom Interaction," *Merrill-Palmer Quarterly of Behavior and Development,* 9 (July 1963), 183–94.

30. Gary Manson and Ambrose A. Clegg, Jr., "Classroom Questions: Keys to Children's Thinking," *Peabody Journal of Education,* 47 (March 1970), 304–5.

31. Norris M. Sanders, *Classroom Questions: What Kinds?* (New York: Harper & Row, 1966); Francis P. Hunkins, *Questioning Strategies and Techniques* (Boston: Allyn & Bacon, 1972).

32. Hunkins, *Questioning Strategies,* p. 9.

33. Jack C. Morgan and Joan E. Schreiber, *How To Ask Questions.* How to Do It Series—No. 24 (Washington, D.C.: National Council for the Social Studies, 1969).

Studying this chapter will enable the reader to:

1. define values and recognize their importance in the day-to-day life of the individual.
2. realize that the school deals with values not because it wishes to overstep its boundaries, but because values facilitate or inhibit the school's basic, and even traditional, functions.
3. realize that values are instrumental in the resolution of issues, a basic concern in contemporary social studies.
4. list in a logical sequence and explain the steps in the process of resolving issues.
5. recognize the similarity between the process of decision making and the process of resolving issues.
6. become familiar with techniques of value clarification and value assessment.
7. design plans for teaching the process of resolving issues to young children.
8. accept that the best way to teach lasting social values is not through direct traditional methods but through values assessment and the application of the rational process.
9. become more aware of the basic social values of U.S. society expressed or implicit in the Declaration of Independence, the Constitution, and the Bill of Rights.

5

DEALING WITH ISSUES,
VALUES,
AND THE VALUING PROCESS

It was argued in Chapter 1 that a social studies program oriented toward developing decision-making abilities must deal with issues. Issues reflect social realities, and failure to deal with them deprives the children both of a rounded treatment of the topics they study and of opportunities to practice decision making and develop the potential to contribute toward solution of social problems.

In Chapter 3 it was demonstrated that every topic or situation under study includes not only generalizations but also issues. Issues are problems, but ones that cannot be resolved with information alone. Usually information adequate for understanding the problem is not enough to support a solution that would satisfy all concerned. There is plenty of information, for example, to show that the elderly in our society do not enjoy the best care, but the available information is not enough to support any one all-satisfying solution.

Although satisfactory solutions are hard to come by, most individuals, faced directly or indirectly with social problems that affect them, must come up with solutions and act upon them. In the United States, for example, no solution has been found to the problem of school segregation, but many Americans have had to vote on whether busing children from one district to another is the way to achieve school integration. We just cannot avoid social problems.

Persons faced with a problem that cannot be resolved by information alone resort to their value systems. From all possible solutions, they select the one most in agreement with their values. Values, therefore, are very important in dealing with issues. The purpose of this chapter is to (a) show what values are, (b) show the importance of values in teaching, and (c) recommend a practical way for dealing with issues, and through them with values.

THE NATURE OF VALUES

The term "value" is difficult to define. David Krathwohl, Benjamin Bloom, and Bertram Masia define values in terms of the process of "internalization." [1] Internalization implies that the individual gradually grows to accept ideas, practices, standards, or sanctions to the point that they become for that person a way of life. The process of internalization proceeds along a continuum, and has been defined by the same authors as follows:

> The process begins when the attention of a student is captured by some phenomenon, characteristic or value. As he pays attention to the phenomenon, characteristic, or value, he differentiates it from the others present in the perceptual field. With differentiation comes a seeking out of the phenomenon as he gradually attaches emotional significance to it and comes to value it. As the process unfolds he relates this phenomenon to other phenomena to which he responds that also have value. This responding is sufficiently frequent so that he comes to react regularly, almost automatically, to it and to other things like it. Finally, the values are interrelated in a structure or view of the world, which he brings as a "set" to new problems.[2]

Krathwohl, Bloom, and Masia do not clearly distinguish the meaning of "value" from that of such other terms as "attitude," "appreciation," "interest," and "adjustment." However, it is clear that a "value" is a commitment that eventually influences and determines behavior. Through internalization, "a given phenomenon or value passes from level of bare awareness to a position of some power to guide or control the behavior of a person."[3]

Louis Raths, Merrill Harmin, and Sidney Simon (discussed in Chapter 1) define values in a similar way:[4] A value is something that (1) is chosen freely, (2) after considering all possible alternatives and (3) the consequences of each alternative; such a choice is (4) cherished by the individual to the extent that (5) the individual is willing to affirm it publicly. Finally, (6) the individual acts upon the choice and (7) does so repeatedly over time. Values grow from experiences and vary among individuals.

Raths, Harmin, and Simon do not advocate any particular set of values, but they believe that students or adults who have used the above process to develop an adequate store of values are "positive, purposeful, enthusiastic, proud." Persons who have not developed an adequate number of values are "apathetic, flighty, uncertain . . . inconsistent . . . drifters, overconformers, overdissenters, or role players."[5] There is, then, a definite relationship between values and behavior.

Milton Rokeach defines values as those inner forces that prescribe the individual's behavior and motivate the individual's striving for achievement of goals in life.[6] Unlike Raths, Harmin, and Simon, Milton Rokeach recognizes a limited number of values that he classifies as being either instrumental or terminal. Instrumental values influence the person's way of life; terminal values influence the person's striving for chosen goals in life.

Rokeach's list of values pertains to adults but it has been modified by Richard Cole[7] and Dave Williams[8] for use in the elementary school, as shown in Figure 5–1.

Figure 5-1
Rokeach Values as Modified by Cole and Williams

Instrumental Values	Terminal Values
loving (affectionate) *	confidence and pride in myself
honest (truthful, sincere)	equal opportunity for all people
creative (imaginative)	freedom and choice of action
helpful (aiding others)	family love and protection
intelligent (smart)	true friendship
capable (able to do things well)	feeling of achievement
dependable (reliable)	peaceful world
self-controlled (self-disciplined)	admiration and respect for others
forgiving (understanding)	pleasure (enjoyable life)
cheerful (light-hearted)	a secure country
ambitious (hard-working)	exciting life (adventurous life)
polite (courteous)	beautiful world
influential (leadership)	religious life
clean (neat and tidy)	prosperous life
brave (courageous)	

* The words in parentheses are those chosen from a number of synonyms by a sample of elementary school children to express the meaning of the respective values.

James Shaver and William Strong suggest that *"values* are our standards and principles for judging worth. They are the criteria by which we judge 'things' (people, objects, ideas, actions and situations) to be good, worthwhile, desirable; or, on the other hand, bad, worthless, despicable; or, of course, somewhere in between these extremes." [9] In *Values Education*, the 1971 yearbook of the National Council for the Social Studies, the term is avoided altogether in favor of value judgments. "Value judgments," writes Jerrold Coombs, "may be defined roughly as those judgments which rate things with respect to their worth." [10] But Shaver and Strong argue that there is a difference between values and value judgments: "The latter are assertions we make based on our values." [11] They point out also that values and attitudes differ, although, the reader may recall, Krathwohl and his associates hardly distinguish between the two. Like Rokeach, Shaver and Strong believe that values underlie attitudes and are the fewer in number.

Shaver and Strong classify three categories of values—esthetic, instrumental, and moral. "Esthetic values are those standards by which we judge beauty—in art, in music, in literature, as well as in personal appearance, nature and even cookery (the culinary art)." [12] Instrumental values are the means used to achieve ends. Their worth as means depends on their effectiveness in achieving specified goals. A teaching method, for example, is valued if it helps to achieve certain educational goals.

Apparently Shaver and Strong consider those values that help the in-

Figure 5-2
Categories of Values According to Shaver and Strong

Categories of Values	Examples of Values
Esthetic: Standards by which we judge beauty	beauty in art, music, literature, personal appearance, nature, cookery
Instrumental: The means we use to achieve ends	a teaching method, a reward, an incentive, is valued if it assists in the achievement of some goal
Moral values: Standards or principles by which we judge whether aims or actions are proper — *Personal preferences:* Important in one's life but not basic to human existence	solitude, playing bridge, hiking, cleanliness, reading books
Middle-level values: More than a matter of personal preference, but people differ as to their importance	honesty, cooperation, patriotism, initiative, hard work
Basic values: Important to human existence	freedom of speech, sanctity of life

dividual make ethical decisions—decisions about proper aims and actions —most important. "Moral values," they write, "are the standards, the principles, by which we judge whether aims or actions are proper."[13] Moral values are ranged in a continuum from personal preferences—like solitude—to values that are considered basic to human existence—like the sanctity of human life. Values such as hard work, honesty, cooperation, and patriotism fall between these poles. Although a particular value may be difficult to classify in the continuum, Figure 5–2 shows Shaver and Strong's categories of values.

Kohlberg's cognitive-developmental approach to moral education yields two kinds of values: those that cause the individual to have moral dilemmas, and those that guide the person's resolution of the dilemma. As to the first category, we saw in Chapter 1 that these values are 10 in number:[14]

1. Punishment
2. Property
3. Roles and concerns of affection
4. Roles and concerns of authority
5. Law

6. Life
7. Liberty
8. Distributive justice
9. Truth
10. Sex

But in Kohlberg's theory, the second category of values is the more important—the reasons for which the individual resolves a dilemma in favor of one or more of the values in the first category. The reasons vary, in six successive stages corresponding to cognitive-developmental levels, and range from blind obedience through the application of universal principles.

For example, a person at stage 5 considers a choice justified when it is based on the society's valuation of individual rights and standards, whereas a person at stage 6, in a conflict situation, makes decisions on the basis of personally chosen ethical principles that the person thinks of as comprehensive, universal, and consistent. The reader can turn to Chapter 1 to review Kohlberg's six stages.

In summary, then, values are universally held to be each individual's inner forces that influence judgment and behavior. According to some experts, values develop through a process that works only with the individual's commitment. Finally, most authorities see values in any society as falling into a hierarchy of more and less important ones, rather than all being of uniform importance. Chief among them in our society, for example, are respect for human life, the dignity of the individual, and preservation of the common good.

VALUES IN TEACHING

While the experts argue about how to define values, teachers and school officials wonder what to do with them. Some urge that teachers teach values or at least deal with them in certain ways. Others insist that values should not be dealt with in schools, but rather in the family and the church.

Yet even when cognitive development held its long sway in the schools, there were attempts to develop values. The methods were usually emotional pleas, appeals to conscience, moralizing slogans, and withholding from the learner information that was considered undesirable. It was also sought to inspire young people through study of the lives of individuals with exemplary value systems and behavior. And quite often children were simply given raw indoctrination.

Such approaches worked in the past probably because the primary objective was conformity to existing social conditions. But conformity implies training, not education, which, says Thomas Ringness,

> demands inner direction and controls. It implies that a person makes his own decisions, thinks for himself, considers alternatives and projects the probable consequences of his choices of behavior. He prizes his individualism and accepts responsibility for his own decisions. He relates his means and ends to his own philosophy of life—his hierarchy of values.[15]

Even the most outspoken critics of American education agree, prizing individual inner-directedness over conformity.

Ringness points out that those who opposed the conformist role of the traditional school, and who valued inner-direction and a dynamic education, turned to the so-called "free schools," where development of individuality supplanted concern for an imposed, prescribed curriculum. However,

> in experimenting, we have thrown out some of the potentially good things of traditional education. Thus we find "freed-up" schools in which children are confused, lacking in self-discipline, and unable to complete tasks. We find that some children in these schools lack consistent value systems. Sometimes we find "cop-outs," "spoiled brats," and others who suffer from too little direction, which may be as evil as too much.[16]

How can schools play a role in values development that avoids the pitfalls of both extremes?

The chief preoccupation of the schools clearly remains cognitive development; that has always been the school's main role in the cooperative educational enterprise that includes the home, the church, peer groups, mass media, and many other entities. Probably this role would not have changed had the end of education remained simply the accumulation of knowledge. But knowledge, though important, is now perceived as a means toward the end of making decisions, thus also involving personal values. Moreover, the cognitive domain came to be seen as interacting with the affective and psychomotor domains. Because physical characteristics, values, and emotions influence the learner's cognitive development, they cannot be ignored—particularly because the other socializing agencies have not taken adequate care of these needs.

Given, then, that the school's emphasis on decision making requires a systematic concern with values, what is the school's proper course of action? Several principles and basic assumptions both define values and clarify their place among the school's objectives. It is all the more important that these be set forth because the area of values in the school is still in a formative, confused stage of development. There are no clear-cut directions. Later in this chapter practical recommendations are made concerning values; they are based on the following assumptions and principles:

1. Values are inner forces influencing the individual's behavior.

2. Because how we confront our life dilemmas and how we make decisions about them are basic manifestations of our behavior, values influence how we make decisions just as knowledge does.

3. Values influence the individual's perception and interpretation of reality.

4. Individuals may or may not be aware of the values that influence their decision making and their behavior in general.

5. The more aware they are of their values, the more able are individuals to control their behavior and, in particular, their decision-making capability.

6. Values are stronger, or more committed to, when they are chosen and accepted freely by use of the rational process.

7. Members of a society must agree on a common core of values if that society is to survive and function well.

8. Various approaches for dealing with values disagree with each other. While all contain many valid assumptions and recommend valuable practices, no one approach appears to be clearly acceptable in its totality to the exclusion of others.

9. In view of the preceding assumption, the practitioner must be eclectic—in other words, must select elements from each theoretical approach on the basis of some criterion that serves a particular purpose.

10. The factors guiding the eclectic approach in dealing with values should be the function and the objectives of the schools. Some call this position relativistic.

Thus, the school must deal with values, not to usurp the role of the home or of any other social institution, but because values are inseparable from knowledge in achieving the school's dynamic objective. This is particularly true with respect to social studies, the purpose of which is to help pupils become functioning members of society. As such, social studies deals with human relationships, which require adequate knowledge and certain abilities, and which often involve conflict. Conflicts give rise to issues. Children must be able to understand the issues and to resolve, or attempt to resolve, their underlying conflicts. Hence, issues supply the context for dealing with values in social studies.

A word of caution is necessary, however: Schools, and social studies in particular, should deal with values only to the extent necessary. They should not become overly enthusiastic and faddish about this or that value-related theory, or implement theories at the expense of the primary function of social studies. For example, these days it is often found that social studies has been neglected in favor of intensive value clarification, or has in fact been replaced by efforts to develop the children's "moral reasoning," per Kohlberg, using artificial value dilemmas rather than real-world, everyday dilemmas and issues. Value clarification and moral reasoning should be seen in proper perspective within the social studies program. They are means, not ends, to enhance rather than replace the social studies objectives.

As was demonstrated in earlier chapters, essential to achieving basic social studies objectives are appropriate topics, with their related generalizations and issues. As we have also seen, whereas generalizations can be developed from knowledge alone, issues involve values. We now discuss how students' personal values are treated in resolving conflicts and in considering social principles.

STEPS IN RESOLVING ISSUES

Issues are resolved by an interplay of knowledge and values. In defining social issues, Byron Massialas and Nancy Sprague implicitly suggest the steps for dealing with issues: "A social issue is a recognizable aspect of a larger social problem in which real and meaningful alternatives are presented for critical analysis, decision and possible action." [17] The process can be anatomized into several steps, about which authorities on the subject are in agreement: [18]

1. Presentation of the issue.
2. Relevant information and value positions are collected and discussed.
3. All possible alternative solutions of the issue are discussed and evaluated in light of the children's values.
4. The consequences, positive and negative, of each alternative solution are thoroughly discussed.
5. The children are given opportunities to choose from the alternative solutions and justify their choices.
6. The children organize for action.
7. The children act.

Figure 5–3 shows the similarities between this process and decision making. Given these steps, how should actual teaching strategies be developed? The seven steps just outlined can now be elaborated.

1. PRESENTATION OF THE ISSUE   A fifth grade teacher may want to introduce the issue: "Should the United States use food surpluses as a diplomatic weapon with other countries?" If the teacher believes that the children will be better motivated to deal with the issue if they themselves raise it (this approach will be more in accord with inquiry), the teacher creates the appropriate climate—say by circulating an account of the 1845–1847 famine in Ireland, in which thousands died of starvation and disease and many others emigrated to the United States, and after which the population dropped, from eight million in 1841 to five million in 1871.

Children, tending to be idealistic and moved by such information, are ready to pay attention to the fact that worldwide food distribution is uneven, and that, while we in the United States have surplus food and waste much food, people in other parts of the world suffer from malnutrition and

Figure 5-3
**Comparative Chart Between Decision Making and the Process
of Resolving Issues**

Decision Making	Process of Resolving Issues
1. Decision-making situation	1. The issue
2. Knowledge and values are examined	2. Information and value positions are collected and discussed
3. Choice from alternatives	3. Alternative solutions are examined
	4. The consequences of each solution are examined
4. Justification of choice	5. Choice is made from alternatives and is justified
5. Action	6. The children organize for action
	7. Implementation of action takes place

outright starvation. The children may be directed, for example, to *Compton's Encyclopedia* or any other encyclopedia to discover that most well-fed people live in North America, parts of South America, Western Europe, Australia, and New Zealand.[19] The rest of the world is ill-fed, consuming on average well below the minimum 2750 calories required each day. Children will also discover that each year enough food to feed the entire U.S. population is destroyed in storage by rats, insects, and mold. Once aware that most of this stored food is in the United States, which uses it quite often as a diplomatic weapon in its relationships with other countries, the children will most likely raise the issue: "Should the United States use the food surplus as a diplomatic weapon in its dealings with other countries?"

2. RELEVANT INFORMATION AND VALUE POSITIONS ARE PRESENTED AND DISCUSSED
Once the issue is presented, the children are directed to search for relevant information, to understand the conditions that underlie the issue. Each issue involves several concepts and generalizations that must be grasped. For example, to deal with the sample issue, the children must learn, among other things, that less than one-third of the earth's land is cultivated or arable; people in nonarable areas must import food or go without. The children need also to learn that the world is divided along ideological and other lines and that food and other resources are usually transferred for reasons other than to alleviate human suffering. Such concepts as "food processing," "sterilization," "advanced farming methods," "conservation," "diplomacy," "diet," and others must also be understood prior to dealing with the issue.

Children may in fact already know much that must be known. But the teacher must be sure to offer whatever additional knowledge is needed, and should supply it by the methods discussed in Chapter 4. Because the conditions that create a problem or issue are real, they can always be demonstrated. It is just as easy to show, for example, that crime among the young is increasing as it is to show that the U.S. family has been transformed from extended to nuclear.

The value positions concerning an issue are also accessible to the children's awareness. With reference to our sample issue, there are those in this country who believe very strongly that to allow human lives to perish for diplomatic advantages is immoral. Others believe that the rest of the world is ungrateful to the United States, which has given more to the world than has any other nation, yet is mistrusted and its integrity questioned. Why, they ask, should we give food to nations that openly dislike us and work against our welfare, as happened in the 1973 oil embargo? Why should we give what others need while, for political and diplomatic reasons, we are intentionally deprived of what we need? Between these two extremes, other positions fall. The children should be made aware of them.

Presenting information and value positions illustrates how knowledge can be used as a means rather than an end. Without this step, issues will be resolved by emotion rather than by informed reason, decision making will be impulsive, and there will be less motivation for lasting commitment to sustained action.

3. ALL POSSIBLE ALTERNATIVE SOLUTIONS OF THE ISSUE ARE DISCUSSED AND EVALUATED IN THE LIGHT OF THE CHILDREN'S VALUES   Faced with an issue relevant to their lives, individuals usually react. Weak ones shun the issue; strong or purposeful ones attempt a satisfactory resolution. The quality of the resolution depends partly on how well the previous step was executed; the more the individual knows about the facts and value positions of an issue, the sounder the resolution.

Facts themselves, however, are open to different interpretations, used to support different positions. A classic example is the riots in the Watts district of Los Angeles, in the 1960s. Witnesses of the initiating incidents differ in their interpretations: Some placed the blame on the police, others placed the blame on black youths. People are led to interpret facts in different ways by their values.

Furthermore, two individuals can study the facts of an issue with equal intensity, agree in their interpretation of these facts, yet resolve the issue differently. The difference is again a matter of personal values. Thus, two persons could study the same facts on the issue of distributing U.S. surplus food abroad and still differ on resolving the issue—say because one values human life most, while the other values national pride most.

People are not always aware of their values—those inner forces that make them behave in a certain way—yet those values influence their decisions nevertheless. Quite often people say: "I am not sure what to do in this situation, but there is something inside me which tells me to decide this way."

Another basic phenomenon is relevant: When a decision must be made, people who are aware of a variety of choices are more likely to find a course of action in agreement with their values. Often people choose one extreme position or another only because they did not have the opportunity or the stimulation to consider other courses of action more in agreement with their own values.

Thus, essential to effective conflict resolution are two conditions: (a) Individuals must be aware of as many of the alternative choices as possible, and (b) they must be as aware as possible of the values that influence them to choose their course of action.

The most practical way to expose children to alternative solutions is to have an open discussion of the issue and allow each child to recommend solutions. To warm up the class to this task, the teacher may summarize the courses of action dictated by the various value positions expressed during information gathering. While the children's positions may at first be other-directed, probably reflecting their parents' positions, they soon begin to propose new and imaginative solutions. The teacher should keep a record of all solutions proposed.

As the children prepare to make a choice, the teacher ought to make sure that they know what values stimulate them to their choices. The process used is *value clarification*, which can be pursued through any of several strategies (which are discussed in more detail later in the chapter). The simplest strategy is the *clarifying response*—a questioning technique directed to what the children say, their choices, and their behavior. This technique helps the children to discover their own values but avoids moralizing or "pushing" them toward adopting specific values.

Another popular value-clarifying strategy is the *value sheet*. For example, a news story—real or fabricated from facts—may be presented in which the U.S. Secretary of State refused surplus food to a country because its government follows policies contrary to what the United States desires. The children study the story and respond to the teacher's questions, which usually require that the children take the place of the persons in the story and try to express those persons' feelings and value positions.

4. THE CONSEQUENCES, POSITIVE AND NEGATIVE, OF EACH ALTERNATIVE SOLUTION ARE THOROUGHLY DISCUSSED   It may not always be best to resolve an issue by selecting the solution that most closely matches one's present value system. The person's value system might be too narrow and the person might desire to expand it. Or the person's values might contradict such

basic values as the sanctity of human life, the rational process, or the common good. Or some individuals might be indifferent about an issue and prior to making a decision would like to know what others think and by what values. Or the applicability or validity of a particular value might be made questionable by new information. The children should be given opportunities to question and analyze not only the facts of a particular issue but also their own values and how these relate to the facts. This scrutiny may lead to changed or new values.

Values can be most practically scrutinized without violating the social studies objectives by projecting the consequences of each alternative solution of an issue. Teachers may do so by a variety of ways. A teacher may, for example, place yard-long pieces of butcher paper around the room where all children can see them. There would be a piece of paper for each solution proposed, written at the top of each sheet.

Taking one solution at a time, the teacher directs a discussion on the consequences, creating an open atmosphere in which the children can feel free to suggest consequences. Using different colors of crayon, the teacher writes the consequences suggested under each alternative, making sure that both positive and negative consequences are proposed and listed. The teacher accepts both types with a neutral attitude, to allow children to express themselves as openly as possible.

Another strategy would be to ask the children to list under a solution they favor as many of its consequences as they can think of. Because they favor the solution, they will most likely list positive consequences. After giving the children time to study all the consequences listed, ask them to select an alternative solution they do not like and write as many negative consequences of it as they can. Make sure all solutions have both positive and negative consequences. Follow this activity with a class discussion in which the children elaborate on the consequences they foresee. Urge them to describe these consequences as convincingly as they can.

This is an important step for the child's value system. Having clarified their values in the previous step, the children are now compelled to assess them while trying to achieve the best match between them and the alternative resolutions to the issue. As they listen to the discussion and survey the alternatives and consequences displayed around the room, they probably see an alternative that they prefer to their original choice. And they probably had never thought of some of the negative consequences attributed to their choice. Indifferent children, upon seeing a series of consequences that they would like to see materialized, will probably no longer be neutral and apathetic and may become committed to a particular resolution.

This process produces information that provokes cognitive dissonance and compels the children to adjust both their values and behavior. Leon Festinger asserts that, before the intrusion of new information, the individual's knowledge, values, and behavior are in equilibrium.[20] Cognitive dissonance—provoked by new knowledge—disturbs that equilibrium, which the individual seeks to reestablish. This is accomplished by one of three strategies: The person tries to block out the new knowledge; makes a change in personal values; or makes a change in behavior. Smokers who find research studies to contradict the evidence that smoking causes cancer are trying to block out disturbing information. The smokers who say, "I'd rather die happy than deprived," so arrange their values that smoking becomes a necessary condition for the value of happiness to be realized. Smokers who quit change their behavior to reestablish equilibrium.

5. THE CHILDREN ARE GIVEN OPPORTUNITIES TO CHOOSE FROM THE ALTERNATIVE SOLUTIONS AND JUSTIFY THEIR CHOICES   Having completed all previous steps, the children can now be encouraged to choose among the alternative resolutions of an issue. Thus far the children have been speculating and making suggestions to get their classmates' reactions. Now the children individually choose a resolution knowing that they will each have to act upon their decision. There is no question that a decision based on exploration of the facts and all possible alternatives and their consequences will be sounder than a decision made otherwise.

Even at this stage, however, the children may still find reason to adjust their position. The teacher provides such an opportunity by asking them to justify their choice. The request must be made in a way that will not make the children feel defensive. (It should always be remembered that there is no right or wrong answer on an issue; a question amenable to such an answer is not an issue.)

As the children justify their choice, the teacher must make sure that all available information is taken into consideration. If the child has reasonably considered all possible alternatives and their consequences and there are no obvious inconsistencies or contradictions, the choice is sound. There can be no other objective criteria by which to evaluate the children's choices.

Although formal research is lacking, informal observations indicate that groups of children using the approach thus far described tend to reach a better consensus on issues than without it. Considering facts and examining relevant value positions pull people together. No one will doubt that consensus is something our society needs badly. This condition is by no means the same thing as conformity, because it is the children themselves who make the decisions; the teacher simply makes sure that as many facts and value positions as possible are examined. It is not the teacher's job to recommend any position. If asked to state a position, the teacher may do so—preferably late in the process—but should stress that it is a personal position alone, and give the reasons for the choice.

6. THE CHILDREN ORGANIZE FOR ACTION   This and the next step bring social studies closer in line with contemporary trends. The social studies of the 1970s requires learners to increase their ability to contribute toward the functioning and improvement of society. As such, social studies is dynamic—chiefly because it addresses issues, which invite knowledge and values to interact—and demands more of the learner than passive acceptance of a body of knowledge.

Lacking opportunity or impetus to act on a decision, individuals will feel less urgency to make the decision that best reflects their strongest values and commitments. People may easily decide that racial discrimination is bad, but when asked to act on this decision by supporting a non-discriminatory housing policy in their neighborhood, they may find all kinds of excuses to evade the challenge. They may say, for example, that they do not mind if blacks or chicanos move into the neighborhood, but they do not want their houses to lose market value.

In the literature, action generated by the resolution of social issues has been called "social action." The term has been misunderstood, however, and during the early 1970s met with some concern. Probably because the concept surfaced during a time when youth was in revolt, it was interpreted to mean advocacy of riots, civil disobedience, and more unrest among youth. Thus did the National Council for the Social Studies substitute the more moderate term "social participation." As defined in the NCSS Curriculum Guidelines, "Social Participation should mean the application of knowledge, thinking and commitment in the social arena." [21]

Because issues have no right or wrong answers, no overwhelming consensus among the children should be expected. But some issue resolutions may occasion a degree of partial consensus. But whether a group of children or only a single child has chosen a particular resolution, action must be planned for it. The children, assisted by the teacher, must ask themselves several questions and consider several factors. Is the action contemplated practical? Can it be done without putting the rest of the school program in jeopardy? Will the action conflict with any community values? Is it legal? What will be the consequences for each of the children and for the school? Are there different ways to accomplish the goal? Which approach is best under the circumstances? Are there any instruments— recording forms, questionnaires, and the like—that must be prepared in advance?

Such questions should be thoroughly considered first to avoid alienating segments of the community. Social action and social change are better executed with support of those around the participants, which often can be maintained simply by avoiding small mistakes, by using sound, often simple procedures of human relations. Some advocate that school children's actions should always be within the law; others object that this dictum does not reflect the American political tradition. But there are no hard and fast rules, and teachers and students should use their judgment in each situation.

Although compromise is acceptable, the class, the teacher, the school officials should not submit to pressure groups with narrow interests. Most important, the schools should not shun issues just because they sometimes lead to controversy. The issues, remember, are the heart of social studies.

7. THE CHILDREN ACT   This, the final step, brings the children in contact with the real world and makes education relevant and meaningful. Suppose that a class pursued our sample issue, "Should the United States use food surplus as a diplomatic weapon with other countries?" this far. After exploring the alternatives and their consequences, some children decide that, sanctity of life being a highly considered value in our society, food should be sent anywhere and without conditions, provided there are assurances that it will be used to save lives. Action could take a variety of forms: Children might write to the State Department and urge our government to adopt this policy; they might also survey the community to find out how many of its people feel as they do, and then organize a campaign to have these people also write to the State Department.

Social action is often controversial—but not always. If the action contemplated is favored by most of the people in the community, there is no problem; it is simply a matter of someone's taking the initiative to get a job done. Everyone is familiar with children's efforts to clean up the school grounds or a nearby creek or park. I will not forget the enthusiasm with which my daughter directed a two-day campaign to rid the house of all fire hazards. When the issue of how to prevent loss of life had been considered in school, she was impressed by a list of household fire hazards that the teacher made available. She took this list and checked the house to make sure everything was in order. It was work for all of us at home, but we were glad to do it and, most of all, we were glad to see her assume the responsibility.

Teachers should always try to help children carry out their actions so that they can grow to view this step as an important part of instruction. Action should not be considered a dispensable step. Following each action the children should be given opportunities to evaluate it for appropriateness. Some children might be dissatisfied with their action or its effects and might decide to reconsider their choice or rethink the entire issue.

A SAMPLE PLAN DEALING WITH AN ISSUE

The following illustrates how a teacher can plan to deal with an issue in the classroom. The plan follows the steps outlined in the preceding pages. Note that the first part deals with facts and follows the same procedures recommended for developing concepts and generalizations. Keep in mind, however, that while a plan must be prepared by following the suggested logical sequence of steps, that sequence can be varied during actual teaching. Remember also that, with respect to a given issue, different children are at different levels; depending on their background, children can begin dealing with an issue at different steps.

Grade Level:	Sixth
Characteristics of Children in Class:	Average heterogeneous group
Area of Study:	The Interaction of World Cultures
Unit Topic:	Forces that Divide the World
Issue:	What can be done to reduce conflict around the world?

INSTRUCTIONAL OBJECTIVES:

Content Objectives

    a. Knowledge—The children will know:
        1. The major conflict areas around the world.
        2. That four of the most important causes of conflict are economics, religion, race, and territorial disputes in border areas.

      3. That conflict is never remote from the affairs of any nation.

      4. Three ways are now used to reduce conflict: the United Nations, summit conferences, personal diplomacy.

  b. Social values—The children will value:

      1. Genuine cooperation among nations.

      2. Nonviolent methods of resolving conflicts.

Process Objectives

  c. Intellectual skills—The children will be able to:

      1. Analyze proposed solutions for reducing conflict and project the consequences of each solution.

      2. Distinguish between behavior motivated by the facts and behavior motivated by values.

  d. Value-clarification skills—The children will be able to:

      1. Express and discuss their feelings about conflicts and the way they are presently handled.

      2. Choose freely an alternative solution to the problem that would be in agreement with their values, and give reasons for their choice.

      3. Take advantage of appropriate opportunities to show the degree of their commitment toward their proposed solution by working toward that solution.

  e. Social skills—The children will be able to:

      1. Work with other children to plan some kind of action toward the solution of their choice.

      2. Work in such a way as to win the support of others around them for their cause.

PROCEDURE

  I. The issue is presented: Use one or more activities such as the following:

    A. Read a vivid account of a conflict that can be found in the local press or a weekly news magazine or any other source.

    B. Ask one or more children to read *Children of Vietnam* (includes an account of the My Lai tragedy) by Betty J. Lifton and Thomas Fox (Atheneum, 1972) and discuss it in class.

    C. Review a few issues of *My Weekly Reader 6* (American Education Press), *Newstime* (Scholastic Magazine), or any other current-events source to persuade the children that conflict is widespread.

    D. With proper questioning lead the children to the issue: What can be done to reduce conflict around the world?

  II. Relevant information and value positions are collected and discussed.

QUESTIONS	LEARNING ACTIVITIES
A. What are the major conflicts around the world?	1. Ask children to look at local newspapers for a couple of days, notice and cut out stories on conflicts around the world—

for instance, at the time of this writing: "Russian buildup noted near China," "Officials discuss Korean security," "Leftists cite two threats in Lebanon," "The spread of nuclear weapons," "Queen visits North Ireland; 15 hurt in Belfast rioting," "South African police fire tear gas on colored youths," " 'Rifle' is Arafat's solution," "Begin flatly rejects efforts to bring P.L.O. into parley," "Rhodesia guerrillas kill doctor, nun," "Somalis repelled, says Ethiopia." [22]

2. Display a world map. Arrange the cutout stories around the map and extend strings from each story to the appropriate place. Make sure the most important conflicts of the time are covered. If the children miss any major conflicts, direct them to or bring in other sources.

3. Briefly discuss each conflict to find out how much the children know about these trouble spots.

B. What are the causes of the various conflicts around the world? What are the value positions of the conflicting parties?

1. Divide the children into groups and have each group explore specific conflicts to find their causes. Guide the various groups to such books as *The Easter Rising: Dublin, 1916,* by Neil Grant (Watts, 1972), and *The Time of Anger,* by Thelma Nuremberg (Abelard-Schuman, 1975). The second book examines the complex problems and feelings of Israeli and Arab students.

2. Ask children to organize short skits to dramatize the conflicts between various groups or nations.

3. To show how basic human values are sometimes overlooked to satisfy personal desires, have the children read *The Lion and the Lily* by James Rosenfeld (Dodd, Mead, 1972). This novel illustrates how a man's thirst for power often comes before his value for human life.

4. If your school is near a university or college, ask foreign students from countries in conflict to come to your class and present the various sides of the conflict.

5. Ask the children to individually look into their experiences and make a list of reasons why people usually argue. Collate their lists into one list. How do the reasons why individuals argue differ from the reasons why nations argue?

C. What effect do these conflicts have upon the United States and the world as a whole?

1. An effective way to respond to this question would be to have the children thoroughly study the Arab oil embargo of 1973 and its effects upon the United States and the rest of the world. Have the children use 1973 newspapers and news magazines as sources.

2. Bring in some parents to talk about the long gas lines and how they felt going through the oil shortage.

III. Alternative solutions are examined.

QUESTIONS	LEARNING ACTIVITIES

A. What is being done to reduce conflict?

1. Prepare a list of debates in the United Nations during the last few years and distribute it to the children, to show how the United Nations is preoccupied with reducing conflict.

2. Study the personal diplomacy of the United States as in the case of the Israel-Egypt Sinai agreement and the diplomatic contacts constantly made by the Secretary of State and the U.S. Ambassador to the United Nations.

3. Leaders of nations constantly come in contact to reduce conflicts. Follow the news and bring such contacts to the children's attention.

B. What more can be done to reduce conflict?

1. Give an opportunity to the children to propose solutions. Make sure you maintain an open atmosphere in which you accept all solutions.

2. Prepare sheets of butcher paper and write each solution—those already implemented as well as those proposed—at the top of a sheet. Display all sheets around the room where they are easily visible. Possible suggestions in addition to what is now being done could be: (a) establish one government throughout the world; (b) give more powers to the United Nations; (c) eliminate small nations by organizing each continent into one nation; (d) all nations agree to allow the principle of self-determination to prevail throughout the world; (e) the super powers take over the small nations by force; etc.

IV. The consequences of each solution are examined.

A. Taking the solutions one at a time, stimulate the children to propose consequences. Solicit both positive and negative consequences. In different colors of crayon, write the consequences below each solution.

B. Give the children time to study the alternatives and the consequences, and opportunities to express their feelings concerning the consequences. Using open-ended value-clarification questions, make sure the children review their positions in light of suggested consequences.

V. Choice is made among alternatives and is justified.

A. Ask the children, who know full well that they will act upon it, to express their choice of alternatives.

B. Make a list of the choices made and organize the class according to these choices.

C. Ask each group to prepare a justification for their choice and have a session in which each group presents their justification to the class.

VI. Action is organized for.

A. Each person or group prepares for action, which may take a variety of forms. Children considering the United Nations as the best hope for reducing conflict may, for example, start a campaign to let the school and the community know more about the organization.

B. The teacher should be aware of all action contemplated and discuss with the children the consequences of each action.

VII. Action is implemented.

A. The various groups or individuals carry out their actions.

B. Upon completion of action teacher and pupils discuss the outcomes and assess the effectiveness of their actions. This might cause them to reassess their choice.

Both sample issues in this chapter are addressed to the upper elementary grades, to balance the use of primary grade examples in the previous chapter. However, the approach described in this chapter can easily be applied in the primary grades as well, provided the issues are relevant to the children's experiential backgrounds and developmental levels.

For some children such substantive issues of wide interest as those used in this chapter are too difficult. When that is so, such issues should be postponed in favor of those more immediately accessible to the children and more personal to them. Chapter 3 contains many such issues. It is hoped, however, that teachers use issues that keep pace with the children's developing abilities. To do otherwise deprives children of opportunities to learn about important realities of their world, and returns social studies to its superficial and too often bland past.

DEVELOPING SOCIAL VALUES

No society can exist without common values. The school has a responsibility to promote the development of such values. This is a difficult notion to advance at a time when the most sacred American values have been questioned and some educators have proposed that the school should not teach values but instead a process of valuing that is "value-free"—one, in other words, that does not lead the student to preconceived values. However, the question is now seen to be not whether we should teach values, but how to teach them. In the past values were perceived as absolutes, as givens that society's members accepted without question. The methods used to transmit values from one generation to the next were barely distinguishable from indoctrination. Children were made to feel duty-bound to accept the values or feel ashamed for not doing so.

The old methods of teaching values are now thought to have not produced lasting commitments in the children. Presented with absolute standards of behavior, children were shaken in their commitment as soon as they observed a contradiction in real life between value and practice. For example, in the late 1960s and early '70s, many young people discovering the existence of discrimination, refused to consider the notion of equality, a value that is believed and practiced by the American society. They overlooked the fact that perfection is unattainable, and were unaware that the United States practiced equality more fervently than many other nations.

If values are to be operative, they must be accepted voluntarily by the children themselves through the rational process. To this end, values assessment seems the best method. The school should directly address the so-called American creed, putting its component values under the children's scrutiny for analysis and evaluation. This is best done by assuming that all values are tentative and using the conflict resolution to decide whether a value is worth maintaining. If the value is decided against, the alternatives are to change it or totally reject it.

Value assessment through conflict resolution involves the following steps:

1. Ask whether it is worth maintaining a particular traditional value.
2. Collect and discuss relevant information.
3. Explore the alternatives, which, for social values, are acceptance, rejection, or some form of change.
4. Explore the consequences of each alternative; how each alternative will affect society.
5. Each child chooses among the alternatives and justifies the choice.
6. Organize for action so that each child demonstrates commitment to an espoused value.
7. Repeatedly apply the value as a standard in everyday life.

Each teacher must be familiar with the values in the American creed and must create occasions to bring these values into focus. There are many lists of the American values in the literature; B. Othanel Smith, William Stanley, and J. Harlan Shores adopt the following list prepared by Harold C. Hand:

1. We hold that all human beings are of supreme and equal moral worth, that human life and well-being are to be valued above all material things, and that the dignity and worth of each person should be equally respected at all times and in all ways. . . .

2. We believe that human beings should be the architects of their own destiny, that they have the capacity to govern themselves wisely, and that the distribution of this capacity does not follow the contours of caste, class, family, ecclesiastical, or property lines. . . .

3. We have faith in human intelligence. We believe that by taking thought man can build a better world. Consequently, we assert that human well-being can best be advanced only if there is an unrestricted play of free intelligence upon all problems and difficulties. . . .

4. We believe in the rule of law; in a written Constitution which brings government and public officials as well as other persons under the rule of law; in law which is made by representatives of our own choosing; in law which prevents the exercise of arbitrary power by persons clothed with the authority of the state; in law which upholds the rights and enforces the obligations of men in their everyday pursuits and associations. Our ideal is a self-imposed type of law and order.

5. We believe in the principle of majority rule with minority protection, that the will of the majority should prevail at any given moment. That any person or group who believes that the operation of the will of the majority is inimical to any democratic principle is morally obligated to attempt to change this will through persuasion based on reason, that all minorities which seek to change this will of the majority through persuasion based on reason should be legally sanctioned and fully protected in their right to do so; but that, except for the minimum violation necessary to induce a test case in the courts, all minorities are obligated to abide by the will of the majority even while they work to change it.

6. Within our own country, we are determined that there shall be freedom for peaceful social change, and insist upon the peaceful settlement under law of all internal disputes; we believe that ballots should be substituted for bullets in resolving internal differences as to policy, and that men should abide by the decisions of the courts in respect to other disputes which they are unable to talk out.

7. We assert the individual's right to freedom in all respects not injurious to the common good; we declare that every person has the right to worship in his own way, think his own thoughts, speak his mind on any matter not causative of some clear and present danger to others, dress in any fashion not corruptive of public morals, seek employment in any lawful occupation of his own choosing, search in whatever social class he will for a marriage partner, and domicile himself in any state in the Union.[23]

Anyone who declines to put the American values to the test of the rational process probably doubts their validity. The American social values are not absolute in time or universal in sway, but they are loyally adhered to by the large majority. Such values are more effectively realized, however, in the hands of citizens who know the alternatives and their consequences. The basic American values can survive the test of rational scrutiny.

If at any time a value fails that test, it must be changed. Changes in circumstances do sometimes necessitate changes in values. For example, personal freedom and individual initiative have always been basic values in our society, but during the last few decades circumstances have forced the government to sidestep these values and exercise increasingly more control over the activities of individuals and groups.

MORE ON VALUE CLARIFICATION AND VALUE ASSESSMENT

The school, it should be clear, is not involved in the direct development of any particular set of social values. The school promotes the valuing process to accomplish two things: (a) to enable children to clarify their values and become aware of how their decisions and behavior are thus influenced; and (b) to guide children in assessing social values, to enable them to decide for themselves which are essential for social well-being. Because value clarification and value assessment are so basic, additional strategies and details merit discussion. Among the most common and effective strategies are the following:

1. Identifying value indicators
2. Value response
3. Value sheet
4. Role playing
5. Moral dilemma discussions
6. The teacher as a model

Among a teacher's most important skills is the ability to recognize and take advantage of children's value indicators, the things they say or do that reflect, however casually, deep-seated values of which they are not aware. A child who tells a teacher, "I have ten dollars and I am going to buy a fishing rod," may reflect a strong value for the outdoors or may have been given the ten dollars and that stipulation on how it should be spent. The teacher must deal with such a comment carefully, listening first and then raising questions that can reveal the background of the comment. If the comment reflects a value, the child should be helped to clarify it.

Raths, Harmin, and Simon recommend the following 30 questions as different ways to respond to value indicators:

1. Is this something that you prize?
2. Are you glad about that?
3. How did you feel when that happened?
4. Did you consider any alternatives?
5. Have you felt this way for a long time?

6. Was that something that you yourself selected or chose?
7. Did you have to choose that; was it a free choice?
8. Do you do anything about that idea?
9. Can you give me some examples of that idea?
10. What do you mean by _____; can you define that word?
11. Where would that idea lead; what would be its consequences?
12. Would you really do that or are you just talking?
13. Are you saying that . . . (repeat)?
14. Did you say that . . . (repeat in some distorted way)?
15. Have you thought much about that idea (or behavior)?
16. What are some good things about that notion?
17. What do we have to assume for things to work out that way?
18. Is what you express consistent with . . . (note something else the person said or did that may point to an inconsistency)?
19. What other possibilities are there?
20. Is that a personal preference or do you think most people should believe that?
21. How can I help you do something about your idea? What seems to be the difficulty?
22. Is there a purpose to this activity?
23. Is that very important to you?
24. Do you do this often?
25. Would you like to tell others about your idea?
26. Do you have any reasons for (saying or doing) that?
27. Would you do the same thing over again?
28. How do you know it's right?
29. Do you value that?
30. Do you think people will always believe that? Or, would Chinese peasants and African hunters also believe that? Or, did people long ago believe that? [24]

The above questions reflect the seven steps of the Raths, Harmin, and Simon model of valuing, defined in Chapter 1. Recall that for something to become a value it must be chosen freely among alternatives, after all consequences of each alternative have been considered; the individual must cherish the choice and be willing to affirm it publicly; finally, the individual must be willing to act upon the choice and do so repeatedly.

Another practical technique for bringing out the children's values and helping them to clarify these values is, again, the value sheet, which can take a variety of formats. J. Doyle Casteel and Robert Stahl write, "The standard format contains two components: a learning resource providing the social or scientific context, and a set of questions." [25] The questions are instrumental in helping the children to comprehend the learning resource, to relate it to broader topics or concepts under consideration, and to express their feelings about it. The learning resource could be a cartoon, poem, magazine or newspaper article, tape recording, filmstrip, graph, chart, picture, personal experience, movie or television show, play, experiment, speech, or the like.

Following is a sample standard value sheet presented by Casteel and Stahl:

RATS

Teacher Preparation

1. Secure sufficient copies of the resource.
2. Decide whether you wish students to respond to the questions individually or in small groups.
3. Develop questions likely to help students relate this value sheet to the unit you are teaching when you use it.

Resource Providing the Social and Scientific Context

Chicago, Illinois—In a very stirring and emotional speech the President last night declared an urgent need for Congress to act on a bill that would provide $237 million for the control of rats and mice in major urban centers. Addressing a fund-raising dinner, attended by persons capable of paying $1,000 for the right to sit at the table, the President said, "This bill is needed and it is needed now. Congress should waste no more time in deliberation. Every minute of congressional inaction and delay increases the threat of major epidemics in our cities."

The President continued his appeal by saying, "Disease spreading rodents continue to flourish with no systematic effort being made to control them. The numbers of wild field mice and rats are at an all-time high. Should these rodents begin to breed with the urban rats, we could well be on our way to a plague unequaled in human history."

To this last appeal, the crowd roared with laughter apparently believing that the President was jesting. However, the President was antagonized and continued to argue his case by. . . .

Discussion Starters

1. Where is the President speaking?
2. What do you know about the President's audience?
3. What bill does the President want passed?
4. In your opinion, should the bill be passed?
5. Suppose the bill is not passed. What effect will this have on those in the President's audience?
6. If the bill is not passed, who are some of the people who will suffer?
7. What are your first feelings when you read that those whom the President was addressing laughed at his arguments?
8. Given what occurred here, could this President serve as an effective leader of the American nation? Explain your answer.[26]

In addition to the standard value sheet, Casteel and Stahl elaborate on several other value sheet formats: the forced-choice, the affirmative, the rank-order, the classification, and the criterion formats. The forced-choice format "focuses on those situations in which the students must make a choice from among a number of almost equally attractive or almost equally unattractive alternatives." [27] The affirmative format, in contrast, puts students in a decision-making situation and asks them to invent alternative solutions. The rank-order format reveals children's values by asking them to rank a list of options. The classification format requires children to classify a number of options into desirable and undesirable. Finally, the criterion format "places students in a close setting. Given a limited number of options, a limited amount of data, and a limited list of criteria, students must make decisions related to both the data and the criteria given." [28] For illustrations of all of these formats the reader is referred to Casteel and Stahl's book.

Role playing places students in different value-laden roles and situations and requires that they act them out. In so doing, students interpret a particular situation on the basis of their values, which thus become evident. A basic source for role playing is *Role Playing for Social Values: Decision Making in the Social Studies*, by Fannie R. Shaftel and George Shaftel (Englewood Cliffs, N.J.: Prentice-Hall, 1967), in which many situations are provided for acting out. More details and illustrations on role playing are provided in Chapter 11.

Moral dilemma discussions are associated with Kohlberg's cognitive-developmental approach to moral education. These discussions require the individual to practice moral reasoning, choosing among two or more conflicting values on the basis of a six-stage hierarchy of reasons (listed in Chapter 1). Kohlberg believes that children can be trained to make moral decisions on the basis of reasons found at stages higher than their present stage. The teacher presents the children with moral dilemmas and, from the reasons they use to resolve the dilemmas, classifies the children in a stage. The teacher attempts to raise the children's level of moral reasoning by exposing them to the moral reasoning characteristic of those one stage above their own.

As to the medium for such training, moral discussion, Barry Beyer elaborates,

> One tested approach for conducting moral discussions requires that the teacher help students engage in sequence in five distinct activities: (1) to confront a dilemma; (2) to recommend tentative courses of action to resolve the dilemma and to justify these recommendations; (3) to discuss their reasoning in small groups; (4) to examine as a class their reasoning and the reasoning others use as they justify recommended solutions to the dilemma; and (5) to reflect on this reasoning as they bring temporary closure to their discussion.[29]

Moral discussion, then, resembles the process advocated in this chapter for dealing with controversial issues and social values. The moral dilemmas could be addressed to the issues themselves or to incidents that reflect the issues. For instance, the children in a class might conduct a moral discussion on how cliques could be discouraged in the class, or they might discuss an incident in which a student's feelings were hurt through rejection by the cliques.

Dealing with values is a difficult and delicate matter. The strategies presented can help children to clarify and to adjust their value systems. One of the most effective strategies, however, is modeling by the teacher. Is the teacher's decision making on day-to-day matters manifestly sound? Is the teacher accepting of the children, and the source of a trusting atmosphere?

In a comprehensive book on dealing with values, Jack Fraenkel gives these suggestions to teachers:

1. Accept all statements that students offer, no matter how silly or unusual they may seem when first presented.
2. Do not require students to talk if they do not want to.
3. When the student is having trouble getting his thoughts out, it sometimes is helpful to restate what he has expressed without indicating approval or disapproval of his idea.
4. Let students know that you want them to offer their ideas by telling them so.
5. Take care not to impose your views on students.
6. Don't hesitate to introduce ideas contrary to those expressed by students in order to bring out other aspects of an issue.[30]

SUMMARY

Understanding of social issues and the ability to contribute toward resolving them are important social studies objectives. Issues, most conducive to developing decision-making skills, come to be understood by the same methods used to develop concepts and generalizations. Evidence of a problem is presented to the children, and their value systems are mobilized to begin the process of resolution.

Because values are influential in decision making, a prime social studies objective, they can no longer be ignored by the school. The school, however, should deal with values only to the extent required by conflict resolution and decision making, never at the expense of the larger social studies program, and never becoming an arbiter of social values.

Yet the school has a responsibility to assist children to develop the basic social values espoused by the so-called American creed—not, however, as absolutes to be accepted without question, but as inheritances to be assessed for their suitability for life today. All values should be presented as questions and be tested by the rational process. Values adopted after scrutiny by the rational process are usually stronger and more lasting than those learned by traditional methods. A value is accepted, modified, or rejected in much the same way that an issue is resolved. Those methods are, in turn, similar to decision making. The steps of conflict resolution are:

1. Presentation of the issue
2. Collection and discussion of information and value positions
3. Presentation of all possible alternative solutions and their evaluation in light of the children's values
4. Consideration of the consequences of each alternative solution.
5. Choice from the alternative solutions and justification
6. Organization for action
7. Action

Conflict resolution demands that children be aware of their values and clear as to what they are. Various value-clarification and value-assessment strategies accomplish these goals; the value response, the valuing sheet, role-playing, and discussions on moral dilemmas are the most common of these strategies. The teacher as a model of sound decision making is also important in the classroom.

ACTIVITIES

1. Respond individually to questions that would reveal your instrumental and terminal values. For example: (a) What is the best way of life for me? (b) How would I like to be remembered when I get old and gray? Submit these responses to a committee anonymously to analyze and compile a list of the expressed values.

2. Arrange with a local classroom teacher to have children respond to the same questions by writing compositions. Analyze the compositions and compile a list of the children's instrumental and terminal values. Compare your values with the children's. What similarities do you notice? What differences? What might account for the differences?

3. Identify those occasions in which your life outlook has changed in some way. What caused each change? Was it something you read, some person you met, some unusual experience? Was the change sudden or gradual?

4. Identify six or seven beliefs, traits, or principles for which you stand as an individual. Rank these characteristics. Think of yourself without each one of them and try to articulate the way you feel. Think of yourself without any of these characteristics and try to articulate your feelings. Usually this exercise persuades participants that they do not wish to arbitrarily give up any element of their value system. The same is true with children. Recall and discuss what teachers usually say or do that forces children to give up elements of their individuality. Discuss the implications of such a practice.

5. Take a basic issue and identify the instructional objectives for both primary and upper elementary school grades. What differences do you notice and why?

6. Take the objectives developed in the preceding activity and indicate what the children may do to reach each objective.

7. Each student should take an issue and develop a complete teaching plan as illustrated in the chapter. Students may coordinate their issues along particular unit topics and develop plans that they can share. Combining these plans with the appropriate plans on generalizations may produce complete units and even complete programs.

NOTES

1. David R. Krathwohl, Benjamin S. Bloom, and Bertram B. Masia, *Taxonomy of Educational Objectives—Handbook II: Affective Domain* (New York: David McKay, 1964), pp. 24–44.

2. Ibid., p. 33.

3. **Ibid., p. 27.**

4. Louis E. Raths, Merrill Harmin, and Sidney B. Simon, *Values and Teaching* (Columbus, Ohio: Charles E. Merrill, 1966).

5. Ibid., pp. 5, 7.

6. Milton Rokeach, *Beliefs, Attitudes and Values: A Theory of Organization and Change* (San Francisco: Jossey-Bass, 1968).

7. Richard A. Cole, "A Study of Values and Value Systems of Pre-Adolescent School Children" (Unpublished Ph.D. thesis, University of Washington, 1972).

8. Dave Williams, "A Study of Pre-Adolescent Value Preferences" (Unpublished Ph.D. thesis, University of Washington, 1972).

9. James P. Shaver and William Strong, *Facing Value Decision: Rationale-Building for Teachers* (Belmont, Calif.: Wadsworth, 1976), p. 15.

10. Jerrold R. Coombs, "Objectives of Value Analysis," in Lawrence E. Metcalf, ed., *Values Education,* 41st Yearbook of the National Council for the Social Studies (Washington, D.C.: National Council for the Social Studies, 1971), p. 2.

11. Shaver and Strong, *Facing Value Decision,* p. 15.

12. Ibid., p. 19.

13. Ibid., p. 22.

14. Lawrence Kohlberg, "The Cognitive-Developmental Approach to Moral Education," *Phi Delta Kappan,* 56 (June 1975), 672.

15. Thomas A. Ringness, *The Affective Domain in Education* (Boston: Little, Brown, 1975), pp. 10–11.

16. Ibid., p. 17.

17. Byron G. Massialas and Nancy F. Sprague, "Teaching Social Issues as Inquiry: A Clarification," *Social Education,* 38 (January 1974), 10.

18. Morris R. Lewenstein, "Teaching Strategies for Discussion of Quality of Life vs. Gross National Product," *Social Education,* 37 (November 1973), 609; Jack R. Fraenkel, "Teaching Procedures for Discussion of Which Way World Peace: Gradualism or Drastic System Change?" *Social Education,* 37 (November 1973), 619; Jerrold R. Coombs and Milton Meux, "Teaching Strategies for Value Analysis," in Lawrence E. Metcalf, ed., *Values Education,* 41st Yearbook of the National Council for the Social Studies (Washington, D.C.: National Council for the Social Studies, 1971), p. 29.

19. "Food and Nutrition—The Key to Healthy Living," *Compton's Encyclopedia,* vol. 10 (Chicago: F. E. Compton, 1975), pp. 326–27.

20. Leon Festinger, *A Theory of Cognitive Dissonance* (Evanston, Ill.: Row, Peterson, 1957).

21. Gary Manson et al., "Social Studies Curriculum Guidelines," *Social Education,* 35 (December 1971), 859.

22. Titles listed are from the *Seattle Times,* September 1 and 2, 1976, and August 9, 1977.

23. B. Othanel Smith, William O. Stanley, and J. Harlan Shores, *Fundamentals of Curriculum Development* (New York: World Book Company, 1957), pp. 76–78; adapted

from Harold C. Hand, *Principles of Public Secondary Education* (New York: Harcourt, Brace, 1958), pp. 43–45.

24. Adapted from Louis E. Raths, Merrill Harmin, and Sidney B. Simon, *Values and Teaching,* pp. 56–62. Reprinted with the permission of Charles E. Merrill Publishing Co.

25. J. Doyle Casteel and Robert J. Stahl, *Value Clarification in the Classroom: A Primer* (Pacific Palisades, Calif.: Goodyear, 1975), p. 13.

26. Ibid., p. 23.

27. Ibid., p. 27.

28. Ibid., p. 127.

29. Barry K. Beyer, "Conducting Moral Discussions in the Classroom," *Social Education,* 40 (April 1976), 196–97.

30. Adapted from Jack R. Fraenkel, *How to Teach About Values: An Analytic Approach* (Englewood Cliffs, N.J.: Prentice-Hall, 1977), pp. 138–41.

Studying this chapter will enable the reader to:

1. argue against the use of any one textbook and in support of the unit plan.
2. outline a unit plan and logically justify the order of its components.
3. recognize the importance of the content objectives in the structure of the unit.
4. realize that process objectives develop as the children attempt to reach content objectives and apply the knowledge acquired.
5. compare and contrast a traditional unit plan with the one presented in this chapter that reflects contemporary educational trends.
6. outline steps that would help the teacher move gradually from using one textbook to using the unit plan.
7. develop a complete unit plan as illustrated in the chapter.
8. define the three most important components of a lesson plan.
9. abstract lesson plans from unit plans and write them in a simple format as illustrated in the chapter.
10. recognize the importance of the children's experiences and of the local environment in the development of unit and lesson plans.

THE UNIT PLAN
AND THE LESSON PLAN:
BRIDGING THE OLD AND THE NEW

We have explored in detail how the overall purpose of social studies can be reduced to instructional objectives, and how concepts, generalizations, and issues can be used as the structural elements of a social studies program intended to develop citizens who can effectively live in contemporary society. In this chapter we will examine how extended and daily comprehensive plans can implement the ideas and procedures discussed thus far.

Teachers usually approach planning and teaching, whether for the short term or the long term, in one of two basic ways: by using a textbook or by using a unit plan. In theory, the only teaching method to be advocated for teaching social studies to young children is the unit plan. But practicing teachers who return to college for refresher courses often laugh at the education professors who anathematize the use of one textbook and favor the unit plan absolutely. The teachers know that in practice most of them continue to teach from one textbook and will probably continue to do so in the future.

This disturbing phenomenon persists not because the teachers are unconvinced of the unit plan's superiority but mainly because it is difficult for them to abandon the textbook entirely and at once. Unfortunately, since the unit plan emerged this is what they have been asked to do—to take a big jump to a place remote from their original base. Because such a daring and impractical suggestion continues to be rejected, there is need of a gradual approach toward the unit plan. This chapter presents such an approach.

There is another problem: Since its conception, the unit plan itself has changed to reflect more recent developments in social studies. So drastic have been those developments that the difference between a typical traditional unit plan and one that reflects recent developments is instructive. Such a contrast is made in this chapter.

WHY ABANDON THE TEXTBOOK?

Teachers and educators in general often become fanatical partisans over unresolved issues. For example, research cannot support the phonics method of teaching reading as superior to the "look and say" method; each method is equally effective in the proper circumstances. Yet some teachers, and even reading supervisors, completely reject one method in favor of the other. On the issue of textbooks versus the unit plan, however, especially in the teaching of social studies, there is no doubt as to the right course. The textbook, as now used, is simply inadequate, and for many reasons.

Again, social studies, in dealing with contemporary human relationships, must deal with conflicts. Undoubtedly, the best way to do so is to present all sides of an issue and help the youngsters to think about them with an open mind. No one textbook can achieve this. Whether intentionally or not, a textbook author tends to bias youngsters' thinking. Moreover, textbook publishers are often forced to accede to local or sectional conditions and pressures to be less than objective or to skimp on certain topics.

Furthermore, reliance on one textbook contradicts a peculiar characteristic of the American educational system: the diversity of abilities present in each grade level. This is a gigantic problem for the teacher. In many parts of the world, where education is by necessity or by design the privilege of the few, this problem is solved by creating homogeneous groups, by eliminating many children from the school. In the United States this cannot—and should not—take place, because here education is a birthright. It is not right under these circumstances to force every child in a grade to follow one textbook written for the average child in that grade. To do so loses the youngsters with below-average ability and bores those who have above-average ability.

Sectional and environmental differences also make the use of one textbook inadequate: Children living in the city need more emphasis on the farm in their studies than do children living on farms, and vice versa; New York children need to study more about oil than do Texas children. Only by departing from the use of one textbook can these adjustments be made.

Another objection is that social studies textbooks rapidly become outdated—sometimes are outdated in certain respects as soon as they are published. Given economic and technological constraints on publishers, it is impossible for them to keep their texts abreast of the rapid, often significant changes in today's world.

Learning from one textbook tends to be dull. Think of children day after day taking turns reading paragraphs out of the same book and then having discussions on what they read. Or they must read a chapter and answer the questions at its end. Children consider this kind of learning a chore, and quite often it is unrelated to their needs and interests. The monotony bores the children and stifles their natural curiosity and creativity. It deprives the children of opportunities to interact and to practice some of what they learn, or should learn. Social skills, for example, are totally neglected. It is no wonder children learning from a textbook usually dislike social studies.

Teaching from a single textbook is easy for the teacher, but the teacher is no longer in control of the teaching situation. By selecting a textbook that is to be followed page by page, the teacher ceases to be a professional and becomes a technician or caretaker. There is no substitute for a committed, self-directed, and creative teacher. During the last 10 to 15 years many so-called teacher-proof materials have been produced, but they proved to be futile. A class of young people is a dynamic situation that cannot be fully predicted and packaged for. Materials are useful, but the teacher's success depends less on the materials than on how they are used.

There is no question that the dynamic nature of social studies is better served through the unit plan and its derivative lesson plans. After a brief account of the unit plan's advantages, its structure is described in detail. The traditional form of the unit plan is then compared with a more contemporary form. Although the contemporary unit plan is presented in its ideal form, methods are discussed that allow teachers to compromise between the textbook and the unit plan. A sample unit is then presented. Finally, the lesson plan is considered in its relation to the unit plan, and a sample lesson plan is abstracted from the unit.

ADVANTAGES OF THE UNIT PLAN

One of the most important advantages of the unit plan is that *it localizes the teaching–learning situation, puts the teacher in control of the learning process, and makes schooling relevant to children's experiences.* Recently the leaders of a small Indian reservation in the Northwest expressed concern that the education of their children, in a school that they controlled, did not reflect their values and way of life. But they also wanted their children to achieve the same educational objectives other children in society were pursuing. They approached me and, with the Native American's traditional wisdom, asked whether society's educational objectives could be achieved through the study of their environment and way of life. Their common sense reflected a basic educational principle.

Funds were secured and 16 teachers were hired during the summer to develop a localized curriculum. First, the objectives of a number of subjects were identified as they appeared in state documents and other national sources. Learning activities that reflected the local environment were then developed for each objective. For example, one objective was to help children understand that "natural resources provide a way of life for people throughout the world." Some of the initial activities suggested were: (1) find out how many people on the reservation have jobs that depend on reservation resources; (2) find out how many of the reservation resources are sold outside the reservation; (3) visit local companies that process reservation resources; (4) respond to the question, "Why do people from other parts of the nation or the globe buy the reservation products?" Another objective was to convince the children that government decisions usually reflect the wishes and values of the people they govern. The teachers decided that the easiest way to reach this objective was to study the decisions of the tribal council and how these decisions were made.

Implementation of the new, teacher-developed units brought excitement among all those concerned—pupils, teachers, and the community. The parents were drawn closer to the school, and the children started feeling good about their local community and about school and learning. No longer bored by the monotonous reading of a textbook, they were out in the community searching for information, observing, talking to older people, taking notes, and using their information to reach conclusions.

Another advantage of the unit plan is that *it facilitates the conceptual approach, to the benefit of all children.* The textbook is the tool of the descriptive approach and describes situations, events, and phenomena in the same way for all children. Children, however, learn differently because their abilities and experiential backgrounds differ. Some children learn through the textbook, others do not. The conceptual approach enables all children to learn in ways most suitable to them. The constant elements in the conceptual approach are the objectives: the concepts and the generalizations to be grasped. But the method of learning these concepts and generalizations varies from child to child. The unit plan, unlike the textbook, makes possible this variation in instruction.

If, for example, children in the primary grades are to learn the concept "change" they do not need a book. Some might learn it from a book, but others might look at a set of pictures of themselves and observe the changes they underwent as they grew. Others might learn what change means by observing the changes in the trees, flowers, the weather, and just about everything around them. A second grade teacher asked her children to list as many changes as they could think of. They came up with about 70 of them, including, "Mother changes when she is pregnant." As explained in Chapter 4, concepts and generalizations develop through examples of what they represent. The children's life and experiential background are a better quarry than any textbook. In higher grades children can strengthen their concept of change by viewing films and observing the changes that have taken place in our country, or by analyzing songs from various periods to determine the changes in people's outlooks.

A third advantage of the unit plan is that *it provides opportunities for decision making.* The unit plan affords two types of decision for the children: substantive decisions and procedural decisions. Textbook learning often brings out the substantive issues, but it is not enough to simply talk about them. If decision-making skills are to develop, children must practice resolving the substantive issues and act upon their resolutions. Because it reflects the local environment, the unit plan makes it easier to carry out decisions made by the children.

The second type of decision, procedural decisions, are required in planning and executing the unit plan. Whereas the textbook spells out in detail what should be learned and how, giving explicit instructions for pupils and teacher alike, the unit plan is open-ended and demands cooperative planning between the teacher and the pupils. In the course of this planning, children make and carry out many decisions that are personal, relevant, and, therefore, powerful.

In addition, the unit plan *makes the learner an active participant in the learning process.* The belief prevailed in the past that students learn from the teacher. John Dewey tried to broaden the avenues of learning, but American educators were not convinced of his ideas until the British implemented them and found them successful. Yes, children learn from the teacher, but they also learn by themselves and from each other. The idea that children can learn by themselves has been systematically promoted during the last few years. Individual *learning contracts* and *learning centers* implement individualized learning by students. Instead of every child in a classroom learning from a textbook, the teacher and individual pupils agree on special individual projects, with special contracts that stipulate what avenue each student should use to achieve the same objectives.

Learning centers are usually sets of materials arranged in some secluded part of the classroom and always available for students to use on their own time or at any time with the teacher's permission. Specific instructions stipulate how explicitly stated objectives are to be achieved, and give ways for the children to evaluate their progress. There can be many learning centers in any unit. Their quantity and quality depend entirely on each teacher's creativity.

Another merit of unit teaching is that *it provides for an unknown number of indirect learnings.* While youngsters are searching the various resources for an answer, they are exposed to considerable ancillary information, some of which might arouse their curiosity and stimulate further reading. Some of it might clear up previous misconceptions.

In summary, the unit plan is an approach that combines the most contemporary principles of education. It not only offers knowledge, it provides opportunities to use that knowledge. In so doing, the children develop their intellectual abilities as well as useful social skills. The unit plan is a rounded experience that resembles important undertakings in real life. The children learn to cooperate with other people; they learn to listen to other people's views; and, most important, they learn how to make decisions.

THE STRUCTURE OF THE UNIT PLAN

Various textbooks and journal articles present the unit plan by listing its structural elements. Such lists show variations one from another, which can confuse the neophyte. But there are no substantial differences from one form to the other. Careful analysis invariably reveals that three basic elements are always present: (1) the objectives to be achieved; (2) the content and its presentation, or the means of achieving these objectives; and (3) the techniques of evaluation, the ways the teacher finds out if the children are reaching or have reached the objectives. Everything else in a unit's structure is part of these three elements or serves an auxiliary function.

The structure presented in this section contains all elements of the traditional unit plan. At the same time, however, these elements reflect the philosophy, objectives, program, and procedures discussed in preceding chapters. Also, the structure is presented in a practical sequence, that is, the sequence that teachers should follow in preparing a unit for a class.

The Title

The first thing a teacher has to do before starting a new school year is to title the units to be taught. This is not easy, because there is much to be taught in limited time. All American history, for example, might have to be taught in one grade. Time not permitting the study of too many details, the teacher would have to be selective. The events most formative of the American nation and the most basic issues, concepts, and generalizations should be selected. Otherwise one aspect of American history might be overstressed while other aspects equally or even more important might be neglected or just touched upon.

Chapter 3 provides specific guidelines for selecting unit topics. (See that chapter for more details on the guidelines and for examples of unit topics for each grade.) Remember that an area of study is treated adequately only if the following are taken into consideration. The topics selected should:

1. Reflect content that is considered important by social scientists.
2. Provide for a comprehensive treatment of the particular area of study designated or selected for that grade.
3. Allow for the consideration of the local scene.
4. Lead to the treatment of important contemporary issues.

Once titles are determined, the teacher should prepare a folder for each title and be alert to materials that can be placed in them. Anything related to the topics is good at this stage—lists of books, book reviews, magazine and newspaper articles, pictures, maps, graphs, lists of films and

149

filmstrips, pamphlets, and other items. These folders, when properly applied, can be used year after year.

When a unit is to be taught, its folder is the starting point. The teacher first reviews the materials to become familiar again with the topic, although usually the teacher goes beyond these materials, seeking optimum mastery of the content and proper enthusiasm in presenting the unit.

The same units need not be taught year after year. As conditions change, the units can change accordingly. For example, a teacher in the 1960s dealing with Southeast Asia probably taught a unit on Vietnam, because of the American involvement there. But earlier than that or since then a unit on Korea or on China might be more appropriate.

The Objectives

Unit plans usually have two types of objectives: general and instructional. When the descriptive approach dominated social studies, general objectives prevailed in the unit plan, and consequently were the same from one unit to the other. Their function was to act as a general framework, keeping the randomly selected specific objectives and the study of each unit within the general scope of social studies.

As decision making has become the emphasis of social studies, general objectives have changed. Gone are the broad, often vague statements formulated by teachers' committees; general objectives are now the basic generalizations and issues from the social sciences and contemporary life conditions from which instructional objectives are derived. As was discussed in Chapter 3, about a half dozen generalizations and about the same number of issues are selected for each unit topic. Some generalizations and issues, remember, may not be completely developed in one unit, but may appear in successive units to accommodate the children's cognitive development.

Students in teacher education programs and teachers returning to the campuses for refresher courses or to pursue graduate programs usually take several social science courses on subjects that deal with many of the units they will be teaching. In such a situation, search for basic generalizations. Seek the advice of your professors to arrive at comprehensive sets of valid generalizations and issues on specific topics. Note the best sources on these topics. When you take a course on the family, for example, identify what are considered to be the five or six basic understandings and five or six basic issues about the American family and ask your professor to verify their validity. Do the same with all of your courses, and be sure to take courses relevant to what you will be teaching.

The second type of objectives in a unit plan are the instructional objectives, also called behavioral, or specific, objectives. Instructional objectives are the changes that are expected to take place in each child. They should not be confused with the activities to be undertaken by the teacher, the pupils, or all working together. (Instructional objectives were discussed at some length in Chapter 2, so much of what follows is in the nature of a review.)

There are five types of instructional objectives:

1. Knowledge—the facts, concepts, and subgeneralizations contained in the generalizations and issues.
2. Social values—the accepted standards of behavior implicit in the generalizations and issues.
3. Intellectual skills—mainly the skills of inquiry.
4. Value-clarification skills—the skills required to enable children to become aware of and clarify their personal values.
5. Social skills—these are the skills that help us conduct our affairs in an orderly fashion, such as cooperation, parliamentary procedure, and the like.

The first two objectives listed are content objectives, the next three are process objectives. Both types are equally important, and all should be developed in any unit plan.

Because the objectives are derived from generalizations and issues, the social science disciplines and the structure of knowledge are seen to be crucial, and are significant in another respect: Years ago, and even today in some so-called alternative schools, if a teacher were asked in September what the objectives were for the year, the answer might be, "I won't know until June." The era is gone in which the children's immediate needs and interests alone determine the objectives of instruction. The teacher, not the children, is most qualified to determine the objectives. The teacher knows not only the immediate interests of children but their present and future needs as well. The teacher knows also the structure and basic elements of the disciplines, as well as the conditions of life today.

If in the past the needs and interests of children were given too much weight in determining the objectives, it was because certain psychological principles were given prominence in the teaching–learning process. Psychologists insist that learning is facilitated, and more permanent, if the children feel a need for what they learn and are interested in it. This is true, but acting on it does not require that structured learning be abandoned. Good teaching can generate both need and interest by relating what the children are to learn with what they already know. Psychological principles should facilitate the achievement of educational objectives, not replace or eliminate them.

Problems and Activities

The objectives having set the direction that the development of a unit must take, the value of content—dictated by the generalizations, the issues, and the social values—becomes obvious. In the traditional form of the unit plan, the content was outlined in considerable detail—which would be useful only if the teacher were to lecture to the class. But good teaching in the elementary school is not lecturing; it is instead providing the children with problems both interesting and basic to a topic and directing their inquiry in finding the solutions.

Thus, in the place of an outline, the teacher converts content objectives into basic problems (as discussed in Chapter 4). These problems should be basic questions, the answers to which lead to the formulation of important concepts and relationships, and the resolution of meaningful conflicts. The concepts are constituents of the generalizations, the issues, and the social values; the relationships are the subgeneralizations derived from the same three sources, while the conflicts to be resolved derive from the issues and their operative social values.

To show how content objectives are closely related to the basic questions that direct the inquiry in a plan, the content objectives and the questions from the sample plans in Chapters 4 and 5 are placed side by side below. The generalization underlying the instructional objectives for the first plan was: "Migration develops cultural diversity within groups and cultural diffusion between groups."

CONTENT OBJECTIVES	BASIC QUESTIONS
A. The children will know that:	
1. People move from one place to another	1. Were all the people in our community born here?
2. There are different reasons for which people move.	2. Why do people move from one place to another?
3. Various ethnic groups eat different foods.	3. How different are the foods we eat and why?
4. People often try foods usually eaten by other ethnic groups.	4. Who eats in the ethnic restaurants?
5. Every cultural group has something to offer to enrich our lives.	5. What would our community be like without the ethnic restaurants?
B. The children will value:	
1. The differences among people.	1. What groups of people are in our community and what new things have they brought to our community?

The instructional objectives for the second plan were derived from the following issue: "What can be done to reduce conflict around the world?"

CONTENT OBJECTIVES	BASIC QUESTIONS
A. The children will know:	
1. The major conflict areas around the world.	1. What are the major conflicts around the world?
2. That four of the most important causes for conflict are economics, religion, race, and territorial disputes in border areas.	2. What are the causes of the various conflicts around the world? What are the value positions of the conflicting parties?
3. That no nation is remote from conflict.	3. What effect do these conflicts have upon the United States and the world as a whole?
4. Three ways presently applied to reduce conflict— the United Nations, summit conferences, personal diplomacy.	4. What is being done to reduce conflict?
B. The children will value:	
1. Genuine cooperation among nations.	1. What more can be done to reduce conflict?
2. Nonviolent methods of resolving conflicts.	2. Are violent or nonviolent techniques more appropriate or more effective?

Questions, which set the stage for learning through inquiry, are only guidelines for the direction the lesson will take. As the plans are discussed with them, the students might raise more questions as appropriate as, or even more so than, the teacher's.

Each problem needs learning activities, which spell out the class-period-by-class-period and day-by-day course of action the children will follow under the teacher's direction. The unit plan represents the broader method of teaching; the activities represent the techniques of teaching. As John McNeil states: "Learning activities—sometimes called learning opportunities, learning experiences, or instructional interventions—are the essence of education. As one wag said, 'Aims and objectives are the menu, learning activities are the meal.' " [1]

To properly formulate learning activities, the teacher must consider two factors: the nature of the children, as individuals and as a group; and the available teaching resources. The teacher should not only know the children's general abilities and experiential backgrounds, but, more important, should thoroughly diagnose their knowledge of the topic to be studied. Such diagnosis helps to avoid unnecessary repetition for some youngsters, and it helps to identify students who can be used as motivating agents.

Social studies resources include the community, trade books and other reading materials, audiovisual aids, current events, maps and globes, games, and dramatic and rhythmic exercises. All can be used to make the study of social studies, or research into basic problems, vivid, realistic experiences. These resources provide diverse avenues toward the same objectives allowing for individual differences in ability (as well as allowing for more than one viewpoint on controversial matters). For the slow child can be found activities less abstract than those for the gifted child. Yet all activities lead to realizing the same goals.

The most convenient way to record a unit's problems and activities is to divide sheets of paper into two columns and record the problems in one column and the activities in the other, as this excerpt from the plan in Chapter 4 illustrates:

PROBLEMS	ACTIVITIES
A. Were all the people in our community born here?	1. Ask children to indicate how many of them were born in the community and how many of them came from other places.
	2. Have children find out how many of their parents were born in the community and how many came from other communities.
B. Why do people move from one place to another?	1. Contact a couple of parents who have moved into the community or who are about to move away from the community to come to class and give reasons for their move.
	2. Stimulate the children to think of other reasons why people move. You might have them think of relatives who live away from the community and recall any particular reasons for their living away.
C. . . .	1. . . .

Student teachers and teachers usually ask two questions about designing learning activities: "How many activities should there be for each problem?" "How detailed should the activities be?" No general answer can be given to the first question because the children's level and experiential background are determinant. As to the second question, the learning activities designer should write them out in enough detail to enable a substitute teacher to follow them. If a film is to be used, for example, the title of the film and how it is to be used should be given in the activities, while the complete bibliographical information concerning the film should be given at the end of the unit. Vague activities such as "The children will do research in the library," or "The children will view a related filmstrip," should be avoided.

The logical flow of the unit plan's elements is obvious: The topic is related to a particular grade level's area of study; generalizations and issues are related to the topic; both the content and process instructional objectives derive from the generalizations and issues. The problems or questions reflect both content objectives—knowledge and social values. All three process objectives—the intellectual skills, value-clarification skills, and the social skills—must be reflected in the activities. As we saw in Chapter 2, skills are most effectively developed by being applied to achieving the content objectives.

The teacher designing learning activities must therefore be directed not only by the questions but by the process objectives as well. Children cannot learn how to clarify values without activities that require value clarification; nor can they develop the skill of analysis unless their activities require it. The same applies for all skills. Unfortunately, it is a commonplace error to have, listed among the instructional objectives, process objectives with no corresponding activities.

There are some teachers who set time aside for teaching, say, inquiry skills, but who do not use the inquiry method of instruction at any other time. Teaching children this way is like instructing a group of undernourished people on proper diet without giving them the proper food. Children cannot be told, for example, to be cooperative; they must learn cooperation —and all other skills necessary for a democratic way of life in a changing world—by practicing them in situations that they see as real-life. The activities in a sound unit plan are nothing more than a well-designed sequence of such situations.

As early as 1960, Wilhelmina Hill gave the following extensive list of types of activities:

1. Reading for information. . . .
2. Viewing informational films and filmstrips.
3. Listening to recordings and people.
4. Carrying out experiments.
5. Taking notes on needed information.
6. Studying maps and globes.
7. Taking field trips to gather information.
8. Making collections.
9. Writing letters for information.
10. Interviewing appropriate people.
11. Studying pictures for information.
12. Reading the landscape for geographic information.
13. Discussing unit problems and progress.
14. Sharing information in small and large groups.
15. Keeping a record of information each child is gathering.
16. Organizing information on charts and graphs.[2]

Jack Fraenkel classifies activities into behaviors, products, and experiences.[3] Behaviors include interviewing, describing, discussing, listing, grouping, explaining, predicting, hypothesizing, summarizing, choosing, and rating. Products include maps, charts, models, outlines, reports, diagrams, essays, murals, poems, songs, and photographs. Experiences include viewing a sunset, listening to a record, attending a ballet, visiting a factory, smelling a flower, tasting a food, watching a demonstration, browsing in a library, seeing a play, holding a kitten, painting a picture, playing a musical instrument, riding a bicycle, talking to an elderly person, playing a game, and walking through a park.

Fraenkel also classifies activities according to the function they serve in the acquisition and application of knowledge. He identifies four different functions: intake, organizational, demonstrative, and creative.[4] The traditional school, which emphasized the accumulation of knowledge, relied mainly on intake activities such as reading, seeing films, listening to records, and the like. With the emphasis now on using knowledge, the other three types of activities assume equal importance. Children, for example, make maps of an area after observing it—an organization activity; they role-play a situation they have studied—a demonstrative activity; or they make a mural to show the steps in a particular process—a creative activity. Teachers never fail to include intake activities in their plans; they should make every effort, however, to include organizational, demonstrative, and creative activities as well. The latter three can help children develop decision-making skills.

An advantage of the unit plan, stressed earlier, is that it allows children to learn by themselves—but only if appropriate activities are designed. Excellent examples can be found in a collection of activities pre-

pared under the direction of Bob Samples by ESSENTIA, a project supported by the National Science Foundation and sponsored by the American Ecological Institute. The activities help children learn a concept, clarify a value or a feeling, or apply a skill. Because they are open-ended, the activities can be executed in any way the child chooses. As the authors state, their activities (or assignments as they call them)

> are permissive slips to openness. The whole project is committed to openness. By openness, we feel that greater responsibility is assumed by young people as they make decisions about what they do. It is this sense of responsibility in learning that is so important to nurturing individual growth and individual distinctiveness. No one likes to be treated like a member of a herd.[5]

Each one of the ESSENTIA activities is on a cleverly designed and illustrated card. On one side is the concept, value or feeling, or skill; on the other side, usually in a squared block, is "the action"—the main activity or activities to be undertaken. Below it, labeled "more," are additional activities. As an example, visualize a five-by-eight-inch card: On one side is the concept *Expectations;* on the other side are:

THE ACTION:

> Figure out what kinds of things people expect you to do without asking their permission.
>
> Figure out things you expect other people to do without asking their permission.

MORE:

> Determine which expectations are fair and which are unfair.
>
> Create "Don't lay that on me" lists that are kept in the room and written on freely.
>
> Do people have a right to expect anything of you?
>
> Do you have the right to expect anything of others? [6]

As can be seen, the assignments are not only open-ended but personalized as well. They involve the children, their experiences, and their relationships with the people around them.

Teachers can prepare their own activity cards—either individual cards or a sequence forming a learning center. (A good source for the design of learning centers is "The Learning Center in the Social Studies Classroom," by James M. Larkin and Jane J. White.[7])

Most activities in a unit are short-range, addressed to one question. But some long-range activities could be designed as ongoing experiences with which to illustrate a number of learnings. Below is an example of such a long-range activity designed, implemented, and described by Dennis Hamburg, a fifth grade teacher:

> During the first quarter of the year, paper play money is given out to the students on a weekly pay ($200) basis. This continues throughout the entire year, and the students keep a bank book to record their debit, credit and balance. With this money, students buy, sell, auction items, and make bets on games, contests, etc. They earn money by being "good" and are fined when "goofing off." This works as a quick easy positive and negative reinforcement. Each year an income tax is held, and the money is handled in as close to the "real business" world as possible with the teacher being the bank. The students usually become very attached to their money and hate to lose any.[8]

Here is Mr. Hamburg's description of how he related the above experience to the study of the American Revolution:

> As an introduction to the causes of the Revolutionary War, the teacher announces the following new rules in regards to the classroom money:
>
> 1. Anyone buying milk must pay an additional ten dollars per day. (similar to English Tea Act)
> 2. The teacher may inspect any personal property of students (desk, closet, coats, notebooks, etc.) and any "illegal" items will be heavily fined. (similar to Quartering of Troops Act)
> 3. All items that are sold or bought by students must be handled through the teacher, and the teacher gets half the profit. (similar to the Revenue Act)
> 4. Anyone out of their seats for any reason (drinks, bathroom, etc.) during classtime will be fined $100. (similar to Proclamation Act)
> 5. Every frowny face put on, incomplete, messy, or bad work gets fined $50. (similar to Stamp Act)
>
> A discussion on each item is then held, with the teacher not "giving an Inch" on the issues. The students of course get very upset, say it's unfair, refuse to obey, plan action against the rules, etc.
>
> The teacher then leads the discussion into the causes of the Revolutionary War. A correlation is drawn between the classroom money and the early colonists. In the end, the teacher announces that the classroom "acts" are not going to be used (which makes the class happy again). The class and teacher can then "peacefully" fight the Revolutionary War.

Initiating and Culminating Activities

Initiating and culminating execution of the unit plan constitute the first and the last activities. These two activities are considered separately because they serve a special function and are not directly related to specific content problems. The teacher has decided in advance what the general objectives, the problems, and to a great extent the activities of a unit will be, yet there must be a planning session with students to motivate them to study the unit and adopt the plans. If this session is successful, the children will want to study the unit topic and will have collectively and voluntarily accepted the proposed course of action.

It is desirable, then, to put the children in the proper mood, by appealing to their emotions and arousing their interest in the topic, or by connecting the new topic with previous learnings. Any clever idea will do the job; to present a list of possible initiation activities would only inhibit the teacher's imagination. Nevertheless, one or two examples should be cited: A unit on Africa could be initiated by showing a film on African life. Then drums, probably made by another class, may be distributed to the children to imitate the music and dancing seen in the film. Such an activity helps children identify with the Africans, promoting enthusiastic discussion about that continent. The study of the Golden Age of the Greeks, to use another example, can lead naturally to the study of what constitutes strong and good government, because without the strong and wise leadership of Pericles there might not have been a Golden Age.

Culminating activities are as crucial as initiating activities. For several days or weeks, the children have been involved in tasks addressed to designated problems. All children's goals were the same, but their individual paths were different. Culminating activities enable the whole class to reflect collectively and relate everything they studied. Life in Africa, for instance, may be portrayed by a series of dioramas. A study on comparative government may be culminated by making and displaying charts depicting the structure of each type of government. Everyone should participate when the unit is culminated. It is rewarding and meaningful for the children to see their own individual work as a part of the total accomplishment of the class. Culminating activities may often produce an exhibit or performance to be viewed by the rest of the school and even the parents. It should be stressed, however, that the chief purpose of culminating activities is not to produce a show or to help teachers gain praise from supervisors and parents, but to bring the learnings into focus for the students.

Evaluation

Student progress in a unit is not evaluated only after the unit is completed (such evaluation, remember, is called summative). Rather, evaluation is also formative—is a part of teaching and is directed toward the children and teacher alike. Everything the teacher does with the class should have an objective. If the objective seems not to have been reached, the teacher should try to revise the teaching techniques. (Both types of evaluation are discussed in detail in Chapter 7.)

A third type of evaluation must be used in developing and teaching a unit: diagnostic evaluation. Children, as individuals and as groups, have diverse backgrounds, sets of knowledge, skills, and talents. Unless diagnostic evaluation of these factors precedes the designing or teaching of the unit, some children will be asked to undertake tasks beyond their abilities, while others will be bored. The lack of diagnostic evaluation was one reason why primary social studies during the 1950s and the early '60s was notorious for its trivial and repetitious content.[9]

It is important to remember that pencil and paper tests are not the only means of evaluation. These tests usually measure only levels of knowledge, but the concerns of social studies also include attitudes, beliefs, and skills, which cannot be so measured. A variety of evaluation techniques is therefore necessary. (These techniques, described in the next chapter, include observation, group discussion, interviews, checklists, scrapbooks, and samples of work.) Techniques of evaluation can differ from one unit plan to the next, according to what the objectives, content, and activities dictate as most appropriate. The teacher should be alert to these indications and register the appropriate evaluative techniques under each unit plan.

Resources

This last component of the unit plan is in effect an appendix in which the resources used in the activities are recorded in standard bibliographical format—in the case of published material—or in full detail—in the case of community resources. They are usually classified as books (for the teacher and for the children), magazines, pamphlets, newspapers and other printed materials, films, filmstrips and other audiovisual materials, places to visit, persons to be invited to speak to the class, and other special resources. It should be emphasized that contemporary social studies uses more social science and humanities resources than in the past—with respect not only to determining topics, generalizations, and issues, but some activities as well.

THE CONTEMPORARY UNIT PLAN COMPARED WITH THE TRADITIONAL

As was mentioned earlier, although the unit plan reflects recent developments in social studies education, it does not depart drastically from the traditional plan. The structure is the same; only the elements have been modified, as shown below:

TRADITIONAL UNIT PLAN	MODIFIED PLAN
1. *Title*—traditionally popular topics, in many cases not all of them related to each other.	*A unit of study* sharing a common theme with the other units of study selected for a particular year and reflecting the contemporary scene.
2. *General objectives*—broad flowery statements, in many cases impossible to reduce to specific behaviors.	*Generalizations and issues* from the social sciences and humanities and sometimes from life situations, capable of providing a structure and a comprehensive treatment for a particular unit of study.
3. *Specific objectives*—mostly content statements to be mastered.	*Specific items of knowledge* to be acquired and *behaviors* to be achieved by children, usually called *instructional objectives*. All derive from the generalizations and the

TRADITIONAL UNIT PLAN	MODIFIED PLAN
	issues and could be divided into content and process objectives. Content objectives include knowledge and social values; process objectives include intellectual, value-clarification, and social skills. The ultimate purpose of these objectives is to enable children to make sound decisions.
4. *Initiating activity*—an activity or activities designed to create a mood in favor of studying a particular topic.	The function of the *initiation activity* remains the same.
5. *Content*—an outline of subject matter; an expansion of the content statements listed as specific objectives.	*Basic questions* derived from the content objectives. Some questions stimulate children to look for evidence, analyze it, and discover relationships. Other questions lead to attempts to resolve issues, while still more questions call for the assessment of social values.
6. *Activities*—an account of types of activities that could be used. Usually the extraordinary type of class undertaking—like a field trip—and not the entire sequence of events required to achieve objectives. Rarely specific enough to give adequate direction to the teacher.	All the specific *learning experiences* needed to provide adequate responses for each of the basic questions. They can actually represent the procedure of specific lesson plans. They are of a wide variety and provide for individual differences. The activities determine whether the process objectives will be developed. Activities could be short- or long-range and many of them duplicate social science methods of inquiry.
7. *Culminating activity*—an activity or activities to help summarize the unit.	*The culminating activity* serves the same purpose.
8. *Evaluation*—a variety of methods to evaluate pupil progress; overemphasis on pencil and paper tests; too often objectives are not clear enough to facilitate evaluation.	*Evaluation* is more precise, directed toward developing specific behaviors. The emphasis on developing processes as well as acquiring content requires a greater variety of informal evaluation techniques. Activities, programs, and teaching procedures are evaluated along with pupil progress. Evaluation is an ongoing process rather than something that takes place at the end of a unit.
9. *Resources*—mostly children's books and commercially developed units. Some audiovisual aids and field trips are used.	Social science *resources* for teachers have become a must, along with all kinds of resources for children, such as the community, reading materials, audiovisual aids, current events, games, and others. Much emphasis is placed on raw data and the children's experiences.

MOVING TOWARD THE CONTEMPORARY UNIT PLAN

The biggest problem in practice is not that the contemporary unit plan is neglected in favor of the traditional but that both are neglected in favor of the textbook. The unit plan has never caught on to the extent that it merits. For approximately 50 years, education theorists have extolled unit teaching, but the teachers have seen only a seeming waste of time, loosening of discipline, and lack of subject matter (pages in a textbook). Obviously, a plan is needed that gradually weans teachers away from the textbook, so that they can see the merits of the unit plan without losing at once the security that the textbook gives them. Such a plan could be comprised of the following steps:

1. In the beginning the teachers could use the textbook to determine the number and the titles of the units to be taught.

2. By considering the local circumstances and the children in the class, the teacher might decide to eliminate a few topics in the textbook and add others which the teacher considers more appropriate. This eliminating and adding of topics is a small but significant step away from the textbook.

3. The textbook could be used in determining the generalizations and issues to be developed. Their validity should be tested by comparing them to other sources.

4. The textbook can also be useful in determining content objectives from the data contained in the text. At least the teacher can begin with what is in the text and go beyond that if there is time or the inclination.

5. For each content problem, the teacher can use other teaching resources along with the textbook. It might at first be only a film, or an interesting current article, or an exciting book, or a set of pictures, or a firsthand report, but it is more than the textbook.

6. As time goes on, more resources will be brought into the teaching process.

7. Eventually, other resources will become as important as the textbook, not only in determining activities but in determining the topics, concepts and generalizations, and issues. The time will come when the textbook will be just another source or will not be needed at all.

8. If content objectives no longer receive all the attention and process objectives begin to receive some as well, the activities are by necessity enriched and more attention is directed to interrelationships.

To provide a more concrete picture of a unit plan, a sample is presented in the following pages.

AN EXAMPLE OF A UNIT PLAN

Grade Level:	Fourth
Characteristics of Children in Class:	Heterogeneous with average ability.
Area of Study:	People Need the Earth
Unit Topic:	The Earth Satisfies Our Needs

GENERAL OBJECTIVES:

1. The earth's resources are used in multiple ways to satisfy people's needs.
2. Humans continuously develop new methods to improve the fertility of the soil to increase productivity.
3. Humans constantly seek to satisfy their needs for food, clothing, shelter, and their other wants; in so doing, they attempt to adapt and exploit the earth.
4. Each culture tends to view its physical habitat differently. A society's value system, goals, organization, and level of technology determine which elements of the land are prized and used.
5. Soils are altered by nature and by people.
6. How can we conserve the earth's resources?
7. How could an even distribution of essential resources be achieved, to better satisfy the needs of the various people around the world?
8. Should some nations be forced to change their techniques of agriculture to increase productivity?

INSTRUCTIONAL OBJECTIVES:

1. Knowledge—The children will know:
   a. At least five different resources from the earth people use to satisfy their needs.
   b. That our lives and the well-being of our nation depend upon the resources we get from the earth.
   c. That fertilizers and new farming methods increase the productivity of the earth.
   d. That in some countries productivity is retarded by the perpetuation of traditional farming methods.
   e. At least five ways in which humans have changed, adapted, or exploited the earth to satisfy their needs.
   f. That technology has made some resources more valuable than others.
   g. At least five ways in which humans abuse the earth to satisfy their needs.
   h. That some resources from the earth are renewable, while others are nonrenewable and their supply can be maintained only through wise use.
   i. Some ways in which the government assists in the wise use of our country's resources.
   j. That the earth's resources are unequally distributed.
2. Social values—The children will value:
   a. Efforts to conserve resources and commit themselves to that end.
   b. The role of the government in conservation.

3.   Intellectual skills—The children will be able to:
   a.   Analyze present circumstances to identify trends.
   b.   Read and develop simple graphs.
   c.   Suggest alternative solutions to social issues.
   d.   Predict the consequences of alternative solutions.
   e.   Develop plans of action for reducing or eliminating social problems.
   f.   Justify their plan of action by showing how its consequences accord with or enhance the common good.
4.   Value-clarification skills—The children will be able to:
   a.   Articulate their feelings concerning the abuse of the earth's resources.
   b.   Express and clarify their feelings about how this nation's food surplus and the excess resources of other nations ought to be used to meet the needs for people around the world.
   c.   Express their feelings about the need for world cooperation in resolving the problems created by the uneven distribution of resources.
   d.   Demonstrate pride in our nation's ability to produce large quantities of food, as well as in their individual efforts to conserve resources.
   e.   Express their feelings concerning the role of government in the conservation of resources.
5.   Social skills—The children will be able to:
   a.   Work together in planning activities.
   b.   Listen carefully to the views of other children even though they might not agree with them.
   c.   Carry out social action plans without offending or while being considerate of other people.

INITIATION   Start a discussion by posing the question, "What would happen if something went wrong with our local water system and we had no water for the next five days?" Allow the children to speculate on this open-ended, divergent thinking question for as long as they seem interested. Also give them opportunities to speculate on what might go wrong with the water system. The question might be given as a theme for a composition, in which case the subject of Language Arts would be appropriately used to develop interest in the unit. After the initiating discussion the teacher may, with proper questioning, lead the children to express a desire to study about the earth's resources and to adopt for this purpose the instructional objectives prepared by the teacher. Any sensible suggestions for modifications should be accepted. At the same time, obtain the *Conservation Posters* from the U.S. Department of Agriculture and display them around the room along with resource maps. Among the posters are "How Trees Grow," "The Tree and the Soil," "What We Get from Forest Land," and "What We Get from Trees."

PROBLEMS	ACTIVITIES
A. What resources do we get from the earth and what role do the resources play in our lives?	1. Examine everything around the room to determine what products used in the room come from the earth.
	2. With suggestions from the children, make a list of natural resources—forests, rivers, farms, etc.—available in the local community and classify them according to the need they satisfy.
	3. Visit one or two places in which important local resources are processed.
	4. What additional resources does the community need and where do they come from? Assign individual children to find out. Have them make wall maps of the United States and of the world and pinpoint the locations.
	5. Have children write a composition on the topic "Life without Natural Resources." Read to the class the most dramatic compositions.
	6. To show that the lives of some people are very much attached to the land, ask the children to read, or read to them, the book *Hoofprints on the Wind.*
	7. Show the films *Water Works for Us* and/or *The Story of Petroleum.*
	8. Urge children to readings such as *Great Heritage, Water—Or Your Life, Wildlife for America, Soil Means Life,* and *The Earth Book.*
B. Why does land in some areas of the world produce more than other areas to satisfy people's needs?	1. Show the film, *India—Writing in the Sand,* and concentrate on the agricultural crisis and how it is interrelated with the social customs.
	2. Contrast the input from the above film with efforts to increase farm production. Show such films as *Grassland* and *Irrigation and Farming.*
	3. Write to the Ford Foundation and obtain for each child a three-page publication entitled *India's "Food Miracle."* This publication tells how sophisticated fertilizers and a revolution in attitudes have begun to increase production in India. Contrast the contents of this publication with the film *India—Writing in the Sand.*
	4. Guide the children to read *Land of Plenty* and discuss the change from hand to power methods in American agriculture.

PROBLEMS	ACTIVITIES
	5. Direct children to encyclopedias to read about food and classify countries into two categories, those that produce enough for their people and those that do not. Do the same with oil.
	6. Ask children to bring in photographs or printed pictures of wilderness, countryside, and urban areas; examine them and make a list of ways in which humans have adapted or exploited the earth to satisfy their needs. List such things as roads, farms, ski resorts, and the like.
C. What is the status of the earth's resources at present? What resources do we value more today and why?	1. Remind the children of the unequal distribution of natural resources around the world and its effects upon the lives of people and upon the relationships of nations. Ask the question: "What resources assume more importance because of technological developments?"
	2. Use natural-resources maps of the world and the U.S.A.
	3. Bring in clippings from 1973 newspapers and magazines to show the effect of the Arab oil embargo and the importance of oil as a source of energy.
	4. Invite the local conservation agent to come and talk to the class about the status of natural resources in the local area.
	5. Alert the children to current conservation articles in the news media.
	6. Write to the National Wildlife Federation and ask for the 12 editorial essays entitled *Count Down to Survival.* Use the essays to make the children aware of the present-day problems of conservation.
	7. From a list of resources—possibly one prepared by the children—have the children classify them as renewable and nonrenewable. Underline the ones considered most needed in everyday life. Are more of them renewable or nonrenewable?
	8. Ask children to look into the future and write compositions on how life will be without the benefit of nonrenewable resources.
D. What have been some of the results of the failure to	1. Point out the effects of the unwise use of forests by showing the film *Forest Conservation.*

PROBLEMS	ACTIVITIES
protect and conserve natural resources?	2. Assign appropriate sections from the books, *First Book of Conservation* and *S.O.S. Save Our Earth.*
	3. Show the films *Seeds of Destruction* and *America's Shame—Water Pollution.*
	4. Ask children to report on the books, *The Treasure of Watchdog Mountain* and *The Shrinking Outdoors,* and continue with a discussion on the interrelation of **plants,** animals, humans, and nature's forces.
	5. Show the film, *Yours Is the Land,* to emphasize the interdependence of natural resources.
	6. Identify cases of misuse of natural resources in the local area and reflect with the class on how these misuses affect the local environment.
E. How can **we** conserve the earth's resources?	1. Present methods of conservation now used to conserve resources by referring **again** to films such as *Grassland* and *Irrigation and Farming* and the book *Conservation: The Challenge of Reclaiming our Plundered Land.*
	2. From the U.S. Department of Agriculture obtain the composite chart *Conservation and Full Utilization of Water.* Use this chart to show all measures for full use of water now being undertaken by various government agencies and departments.
	3. Certain children may be stimulated to read and report on "A River is Tamed: The Story of TVA," in *Our Wonderful World* and *Our Country's National Parks.*
	4. Show the film *Life in the Central Valley of California* and discuss methods of conservation used.
	5. Children may now prepare charts showing the misuses as well as the methods of conservation of natural resources used presently and in the past.
	6. At this point, ask children to propose their own alternative solutions to the problem. One way would be to have children design a conservation pledge that would reflect their own feelings and views. As a sample, show them the single sheet, *Conservation Pledge,* available from the Soil Conservation Service, U.S. Department of Agriculture.

PROBLEMS	ACTIVITIES
	7. After the children have had an opportunity to express their solutions, review all solutions and make a master list.
	8. Provide opportunities for the children to examine the consequences of each solution. The teacher could use a variety of ways to accomplish this, but make sure positive as well as negative consequences are pointed out and discussed.
	9. Following the examination of consequences, give the children an opportunity to say what solution they prefer and why. Allow children to clearly express how they feel about their chosen solution(s).
	10. Most likely not all children have chosen the same solutions. Urge them to organize for action. To steer them in this direction make available a publication of the U.S. Environmental Protection Agency entitled *71 Things You Can Do to Stop Pollution.*
	11. Facilitate the children's efforts to implement their solutions.
F. How could a distribution of essential resources be achieved to better satisfy the needs of the various peoples around the world?	1. The uneven distribution of natural resources has already become obvious. The children are asked to consider what should be done about it.
	2. To dramatize the issue, concentrate on the oil situation and on the food surplus in the United States.
	3. Contrast pictures of silos in the Midwest with pictures of starving people in other parts of the world.
	4. Encourage children to suggest solutions and keep record of them.
	5. Organize the class to consider the consequences of each solution. Discuss the consequences with the whole class and allow the children to express their feelings.
	6. Urge the children to consider possible actions and help them to carry out their plans.
G. Should some nations be forced to change their techniques of agriculture to increase the land's productivity?	1. Make sure the children understand that the choice is between preserving tradition and preserving human lives. It is expected that human lives will be placed higher than tradition, but the children must be voluntarily convinced of this. No pressure should be exercised.

PROBLEMS	ACTIVITIES
	2. Urge children to study the efforts of the United Nations in this respect. Also have them study about the Peace Corps.
	3. If the class is divided on the issue, organize a debate to argue the pros and cons of both sides.
	4. Urge the children to promote some kind of action. For instance, express approval or disapproval of the Peace Corps.
H. What should the role of the government be in the conservation of the earth's resources?	1. The children have already been exposed to what the government is now doing. Also, they have seen what the individual can do by considering what they themselves can do. They have adequate background at this point to consider the question of what more the government can do.
	2. Prepare data cards on those who say that the government is doing too much, on those who want the government to do more, on the industry's position, on the environmentalists' position, and set up a role-playing situation.
	3. Following this, urge the children to choose from alternative solutions. Make sure they are aware of the consequences of each.
	4. Urge children to write to politicians or undertake other actions to promote their chosen solution(s).

CULMINATING ACTIVITY   Organize an exhibit on the earth's resources and how people use them. Indicate the renewable and nonrenewable resources and the need for conservation. Relate this to local resources and make presentations to community groups to urge all citizens to do their part to conserve resources.

EVALUATION   Before designing the unit's objectives, the teacher should survey the children's background knowledge on the topic. Whatever the children already know should be used as a stimulus and an avenue toward what they do not know. The teacher should also become aware of the children's social and intellectual skills so that assignments do not exceed them. Simple discussions and examination of the children's experiential background are helpful.

As the unit progresses, evaluation should be an integral part of instruction. The teacher should constantly observe the children's behavior to notice the effects of teaching, and should examine their written work and other projects to evaluate their progress. The teacher should sequence the learnings and move from one step to the next only after making sure that the children have reached the first step. For example, a class should not be proposing solutions to an issue unless all children already have adequate information to understand the issue; nor should children be making decisions unless all possible solutions and their consequences have been presented and been understood.

Finally, summative evaluation could take a variety of forms. The culminating activity provides a good opportunity for children to show what they learned. The attitude of children toward conservation is observed as much as possible in everyday life. Pencil and paper tests may be used. Also, carry-over from this to other units and subjects can be scrutinized.

One of the fundamental characteristics of the unit plan is student involvement. Throughout the unit—including the evaluation stage—children are involved in many activities using a variety of resources. The last part of the sample plan is a complete list of all the resources used.

RESOURCES

A. Books and pamphlets
1. "A River Is Tamed: The Story of TVA," *Our Wonderful World,* Vol. 8, p. 38.
2. Carhart, A. H., *Water—Or Your Life.* Philadelphia: Lippincott, 1951.
3. Clapper, Louis S., *America's Shame—Water Pollution.* Washington, D.C.: National Wildlife Federation.
4. Clark, Ann N., *Hoofprints on the Wind.* New York: Viking, 1972.
5. Dunbar, Ernest, *India's "Food Miracle."* New York: Ford Foundation, 1968.
6. Ever, A., *The Treasure of Watchdog Mountain.* New York: Macmillan, 1955.
7. Graham, H. E., and W. R. VanDersal, *Wildlife for America.* New York: Oxford University Press, 1949.
8. Griffin, Fair C., *Soil Means Life.* Washington, D.C.: National Wildlife Federation.
9. Harrison, C. W., *Conservation—The Challenge of Reclaiming Our Plundered Land.* New York: Messner, 1973.
10. Jennings, Gary, *The Earth Book.* Philadelphia: Lippincott, 1974.
11. Jennings, Gary, *The Shrinking Outdoors.* Philadelphia: Lippincott, 1972.
12. Keen, Martin, *The World Beneath Our Feet.* New York: Messner, 1974.
13. *Land of Plenty.* Omaha, Neb.: Farm and Industrial Equipment Institute.
14. Massini, Giancarlo, *S.O.S. Save Our Earth,* New York: Grossett & Dunlap, 1972.
15. Melbo, I. R., *Our Country's National Parks.* Indianapolis, Ind.: Bobbs-Merrill, 1950.

16. *71 Things You Can Do to Stop Pollution.* Washington, D.C.: U.S. Environmental Protection Agency.

17. Shippen, K. B., *Great Heritage.* New York: Viking, 1947.

18. Smith, F. C., *First Book of Conservation.* New York: Franklin Watt, 1954.

19. Swift, Ernest, *Count Down to Survival.* Washington, D.C.: National Wildlife Federation.

B.   Charts and Posters

1. *Conservation Posters:* "How Trees Grow" (No. D-8), "What We Get from Forest Land" (No. D-9), "What We Get from Trees" (No. D-5). Washington, D.C.: U.S. Department of Agriculture.

2. *Conservation and Full Utilization of Water.* Washington, D.C.: U.S. Department of Agriculture.

3. *Conservation Pledge.* Washington, D.C.: U.S. Department of Agriculture.

C.   Films

1. *Forest Conservation.* Encyclopaedia Britannica Films, Inc., sound motion picture, color, 11 minutes.

2. *Grassland.* U.S. Department of Agriculture, sound motion picture, black and white, 11 minutes.

3. *India—Writing in the Sand.* National Educational Television, Indiana University, sound motion picture, color, 30 minutes.

4. *Irrigation Farming.* Encyclopaedia Britannica Films, Inc., sound motion picture, black and white, 10 minutes.

5. *Life in the Central Valley of California.* Coronet Films, sound motion picture, color, 11 minutes.

6. *Seeds of Destruction.* Encyclopaedia Britannica Films, Inc., sound motion picture, color, 10 minutes.

7. *The Story of Petroleum.* Encyclopaedia Britannica Films, Inc., sound motion picture, black and white, 11 minutes.

8. *Water Works for Us.* Young America Films, sound motion picture, black and white, 10 minutes.

9. *Yours Is the Land.* Encyclopaedia Britannica Films, Inc., sound motion picture, color, 20 minutes.

THE LESSON PLAN

The lesson plan is a subdivision of the unit plan; it covers only one class period, while the unit extends over several days or even weeks. The basic elements of the lesson plan are, again, the objectives, the procedure, and the techniques of evaluation. Objectives are determined by the same guidelines used for the unit. They should not simply be pages to be covered or exercises to be done but should be understandings of verbalized relationships that enable the children to make intelligent decisions and to continue to learn. Lesson plan objectives also should be directed toward clarifying and assessing values—personal as well as social—and toward acquiring certain social skills. The objectives of each lesson plan are the same as those for that unit, although often they are written in more detail and are fewer in number.

As in the unit, the lesson plan procedure comprises the problems and activities. Again, the procedure should not be simply a content outline. Instead, it should be everything the teacher plans to do with the class to reach the predetermined objective or objectives—for example, maps to identify a relationship; a planning session; a report by the children on their research. Clearly, even in lesson plans, activities may extend to more than one day in duration.

If a teacher develops a unit as suggested in this chapter, lesson plans for it will already have been prepared to a great extent: The objectives are all identified and stated; one or two content problems and the related activities will constitute the main part of the procedure; some activities might need to be spelled out in more detail; the evaluation techniques have also been spelled out in general terms, needing, in the lesson plan, only detailed implementation; the specific behaviors that indicate achievement of a specific objective must be identified.

Available lesson plan forms include other structural elements besides the three just enumerated. Initiation and follow-up activities are occasionally identified separately. Materials to be used—even the blackboard—are sometimes described in more detail than is necessary. Objectives are often stated in all kinds of "hair-splitting" subcategories, the differences between them sometimes being so fine that even the best teachers have difficulty distinguishing them. It seems preferable to eliminate all such secondary structural elements and concentrate on the objectives, procedure, and techniques of evaluation. Teachers are too busy to make lesson plans that involve more than the necessary structural elements, and proposing that they do so is one sure way to discourage them from preparing such plans at all.

AN EXAMPLE OF A LESSON PLAN

The following lesson plan is abstracted from the beginning of the unit plan displayed earlier in this chapter.

Grade Level:	Fourth
Characteristics of Children:	A heterogeneous class of children with average ability.
Area of Study:	People Need the Earth
Unit Topic:	The Earth Satisfies Our Needs

OBJECTIVES

1. The children will know that all wood, metal, and many other products used in the room come from the earth.
2. The children will know that the water we drink and most of the food we eat comes from the earth.
3. The children will be able to make a chart to classify earth products found around the school and the house according to their origin.

PROCEDURE

1. The children will be directed to examine everything around the room to identify those things that come from the earth and to each prepare a list.
2. A class discussion will take place to pull together the individual lists. Make sure you give opportunities to all children to make contributions.
3. Expand the common list by asking children to suggest other items that are used around the school and the home.
4. Distribute a form that has been prepared in advance and ask children to classify the products. The form might look as follows:

Origin of product / Need of product	Forests	Farms	Underground
To satisfy basic need			
To satisfy a want			

5. As the children work on their forms, wander around the room and provide individual assistance as needed. Instruct children who finish early to start thinking about those items that are produced in the local community. (This can be used as an introduction to the next lesson.)

EVALUATION

1. During the discussion, the children will correctly suggest the origin of specific items for which they volunteer.
2. The children will be able to correctly classify on the form all items in the class list.

SUMMARY

Unit teaching appears to be most exemplary of contemporary theories of learning and the best method of teaching contemporary social studies. It is, however, more difficult than textbook teaching. To suggest that teachers abandon the textbook immediately for unit teaching is impractical. A gradual changeover from one to the other is needed.

The main structural elements of the unit are the objectives (general and specific), the problems and activities, and the evaluation techniques. An initiation activity to arouse the children's interest in studying the unit is recommended, as are culminating activities to summarize for all children the unit's outcomes. In writing a unit the teacher lists all resources to be used.

The lesson plan, a strategy covering a shorter time, has the same structure as the unit plan: objectives, procedure (the equivalent of problems and activities in the unit), and techniques of evaluation.

ACTIVITIES

1. Make a list of contemporary educational principles and identify which components of the unit plan implement these principles.

2. Ask your instructor for a random list of the components of a unit plan and put them in their logical order.

3. Prepare a checklist with the types of activities afforded by the unit plan (you may use Fraenkel's recommended activities), and make arrangements to observe in a classroom to determine which activities are emphasized and which are not used. What implications do your observations have for learning outcomes? Are any important learnings neglected?

4. Prepare as many activity cards as possible similar to the ESSENTIA cards.

5. Identify an instructional objective from a particular unit plan and develop a learning center. Consult the appropriate article in the November-December 1974 issue of *Social Education* for this activity.

6. Develop a complete unit plan as illustrated in this chapter. Students may wish to pull together plans they developed in activities of previous chapters to make units.

7. Abstract lesson plans from completed unit plans. Try some of these plans in actual classrooms (whenever possible) to determine their appropriateness.

NOTES

1. John D. McNeil, *Designing Curriculum: Self-Instructional Modules* (Boston: Little, Brown, 1976), p. 3.

2. Wilhelmina Hill, *Social Studies in the Elementary School Program,* Bulletin No. 5 (Washington, D.C.: U.S. Office of Education, 1960), p. 50.

3. Jack R. Fraenkel, "The Importance of Learning Activities," *Social Education,* 37 (November 1973), 675.

4. Ibid., p. 677.

5. Bob Samples and Bob Wohlford, *Essencetwo* (Washington, D.C.: American Geological Institute, 1972), p. 1.

6. Bob Samples, director, *Environmental Studies* (Washington, D.C.: American Geological Institute, 1971). Similar cards developed by the same project are now distributed commercially by Addison-Wesley Publishing Company.

7. James M. Larkin and Jane J. White, "The Learning Center in the Social Studies Classroom," *Social Education,* 38 (November-December 1974), 697–710.

8. Dennis Hamburg, Kenmore Elementary School, Bothell, Washington. Letter to author.

9. Theodore Kaltsounis, "A Modification of the 'Expanding Environment' Approach," *The Social Studies,* 35 (March 1964), 99–102; Theodore Kaltsounis, *Teaching Elementary Social Studies* (West Nyack, N.Y.: Parker, 1969), pp. 48–50.

OBJECTIVES

Studying this chapter will enable the reader to:

1. realize that evaluation is an integral part of instruction.
2. define and distinguish among diagnostic, formative, and summative evaluation.
3. define such terms as mastery learning, validity, reliability, norm-referenced tests, criterion-referenced tests, and the like.
4. distinguish between evaluation and measurement.
5. distinguish between informal and formal techniques of measurement and list the most important of each category.
6. realize that the most valid techniques of measurement for the elementary school are the informal ones.
7. prepare materials and instruments to implement informal and formal techniques of measurement.
8. list some of the major tests available commercially.
9. name publishing companies that have developed tests to accompany their social studies programs.
10. realize that the most valid and reliable instruments of measurement are those developed locally from appropriate guidelines.
11. become familiar with the guidelines of the National Council for the Social Studies for evaluating social studies programs.

PUPIL PROGRESS
AND PROGRAM EVALUATION

The quality of the social studies program depends to a great extent on the quality of evaluation. Quite often "evaluation" means collecting information about pupil progress to assign grades. But that is only one function of evaluation. As Norman Gronlund states,

> Evaluation plays an important role in many facets of the school program. It contributes directly to the teaching–learning process used in classroom instruction, and it is useful in programmed instruction, curriculum development, accountability programs, marking and reporting, guidance and counseling, school administration and school research programs.[1]

This chapter explores evaluation as a means of assessing and reporting pupil progress, with specific concentration on evaluation of social studies programs in the last part of the chapter.

TYPES OF EVALUATION AND THEIR PLACE IN THE TEACHING–LEARNING PROCESS

In this book "instruction" has been used to mean the involvement of children in designed and redesigned learning activities for the attainment of predetermined educational objectives. In other words, the first steps a teacher must take are to set objectives and design learning activities, in which the children are then involved. If the activities are appropriate, the children reach the objectives; if the activities are not appropriate, the teacher must redesign them. Because it is the information supplied by evaluation that dictates whether activities must be redesigned, evaluation is an integral part of instruction. Figure 7–1 is a model showing the various forms evaluation takes in the process of teaching and learning.

To begin with, there are the social studies program goals formulated by the professionals and transmitted to teachers by teacher education institutions and professional experiences. These goals are contrasted with the local community's demands and requirements. A teacher must be aware of local values and pressure groups. (For example, most school systems are required to teach about the home state.) A teacher wishing to avoid conflict must reach a compromise with the local people. This does not mean, of course, that the teacher should indiscriminately submit to pressures—

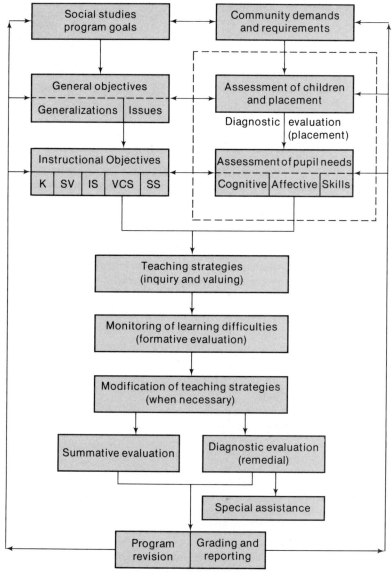

Key: K = Knowledge; SV = Social Values; IS = Intellectual Skills;
VCS = Value Clarification Skills; SS = Social Skills

Figure 7–1
A Model of Evaluation as an Integral Part of the Teaching–Learning Process

sometimes indeed the teacher has to convince some segments of the community that certain goals are valid. There are times when compromise is impossible, and the teacher faces a moral dilemma: Either sacrifice what the teacher believes is professionally sound or move to another community. A strong professional person reasons with the people in the local community but does not easily submit to pressure groups. Such a person listens to the arguments but evaluates them by the criteria of the rational process, the dignity of every individual, and the common good.

The next step in the model is the development of general objectives for the proper developmental level or grade. To avoid the vagueness of traditional general objectives and to provide for substance in social studies, general objectives should consist of generalizations and issues from the social science disciplines and the humanities. These generalizations and issues should be tied to relevant topics, those that comprehend an area of study and that address the important matters of the contemporary scene.

The third major step in the teaching–learning process is to determine the instructional objectives, the changes in the children's behavior that should result from teaching social studies. These objectives, some short-range, others long-range, should be derived from the generalizations and issues. The five types of instructional objectives, remember, are: knowledge, social values, intellectual skills, value-clarification skills, and social skills, all five of which are essential. There can be no sound evaluation without instructional objectives that can be observed as changes in behavior. Gronlund points out: "Only by identifying instructional objectives and stating them clearly in terms of specific behavior can we provide direction to the teaching process and set the stage for ready evaluation of learning outcomes." [2] And Cecil Clark states: "Using instructional objectives places greater emphasis on evaluation and on a clear relationship between objectives and evaluation." [3]

For determining how appropriate an instructional objective is for the students, Clark suggests the following five questions:

> (1) Does the instructional objective seem relevant to the student? (2) Does the instructional objective itself provide any motivation for or is it at least attractive to the student? (3) Is the instructional objective appropriate for the needs of the student? (4) Will the objective be used frequently enough by the student to make its attainment worthwhile? (5) Can the instructional objective be attained by the student within the time allotted? [4]

To be sound, instructional objectives must meet all the requirements implied in these questions. Teachers therefore must carefully assess the children's educational needs. Some children will be closer to the expected outcomes than others; many will have better developed certain basic skills than others have.

The same function is served by assessing the children's characteristics to determine the relevance of the general objectives and by assessing the children's educational needs to make sure the instructional objectives are valid and instruction is appropriate. Such assessments involve *diagnostic evaluation,* here called *placement diagnostic evaluation* to distinguish it from *remedial diagnostic evaluation* (see Figure 7–1) intended to discover the causes of persistent failures to reach expected outcomes.[5]

The concepts of continuous progress—as opposed to having children go back and repeat a grade—and individualization of instruction have obviously made diagnostic evaluation important. As Peter Airasian and George Madaus indicate: "Based on prior achievement or the presence of certain cognitive and affective characteristics, a student can be placed (a) at the most appropriate point in an instructional sequence, (b) in a particular instructional method, or (c) with an appropriate teacher." [6] Rita Dunn, Kenneth Dunn, and Gary Price assign diagnostic evaluation another function: By applying systematic diagnostic evaluation and determining each child's learning potential, teachers can avoid malpractice suits, which have become fashionable. "With both the judiciary and the legislative sectors supporting parental efforts to obtain redress whenever students do not achieve on an academic level deemed to be 'average,' 'normal,' or 'on grade level,' educators had better reassess their expectations for children of a given age." [7] They recommend that the student's potential be diagnosed by agreed-upon criteria such as "baseline achievement data, comparative socioeconomic status, IQ scores, motivation assessments, or personality profiles." [8] Accountability is then tied to the potential of each child rather than to an average expectation that quite often is not possible for some children.

Using diagnostic evaluation to place students at the appropriate level is especially sound at the beginning of the child's school years. Remember that kindergarteners and first graders come from a variety of home experiences and backgrounds; some children are equal, or nearly so, to the system's expectations, while others, who come from homes deprived of the typical elements of the school culture—books, magazines, conversations on school topics, educational games, and the like—are well below "average" expectations. It is unfair to assume that all children of the same age are in the same category and are capable of achieving at the same level. Such an approach cannot provide equal educational opportunity for all children, and has been condemned by many, especially by minority groups, as discriminatory and an example of institutional racism.

The next step in the teaching–learning process is to formulate teaching strategies for reaching the objectives. For concepts, examples must be produced; for generalizations, illustrations of the implied relationship(s) must be adapted to the children's level; for issues, which are open-ended, guidance must be given toward understanding the issue, examining all possible alternative solutions and their consequences, exploring feelings about each solution, and, finally, choosing a solution. Proper execution of all these steps requires correct teaching strategies.

Though all children in a class may work toward the same general objectives, the instructional objectives and teaching strategies will vary—perhaps from child to child or from one group to another—to allow the teacher to reach all children. But not even planning with the utmost care assures success. Thus, the effectiveness of each teaching strategy must be monitored and achievement of an objective confirmed before the next objective is broached. For example, the concept of day and night cannot be taught unless the children have already learned that the earth rotates on its axis. If a strategy is judged ineffective, new methods and probably new materials must be designed and implemented.

Monitoring the effectiveness of teaching strategies is called *formative evaluation*. About this type of evaluation Benjamin Bloom, J. Thomas Hastings, and George Madaus state:

> We regard formative evaluation as useful not only for curriculum construction, but also for instruction and student learning. Formative evaluation is for us the use of systematic evaluation in the process of curriculum construction, teaching, and learning for the purpose of improving any of these three processes. Since formative evaluation takes place during the formation stage, every effort should be made to use it to improve the process.[9]

Although instructional objectives must vary as children's needs and characteristics vary, any unit has basic instructional objectives that all children should reach. Thus, *mastery learning* is required: That is, all children should develop the objectives to the same predetermined degree of proficiency. For example, if a unit in geography requires that specific places be located on a map, all children must learn the cardinal directions; or if concept formation is to be promoted, all children must be able to classify items by common characteristics.

Mastery learning requires continuous formative evaluation. According to Bloom, Hastings, and Madaus, "Frequent formative evaluation tests pace the students' learning and help motivate them to put forth the necessary effort at the proper time. The appropriate use of these tests helps ensure that each set of learning tasks has been thoroughly mastered before subsequent tasks are started." [10]

The method for achieving mastery learning is implicit in that statement. A teaching unit or teaching component is broken into smaller parts arranged sequentially. The teacher monitors the children's progress to make sure they have learned each part before moving to the next. When difficulties are indicated, the student repeats the same process, or uses supplementary materials, or is tutored. The student is not advanced to the next step until a predetermined degree of proficiency has been reached.

In most school districts, objectives are stated as a minimum level of performance. In view of this and the accountability movement, some believe that mastery learning should apply to everything the schools attempt to teach. They see little sense in teachers' expectations that about one-third of their students will do well, one-third will perform at about "average," and one-third will fail or barely pass. Bloom, Hastings, and Madaus state:

> This set of expectations which fixes the academic goals of teachers and students is the most wasteful and destructive aspect of the present education system. It reduces the aspirations of both teachers and students, it reduces motivation for learning in students, and it systematically destroys the ego and self-concept of a sizable group of the students. . . .[11]

Nevertheless, even when instruction methods have been modified to overcome learning difficulties and to achieve predetermined instructional objectives, some children, despite repeated efforts, will be unable to reach certain objectives. *Remedial diagnostic evaluation* is then needed to find the causes. Such evaluation is usually directed to few children and is more intensive than placement diagnostic evaluation. Indeed it often requires that evaluators more expert than the teacher become involved.

The common causes of persistent failures tend to be outside the classroom. Among such causes Airasian and Madaus include "physical, environmental, emotional, or psychological factors generated outside the classroom." [12] A hungry child, for example, or a child with a hearing or sight difficulty may have problems with school work. Remedial diagnostic evaluation usually must be followed by special assistance, directed either to eliminating the impairment or adjusting instruction to it.

The final form of evaluation in the teaching–learning process is *summative evaluation,* which takes place when instruction of a unit or course is completed. Summative evaluation assesses the final outcomes of instruction for two specific purposes: (a) to assign grades to students, to be reported to parents, and (b) to determine the effectiveness of the program. Summative evaluation is the type of evaluation most familiar to teachers.

The model of evaluation in Figure 7–1 identifies, then, four types of evaluation:

1. *Placement diagnostic evaluation*, which is used early in the instructional process to identify the children's needs and characteristics, to which general objectives and instructional objectives alike should be adjusted. This type of evaluation is used to place students at various levels to facilitate instruction.
2. *Formative evaluation*, which continuously provides feedback on the effectiveness of instruction. It detects difficulties in the process of reaching objectives and helps the teacher to make curricular and instructional decisions. Formative evaluation is basic in the teaching–learning process, but it is especially important to mastery learning.
3. *Remedial diagnostic evaluation*, which is used to identify causes of persistent difficulties, usually found outside the classroom.
4. *Summative evaluation*, which takes place at the end of a unit or a course and assists in assigning grades and in judging the effectiveness of the overall instructional program.

Clearly, then, evaluation is an integral part of instruction; evaluation and instruction are inseparable.

TECHNIQUES OF MEASURING PUPIL PROGRESS

Evaluative decisions are made from information about how well or how nearly pupils have attained instructional objectives. Obtaining such information and assigning values to it is called measurement, an essential component of evaluation. Measurement is used to mean the collection of evidence of progress (or its lack) toward objectives in three domains—cognitive, affective, and psychomotor. Evidence can be collected and value assigned to it, by informal as well as formal techniques.

During the last 10 to 15 years many educators have speculated as to whether progress toward all instructional objectives can be measured. Some advocate that objectives that cannot be measured should be rejected entirely; which, and how many, these are depends on how strictly measurement is defined. Yet we have seen that not all instructional objectives of a social studies lesson or unit can be measured at the end of that lesson or unit—there are short- and long-range objectives. Nor can progress toward all objectives be measured with equal precision. Short-range objectives are easier to measure than long-range objectives, because they are stated in terms of precise behaviors that can be observed within a short period of time.

Informal Techniques of Measurement

Informal measurement can be done by observation, discussion, conferences with pupils and parents, examination of samples of children's work, anecdotal records, rating scales, checklists, sociometric devices, and self-reporting. Each of these techniques will be briefly discussed after the importance of informal measurement for the elementary school is explained.

Informal measurement techniques are valuable for two reasons. First, the psychomotor and affective domains, the latter especially, are not readily measured by formal techniques. Children's commitments, values, dispositions, and democratic behavior cannot be so measured. For example, youngsters can be tested to see how well they know the Bill of Rights, but their commitment to and respect for these rights cannot be tested. Each child has to be examined individually and informally in as many situations as the teacher can observe. Most affective and skills objectives are long range and are best assessed by informal techniques, as indeed are the abilities involved in decision making.

The second reason why informal measurement techniques are valuable in the elementary school is that students, especially in the primary grades, cannot perform the tasks involved in formal measurement techniques. For example, they cannot read well, they lack the required attention span, and they cannot follow directions as well as is required.

OBSERVATION   Probably the most venerable and most used technique of collecting evidence for educational measurement, and for many other purposes, is observation. To be useful, observation must be guided by clearly defined instructional objectives. Every observation of behavior involves a value judgment. How accurate was the observation on which the value judgment was based? Such a judgment is subjective, but often no better method can be used, as Gronlund points out: "Our choice is simple: either we use these techniques in an attempt to evaluate each learning outcome and aspect of development as directly and validly as possible or we neglect those that cannot be measured by paper-and-pencil tests." [13]

Observation can be casual or systematic, and can be done in the classroom or outside it. The teacher should keep notes of observations and follow the children's progress toward specific objectives. Systematic observation is done at regular intervals or under specified conditions. Other techniques of informal evaluation, such as anecdotal records and checklists, require the use of observation.

DISCUSSION   Discussion provides excellent opportunities for the teacher to determine progress toward short- as well as long-range objectives. A specific topic or question may be discussed, to assess how well students have acquired a body of content. In the course of a discussion the teacher may also find out how well the children have developed such long-term objectives as getting along with each other, participating in orderly discussions, staying with the subject under discussion, etc. The teacher should maintain an atmosphere that allows all children to express themselves.

CONFERENCES WITH PUPILS AND PARENTS   Most conferences with parents are in effect progress reports on their children. Conferences are also useful in evaluating pupil progress, especially at the stages of diagnostic and formative evaluation. By talking to parents, and the students themselves, teachers can determine how well children sustain their commitments and pursue their interests outside the classroom. They can identify strengths and weaknesses as well as the causes of any difficulties. About the importance of the teacher-parent conferences one school district policy maker says to parents: "Because you are closest to your child, only you can give the teacher an important behind-the-scenes glimpse into your youngster's life. No one can take the place of a child's parents; no one can know the child as well as you do." [14] The same school district gives its teachers the following advice for conducting parent-teacher conferences:

CONFERENCE IDEAS FOR TEACHERS

The parent conference is held so that parents and teachers can *exchange* information about the child so that both may better serve his needs. In order for this exchange to occur the conference must take place in a friendly, relaxed, unhurried atmosphere. It must also be a carefully planned and well organized situation. Enjoy your conferencing; it will be one of the most important activities of your year.

Be Professional

Observe professional ethics at all times. Don't comment about other children even if the subject is introduced by the parent.

If a former teacher or school is brought into the conversation, let your attitude reflect only good.

Treat These Conferences as Highly Confidential

Never repeat any matters of personal nature about a child or family to other parents, even teachers, except when professionally necessary.

Parts of the Conference

The parent contributes information about the child to aid the teacher in understanding him.

The teacher tells the parent about his child's progress in school, his work study habits, and social and personal growth.

Recommendations for the continued growth and progress of the child are discussed by parent and teacher.

Preparing for the Conference

Be informed about school purposes, methods and program.

File representative samples of the pupil's work over a period of time. Children can participate in choosing samples of their work.

Review your record of significant observations of the child's attitudes and actions.

Review data in the pupil's cumulative folder.

Evaluate recent test data in light of the pupil's performance. (Compare test results with daily work.)

Try to conference with the pupil before the parent conference.

Conducting the Conference

Let the parent know what you would like to accomplish during the conference.

Establish a friendly atmosphere. Remember you are a host or hostess just as though you were in your home. The parent may be uneasy and fearful about the conference.

Have an informal setting. *Sit on the same side of the table* with the parents, rather than at your desk. The desk between you is a barrier to free and fruitful exchange of ideas.

Remember that you are dealing primarily with one individual child, not comparing him with other members of his or her class.

Be positive. Begin and end by enumerating favorable points. Stress the strengths.

Help parents to achieve a better understanding of their child as an individual. Don't attempt to interpret the curriculum in a short conference. This is more appropriate for a group conference.

Be sure to have at hand samples of the child's work—the whole range, not just those you consider adequate or inadequate.

Base your judgments on all available facts and on actual situations. Preparation should be made to discuss any standardized group tests that are available.

Keep vocabulary simple; explain new terminology.

Accept the parent's reason for a child's behavior without showing signs of disapproval or surprise. If necessary, lead the discussion into additional possible causes of action or attitude.

Be truthful, yet tactful. The parent should be aware of the child's weaknesses, but nothing is gained by an unkind remark or by putting parents on the defensive.

Remember that parents are subjective and emotional about their children. Put yourself in the place of the parent and try to see what effect a given remark would have on you as a parent.

Don't use expressions that imply placing of blame for unacceptable performance.

Remain poised. Avoid defensive arguments. Talk calmly.

Select for emphasis from among the child's weaknesses only those the child
and parent are ready to deal with constructively.

Be constructive in suggestions. Don't "load" parents with suggestions.
A few are more effective than many.

Help parents to find their own solutions to problems. Agree upon action
needed. Go only as far as the parent is ready to accept. We are all afraid of
ideas we do not understand.

At the close of the conference summarize points covered and suggestions
agreed upon.

Set a time limit. If another parent is waiting, tactfully conclude the conference;
suggest a further conference at another time if the parent wishes.

End on a note of continuing cooperation. Cordially invite parents to visit school.
(You will probably wish to ask for prearrangement.)

The Parent's Contribution

Encourage the parent to talk. Be a good listener. You are interested in the
information the parent brings to you about this child.

Focus upon areas about which you or the parent are most interested for
the particular child. For example: If the child seems worried you might ask:
How is his health? Any recent illness, accident, etc.? Any problems concerning
sleep, bad dreams, etc.? Any early illness or noteworthy experience?

As a result of information received, don't diagnose health conditions or
suggest treatment. Keep discussion to such aspects as fatigue, restlessness,
irritability.

Problems too severe for the school to give sufficient help should be
referred to the principal.

Respect information as confidential. Don't pry.[15]

The value of conferences between the teacher and each pupil individually should also be emphasized. Such conferences should not be limited
to problem situations. To have rapport with the students, the teacher should
have informal discussions with each one of them. The children should be
informed of objectives they are expected to achieve and, from time to time,
of their progress. They should be advised on how to overcome their weaknesses and deploy their strengths. Often teachers use such conferences to
draft individual contracts with the students; performance contracts are
popular in programs that stress continuous progress and individualization
of instruction.

EXAMINATION OF SAMPLES OF CHILDREN'S WORK   As will be seen in the next
chapter, all textbook publishers now produce spirit masters that enable
teachers to duplicate materials and have children engage in individual activities applying what they learn. Also, a well-organized classroom usually
has several learning centers offering many learning tasks for children to
do on their own during free time. Children are usually required to record
in some form the results of their work. All of these tasks are in addition

to such group assignments as reading stories, writing reviews, and making maps. Most teachers also administer a variety of tests.

Everything the children produce in connection with the above activities should be filed in chronological order in a special folder, and preferably kept in the children's desks. Such samples provide an excellent means for assessing each child's progress, and are often useful in parent-teacher conferences. Without question they are more meaningful for everyone concerned than scores on standardized normative tests. If parent-teacher conferences are infrequent or impossible, packages of work samples are sent home so that the parents can observe their children's progress.

ANECDOTAL RECORDS   Gilbert Sax defines anecdotal records as "continuous, objective descriptions of behavior as it occurs at a given time, place and circumstance." [16] According to Sax, episodes to be observed are selected because they elicit the kind of behavior the teacher needs to observe, or such episodes simply occur at regular intervals for specific periods, during which any and all behavior is observed. For instance, a teacher, wanting to know how well a child has developed social skills to date, describes every episode in which the child cooperates with others, takes turn in class discussions, or exhibits any of the social skills promoted by the school program. Because the content of anecdotal records may vary from one observation to the next, no one record reveals the child's typical behavior. Thus, a child must be observed several times for there to be an accurate overall description.

To produce sound anecdotal records, a number of rules must be observed:

1. The description of the behavior must be kept separate from any interpretation.
2. Words should have precise meanings; "aggressive," for example, has different meanings for different people.
3. Notes should be discreetly taken to record particulars of the observation. The report should be written immediately after the observation to avoid memory errors.
4. Uniform cards should be used to record the observations. The name, sex, chronological age, and grade level should be recorded on the top of each card. Also, the day, date, time, and location of the observation should be recorded. The name of the observer should also be clearly stated. The card should be divided into two parts, one labeled *description*, the other *interpretation*. The objective description is more important than the interpretation, which is subjective.
5. Cards with recorded episodes should be filed chronologically for easier assessment of the child's progress.

RATING SCALES   In rating scales, a desired behavior is broken into several stages of development, each with a numerical value. For example, say a teacher wants to determine how well a child is now able to make decisions. An appropriate rating scale might look as follows:

THE CHILD MAKES DECISIONS AFTER CONSIDERING THE CONSEQUENCES OF ALTERNATIVE SOLUTIONS:

5 Almost always
4 Most of the time
3 Half the time
2 Quite rarely
1 Almost never

The lowest degree of development has a value of 1, the highest, 5. But degrees of development may encompass as few as 2 or as many as 10. Sax, who calls degrees of development categories, says: "Rating scales, like test scores, tend to increase in reliability as the number of ratable categories and items increases." [17]

Rating scales may also be designed graphically, with or without numerical values. The above example would then look as follows:

THE CHILD MAKES DECISIONS AFTER CONSIDERING THE CONSEQUENCES OF ALTERNATIVE SOLUTIONS:

/	/	/	/	/
Almost always	Most of the time	Half the time	Quite rarely	Almost never

If rating scales are to be reliable measures, Sax recommends avoiding the following errors:

a. Lack of training. Observers must be thoroughly familiar with scale items and the methods used to record observations.
b. The halo effect, or the tendency to rate a specific trait on the basis of general impressions. . . .
c. The generosity or leniency error, which is the tendency of raters to avoid using the most negative ends of a rating scale. . . .
d. The error of central tendency, which occurs when raters avoid both the high and the low extremes of a rating scale.[18]

CHECKLISTS Checklists are used to indicate whether a desired behavior has or has not been developed. In diagnostic evaluation, checklists are used to indicate the presence or absence of a specific trait, value, or characteristic. Say, for example, a second grade teacher wants to assess the social development of the class at the beginning of the school year. The form in Figure 7-2 could be developed and filled in for each child during the first month.

Checklist on Social Development		
Name_____ Grade_____ Sex_____		
Date_____ Time_____		
Critical Behaviors	Yes	No
Assumes responsibility		
Participates in discussion		
Contributes to the group		
Accepts criticism		
Works well with others		
Carries out assignments		
Follows school rules		

Figure 7-2

To construct usable checklists the teacher must be able to determine the critical behaviors associated with a desired objective. To develop a checklist on the democratic way of life, for example, one needs to know clearly what specific behaviors constitute the democratic way of life.

SOCIOMETRIC DEVICES   The main focus of social studies is human relationships. Teachers rely heavily on group work to facilitate the development of behaviors that promote harmonious human relationships. How well a group works depends on how carefully it is structured. To form effective groups, the teacher must know the social structure of the class—who are the leaders, who are the friendless or rejected or isolated ones, who form cliques, and who choose whom as companions. To find out these facts, teachers may use sociometric techniques.

One use of a sociometric device would be, for example, to ask the children in a class whom they would like to have as a copilot on a space mission. The children selected by the most classmates are the stars or leaders in the class. A small group of children who tend to keep their selections among themselves constitute a clique. In the elementary school years boys sometimes tend to avoid selecting girls and vice versa. This tendency forms two cleavages—the boys and the girls. Cleavages may also result from other factors. A child who is not selected by any classmates is considered to be an isolate and requires careful attention.

Sociometric results can be put to many uses. Gronlund lists four major ones: "(1) organizing classroom groups, (2) improving the social adjustment of individual pupils, (3) improving the social structure of groups, and (4) evaluating the influence of school practices on pupils' social relations."[19]

SELF-REPORTING TECHNIQUES   Excepting sociometric devices, and to some extent teacher-pupil conferences, most of the techniques of measurement discussed thus far rely on observation by the teacher, the parents, or some other adult. But some educationally relevant aspects of the child's life cannot be observed—past behaviors and the child's feelings, attitudes, values, opinions, and the like. Self-reporting techniques are often used to identify these important elements and make the children aware of what expectations they have accomplished and what they still need to accomplish. Figure 7-3 is a form one teacher has her children use weekly to evaluate their work habits and their behavior in general. The children sign the forms after completing them and take them home along with their weekly samples of work.

Figure 7–3

<u>WEEKLY EVALUATION*</u>

Remember what you have done this last week (look through your work and answer the following as honestly as you can).

1. I turned all my work in on time. Yes _____ No _____

2. My work is neat. Good _____ Fair _____ Poor _____

3. I obeyed the school and room rules and did not get into trouble.
   Good _____ Fair _____ Poor _____

4. I worked quietly by myself and did not bother others.
   Good _____ Fair _____ Poor _____

5. I did my best to get along with everyone.
   Good _____ Fair _____ Poor _____

6. My papers were done as well as I wanted. Yes _____ No _____

7. These are some of the things I did during my free time. List three.

8. List some things you are going to improve on next week.

Signed _____ Date _____

*Used by Mrs. Candace LaMonte a fourth grade teacher at Kenmore Elementary School, Kenmore, Washington.

Self-reporting techniques may be less structured, as when children respond to such questions as:

1. What is the best way to behave?
2. What would you like to be when you grow up and why?
3. What does democracy mean to you?
4. What makes you sad?
5. What do you best like about school?
6. What are some of your best experiences?

Or they may be quite formal like interest inventories and attitude scales (both briefly discussed in the next section).

Formal Techniques of Measurement

Formal techniques of measurement usually involve having the subject perform a series of specific tasks at a specified place and time. These techniques are used to gather information that cannot usually be obtained by observation and other informal techniques. Sometimes, of course, information obtained through formal techniques is used to supplement what was gathered by informal techniques. With the exception of interest inventories and attitude scales, most formal techniques are achievement tests —widely and frequently used in school, mainly to assess the children's progress in cognitive objectives.

The tests most commonly used by elementary school teachers are: (1) true-false, (2) multiple-choice, (3) matching, (4) completion or short answer, and (5) essay tests. Tests should not be used only for summative evaluation. Like the entire process of evaluation, testing is an important part of instruction and should occur throughout, including the diagnostic and formative stages. As Gronlund says:

> All too frequently, achievement testing is viewed as an end-of-unit or end-of-course activity that is used primarily for assigning course grades. Although this is a necessary and useful function of testing, it is just one of many. As with teaching, the main purpose of testing is to improve learning, and within this larger context there are a number of specific contributions it can make.[20]

Before types of tests are discussed, *norm-referenced tests* and *criterion-referenced tests* must be briefly distinguished. (These terms have assumed much significance within the contexts of accountability, continuous progress and individualization of instruction.) Until recently, most tests were norm-referenced: They measured how well a class or a child did in relation to the average performance of children of that age or in that grade. Designers of standardized tests would give a newly developed test to a nationwide sample of elementary school children and from their performance would determine the average performance, or norm, for each grade. That norm then became the standard against which all children in that grade would be compared.

A standardized test, or any other norm-referenced test, may help place a child in some rank order, but it does not give a precise description of what that child has learned or not learned, and what tasks have been mastered or not mastered. True accountability, however, demands that teachers have such precise information. Those concerned about a child's progress want to know what and how much of what the child was expected to learn has in fact been learned. Educators thus had to produce a new type of test—criterion-referenced tests. The criterion, the standard against which the performance is measured, is not some norm, but whatever the instructional objectives and the expected outcomes are for a particular grade or child.

Robert L. Ebel, a distinguished authority on evaluation, differentiates between norm-referenced and criterion-referenced tests thus:

> A norm-referenced test is so called because it interprets the test score of a particular pupil in relation to norms established by testing other similar pupils. Most norm-referenced tests also sample the domain of a particular achievement diffusely. A criterion-referenced test reports which, or how many, of a set of specific goals for achievement a particular pupil has reached. Instead of sampling diffusely the multitude of elements of knowledge or skill included in a domain of achievement, the criterion-referenced test concentrates on a limited number of specifically defined goals, testing each of these repeatedly to make certain that the particular goal has actually been achieved.[21]

Most tests constructed and used by teachers are the criterion-referenced type.

TRUE-FALSE TESTS   True-false tests, which present declarative statements for the student to judge true or false, are most appropriate for making the student decide whether:

1. an object does or does not belong to a certain category
2. a rule does or does not apply
3. something is a fact or an opinion, and
4. arguments are relevant or irrelevant.

Sax recommends the following guidelines in writing true-false test items:

1. Construct items that measure important objectives.
2. Avoid the use of specific determiners. . . . Test-wise students have learned that sweeping generalizations, indicated by such absolute terms as *always*, *all*, and *never*, are likely to be keyed *false*.

3. Approximately half the statements should be false.
4. Each statement should be unequivocally true or false.
5. State each item positively if possible.[22]

True-false tests have disadvantages: They emphasize rote memory; they encourage absolute judgments; and they allow much guessing. Correction methods are sometimes used to reduce guessing, the most popular being to score a test by subtracting the wrong from the right answers. For example, if on a test of 100 items a student answered 60 correct, 20 incorrect, and omitted 20, the score would be $60 - 20 = 40$ (omitted items are disregarded).

MULTIPLE-CHOICE TESTS   Multiple-choice tests are probably the most widely used in social studies and especially in grades four through six. They test mainly for information recall, but also for understanding and other higher-level abilities. Lena Boyd Brown says:

> Specifically, the multiple-choice item can measure skills of analysis and interpretation of written material such as documents, statistical tables, charts and maps unique to the social studies. In addition answering the multiple-choice item requires skill in critical thinking abilities such as recognizing relationships, making valid generalizations, drawing inferences and evaluating evidence.[23]

The following multiple-choice test items require more than recall of information: [24]

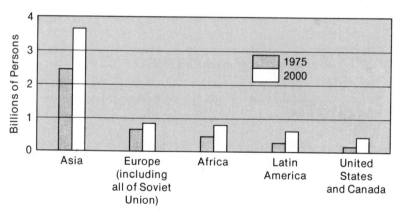

Use the graph above for numbers 18 and 19. The graph shows about what the populations were in 1975 and what they may be in the year 2000.

18. In the year 2000, which region will have gained the most people since 1975?
   a. Africa
   b. Asia
   c. Europe
   d. Latin America

19. In the year 2000, which of the following will be true?
    a. United States and Canada will have the most people.
    b. Africa will have the largest population.
    c. The populations of all the regions will be larger than they were in 1975.
    d. The population of Europe will be twice as large as it was in 1975.

Another example: [25]

The table below shows the major sources of the world's oil. Which of the following statements is supported by the facts in the table?

a. The Soviet Union produces more oil than any other country.
b. The oil resources of the world are found in one area.
c. The figures show that there is no shortage of oil.
d. The desert lands of Saudi Arabia, Kuwait, and Libya together produce more oil than the United States does.

Oil Production by Country * (thousands of barrels)

United States	3,500,000
Soviet Union	2,900,000
Saudi Arabia	2,200,000
Iran	1,800,000
Kuwait	1,200,000
Venezuela	1,200,000
Libya	800,000
Nigeria	700,000

* Figures rounded to the nearest hundred thousand.

Gronlund recommends the following rules for constructing multiple-choice items:

1. Design each item to measure an important learning outcome.
2. Present a single clearly formulated problem in the stem of the item.
3. State the stem of the item in simple, clear language.
4. Put as much of the wording as possible in the stem of the item.
5. State the stem of the item in positive form, whenever possible.
6. Emphasize negative wording whenever it is used in the stem of an item.
7. Make certain that the intended answer is correct or clearly best.
8. Make all alternatives grammatically consistent with the stem of the item and parallel in form.
9. Avoid verbal clues that might enable students to select the correct answer or to eliminate an incorrect alternative.
10. Make the distracters plausible and attractive to the uninformed.

11. Vary the relative length of the correct answer to eliminate length as a clue.
12. Avoid using the alternative "all of the above," and use "none of the above" with extreme caution.
13. Vary the position of the correct answer in a random manner.
14. Control the difficulty of the item either by varying the problem in the stem or by changing the alternatives.
15. Make certain each item is independent of the other items in the test.
16. Use an efficient item format. The alternatives should be listed on separate lines, under one another. . . .[26]

MATCHING TESTS   Matching items are similar to true-false and multiple-choice items. True-false items are usually a declarative statement and two response options; multiple-choice items are a stem (a question or an incomplete statement) and usually about four response options. In other words, there is only one stimulus option and two or more response options. "On a matching item, on the other hand," says Lewis Aiken, "there are multiple stimulus options and multiple response options, and the examinee's task is to indicate which response option(s) goes with which stimulus option(s)." [27]

Aiken recommends the following guidelines for constructing matching items:

1. Place the stimulus and response options in a clear, logical order, with the response options on the right.
2. List between six and fifteen options with two or three more response options than stimulus options.
3. Clearly specify the basis for matching.
4. Keep the entire item on a single page.[28]

COMPLETION OR SHORT-ANSWER TESTS   A completion, or short-answer, item consists of a question or an incomplete statement to which the pupil responds. As such, it resembles a multiple-choice item but instead of providing alternative responses it usually provides blanks in which to write the responses.

ESSAY TESTS   True-false, multiple-choice, matching, and completion or short-answer tests are usually called objective tests. The correct response in each item is predetermined and there is little or no flexibility. The essay test, on the other hand, allows much flexibility, and the response tends to be subjective, reflecting each child's ability to be original and creative. The essay test is subjective also in that the rules for scoring the responses are not as precise as in objective tests; the score depends much on the teacher's or scorer's judgment.

"The most important advantage of essay items," writes Aiken, "is that they can measure the ability to organize, relate, and communicate—

behaviors not so easily assessed." [29] Lena Boyd Brown quotes Frederick G. Brown: The advantages of essay questions are

> that they require the student to compose his own answer rather than select among alternatives; that writing an acceptable essay requires the student to utilize certain skills—e.g., organizational ability, integration, evaluation, summarization, writing ability—which cannot be tested by other items; that the essay format is flexible; and that a topic can be probed in depth, with the student being able to explain and defend his reasoning.[30]

The following guidelines should direct the teacher in constructing and using essay tests:

1. The questions should represent clearly defined objectives.
2. The format of the question should vary with the purpose of the question. Not all essay questions have to start with the usual commands: discuss, explain, describe. . . .
3. While constructing the questions, outline the expected acceptable answers. This outline can be used as the standard against which to grade the test as well as a means to avoid writing vague questions.
4. Determine the degree to which the pupil should be restricted in responding. Questions with too much freedom are difficult to grade.
5. Make sure the questions can be answered in the time allocated.
6. Try to make the examination more comprehensive by constructing shorter questions rather than a few long questions.
7. Children should be informed of the ground rules such as the points each question is worth and the time limits.
8. The same standards should be used for all children. Avoid being influenced by such factors as personality and handwriting. One way to achieve this is by constantly reviewing the standards and by covering the names of the students until the reading of all papers is completed.

Most formal techniques of measurement are tests of cognitive abilities. But, as was mentioned earlier, two formal techniques measure elements of the affective domain: interest inventories and attitude scales.

INTEREST INVENTORIES   Interest inventories are usually used to help adults choose the most suitable careers and vocational goals. But interest inventories can also be used in the elementary school as a means of grouping children and of motivating them. In the study of a unit, the teacher may want to group children according to their common interests, or may want to use the children's interests as a starting point. Interest inventories can also help determine children's interest in helping others, in participating in the affairs of the community, and in other aspects of good citizenship.

Unfortunately, little has been done to develop standardized interest inventories for the elementary school. Teachers have to develop their own inventories for their objectives.

ATTITUDE SCALES   Attitude scales were developed in the belief that "attitudes are tendencies to act for or against something. . . ."[31] A child's manifest attitudes toward something are usually interpreted to mean that the thing is either valued or not. Any textbook on measurement and evaluation contains many attitude scales, but nearly all of them are for high school students and adults. Elementary school teachers must design their own.

In general, attitude scales resemble rating scales, the main difference being that in rating scales the teacher or scorer does the rating while in attitude scales the person filling in the scale does the rating. A typical item in an attitude scale is:

WHICH ITEM BEST DESCRIBES YOUR ATTITUDE TOWARD SOCIAL STUDIES?

1. Social studies is for sure the most important subject.
2. Social studies is for me one of the best subjects.
3. Social studies is of some value to me.
4. Social studies is of very little value to me.
5. Social studies is useless to me.

Another type of frequently used attitude scale is the *semantic differential* scale, on which a child rates a series of concepts on a number of bipolar scales that range from negative to positive. A typical item is:

SCHOOL

Bad	/	/	/	/	/	Good
Unpleasant	/	/	/	/	/	Pleasant
Ugly	/	/	/	/	/	Beautiful
Weak	/	/	/	/	/	Strong
Slow	/	/	/	/	/	Fast

In the elementary school attitude scales are most often used to assess the children's self-concepts. Several such scales have appeared in recent years. Typical are *About Me*, developed by James Parker, and *How I See Myself*, developed by Ira J. Gordon.[32] Parker's test has about 30 items appraising 5 areas: the self, the self in relation to others, the self as achieving, the self in school, and the physical self. A typical item is:

I'm friendly				I'm not so friendly
1	2	3	4	5
( )	( )	( )	( )	( )

Gordon's test includes both elementary and secondary forms. The elementary form contains 40 items arranged as follows:

1.	Nothing gets me too mad	1 2 3 4 5	I get mad easily and explode
6.	I worry a lot	1 2 3 4 5	I don't worry much

Richard Cole and Dave Williams modified Milton Rokeach's adult value survey forms for use with children in the elementary school.[33] These surveys assess children's terminal and instrumental values by asking them to rank the two types of values, listed randomly below. The children are asked to rank the values from most to least important for them.

Items of Modified Rokeach-Type Value Survey

Terminal Values	Instrumental Values
Beautiful world	Ambitious (hardworking)
Admiration and respect of others	Brave (courageous)
Feelings of achievement (lasting contribution)	Capable (able to do things well)
A secure country	Cheerful (light-hearted)
Peaceful world	Clean (neat, tidy)
Confidence and pride in myself	Creative (imaginative)
Equal opportunity for all people	Dependable (reliable)
Exciting life (active, adventurous life)	Forgiving (understanding)
Family love and protection	Helpful (aiding others)
Freedom of choice and action (independence)	Honest (truthful, sincere)
Pleasure (enjoyable life)	Influential (leadership)
Religious faith	Intelligent (smart)
True friendship	Loving (affectionate)
A prosperous life (wealth and comfort)	Polite (courteous)
	Self-controlled (self-disciplined)

Terminal values are the goals people have for their lives; instrumental values are what influence how people behave and conduct their lives. Both Cole and Williams found elementary school children to be quite sociocentric rather than egocentric. From the terminal values, they ranked family love and protection, and equal opportunity for all people the highest. From the instrumental values, they ranked loving (affectionate), honest (truthful, sincere), and helpful the highest; the more egocentric values—prosperous life, exciting life, feeling of achievement, influential, and creative—were ranked the lowest.

In view of the stress on accountability, a welcome recent development is that most textbook series now provide tests to assess progress in
acquiring content and skills contained and promoted in their books. Of the
nine most commonly used programs only one, *Our Working World*, published by SRA, has no tests. *Concepts and Inquiry*, published by Allyn
and Bacon, has tests for grades K–6; *Windows on Our World*, published
by Houghton Mifflin, has tests for grades 1–6; the rest of the programs
have tests only for grades 3–6.

Moreover, there are several standardized tests for the elementary
school. Most of them, however, are for the intermediate grades. Chiefly
because young children cannot read, relatively few tests are available for
grades K–2. Following is a list of elementary social studies standardized
tests published since 1960, arranged according to grade level sequence. (For
more information and reviews consult Oscar K. Buros, ed., *Social Studies
Tests and Reviews* [Highland Park, N.J.: Gryphon Press, 1975].)

1. *Tests of Basic Experience: Social Studies.* Prekindergarten,
   kindergarten–grade 1. (TB/McGraw-Hill, 1970–72.)
2. *Primary Social Studies Test.* Grades 1–3. (Houghton Mifflin, 1967).
3. *Comprehensive Test of Basic Skills (CTBS) Expanded Forms: Social
   Studies.* Grades 2–6. (TB/McGraw-Hill, 1974.)
4. *Primary Test of Economic Understanding.* Grades 2–3. (Joint
   Council on Economic Education, 1971.)
5. *Sequential Tests of Educational Progress: Social Studies.* Grades 4–6.
   (Cooperative Tests and Services, 1956–72.)
6. *SRA Achievement Series: Social Studies.* Grades 4–9. (Science
   Research Associates (1963–69.)
7. *Tests of Elementary Economics.* Revised Experimental Edition.
   Grades 4–6. (Joint Council on Economic Education, 1971.)
8. *Hollingsworth-Sanders Geography Test.* Grades 5–7. (Bureau of
   Educational Measurements, 1962–64.)
9. *Hollingsworth-Sanders Intermediate History Test.* Grades 5–6.
   (Bureau of Educational Measurements, 1962–64.)
10. *Stanford Achievement Test, 1964 Edition: Social Studies Test.*
    Grades 5.5–6.9. (Harcourt Brace Jovanovich, 1940–68.)

Tests that accompany a textbook series differ from the standardized
tests. Textbook-based tests reflect the content in the textbooks—indeed
question order often reflects the text's content arrangement, making the
questions useful instruments of formative evaluation. Most publishers also
have comprehensive tests for summative evaluation. Knowing the exact
body of content that the tests address enables the teacher to determine
whether progress toward the intended objective is in fact being tested for.

Most standardized tests, on the other hand, include about 40 items that cover anywhere from two to four grades. Given the diversity of the social studies curriculum, no teacher can easily ascertain whether those 40-odd items are indeed representative of what had been taught. If they are not representative, the test is invalid—and is unfair to the students, who are being ranked on the basis of something they have not been taught. Standardized tests, therefore, are of poor validity and should be used with extreme caution in the elementary school.

The best formal instruments of measurement for the elementary schools, then, seem to be those developed by the teachers themselves for their own use. To produce sound instruments of measurement, teachers must address two basic concerns: reliability and validity. "Measurements are reliable," says Sax, "if they reflect 'true' rather than chance aspects of the trait or ability measured." [34] In other words, is a test score true and realistic, or has it been influenced by such factors as ambiguous items, trick questions, poorly worded directions, student fatigue, boredom, lack of motivation, and carelessness?

Again, if test items are not representative of the objectives or content students had been working on, the test is not valid. "Validity," says Sax, "can be defined as the extent to which measurements are useful in making decisions relevant to a given purpose." [35] Teacher-made measuring instruments can be more valid than any standardized instrument. The teachers, knowing their objectives and their pupils, can make the instruments more relevant to both.

Again, standardized tests and other instruments of formal evaluation should be used with caution. Districts and schools that wish to initiate a system of accountability would do best to clarify their objectives, determine their curriculum, and develop their own tests and other instruments of measurement. The three types of evaluation—diagnostic, formative, and summative—discussed in this chapter deserve more attention at the local level than they have had in the past. It makes little sense to invest resources to develop curriculum guidelines without the appropriate instruments to determine progress toward the objectives.

PROGRAM EVALUATION

This section might be better titled "More on Program Evaluation" because, as it should now be clear, a main function of all evaluation is to help make decisions about the program. If informal and formal techniques of measurement indicate that the children are not progressing toward the objectives, the program must be modified.

There are occasions, however, when schools or school systems want to take an intensive overall look at their social studies program. (Such scrutiny is especially advisable for districts and schools in which the program is believed to have changed little in the last 10 to 15 years; such schools may not have benefited from the ferment in social studies during the 1960s and '70s.) An assessment requires criteria or guidelines. Fortunately, the National Council for the Social Studies developed one such set of guidelines, which, as it happens, reflect most of the ideas expressed in this book. There are nine basic guidelines, designed specifically to evaluate K–12 programs: [36]

1.0   The Social Studies Program Should Be Directly Related to the Concerns of Students.

2.0   The Social Studies Program Should Deal with the Real Social World.

3.0   The Social Studies Program Should Draw from Currently Valid Knowledge Representative of Man's Experience, Culture and Beliefs.

4.0   Objectives Should Be Thoughtfully Selected and Clearly Stated in Such Form as to Furnish Direction to the Program.

5.0   Learning Activities Should Engage the Student Directly and Actively in the Learning Process.

6.0   Strategies of Instruction and Learning Activities Should Rely on a Broad Range of Learning Resources.

7.0   The Social Studies Program Must Facilitate the Organization of Experience.

8.0   Evaluation Should Be Useful, Systematic, Comprehensive, and Valid for the Objectives of the Program.

9.0   Social Studies Education Should Receive Vigorous Support as a Vital and Responsible Part of the School Program.

Each guideline includes several more specific items. For convenience to users, a practical checklist was developed. This checklist, reproduced below, "will furnish a profile of a program as it is. . . . The outline can be used for a given grade level or for a school or a district-wide program." [37] Data elicited by the questions in the checklist must come from many sources. The letters following each question indicate the best source:

"R" = curriculum materials, such as local and state curriculum guides, faculty and student handbooks, available curriculum materials, samples of children's work and other data on student progress, minutes of curriculum committee meetings, and other similar materials;

"T" = teachers;

"S" = students;

"C" = the community, especially parents;

"O" = direct observation inside and outside the classroom.

Evaluation Checklist *

Rating			
Strongly	*Moderately*	*Hardly at all*	*Specific Guidelines*
			1.1 Are students involved in the formulation of goals, the selection of activities, and the assessment of curriculum outcomes? S T
			1.2 Do the school and its teachers make steady effort, through regularized channels and practices, to identify areas of concern to students? S T
			1.3 Do students have choices within programs? S T
			1.4 Do all students have ample opportunity for social studies education at all grade levels? R T
			2.1 Does the program focus on the social world as it actually is? R T C
			2.2 Does the program emphasize pervasive and enduring social issues? R T
			2.3 Does the program include analysis and attempts to formulate potential resolutions of present and controversial problems such as racism and war? R T
			2.4 Does the program provide intensive and recurrent study of cultural, racial, religious and ethnic groups? R T C
			2.5 Does the program offer opportunities to meet and work with members of racial and ethnic groups other than their own? R T C
			2.6 Does the program build upon the realities of the immediate school community? R T C
			2.7 Is participation both in school and out considered a part of the program? R T C
			3.1 Does the program emphasize valid concepts, principles, and theories in the social sciences? R T
			3.2 Does the program develop proficiency in methods of inquiry in the social sciences and in techniques for processing social data? R T O

	Rating		Specific Guidelines
Strongly	Moderately	Hardly at all	
			3.3 Does the program develop students' ability to distinguish among empirical, logical, definitional, and normative propositions and problems? R T O
			3.4 Does the program draw upon all of the social sciences and the history of the United States and the Western and non-Western worlds? R T
			3.5 Does the program draw from what is appropriate in other related fields such as psychology, law, communications, and the humanities? R T
			3.6 Does the program represent some balance between the immediate social environment of students and the larger social world? R T
			3.7 Does the program include the study of man's achievements and those policies contrary to present national goals? R T
			3.8 Does the program include a careful selection of that knowledge of most worth? R T
			4.1 Are objectives carefully selected and formulated? R T
			4.2 Are knowledge, abilities, valuing, and social participation all represented in the objectives of the program? R T
			4.3 Are general statements of goals translated into specific objectives conceived in terms of behavior and content? R T
			4.4 Are classroom instruction and materials based upon clearly stated objectives? R T O
			4.5 Does classroom instruction enable students to see their goals clearly in brief instructional sequences and lengthy units of study? T S
			4.6 Are objectives reconsidered and revised periodically? R T
			5.1 Do students have a wide and rich range of learning activities appropriate to the objectives of their program? R T

	Rating		
Strongly	Moderately	Hardly at all	Specific Guidelines
			5.2 Do activities include formulating hypotheses and testing them by gathering and analyzing data? R T O
			5.3 Do activities include the processes of making decisions about socio-civic affairs? R T O
			5.4 Do activities involve students in their communities? S T C
			5.5 Are learning activities sufficiently varied and flexible? T S
			5.6 Do students perceive their teachers as fellow inquirers? S
			5.7 Are activities carried on in a climate which supports students' self-respect and opens opportunities to all? S T O
			6.1 Does the program have a wealth of appropriate instructional resources? R T O
			6.2 Do printed materials accommodate a wide range of reading abilities and interests, learning activities, and sources? R O
			6.3 Is a variety of media available for learning through many senses? R O
			6.4 Do classrooms draw upon the contributions of many kinds of resource persons and organizations representing many points of view? T O C
			6.5 Do activities use the school and community as a learning laboratory? T O C
			6.6 Does the program have available many kinds of work space? R O
			7.1 Does the program help students organize their experiences? R O
			7.2 Are learning experiences organized in such fashion that students learn how to learn? R O
			7.3 Does the program enable students to relate their experiences in social studies to other areas of experience? T S O
			7.4 Does the formal pattern of the program offer choice and flexibility? R S
			8.1 Is evaluation based primarily on

	Rating		Specific Guidelines
Strongly	Moderately	Hardly at all	
			the school's own statements of objectives? R
			8.2 Does assessment include progress in knowledge, abilities, valuing, and participation? R
			8.3 Do evaluation data come from many sources, inside and outside the classroom? R
			8.4 Are evaluation procedures regular, comprehensive, and continuous? R
			8.5 Are evaluation data used for planning curricular improvement? R T
			8.6 Do evaluation data offer students help in the course of learning? T S
			8.7 Are both students and teachers involved in the process of evaluation? S T
			8.8 Is regular re-examination of basic curricular goals an integral part of the evaluation? R T
			9.1 Does the school provide appropriate materials, time, and facilities for social studies education? R T C
			9.2 Do teachers try out and adapt for their own students promising innovations? R T

* Gary Manson et al., *Social Studies Curriculum Guidelines* (Washington, D.C.: The National Council for the Social Studies, 1972), pp. 28–31. Reprinted with permission of the National Council for the Social Studies.

SUMMARY

Evaluation as described in this chapter is a process of assessing pupil progress and, thereby, the effectiveness of teaching and learning processes. As such, evaluation is an integral part of instruction; it should not take place only at the end of a unit or of a course. Evaluation starts at the beginning of the instructional process, when information about the children's needs and the characteristics is collected. Without such information it is impossible to select appropriate generalizations, issues, or meaningful instructional objectives. Evaluation for this purpose is called *placement diagnostic evaluation.*

As instruction proceeds, so does evaluation. Recent thinking requires that the instructional objectives, as well as instruction itself, be subdivided into more specific components that are logically sequenced so that the understanding of one leads to the next. No new component is broached unless each child understands its antecedent. It is in this context that the concept of *mastery learning*—children achieving objectives to the same predetermined degree of proficiency—has been advanced. Assessment of pupil progress and the consequent decisions are called *formative evaluation.*

Some children have difficulty reaching certain instructional objectives despite repeated efforts and the best possible instructional techniques. When this occurs, the children must be extensively examined to determine the underlying causes of the difficulties. This evaluation is called *remedial diagnostic evaluation.*

Summative evaluation takes place at the end of a unit or a course of instruction. Like the traditional form of evaluation, its function is to assign students' grades or scores and to determine the program's quality and effectiveness.

The process of collecting and assigning values to data for any type of evaluation is called *measurement,* of which there are *informal* and *formal* techniques. Among the informal ones are: (1) observation, (2) discussion, (3) conferences with pupils and parents, (4) examination of samples of children's work, (5) anecdotal records, (6) rating scales, (7) checklists, (8) sociometric devices, and (9) self-reporting. Among the formal techniques of measurement are: (1) true-false tests, (2) multiple-choice tests, (3) matching tests, (4) completion or short-answer tests, (5) essay tests, (6) interest inventories, and (7) attitude scales.

Informal techniques of measurement rely mostly on observation and can take place any time the children can be observed individually or in groups. They are more appropriate for the elementary school than the formal techniques are. Informal techniques are helpful in assessing the children's progress not only in knowledge and intellectual skills, but in values objectives, value-clarification skills, and social skills objectives as well. Formal techniques, on the other hand, involve tasks the children must perform at a specified time and place. With the exception of interest inventories and attitude scales, they measure mainly progress toward cognitive objectives—knowledge and intellectual skills.

There are some commercial and standardized instruments of measurement for the elementary school, but teachers do better designing their own. Standardized instruments are *norm-referenced;* they tend to rank children on the basis of the average performance of a large, representative sample of other children. Teacher-made instruments are *criterion-referenced;* they are designed to assess progress toward specific content and objectives appropriate for specific children.

Although pupil-assessment is meant to improve the social studies program, it is recommended that from time to time social studies be evaluated from an overall point of view. The National Council for the Social Studies has developed basic guidelines for such program evaluation.

ACTIVITIES

1. Secure available social studies tests and classify those items that test for content objectives and those that test for process objectives. Is there a balance?

2. Interview a teacher to determine what techniques are used for diagnostic, formative, and summative evaluation. Share the findings with your classmates.

3. As often as possible practice informal techniques of measurement. Videotape the practice sessions when possible or ask fellow students to observe your practices and give suggestions.

4. Visit schools and ask for permission to sit in on parent-teacher conferences.

5. Visit a school and ask a teacher to show, and explain, how a child's progress can be assessed by samples of work.

6. Develop as many instruments of formal evaluation as you can, using the guidelines in this chapter.

7. Familiarize yourself with the social studies program of a particular school. Then examine the items in a standardized test to determine how well it tests for the school's objectives.

8. As a class, secure permission from a local school and organize to evaluate their social studies program on the basis of the National Council for the Social Studies guidelines.

9. Collect various instruments of measurement and evaluation and prepare a file for later reference.

NOTES

1. Norman E. Gronlund, *Measurement and Evaluation in Teaching, 3rd ed.* (New York: Macmillan, 1976), p. 7.

2. Ibid.

3. D. Cecil Clark, *Using Instructional Objectives in Teaching* (Glenview, Ill.: Scott, Foresman, 1972), p. 38.

4. Ibid., pp. 51–52.

5. For details on the difference between the two types of evaluation, see Peter W. Airasian and George F. Madaus, "Functional Types of Student Evaluation," in William A. Mehrens, ed., *Readings in Measurement and Evaluation in Education and Psychology* (New York: Holt, Rinehart & Winston, 1976), pp. 9–25.

6. Ibid., p. 11.

7. Rita Dunn, Kenneth Dunn, and Gary E. Price, "Diagnosing Learning Styles: A Prescription for Avoiding Malpractice Suit," *Phi Delta Kappan,* 58 (January 1977), 418.

8. Ibid., p. 419.

9. Benjamin S. Bloom, J. Thomas Hastings, and George F. Madaus, *Handbook on Formative and Summative Evaluation of Student Learning* (New York: McGraw-Hill, 1971), p. 117.

10. Ibid., p. 54.

11. Ibid., p. 43.

12. Airasian and Madaus, "Functional Types," p. 16.

13. Gronlund, *Measurement and Evaluation,* p. 428.

14. *Teacher's Tentative Guide to Reporting Practices, Policies and Procedures—Kindergarten Through Six* (Bothell, Wash.: Northshore School District, 1974), p. 30.

15. Ibid., pp. 7–9 (by permission of Northshore School District).

16. Gilbert Sax, *Principles of Educational Measurement and Evaluation* (Belmont, Calif.: Wadsworth, 1974), p. 477.

17. Ibid., p. 483.

18. Ibid., p. 503.

19. Gronlund, *Measurement and Evaluation,* p. 463.

20. Norman E. Gronlund, *Constructing Achievement Tests,* 2nd ed. (Englewood Cliffs, N.J.: Prentice-Hall, 1977), p. 1.

21. Robert L. Ebel, "Educational Tests: Valid? Biased? Useful?" *Phi Delta Kappan,* 54 (October 1975), 85.

22. Adapted from Gilbert Sax, *Principles,* pp. 81–84.

23. Lena Boyd Brown, "What Teachers Should Know About Standardized Tests," *Social Education,* 40 (November–December 1976), 509.

24. Susan Y. Klein, *Performance Tests PEOPLE AND IDEAS* (Morristown, N.J.: Silver Burdett, 1976), p. 36.

25. Beverly S. Almgren, *Performance Tests THIS IS OUR WORLD* (Morristown, N.J.: Silver Burdett, 1975), p. 25.

26. Adapted from Norman E. Gronlund, *Constructing Achievement Tests,* 2nd ed. (Englewood Cliffs, N.J.: Prentice-Hall, Inc., 1977), pp. 39–53. Reprinted by permission of Prentice-Hall, Inc.

27. Lewis R. Aiken, Jr., *Psychological Testing and Assessment,* 2nd ed. (Boston: Allyn & Bacon, 1976), p. 35.

28. Ibid.

29. Ibid., p. 32.

30. Lena Boyd Brown, "What Teachers Should Know," p. 511.

31. Lewis B. Mayhew, "Measurement of Noncognitive Objectives in the Social Studies," in Harry D. Berg, ed., *Evaluation in Social Studies.* 35th Yearbook of the National Council for the Social Studies (Washington, D.C.: National Council for the Social Studies, 1965), p. 120.

32. James Parker, *About Me.* Available in mimeographed form from Dr. Parker, Box 374, Cordele, Georgia 31015. Ira J. Gordon, *How I See Myself* (Gainsville: Florida Educational Research and Development Council, College of Education, University of Florida).

33. Richard A. Cole, "A Study of Values and Value Systems of Pre-Adolescent School Children" (Unpublished Ph.D. thesis, University of Washington, 1972); Dave Williams, "A Study of Pre-Adolescent Value Preferences" (Unpublished Ph.D. thesis, University of Washington, 1972).

34. Sax, *Principles,* p. 172.

35. Ibid., p. 206.

36. Gary Manson, Gerald Marker, Anna Ochoa, and Jan Tucker (NCSS Task Force on Curriculum Guidelines), *Social Studies Curriculum Guidelines* (Washington, D.C.: National Council for the Social Studies, 1972). Reprinted with permission of the National Council for the Social Studies.

37. Ibid., p. 28.

Instructional Resources
for Social Studies

Studying this chapter will enable the reader to:

1. name the most important elementary school social studies curriculum projects developed during the 1960s.
2. recognize some of the basic concepts taught through the major projects.
3. realize the important role social science disciplines played in the development of the projects of the '60s.
4. identify some of the basic characteristics of each project.
5. name the textbook series most widely used throughout the country.
6. identify some of the basic similarities and differences between the various textbook series.
7. identify the important characteristics of contemporary social studies programs and use these characteristics as criteria to evaluate textbook series.
8. realize the important role that reading materials other than textbooks play in the design and development of learning activities.
9. locate relevant reading materials for children at the various levels.
10. identify several special skills that children need if they are to take advantage of the variety of reading materials.
11. use at least one method to determine the readability level of a particular written communication.

PROJECTS, TEXTBOOKS,
AND OTHER
READING MATERIALS

During the 1960s and well into the 1970s, as the social studies program underwent major changes, social studies textbook series were revised accordingly, and several new ones appeared. Likewise, children's trade books (that is, nontextbooks) were reexamined in the light of developments and an abundance of new ones were written to faithfully project social realities and the complexities of human relationships.

In this chapter we briefly examine the projects that have most affected elementary social studies, the textbook series most widely used throughout the nation, and other types of reading materials used to enrich the teaching of social studies. Next we consider criteria for selecting textbooks and other reading materials, and survey the most important reading skills. The chapter concludes with instructions on how a teacher can determine the readability of the materials planned to be used in the classroom.

It is hoped that this chapter will have several effects: (1) Once aware of the projects that triggered the new social studies, teachers will become more committed to their philosophical premises; (2) teachers might look closer at the materials available through these projects and decide to use them, or use them as prototypes to develop their own; (3) teachers will be able to see the relationship between the curriculum projects and the revised or new social studies series; (4) finally, teachers will select reading materials more carefully for their suitability to meeting the objectives of social studies.

THE CURRICULUM PROJECTS

The entire November 1972 issue of *Social Education* is devoted to an evaluation, by the staff of the Social Science Education Consortium under the direction of Irving Morrissett, of curriculum projects, programs, and materials. Much in the project summaries that follow is based on that issue. Of the 26 projects reviewed, 9 are either designed entirely for the elementary school or are comprehensive programs covering K–12 or 14. Some programs cover all elementary school levels, whereas others cover one grade or a few units that can be used in one or several grades. Moreover, some projects are interdisciplinary whereas others focus on one discipline. But all projects are conceptually designed and for all the inquiry method is the most appropriate for teaching social studies. We examine first the comprehensive programs, most of which were already mentioned in Chapter 3.

The Comprehensive Programs

There are four comprehensive programs, all developed during the 1960s:

1. PROJECT SOCIAL STUDIES OF THE UNIVERSITY OF MINNESOTA   Project Social Studies is an interdisciplinary comprehensive K–12 program, developed at the University of Minnesota under the direction of Edith West, and funded by the U.S. Office of Education. As seen in Chapter 3, the Minnesota Project Social Studies departs very little in scope and sequence from the traditional social studies program. It starts with the study of the American family in the first grade, moves into family life around the world in the second grade, and studies various types of communities in the third and fourth grades. Grades five and six cover the Western Hemisphere, with emphasis on U.S. history.

Like all social studies projects of the 1960s, the Minnesota Project involved social scientists, who determined the concepts and generalizations to be the backbone for the topics proposed in each grade. Teachers and social studies educators then collected resources and designed appropriate learning activities for each concept and generalization. Even today the Minnesota Project units remain a rich source of generalizations, activities, and the like. All units are available from Green Printing Company, 631-8th Avenue North, Minneapolis, Minnesota 55411.

The program has been recently rewritten by Charles L. Mitsakos, Social Studies Coordinator for the Chelmsford (Massachusetts) Public Schools, and, as *The Family of Man,* is published and distributed by Selective Educational Equipment Inc. (SEE). As SEE advertises, each unit consists of a learning system that incorporates:

> A *Teacher's Resource Guide* which makes the unit far more than just a collection of realia and audio-visual materials and includes an historical background paper, Behavioral Objectives, Outline of Content, 30–55 fully developed suggestions for teaching, and a detailed appendix with classroom activities such as stories, games, recipes, songs, additional teaching information, and much more.
>
> A *Media Package* which includes a wide variety of elements such as artifacts and other objects, study prints, filmstrips, children's books, audiotapes, simulation games, primary source readings, maps, sort cards, and printed originals for making student handouts and overhead transparencies.[1]

Thus far 12 units have been completed, classified in 4 levels:

Level I:	1.	Hopi Indian Family
	2.	Japanese Family
	3.	Ashanti Family of Ghana
Level II:	4.	Family of Early New England
	5.	Kibbutz Family in Israel
	6.	Russian Family in Moscow
Level III:	7.	Contrasting Communities in the United States
	8.	The People of Paris
	9.	Early California Gold Mining Camp
Level IV:	10.	Our Own Community—Economic Aspects
	11.	Village in India
	12.	Economic Life in the People's Republic of China

As an example of the variety of resources in each unit, the Hopi Indian Family unit includes:

1. Four authentic Hopi Indian artifacts: Kachina doll, pottery bowl, sifting basket, and Hopi toy.
2. A set of two full-color filmstrips depicting Old Oraibi, the Hopi Land (mesa, canyon, desert), the events of the Hopi calendar, the Hopi at work making piki, making pottery, and weaving baskets and rugs.
3. A set of 30 study prints (11" $\times$ 14") with details of the family and its members, the home, festivals and ceremonies, buildings and local scenery.
4. An audiotape cassette of Hopi legends and music.
5. A package of printed originals for making student handouts and overhead transparencies, including an outline map, Hopi symbols, and Hopi songs.
6. A set of nine children's books including stories about Hopi life, crafts, and children's roles.
7. A complete teacher's resource guide as described earlier.
8. A rationale and overview of the program prepared by Dr. Edith West, who originally developed it.

Obviously, there is a big difference between the program's original format and SEE's format. The original format provides directions, but the teacher must gather the resources and prepare the materials needed to carry out the suggested activities. SEE makes the units ready for use in the classroom. *The Family of Man* being inquiry-oriented, the types of materials it uses make it an open-ended program in which a variety of issues could be raised.

2. TABA SOCIAL STUDIES CURRICULUM PROJECT   This project was directed by the late Hilda Taba while a professor of education at San Francisco State College. Its format resembles that of the Minnesota Project. Its primary

objective is to develop concepts and generalizations through the use of a variety of resources in inquiry-oriented learning activities.

Like the Minnesota Project, the Taba Program does not radically depart from traditional scope and sequence. In each grade, however, the program continues advancing the development of several concepts in more depth. Children are given opportunities to see illustrations of the concepts in different situations as their field of experience expands. For example, the concept of interdependence is illustrated in the first grade as the children recognize the interdependence among members of the family. The understanding of this concept becomes deeper in the third and fifth grades as the children realize that communities and nations as well are interdependent in many ways. Curriculum development in which the same concepts are studied in more depth as the children's experience expands came to be known as the *spiral approach*. The basic concepts in the Taba Program are causality, conflict, cooperation, cultural change, differences, interdependence, modification, power, societal control, tradition, and values. There is no society or period in history through which these concepts cannot be taught.

One of the most important aspects of the Taba Program is that the method of teaching that it reflects is based on extensive study and experimentation. As seen in Chapter 4, Taba developed her own style of inquiry that has become one of the most popular in the elementary school. Consisting of three cognitive tasks, it moves from concept formation to explaining, interpreting, and generalizing, and, finally, to applying known facts and principles. The rationale for Taba's program and a detailed description of her method are found in her valuable handbook for teachers.[2]

The original Taba Program materials were published in paperback, mainly as teacher's guides, by Addison-Wesley Publishing Company. Since 1972, under the consulting editorship of Mary C. Durkin et al., the program has been expanded to include children's texts and other materials made commercially available through the same company. More on the program's commercial form is provided in the next section of this chapter.

3. GREATER CLEVELAND SOCIAL SCIENCE PROGRAM   This program, developed originally by the Educational Research Council of Greater Cleveland (now the Educational Research Council of America), is conceptual and was designed and written mainly by social scientists. The program was tested in the schools of the Greater Cleveland area and is now commercially available as *Concepts and Inquiry*, from Allyn and Bacon.

The Greater Cleveland Social Science Program is probably the only comprehensive program developed during the 1960s that departs from the traditional scope and sequence. This change has no compelling or convincing rationale. Whereas traditional social studies dealt with the home and family in kindergarten and the first grade, the Greater Cleveland Program starts with an overview of the world and deals with children in other lands. The first grade program introduces children to the United States and deals with the lives of explorers and discoverers all the way from Balboa and Columbus to John Glenn and Martin Luther King, Jr. The second and third grades return to the traditional framework, comparative studies of the community. The fourth grade continues this study, adding the history of Anglo-America, an area that the traditional program usually places in the fifth grade. Some attention is also given to industrialization in the fourth grade. In the fifth grade the program is also historical, ranging from ancient civilizations to modern cultures.

Originally, the Greater Cleveland Program was rather high-level in its content, reflecting the social scientists' ambitions to turn elementary school children into little social scientists. The program has since been much improved as published by Allyn and Bacon. It too is further discussed in the next section.

4. THE ELKHART, INDIANA, EXPERIMENT IN ECONOMIC EDUCATION   This project, directed by the economist Lawrence Senesh and funded by the Carnegie Foundation, was intended to teach basic economic concepts to first graders. Not knowing much about education and first grade children, Professor Senesh spent much time in the first grade classrooms of the Elkhart, Indiana, school system. He tried to find out what the first graders were doing, what they were studying, what books they were reading, and what their interests were. He used what the children did as a means to teach economic concepts. Professor Senesh found out, for example, that first graders spent much time before Christmas making gingerbread. He used this activity to teach economics, introducing the concepts of assembly line and specialization. He separated the children into two groups: one group functioned as an assembly line, while each child in the other group individually made gingerbread. They thus became familiar with the nature of the assembly line and specialization, and with some of the advantages and disadvantages of each.

The main focus in the Elkhart Program, called *Our Working World*, was work and the production of goods and services. In each grade this focus was fitted to the traditional scope and sequence: in the first grade, *Families at Work*; in the second grade, *Communities at Work*; and in the third grade, *Cities at Work*.

Although Professor Senesh's original intent was to introduce economics in the elementary school, he also dealt with sociology, political science, and the other social sciences. Professor Senesh compares teaching social studies in the elementary school to directing an orchestra. The instruments are the numerous social sciences addressed to a variety of themes relevant to the children. Various disciplines play solo parts from time to time. The sound concept of the "orchestrated curriculum" is attributed to Professor Senesh.

Curriculum development having proved to be stimulating and rewarding for Professor Senesh, he reached an agreement with the publishers Science Research Associates (SRA) and developed his program into a complete, interdisciplinary elementary school program (discussed further later in the chapter).

Programs Limited to One Grade or One Discipline

In addition to these four comprehensive elementary school programs, five other programs developed in the '60s address one or a few disciplines or grades. Some are still going strong, while others proved to have serious weaknesses. But all are quite useful to the eclectic teacher wishing to be updated. All limited programs demonstrate some kind of strength: Some demonstrate the value of disciplines in determining the curriculum and designing learning activities; others present excellent examples of the multimedia approach to teaching social studies; whereas still others incorporate not only the social sciences but also elements from the behavioral sciences, a trend that has been emphasized during the 1970s. Following are brief descriptions of the most important limited programs.

1. MAN: A COURSE OF STUDY (MACOS)   This program, probably the most exciting of those developed in the 1960s, is also one of the most controversial programs in the history of American education. Developed by the Educational Development Center, it reflects the instructional theories of Jerome Bruner, the Harvard psychologist considered by many the founder of the conceptual approach, with the publication of his classic *The Process of Education*.[3]

Man: A Course of Study is a fifth grade program that addresses three questions:

1. What is human about human beings?
2. How did they get that way?
3. How can they be made more so?

The course is not designed to give final answers to these questions—for no one completely understands the nature of human beings—but rather to get the children thinking about the concept of humanness.

Throughout the course contrasts are used: Children begin learning about animals—the salmon, the herring gull, and the baboon—as an introduction to the study of humans. Next, many questions are raised about things that children take for granted about themselves. Most important are the human need for learning, the ever-presence of parents, the helplessness of babies, and the power of language.

From the animal materials the course leads into an intensive study of one human society—the Netsilik Eskimo of Canada. The remote setting of this people focuses attention on the extraordinary resourcefulness of human beings and their flexibility in technology, their capacity for interchange in social organization, and their fertility of mind as they design and abstractly express their views of the world.

The design of the material favors an open-ended strategy. As Peter Dow points out,

> This open-ended teaching strategy is supported by a collection of booklets that presents information in many different ways and accommodates a diversity of learning styles in contrast to the undifferentiated approach of a textbook. A data book, a set of field notes, an ethnography, a novel, a book of poems, a collection of myths, an "Observer's Handbook," a variety of concept books, and a collection of fact-filled "mini-texts" all foster this diverse approach.[4]

In addition, among the materials are several films that have become classics for their open-ended content.

The program was originally disseminated, under National Science Foundation funding, through six university-based regional centers throughout the country. The multimedia approach of the program was so novel that no publisher was willing to undertake commercial marketing. However, following its enthusiastic reception by teachers, Curriculum Development Associates (CDA) of Washington, D.C., has made the program commercially available since 1972.

Teachers trained to teach MACOS and children who have experienced the program favor it highly. As Peter Dow writes, "the strongly positive response [the program] has received from students and teachers suggests that we must take seriously the search for new and more powerful ways of helping children think about human nature."[5] However, the program has been attacked recently by many parents and organized groups, including the Council for Basic Education. A sharp debate was generated that reached even the halls of the U.S. Congress.

One main objection is that the program deals with controversial issues, usually in the form of such questions as: "Should one ever be cruel? Who am I? What makes me human? What generalizations can we make about family behavior in our society? Do all animals marry? What would you say is the difference between human marriage and the marriage of other animals? Is there agreement about the best way of taking care of people who are old? Interview your mother if you are a girl, or your father if you are a boy, on the question: In what ways do you want me to be like you when I am grown up?" Citing the above questions, George Weber, Associate Director of the Council for Basic Education, asked: "Just why are such young children subjected to this controversial material?"[6]

The prevalent nationwide objections to the program are summarized by Congressman John B. Conlan of Arizona:

> The program allots half a year to study the social behavior and mating habits of birds, fish and baboons, with the implicit view that man not only evolved from lower animals, but also derived his social behavior from them.
>
> Children are then exposed for a full semester to the alien Netsilik Eskimo subculture, in which the following practices are rationalized and approvingly examined in free-wheeling classroom discussions: killing the elderly and female infants; wife-swapping and trial marriage; communal living; witchcraft and the occult; cannibalism.[7]

Peter Dow responds to the criticisms:

> Much has been said in the current discussion about the dangers of exposing young children to alleged issues of adultery, bestiality, cannibalism, infanticide, and senilicide in the MACOS materials, but these horrors are in fact the daily fare of our television screen and are shown presumably with no larger purposes than to "entertain" millions of viewers who daily gawk over lurid scenes of man's inhumanity to man without ever being asked to contemplate the relationship between these behaviors and our elusive search for human understanding. In contrast, MACOS may raise troubling questions about the significance of killing, the importance of the partnership between male and female, and the moral dilemmas all societies face in caring for the very young and the very old; but these questions are always considered in the context of what they tell us, or fail to tell us, about how humankind can better understand itself and thus improve its plight. This is the overriding goal of social education, and it is against the success or failure in achieving this goal that *Man: A Course of Study* should be judged.[8]

Whether a school or district ought to use MACOS depends on the judgment of local school authorities. Nevertheless, as a teaching approach, MACOS is contemporary and is one of the best, if not the best program available. It conveys sound knowledge, it helps children discover and clarify their values, and it develops their thinking abilities. Teachers and prospective teachers are advised to study it carefully and learn from it; numerous teaching ideas can be found in it. Though the program is most suitable for the fifth grade, it is flexible enough to use successfully in any grade from the fourth to the eighth.

2. SOCIAL SCIENCE LABORATORY UNITS   This program consists of seven units that can be used as the program for any grade between third and seventh, or its units can be spread among the elementary school upper grades as a supplement to an ongoing social studies program. The units were developed at the University of Michigan under the direction of professors Ronald Lippitt and Robert Fox; among the main writers was Lucille Schaible. With

the unit booklets are five records and two guides for the teacher, all available commercially through Science Research Associates.

The content of the units is behavior-oriented and stresses student involvement. Through workbook-like exercises children learn about behavior and how it is influenced and shaped. The content makes the units quite popular with teachers in urban areas, who are usually confronted with behavior problems. The titles of the seven units are:

1   Learning to use social sciences
2. Discovering differences
3. Friendly and unfriendly behavior
4. Being and becoming
5. Individual and group
6. Deciding and doing
7. Influencing each other

Whereas most programs developed in the 1960s concentrated on the social sciences and emphasized the development of concepts and generalizations, the Social Science Laboratory Units derived content from the behavioral sciences as well. With today's emphasis on values and decision making, the behavioral sciences are now well represented in current social studies programs, but in the 1960s MACOS and the Social Science Laboratory Units were the ground breakers.

3. MUSEUM MATERIALS AND ACTIVITIES FOR TEACHERS AND CHILDREN (MATCH) This is another interdisciplinary program that is limited to several units. Developed by the Boston Children's Museum under the direction of Frederick H. Kressee, the units were produced by American Science and Engineering of Boston. Its format resembles that of *The Family of Man* units. Each unit is taught through a variety of realia, films, filmstrips, pictures, maps, games, records, reference books, and a Teacher's Guide, distributed in containers called MATCH Boxes.

The first units to be developed were *The City, A House of Ancient Greece,* and *The Japanese Family.* The MATCH Boxes are expensive, but only one of each unit is needed for an entire class or even an entire school. They are what a multimedia approach should be, and the Teacher's Guide includes many ideas for promoting the inquiry method through the use of nonprint materials.

4. ANTHROPOLOGY CURRICULUM PROJECT This project is one of several developed to introduce specific disciplines in the elementary school. It deals with concepts and methodologies of physical, cultural, archaeological, and linguistic anthropology organized sequentially from kindergarten through

senior high school. The materials are designed in units to be used as supplements to an existing social studies program. This particular project stresses concepts, and the reading materials have proved somewhat difficult for elementary school children.

The Anthropology Curriculum Program was developed at the University of Georgia under the direction of Marion J. Rice and Wilfrid C. Bailey. Although it is not published commercially, the project directors themselves will supply any units desired; also available are sample sets for each grade.

5. ELEMENTARY ECONOMICS PROJECT   As the title indicates, this project produced materials in economics suitable for elementary school children. These materials were produced at the Industrial Relations Center of the University of Chicago under the direction of William D. Rader, from whom information concerning the availability of materials can be obtained.

MAJOR TEXTBOOK SERIES

In 1972, Social Science Education Consortium (SSEC), in cooperation with the journal *Social Education*, started a Curriculum Information Network (CIN) to produce evaluative information about social studies materials and procedures used throughout the country. Two of the surveys dealt specifically with social studies textbook series and other types of curriculum materials.[9] Respondents were asked to evaluate up to three materials packages they used on the basis of three questions:

1. How well did these materials work with your students?
2. How do these materials compare with other social studies materials?
3. Would you recommend these materials for use by others? [10]

The first report produced 22 materials packages that were evaluated by five or more respondents, the second report produced 24. The same five comprehensive elementary school textbook series appeared in both lists of materials produced by the surveys:

1. Concepts and Inquiry (Allyn and Bacon)
2. Field Social Studies Program (Field, purchased by Addison-Wesley)
3. Holt Databank System (Holt, Rinehart and Winston)
4. Taba Program in Social Science (Addison-Wesley)
5. The Social Sciences: Concepts and Values (Harcourt Brace Jovanovich)

It is safe to say that the above are among the most popular textbook series. Two programs are based on two of the four major comprehensive projects of the past: Concepts and Inquiry is based on the Greater Cleveland Program (which later became the Educational Research Council Social Science Program), and the Taba Program in Social Science is based on the program Dr. Taba developed for Contra Costa County, in California. The chart on pages 226–27 compares the five programs on areas of study recommended for each grade.

In addition to the five programs already mentioned, the following textbook series are currently in wide use throughout the country:

1. Contemporary Social Science Curriculum (Silver Burdett Company). This program deals with: *The Earth, Home of People* in kindergarten, *Living in Families* in the first grade, *Living in Communities* in the second grade, *People and Resources* or *People and Regions* in the third grade, *People and Regions* or *People and Ideas* in the fourth grade, *People in the Americas* in the fifth grade, and *People and Change* in the sixth grade.

2. Focus on Active Learning (Macmillan). The Macmillan social studies series has no kindergarten program, but deals with: *You and Me* in the first grade, *One plus One* in the second grade, *The Third Planet* in the third grade, *Web of the World* in the fourth grade, *Lands of Promise* and *This Favored Land* in the fifth grade, and *The Ways of Man* and *In A Race with Time* in the sixth grade.

3. Our Working World (Science Research Associates). Another program based on a project of the 1960s, it is an outgrowth of the Experiment on Economic Education conducted by Lawrence Senesh. Areas of study are: *Families* for the first grade, *Neighborhoods* for the second grade, *Cities* for the third grade, *Regions of the United States* for the fourth grade, *The American Way of Life* for the fifth grade, and *Regions of the World* for the sixth grade.

4. Windows on Our World (Houghton Mifflin). This is one of the newest programs and its areas of study present an interesting framework: *Me* in kindergarten, *Things We Do* in the first grade, *The World Around Us* in the second grade, *Who Are We?* in the third grade, *Planet Earth* in the fourth grade, *The United States* in the fifth grade, and *The Way People Live* in the sixth grade.

Unfortunately, very little evaluative information is available about these series. True, in the annual meetings of the National Council for the Social Studies and in the various regional, state, and local meetings, new textbook series are exhibited and presentations are often made, but they are usually descriptive, or the developers expound only on the merits of their products. The two surveys by Irving Morrissett and the staff of *Social Education* are thus far the only beginnings—and modest ones at that —of such evaluations. The results of these surveys, however, are not reliable, because their sampling was not representative and their respondents were few.

Social studies educators have not yet produced a person or group that systematically evaluates social studies materials in the same way that Oscar Buros, for example, evaluates testing instruments. Teachers, administrators, and textbook selection committees throughout the country draw no substantial help from the profession, and often are subjected to the nonprofessional, often questionable, selling tactics of publishers' marketing departments. The Social Science Consortium in Boulder, Colorado, tried to fill this vacuum with their *Social Studies Curriculum Materials Data Book* (an ongoing looseleaf publication), but most of its information is only descriptive.

Lacking evaluative information, the most that can be done at this point is to describe the basic characteristics of various textbook series and to list criteria to be used in selecting textbooks.

Basic Characteristics of Social Studies Textbooks

1. All textbook series are claimed to deal with the development of the cognitive, the affective, and skills areas. Yet programs developed in the '60s were concerned mainly with the cognitive area and with developing intellectual skills. Values, value clarification, and social skills were neglected. In subsequent revisions these elements were incorporated, but not as successfully in all of them as in some of the more contemporary series.

2. In the '70s, with their emphasis on developing decision-making abilities, textbooks address issues, but still the development of concepts and generalizations dominates most. Many issues are controversial, and textbook publishers prefer to omit them to satisfy a variety of pressure groups. Decision making is a broad creative ability, but recent attention to the "basics" and to accountability has promoted a narrower, mechanical form of decision making within specific social contexts. For instance, it is now often considered important for children to learn how to balance a checkbook, find a job, or deal with the law.

3. There is considerable emphasis on map skills, which begin to be taught as early as kindergarten.

4. The content of all textbook series is derived from basic concepts, generalizations, and issues as defined by the social science disciplines. Most teacher's guides outline the concepts, generalizations, and selected basic questions for each level of the series. Again, the more contemporary programs give more attention to the issues.

5. All programs are interdisciplinary or multidisciplinary. This characteristic is now being challenged. With the return to "the basics," some would like to see the old social studies reconstituted as history and geography. Indeed, Ginn and Company has already reprinted an old series

A Comparative Chart of Five of the Most Popular Textbook Series on the Basis of the Areas of Study for Each Level

Recommended Grade Level	Concepts and Inquiry (Allyn and Bacon)	Field Social Studies (Addison-Wesley)	Holt Databank (Holt, Rinehart & Winston)	Taba Program (Addison-Wesley)	Concepts and Values (Harcourt Brace Jovanovich)
K	Learning About the World; Children in Other Lands		Inquiring About Myself	Amek's Family of Bali	Children interact with their physical and social environment.
1	Our Country; Explorers and Discoverers	Working, Playing, Learning	Inquiring About People	People in Families	Responsibility for people and their environment—through adaptive behavior of the individual within the group
2	Communities at Home and Abroad; American Communities	People, Places, Products	Inquiring About Communities	People in Neighborhoods	Responsibility for people and their environment—through adaptive behavior of the basic group.
3	The Making of Our America; The Metropolitan Communities	Towns and Cities	Inquiring About Cities	People in Communities	Responsibility for people and their environment—through adaptive patterns of the larger group.
4	Agriculture: People and the Land; Industry: People and the Machine; the Indian Subcontinent	Regions Around the World	Inquiring About Cultures	People in States	Responsibility for people and their environment—through adaptive patterns of behavior.

Recommended Grade Level	Concepts and Inquiry (Allyn and Bacon)	Field Social Studies (Addison-Wesley)	Holt Databank (Holt, Rinehart & Winston)	Taba Program (Addison-Wesley)	Concepts and Values (Harcourt Brace Jovanovich)
5	Ancient Civilization; Four World Views; Greek and Roman Civilization; Medieval Civilization; Lands of the Middle East	America: In Space and Time	Inquiring About American History	People in America	Responsibility for people and their environment—through cultural patterns of behavior.
6	The Age of Western Expansion; New World and Eurasian Cultures; The Challenge of Change; The Interaction of Cultures; Lands of Latin America	The Human Adventure	Inquiring About Technology	People in Change	Responsibility for people and their environment—through development of systems of behavior.

developed by Ernest W. Tiegs and Fay Adams; other companies are con-templating similar ventures.

6. The textbook series make an effort to represent our society as it is. Its multi-ethnicity is now acknowledged in all textbooks. Although this was often done in an artificial way in the 1960s, in the '70s the minorities, including women, are given genuine recognition. Few publishers release textbooks these days unless they have been scrutinized and approved by scholars committed to the causes of the various minority groups.

7. Current textbooks provide for a world-view, with more emphasis than hitherto on the non-Western world. The expanding horizons ap-proach, which confined primary children to the geographic boundaries of the local community, is no longer considered valid. In some programs chil-dren begin to study about distant places as early as kindergarten.

8. Most programs are largely similar in scope and sequence. The family and community studies are dealt with in the primary grades, cul-tural geography in the fourth grade, the United States and the rest of the world in the fifth and sixth grades. The programs that deviate most are *Concepts and Inquiry* (Allyn and Bacon) and *Windows on Our World* (Houghton Mifflin), the first using an historical approach, the second em-phasizing the development of process objectives, through content that comes from all social and behavioral sciences and defies the traditional topics.

9. All series are claimed to match vocabulary to the children's read-ing level. Allyn and Bacon call their latest edition "learner-verified," while Macmillan provides special materials for both slow and more advanced learners. Nevertheless, readability remains a big problem—most social studies textbooks are too difficult for the children.

10. The inquiry method is advocated by most if not all series. In-quiry, however, is defined in many different ways, and teachers must clearly define inquiry for themselves to determine how well a textbook series matches their needs. Moreover, because many teachers find it difficult to use an inquiry-oriented series (Holt Databank, for example), most series try to strike a balance between inquiry and the expository approach.

11. All series provide a variety of teaching aids to supplement the text. (See the chart on page 229.)

12. Recently some textbook series have been accompanied by in-struments of formative and summative evaluation. As the chart shows, not all programs have tests, and those that do concentrate mainly on grades three through six. *Concepts and Inquiry* (Allyn and Bacon) and *Windows on Our World* (Houghton Mifflin) are the only two programs that have tests for grades one and two; *Concepts and Inquiry* includes a test for kindergarten as well.

13. Most of the current textbook series favor use of a specific teach-ing strategy, and they are packaged in a way that makes them more diffi-

Materials	Concepts and Inquiry (Allyn & Bacon)	Field Social Studies (Addison-Wesley)	Holt Databank (Holt, Rinehart & Winston)	Taba Program (Addison-Wesley)	Concepts & Values (Harcourt Brace Jovanovich)	Contemporary Social Science (Silver Burdett)	Focus on Active Learning (Macmillan)	Our Working World (SRA)	Windows on Our World (Houghton Mifflin)
Kindergarten program	X		X	X	X	X			X
Child's text	X	X	X	X	X	X	X	X	X
Teacher's edition or guides	X	X	X	X	X	X	X	X	X
Activity book or sheets		X		X (3–5)					
Tests	X (K–6)	X (3–6)	X (3–6)	X (3–6)	X (3–6)	X (3–6)	X (3–6)	X	X
Sound filmstrips	X				X				X (1–6)
Tapes				X	X	X		X	
Records				X	X	X		X	
Data comix			X						
Data foldouts			X						
Data masters			X	X (tests)		X	X	X	
Data cards			X						
Games and simulation	X		X				X		X
16mm Films			X						X
Posters	X								
Enrichment booklets	X					X			
Filmstrips	X							X	X
Vocabulary exercises	X								
Overhead visuals							X		X
Student record form							X		
Reading provisions for slow and advanced readers							X		
Individualized learning packages							X		

* Prepared from publishers' 1976 and 1977 catalogues.

cult to implement than the traditional descriptive textbooks with questions at the end of the chapter. As a result, teachers must adapt themselves to the new series. In fact, some programs during the 1960s (the Taba Program and *Man: A Course of Study*) were not made available to a district unless the teachers were first specifically trained to use their materials properly. This need still exists: Before teachers can use a current series, they need to understand, for example, such concepts as generalizations, the conceptual approach, inquiry, the valuing process, and so on. They should also be able to use the various media in ways that help children relate what they learn with their own experiences and to develop their self-concepts and abilities.

Criteria for Selecting Textbooks

If textbook series have improved over what they once were, some nevertheless are better than others. Because no authoritative evaluative information is available, school administrators, and especially teachers, must decide on their own which materials to use. Following are three sets of criteria that could be useful in selecting textbooks.

The first set of criteria, proposed for the '70s by Arthur Nichols and Anna Ochoa, emphasizes the importance of knowledge and the intellectual component of the program:

I. The Knowledge Component
   A. Social Issues: Does the knowledge presented in the textbook support the understanding of complex and persistent social issues?
   B. Interdisciplinary, Conceptual Organization: Does the textbook emphasize conceptually organized knowledge from many disciplines and fields of study?
   C. Recency: Does the knowledge presented reflect the most recent scholarly findings?
   D. Bias: Is the information in the textbook objectively presented?
II. The Intellectual Component
   A. Analytic Mode: Can the textbook serve as the basis for inquiry?
   B. Higher-Level Questions: Do the questions presented in the textbook support the use of intellectual processes above the memory level?
   C. Decision-Making: Can the textbook function as a basis for decision-making?
   D. Establishing a Direct Relationship with the Learner: Does the textbook consistently demonstrate the relationship between the knowledge presented and the immediate life-space of the learner? [11]

Another, more-comprehensive, set of criteria was published in 1973, by Barbara Capron, Cheryl Charles, and Stanley Kleiman:

1. Does the textbook have a clear statement of rationale and clearly state objectives which are consistent with the rationale?
2. Do the objectives span the range of cognitive and affective taxonomies, or do they, for example, stress low-level cognitive skills such as recognition and factual data?
3. Does the textbook reflect a recognition of individual differences in students' learning style? Does it include a wide range of alternatives for individualization of instruction as an integral part of the book and/or its support materials?
4. Does the textbook incorporate means for students to acquire and use inquiry skills?
5. Is the content based upon fundamental concepts of the social science disciplines?
6. Does the content emphasize the values implications, both individual and societal, of social problems?
7. Does the content focus on issues and problems of concern to students and does it do so in an interesting and stimulating way?
8. Is the textbook accompanied by multimedia resources for both teachers and students? A teacher's guide? Filmstrips? Instructional games? Readings from primary sources? Tapes? Artifacts?
9. Is the wider community suggested as a resource for student learning and involved as a focus of study?
10. Are evaluation data on the use of the textbook available to the general public? [12]

A third set of criteria was developed by a group of teachers representing the teachers' association of a large school district in the Northwest. Dissatisfied with the quality of social studies textbooks adopted by the school administration, the teachers suggested that all adopted textbooks be evaluated on the basis of the following criteria:

I. Content
    1. Are the major purposes of the content clearly stated in terms of pupil behavior, realistically attainable, and consistent with the philosophy of the school district?
    2. Is the content designed to serve students of particular ethnic groups, and also to acquaint others with the history of various ethnic groups?
    3. Does the content show evidence of providing for balance in its attention to cognitive, affective, and skills objectives?
    4. Does the content provide for sequential and systematic development of concepts and skills that are believed to be important?
    5. Are the criteria for the selection of substantial content clearly specified?
    6. Is the content of instruction relevant to the lives of the pupils?
    7. Is the scope of the content realistic in terms of the contemporary world and the background of today's pupils?

8. Are the learning activities and instructional resources consistent with the stated purposes of content?

9. Does the content provide adequately for differentiated instruction?

10. Is the content one that teachers can understand and be able to implement?

11. Are the curriculum documents sufficiently structured to provide the teacher with direction, yet flexible enough to allow teacher-pupil initiative and creativity?

12. Is it possible to evaluate the content in order to establish the extent to which major purposes have been achieved?

13. Is the vocabulary too difficult for the reading ability of the average pupil?

14. Do content and methodology vary enough to maintain motivation and interest?

II. Format

1. How durable are texts and other materials of a series?

2. Is the print easily readable?

3. Consider the accuracy, currentness, and ease of use, organization and attractiveness of
   a. Maps
   b. Illustrations
   c. Charts and Graphs
   d. Index
   e. Table of Contents
   f. Reference Tables
   g. Glossary
   h. Pupil Bibliography
   i. Filmstrips
   j. Records

III. Remarks

1. Please elaborate or qualify any checked items.

2. Please include other criteria that you consider important.[13]

OTHER READING MATERIALS

In the various projects, especially the textbooks, reading materials are systematically organized to teach social studies in a particular way. A wide variety of other types of reading materials can enrich the teaching of social studies. About these materials three questions must be asked:

1. What is the most effective way to use them?

2. What reading materials are available and how can the teacher locate them?

3. What skills must the children develop to benefit from them?

The method of using reading materials is dictated by the method of teaching advocated throughout this book and summarized as follows:

1. The teacher selects a basic area of study that will pervade the year's work and specifies five or six topics for which units of teaching are then designed.
2. For each topic, the concepts, generalizations, and issues to be taught are identified.
3. The concepts, generalizations, and issues are translated into specific behaviors to be developed in the children.
4. Content problems are formulated, the solutions of which will lead to realizing the objectives.
5. The teacher and the children plan a variety of activities, or learning experiences, through which the children will find solutions to the problems.

The unit method, as explained in Chapter 6, reflects the steps outlined above. The unit title signifies the area of study. The instructional objectives are the specific behaviors to which concepts, generalizations, and issues have been reduced. The problems are formulated by converting the content objectives into basic questions. As a final step in preparing a unit, the teacher designs the learning activities, for which a variety of resources may be used. Directing the youngsters to various reading materials provides them with one type of learning activity.

Teachers use reading materials to serve a variety of functions, such as:

1. To motivate the children toward the study of a topic. Many teachers have an area in which they display books before undertaking the study of a topic. The children become interested in these books, browse through them, and are stimulated to raise questions.
2. To find specific information such as dates, names, and locations.
3. To enable the children to expand on a particular concept.
4. To obtain many points of view on an issue.
5. To collect information to write a report or to prepare a skit.
6. To study and analyze a specific situation described in a written communication.

Reading-material assignments should follow several guidelines:

1. Different children have different reading abilities. Reading materials should cover a wide range of difficulty.
2. Some children can benefit more from picture books and books with colorful illustrations.

3. The teacher should check the load of new words and help the children with the most difficult ones.

4. Although the materials vary to reflect children's differences, the overall objectives do not have to vary. All children should feel that they are members of the same class and are all working toward the same goals.

5. Reading should be done in such a way and context as to be pleasurable and not a chore.

What Reading Materials Are Available and How Can the Teacher Locate Them?

A vast amount of reading materials is available. Many have to be purchased, while others reach the classroom unsolicited. The teacher's choices must fit budgetary limitations and the children's abilities, and should exclude propaganda materials with no educational value. A number of references, sources, and books can help the teacher locate and select reading materials:

1. *Reference materials*

   Facts on File, Inc., recently published a brochure, "A Student's Guide to Library Reference Materials," in which the following reading references or reference materials are recommended:

   a. General information (historical and contemporary)

      The Reader's Guide to Periodical Literature

      The Social Sciences and Humanities Index

      The Art Index

      The Education Index

      Encyclopaedia Britannica

      Britannica Junior Encyclopaedia

      Encyclopedia Americana

      Compton's Encyclopedia

      Collier's Encyclopedia

      The World Book Encyclopedia

      The Book of Knowledge

   b. Resources for facts

      The World Almanac

      Information Please Almanac

      The Reader's Digest Almanac

      The Canadian Almanac and Directory for the Year . . .

      Facts on File Yearbooks

      News Dictionary

      The Britannica Book of the Year

      The United Nations Yearbook

      The Statistical Abstract of the United States

3. Magazines and newspa...
   a. *Children's Diges*... Bergenfield, N.J.
   b. *Highlights for Ch*...
   c. *Junior Scholasti*... Englewood Cliffs...
   d. *National Geogra*... Bulletin, 17th an...
   e. *Sesame Street M*...
   f. *The Weewish Tr*... People, America... Avenue, San Fra...
   g. All adult magaz... *Geographic*, and... teaching social...

4. Sources of trade books
   a. *Children's Catal*... issues combined
   b. *Books for Young*... Geographic. (Co... studies topics.)
   c. *Books for Young*... Inc. (Annual cat...
   d. *Dell Paperbacks*... Publishing Co. ... listed that are...
   e. *Messner Books*... Messner and Si... with books appr...
   f. *Pleasure Readi*... (About 40 titles...
   g. "Notable Childr... *Social Educatio*... journal of the... are annotated a... classified into t... next. For exam... American Herita... Native American... and Social Just... Social Justice;... Houses, Cities,... Caribbean; Wor... Areas: Middle... World Areas: E... The April 1976... Ancient and Me... Contemporary...

...ve Americans; Understanding Oneself and ...rld Areas; and World of Work.

...on publishes special features on specific ...ed trade books and other resources are listed ...example, the February 1971 issue deals with ...ulum." Among the articles is an annotated ...n, Folklore, Poetry: Three Routes to Africa."

... deals with "Teaching About Ancient ... articles is "Sources and Resources for ...ient Greece."

...*Education*, the teacher may find recommended ...n such teachers' magazines as *Teacher*, ...*ing*.

..."social studies reading skills" seems mis-...kills needed in social studies are no dif-...erstand any other written communication. ...ent in social studies are highly correlated. ...ditionally taught in North America," June ... out, "reading has always been the essen-...students. . . . A major reason for failure ...(ing ability of students." [14]

...eading skills must be emphasized, because ...n social studies than in other content areas ...tudies deals mostly with conflicts, authors ...color their writings with their own opin-...ident should be able to evaluate reading ...ts.

...ocial studies could be classified in three ...eading information; (2) understanding it;

Such skills would include:

...eral idea about the content of a written ...specific information.

...rms of knowing what the holdings of a ...use the card catalog as well as the

The use of the table of contents and indexes are simple skills that require practice. Like all skills, they do not develop through lecturing about them. Practice needs to be meaningful, as in the following example: Quite often teachers explain the table of contents in the first grade by making a book of the experience charts to which they attach a table with all the titles of the charts.

Practice in using tables of contents and indexes introduces the children to the skill of skimming. In skimming a text, the reader is aided by subheadings, pictures, illustrations, maps, tables, graphs, diagrams, and charts. In some books or other written communications, summaries help give a general overview.

Skimming helps children develop their ability to make inferences from a few clues. It is a difficult skill to master, and children should be closely guided in developing it. One teacher had her students practice skimming by playing a guessing game. She gave them a book and asked them to suggest clues as to its content by skimming. She wrote these clues on the blackboard. The children were then asked to guess from these clues what the book was about. After all guesses were recorded, the children were asked to read the book and decide which guess was most nearly correct.

Another important skill in locating information is using the library, which first requires an enthusiasm for books, something often transferred from the teacher to the children. Only if the teacher uses a variety of reading resources available in the library will children see the value of the library. The teacher planning a unit or lesson should have read much of the locally available related materials. Only then will students be successfully directed to reading beyond the textbook.

Some teachers, trying to be progressive, have the children write reports on various topics, but give them no directions as to resources. From the only encyclopedia that happens to be available, the children then copy statements that they do not understand. The teacher who knows not only the holdings on various topics but also their levels of difficulty will be able to distribute reading materials properly.

In the beginning stages of the children's development, teachers should not send them to the library to find materials on their own. Not knowing the procedures, they might become frustrated and give up forever. Whenever children need materials, take them by the hand and go through the procedure together. Make sure the use of the library is taught within the context of problem solving situations. Avoid making it an academic exercise.

The last skill in locating information is taking notes to easily relocate information. From most reading not done entirely for pleasure, information gained is usually put to some later use; notes obviate the need to re-

locate it. Some pitfalls should be avoided in note taking: Some people tend to take too many notes while others take too few. The first thing to remember is the purpose of the reading: If done to locate specific information, notes should be taken only on that information. But if the child is interested in an entire written communication, all of its basic elements must be noted. To do so, the child must be able to discover its main and subordinate ideas. More about this is presented in the following section.

UNDERSTANDING READING INFORMATION   Such skills would include:

1. Attacking new words.
2. Discovering the organization of ideas.
3. Seeing relationships.
4. Making inferences.

Many social studies concepts are intangible and therefore difficult. Knowing the meaning of one such concept could often be the key to understanding an entire passage. It is therefore imperative that children know how to attack new words through clues, context, and other means. Here the teacher could correlate the teaching of reading skills—another subject —with social studies.

Another reading skill is discovering the structure of the author's ideas. The children should get practice in identifying the overall theme of the book, the main idea and the subordinate ideas in each section, chapter, and paragraph. By so doing, they become able to reduce a written communication to a skeletal outline.

Discovering the structure of reading information leads to another skill: seeing relationships. A child reading a book about a boat and able to describe the bridge and the engine room in detail has not gone very far. The child must see the *relationship* between the two. When children first begin to talk, "why" is always on the tip of their tongues. What happens to them after they go to school? Teachers should encourage the children to continue asking "why" and should provide situations for doing so.

One relationship children should be able to discover is cause and effect. Once they learn that drought in Kansas, for example, causes reduced grain production, they should be able to predict and explain what will happen if India had a drought. Seeing cause and effect relationships enables the youngsters to make inferences.

CRITICALLY EVALUATING READING INFORMATION   Such skills would include:

1. Distinguishing between fact and opinion.
2. Recognizing propaganda.
3. Discovering contradictions and examining their causes.
4. Detecting the authors' biases.

It used to be that whatever was put in print was considered to be the final word. This is no longer so, and the children should realize it. They must be able to read critically.

The most practical starting place for teaching how fact and opinion differ is the local newspaper. Point out how reports on actual events and the views expressed on the editorial page differ. Illustrate that whereas almost everyone agrees on the facts, not everyone shares the same opinion. Children should understand that opinions must be intelligent statements based on facts. Also, children should favor the holding of opinions and should be encouraged to express their own on issues. Courage and ability to express one's opinion develop the ability to formulate hypotheses.

Another skill to be developed in children is recognizing propaganda. Most people think of all propaganda as distortion. This is not necessarily correct. The common feature of all propaganda is the intent to convince. There is nothing wrong with propaganda that does so without distorting reality. Only when the truth is twisted in an effort to convince does propaganda become objectionable.

Unfortunately, much untrue propaganda reaches the children and they should be taught how to protect themselves from it. But evaluating reading materials by sound criteria and comparing their content with authentic resources is a demanding intellectual activity.

The children's ability to read critically will be enhanced by making them sensitive to contradictions within a written communication or between two or more of them on the same subject. Among the causes for such contradictions, the author's bias or confusion is probably most common.

Critical-reading skills do not develop overnight. Nor are they fully developed when students leave elementary school. Yet a conscious effort to develop them should be made as early as possible. Children's understanding of their social environment and their self-development depend much on what they read and how. (For further insights on reading and the social studies, see writings by Harold Herber, John Lunstrum, and Ralph Preston,[15] and the January 1978 issue of *Social Education*.)

The Problem of Readability

The three sets of criteria for selecting textbooks apply for the most part to selecting other types of materials as well. Readability is a crucial criterion, and a couple of methods can help determine the reading level of given material.

One method is the *cloze procedure*. Words are systematically deleted from representative passages of specified lengths. The student's task is to replace them. Replacement of less than 44 percent of the deleted words indicates a *frustrational* level (some use 40 percent or less); 44–57 percent would indicate an *instructional* level; and 57 percent or more would indicate an *independent* level, which is the highest level to be attained.[16] The cloze procedure is applied by the following steps:

1. Select a passage of at least 250 words from what you plan to use for instruction. Try to find a passage that is relatively complete in itself.
2. Delete every fifth word (but do not delete proper nouns).
3. Type the passage, with uniform-length blanks for those words deleted.
4. Ask students to write in the blanks what they think the words should be. This task is not timed.
5. Score the students' performance by counting correct every word that is exactly the same as the original text. While exact percentages vary, usually better than 40 percent correct establishes an instructional reading level.

Another method of determining readability is the so-called Fry's Readability Graph (as shown on page 242).[17] The steps are:

1. Select three 100-word passages from the reading material you plan to use in social studies.

2. Count the total number of sentences in each sample (estimate to the nearest tenth of a sentence). Average these three numbers by summing them and dividing by three.

3. Count the total number of syllables in each sample. Average these three numbers by summing them and dividing by three. (A syllable equals a vowel sound: cat—1, blackbird—2, example—3, polio—3, fooled—1, through—1, continental—4, bottle—2.)

4. On the graph (see below), plot the average number of sentences and the average number of syllables per hundred words. Their point of intersection indicates the approximate grade difficulty of the material.

**Fry's Readability Graph—
Extended Through Preprimer Level
(Average number of syllables per 100 words)**

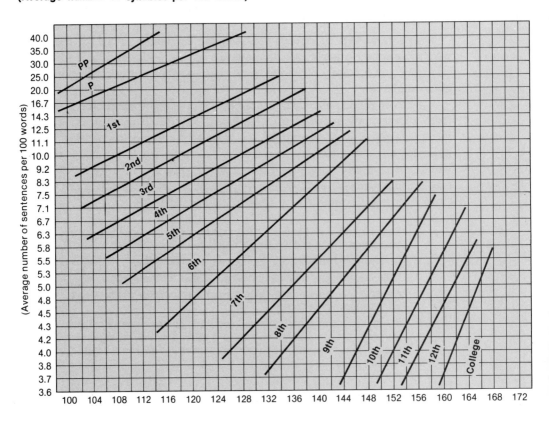

For example:

Samples	# Sentences	# Syllables
Sample #1	8	112
Sample #2	11	128
Sample #3	10	116
Average	9.7	118.7

Readability = Third grade (see graph).

SUMMARY

The change in social studies from a descriptive to a decision-making approach was accomplished through the projects of the 1960s and '70s that influenced the textbooks now in use throughout the country. The most important projects were: (1) Project Social Studies of the University of Minnesota, (2) The Taba Social Studies Curriculum Project, (3) The Greater Cleveland Social Science Program, (4) The Elkhart, Indiana, Experiment in Economic Education, (5) Man: A Course of Study, (6) The Social Science Laboratory Units, (7) The Museum Materials and Activities for Teachers and Children, (8) The Anthropology Curriculum Project, and (9) The Elementary Economics Project.

Among the major textbook series influenced by the projects are: (1) *Concepts and Inquiry* (Allyn and Bacon), (2) *Field Social Studies Program* (Addison-Wesley), (3) *Holt Databank* (Holt, Rinehart and Winston), (4) *Taba Program in Social Science* (Addison-Wesley), (5) *The Social Sciences: Concepts and Values* (Harcourt Brace Jovanovich), (6) *Contemporary Social Science Curriculum* (Silver-Burdett), (7) *Focus on Active Learning* (Macmillan), (8) *Our Working World* (Science Research Associates), and (9) *Windows on Our World* (Houghton Mifflin). All have common characteristics, identified in this chapter, and differences. Criteria are provided to help teachers and administrators make sound selections among texts.

Other reading materials are important as well, requiring that teachers be guided by three questions: (1) What is the most effective way to use reading materials? (2) What reading materials are available and how can the teacher locate them? and (3) What skills do the children need to benefit from reading materials? Finally, the problem of readability is emphasized and ways for quantifying it described.

ACTIVITIES

1. Examine at least one of the major social studies curriculum projects of the '60s. Pay special attention to *Man: A Course of Study*. How different is the program advocated by these projects from the social studies program you experienced as an elementary school student? Discuss your impressions.

2. If the materials are available in your library, compare the original version of a project with a recent edition of a textbook series based on it. What changes do you notice? What might have prompted them?

3. Use one of the sets of criteria to evaluate a recently published textbook series.

4. Using the topics in the scope and sequence suggested in Chapter 3, search the last five issues of *Social Education, Instructor, Learning, Teacher,* and other sources to compile a list of reading materials relevant to those topics. The class may be divided into grade levels so that lists for all elementary grades are compiled.

5. Survey a local school library and identify the various types of materials there. Are the materials adequate for the social studies program? Are there any important omissions?

6. By one of the two methods suggested in the chapter, determine the readability level of a textbook or some other publication.

NOTES

1. *The Family of Man: A Social Studies Program* (Newton, Mass.: Selective Educational Equipment, Inc., 1975), p. 1.

2. Hilda Taba, *Teacher's Handbook for Elementary Social Studies* (Reading, Mass.: Addison-Wesley, 1969 or 1972 edition).

3. Jerome Bruner, *The Process of Education* (New York: Vintage Books, 1969).

4. Peter B. Dow, "MACOS Revisited: A Commentary of the Most Frequently Asked Questions About 'Man: A Course of Study,'" *Social Education,* 39 (October 1975), 394.

5. Peter B. Dow, "MACOS: The Study of Human Behavior as One Road to Survival," *Phi Delta Kappan,* 57 (October 1975), 80.

6. George Weber, "The Case Against *Man: A Course of Study," Phi Delta Kappan,* 57 (October 1975), 82.

7. John B. Conlan, "MACOS: The Push for a Uniform National Curriculum," *Social Education,* 39 (October 1975), 388.

8. Dow, "MACOS: The Study of Human Behavior," p. 80.

9. Irving Morrissett, "CIN (Curriculum Information Network). First Report: Evaluations of Curriculum Materials," *Social Education,* 37 (November 1973), 665, 667; Irving Morrissett, "CIN (Curriculum Information Network). Third Report: Ratings of 24 Social Studies Materials," *Social Education,* 39 (February 1975), 96–99.

10. Morrissett, "Third Report," p. 96.

11. Arthur S. Nichols and Anna Ochoa, "Elementary Textbooks for Elementary Social Studies: Criteria for the 'Seventies," *Social Education,* 35 (March 1971), 291–92.

12. Barbara Capron, Cheryl Charles, and Stanley Kleiman, "Curriculum Reform and Social Studies Textbooks," *Social Education,* 37 (April 1973), 284–85.

13. "Seattle Alliance of Educators Elementary Social Studies Fact-Finding Report," *STA* (Seattle Teachers' Association) *News* (December 1974), 11.

14. June R. Chapin and Richard E. Gross, *Teaching Social Studies Skills* (Boston: Little, Brown, 1973), p. 23.

15. Harold L. Herber, "Reading in the Social Studies: Implications for Teaching and Research," in James L. Laffey, ed., *Reading in the Content Areas* (Newark, N.J.: International Reading Association, 1972); John P. Lunstrum, "Reading in Social Studies: A Preliminary Analysis of Recent Research," *Social Education,* 40 (January 1976), 10–18; Ralph C. Preston, ed., *A New Look at Reading in the Social Studies* (Newark, N.J.: International Reading Association, 1969).

16. John Bormuth, "The Cloze Readability Procedure," *Elementary English*, 45 (April 1968), 429–36.

17. Adapted from a graph by Edward Fry; reported by G. H. Maginnis in "The Readability Graph and Informal Reading Inventories," *The Reading Teacher*, 22 (March 1969), 516. By permission of the International Reading Association.

Studying this chapter will enable the reader to:

1. define community resources.
2. articulate the reasons why community resources are valuable in the teaching–learning process.
3. identify specific community resources and activities that are appropriate at the various grade levels.
4. be convinced of the need to get to know the community in which teaching is done or planned to be done.
5. identify some ways in which the teacher can study the local community.
6. become familiar with several models for systematically using the local community in the teaching–learning process.
7. list the essential tasks in planning and carrying out a field trip.
8. define current events and articulate their importance in social studies.
9. view current events as a resource in the teaching of a structured social studies program and explain why.
10. list the major commercial programs for dealing with current events.
11. identify ways to organize and deal with current events.
12. locate useful government publications to provide background information on current events.

COMMUNITY RESOURCES
AND CURRENT EVENTS

This chapter continues the consideration of resources useful in the teaching–learning process. Community resources and current events are considered. Though at times current events are a community resource for the teacher, they usually involve more than the local community. In some elementary schools current events have replaced the entire social studies program. Several commercial programs have been developed to help the teacher make use of current events, but none to help apply community resources; these are left mainly to the discretion and abilities of the teacher. For these reasons, community resources and current events are treated separately in this chapter.

COMMUNITY RESOURCES

Community resources include everything in the community that can be used to illustrate a concept, generalization, value, or human conflict. Such resources include every community situation in which the children apply an intellectual or social skill and every experience that allows them to express their feelings and clarify their values.

The Significance of Community Resources

There are four main reasons why community resources are valuable:

1. Teaching and learning become relevant, because they are conducted through the children's experiences.
2. The community provides excellent opportunities for social action and for the development of intellectual and social skills.
3. The school and the community grow closer together.
4. The children learn more about the community, become involved in its affairs, and therefore may become better citizens than otherwise.

Educational theorists have long believed that using the children's experiences and the familiar as stepping stones to the unfamiliar is a sound and powerful approach—definitely more so than the more convenient reliance on one textbook. This point has been elaborated on throughout this book and the following model helps to summarize it: [1]

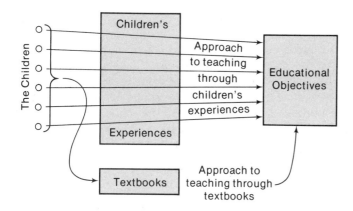

Using the children's experiences makes social studies relevant and allows the individualization of instruction. Miller Collings asserts: "Educators increasingly recognize the principle that schools need contact with the realities of life; that curricula are most effective when closely related to the community they serve; and that boys and girls learn best when dealing with direct, concrete experience."[2] If, on the other hand, one textbook is used as the main approach to learning, children are forced to conform to a single method and are led toward the objectives by a long, often tiresome way through unfamiliar ground.

The significance of community resources became indisputably clear to me during the development of social studies programs for schools attended mostly by American Indian children. Formerly, Navajo children studied about the family, but rarely were Navajo families used as a reference point. While they studied the relationship between human beings and the land, their relationships with their own tribal land were ignored. Northwest Indians used to study principles of government, but their own tribal government was never thought of highly enough to be used as an example. Consequently social studies was an uninspiring subject for these children.

This changed when the concept of family was studied by starting with their own families. Excitement was evident among children and parents alike, when the children were guided to explore the local tribal government system to determine, among other things, the extent to which it governed in response to people's wishes and values. The children on a particular reservation felt pride in the achievements of their community after learning economic concepts through the local resource-development programs sponsored by the tribe. The community is indeed the best laboratory for the teaching of social studies; virtually every concept or generalization regarding human relationships can be taught through reference to it.

It is well established that social studies ought to teach more than concepts and generalizations; students must also deal with immediate, compelling issues and learn how to make decisions and resolve conflict. The local community provides many opportunities for the kind of involvement

249

required. Whether to understand an issue or to reach or implement a decision, the children seek and analyze information, make predictions, develop commitments, and act. Social action must come to be valued by the children through their guided involvement in the affairs of the community.

The possibility of drawing parents closer to the school and encouraging them to participate actively in their children's education is another vital by-product of using community resources. In these days of accountability and of mistrust of the schools, recruitment of the public's support can be rewarding.

Finally, we live in an age of indifference and alienation. The poor voting record of 18-year-olds seems to be an indication that schools have failed to inspire young people to participate in the affairs of society. Could this failure be due to the schools' overwhelming reliance on books and other abstract methods and neglect of opportunities for the children to apply the knowledge they acquire? Making the community a laboratory for practicing intellectual and social skills from an early age might change the picture. The children will learn more about the community—its problems as well as its aspirations. The children will become accustomed to problems, and will develop skills necessary to solving, or at least attempting to solve them. More important, they will begin to identify with their community and develop pride in it. This is especially important where community spirit is now low.

Summarizing the contributions of community resources to learning, Collings outlined the following:

1. In-school work becomes more meaningful because of out-of-school experiences. Concrete situations form bases from which to build new learning concepts.
2. There is general improvement in citizenship as students become aware that they are actually involved in meaningful learning experiences.
3. Students demonstrate greater proficiency in problem solving. Experiences in real situations such as selecting the appropriate visit, making arrangements, and carrying on the follow-up activities are actual living, not playing at living.
4. Groups show superior ability in getting along with others. Better human relations are demonstrated.
5. An increased interest in school is evident. Pupils are rarely absent on the day of a trip. General attitude is better.
6. Students are increasingly aware of the ability of many groups to contribute to the total community good.
7. Increased cooperation results in better understanding of the school and its problems on the part of the parents and others in the community.
8. Students acquire greater knowledge of the functions of civic and governmental agencies and the specific services of these agencies to the local community.

9. Students gain firsthand experiences in determining available job opportunities, necessary qualifications, working conditions, remuneration, existence of employee benefits, and retirement plans.

10. Students acquire the concept of giving something to their community through participation in appropriate volunteer service activities and membership in community organizations. They obtain enriched understandings of the possibilities within the community for profitable use of leisure time.[3]

The Variety of Community Resources

It is difficult to visualize the enormous variety of learning resources available in any community. Following is a list of community resources and learning activities adapted from a more specific list developed by two practicing teachers.[4] Resources and activities are classified according to the areas of study recommended in this book for each grade.

GRADE LEVEL: Kindergarten
AREA OF STUDY: Me and Others
RESOURCES AND ACTIVITIES IN THE COMMUNITY:

---

1. Children bring pictures of themselves for a bulletin board on "ME."
2. Mothers and fathers visit school and share what they do as a family.
3. Have foreign visitors or recent immigrants show pictures of children in other cultures and their activities. Share songs, games, stories, and dances from other cultures.
4. Take a trip to the local zoo or aquarium.
5. Visit the community park and discover the many things to do there.
6. Invite a police officer, firefighter, nurse, or other community helper to talk about safety for children. Note that these are jobs that parents do to earn money for families. Also, these are things children can do when they grow up.
7. Tour your own school. Meet all the helpers (principal, secretary, etc.) and learn about their jobs. Learn about the rules around the school.
8. Visit the local library. Find the children's books and show them who can help them to check out books.
9. Invite a puppetteer (if available) to do a puppet show in class.
10. Visit the children's theater (if available) and see a performance.
11. Have a grandmother or grandfather visit the class to describe a hobby and tell a story. Let the children sing a song or make a gift for these visitors.
12. Ride a city bus on one of your out-of-school activities.
13. Have the children bring collections or hobby activities to class. Have people from various hobby clubs come into class and show what they do.
14. Visit a farm and show the children as many activities as possible.

GRADE LEVEL: First
AREA OF STUDY: My Family and Other Families
RESOURCES AND ACTIVITIES IN THE COMMUNITY:

1. Have a newlywed couple visit the class to show wedding attire and pictures, and to tell about future plans—setting up a home, etc.

2. Have both parents of a student visit the class and as a family group have them talk about their recreation activities, work, responsibilities, problems and the way they solve them. Allow children to ask questions.

3. Invite a mother to bring a baby to class and show how she cares for its needs. Note how the baby is dependent on the older members of the family.

4. Invite fathers and mothers to come to class to describe their jobs and show things related to their jobs. Emphasize the necessity of work in order to earn money for the needs of the family.

5. Visit some parents in their places of work in the community.

6. Invite grandparents to tell about the kind of work they used to do. Note if any of those jobs no longer exist.

7. Have children bring animal babies and their parents to class and observe care of the young. Compare to human family.

8. Have visitors from different ethnic or cultural groups bring in special artifacts and share different family customs.

9. Organize the children to exchange visits between the various cultural groups represented in the class.

10. Take a walk through the school neighborhood and notice the different types and styles of homes, and, if possible, the types of families living in them. Discuss the similarities and differences.

11. If you live in a city, visit a rural family and notice the differences. Do the opposite if living in a rural area.

12. Visit a museum and compare family life in the past with family life in our day.

13. Take part in cultural activities in the community—especially those sponsored by various ethnic and cultural groups.

14. With the cooperation of the parents, organize the children to make exchange visits to various churches to which the children belong.

15. Invite children from various youth organizations, like Boy Scouts, Camp Fire Girls, Girl Scouts, 4-H Clubs, to describe and explain some of their activities.

GRADE LEVEL: Second
AREA OF STUDY: My Community and Other Communities
RESOURCES AND ACTIVITIES IN THE COMMUNITY:

1. Visit a local department store.

2. Visit local factories.

3. Visit a local fire station.

4. Visit a local police station.

5. Visit a local bank.

6. Visit a public utility plant.
7. Visit a public library.
8. Visit a local hospital.
9. Visit the local post office.
10. Invite various community service and professional people to visit class and share how their jobs help the community.
11. Visit local museums to study the history of the community.
12. Visit the local radio station, or a newspaper.
13. Invite people from different cultural groups to describe how they contribute to the community.
14. Have local writers, artists, or craft workers describe their contributions to the community.
15. Have old-timers share memories of the old days in your community.
16. Visit a nursing home to determine the advantages and disadvantages of the living conditions for the elderly.

GRADE LEVEL: Third
AREA OF STUDY: People Move In and Around the Cities
RESOURCES AND ACTIVITIES IN THE COMMUNITY:

1. Have children write or visit the chamber of commerce to acquire information about the city. Note the characteristics of the city as portrayed in the materials.
2. Take a bus trip through the various parts of the city—central business district, industrial area, ethnic neighborhoods, suburbs, etc. Discuss the differences.
3. Visit an industrial plant.
4. Visit the city hall.
5. Visit the municipal court.
6. Visit various transportation facilities—airport, ferry terminal, shipping company, trucking company, bus depot, railroad station, and others.
7. Visit TV stations.
8. Visit a high school and a local college or university.
9. Visit the weather station.
10. Visit parks and attend sports events.
11. Visit cultural centers such as theaters, art galleries, museums, etc.
12. Visit historical places.
13. Visit public markets.

GRADE LEVEL: Fourth
AREA OF STUDY: People Need the Earth
RESOURCES AND ACTIVITIES IN THE COMMUNITY:

1. Invite the local Audobon Society to send representatives to talk to your class about their activities and share their materials.
2. Visit special farms in the area to see how they use and treat the land.
3. Visit a fish hatchery (if available) or a game farm.

4. Invite the Sierra Club to talk to the class about their activities.

5. Visit an historical museum to study the use of the land in the past and compare with the present.

6. Visit a nearby forest or a state park.

7. If practical, visit a wildlife refuge.

8. Visit a highway construction site to observe the alteration of the land.

9. Visit a gravel pit.

10. Visit a dam and describe what the area was like before the dam was built.

11. Find some old pictures of newly inhabited areas and show and discuss the differences between then and now.

12. Have the children observe the sizes of store parking lots in the suburbs and in the central business district. Discuss the reasons for the differences.

13. Visit an irrigation system.

14. Bring to class and observe different types of soil.

15. Bring in samples of crops produced in the area and prepare an exhibit.

16. Go to the county or state fair and make a list of the products exhibited.

GRADE LEVEL: Fifth
AREA OF STUDY: Development of Our Nation
RESOURCES AND ACTIVITIES IN THE COMMUNITY:

1. Visit American Indian centers or reservations.

2. Visit old buildings.

3. Visit historical museums and museums of industry.

4. Invite representatives of historical associations to speak to the class.

5. Study the history of various industries in the community.

6. Trace the history of various monuments in the community.

7. Visit old churches and cemeteries.

8. Visit the headquarters of various benevolent associations.

9. Attend various calendar events of local significance.

10. Invite veterans of various wars to talk to the class.

11. Interview individuals who lived during the Great Depression.

12. Interview elderly immigrants.

13. Ask retired politicians to speak to the class.

GRADE LEVEL: Sixth
AREA OF STUDY: Interaction of World Cultures
RESOURCES AND ACTIVITIES IN THE COMMUNITY:

1. Visit the so-called international districts in your city and observe the presence of many subcultures.

2. Visit the airport and observe international arrivals and/or departures.

3. Locate the foreign consulates in your community or the nearest ones to your community and write for information on their countries.

4. Find out how many of the children in your class have relatives living in other countries.

5. Ask how many children have clothes made in other countries.

6. Find out how many children visited other countries and have them explain the reasons for their visits.

7. Visit a grocery store to determine how many products are imported.

8. Invite immigrants to talk about their "old countries."

9. Consult with a local freight or shipping company to find out what our country exports to other nations.

10. Invite former Peace Corps members to talk about their experiences.

11. Visit a travel agency and collect brochures that describe other countries.

12. Invite international students and/or scholars from a nearby college or university to speak to the class about their country.

13. Read books and view films on other countries found in the local library.

Get to Know the Community

The list above is only partial. Teachers must study their own community to become fully aware of what is available. But many teachers do not reside in the community in which they teach. In the big cities, especially in the poorer neighborhoods, many teachers make every effort to ignore their students' living conditions—and their values as well. Their teaching, too often based on a context different from the children's, fails to reach the children, who are then usually blamed for not learning.

All teachers—the commuters and the residents, those who identify with the social environment of the children and those who do not—must get to know thoroughly the community in which they teach. Every teacher must make a community survey to answer the following questions:

1. What are the people like in this community—their occupations, interests, recreations, attitudes, cultural and historical backgrounds, civic mindedness, conflicts and problems?

2. What are the basic social functions in the community like—government, recreation, transportation, communication, religious expression, food production and supply, attitude toward and provisions for health?

3. What are the community's history, important geographic features, and industries?

There are established techniques for surveying the community, such as interview, observation, and documentary analysis. A teacher may learn much about the community by taking walks around town, eating in restaurants, and riding buses; by attending business and social gatherings, scout meetings, and even various church services and functions; by visiting the local library and museums and finding out about their services to the community. Also, a teacher may obtain valuable information and materials by visiting the chamber of commerce and by interviewing various eminent or influential persons in the community. A good way to become more familiar with the children's neighborhoods and homes is to ride the school bus. Of course, students and parents are among the best avenues to insights about the community.

A teacher studying a community should develop a file of community resources. To assure the availability of adequate information on the community's educational resources, Collings advises that a 10-point system be used: [5]

1. Location
2. Telephone number
3. Contact person
4. Time to call
5. Length of visit
6. Number of students
7. Materials available
8. Services available
9. Trip outline
10. Dates of trips, other comments

School districts wishing to systematically develop comprehensive guides to community resources should consult those developed in three areas: the Boston metropolitan area; the Catskill area around Oneonta, New York; and South Bend, Indiana.

The Boston guide, funded by the U.S. Office of Education and developed under the direction of Alberta P. Sebolt of Sturbridge, Massachusetts, includes details on the various resources, criteria for selecting them, and practical suggestions on planning and evaluation.[6] The Catskill area guide, also funded by the U.S. Office of Education, and developed by the Catskill Area School Study Council of Oneonta, New York, is an extensive listing of resources in several counties in the state of New York.[7] The South Bend guide, a joint project of Indiana University at South Bend and the South Bend Community Corporation under the direction of Charles T. Duvall and Donald W. Truex, is distinctive in that the resources have been computerized to make them more accessible to teachers.[8] Also helpful in developing a guide or in using community resources are articles by J. Pope Dwyer, Joel Eastman, Bernard Kravitz, George Lindemer, and Ralph Cordier, which deal with the use of specific community resources.[9]

JoAnn Buggey recommends that the teacher not list only those community resources that can be used whenever convenient: "Community involvement in citizenship education must not be left to chance." [10] She favors total involvement and wants the teacher and the school, the students, and the parents and the community to work together on the basis of a three-stage model: [11]

STAGE I: Organization

---

    a. Identify the citizenship goals for the school/community.

    b. Clearly state objectives for each grade level or school division based on the goals identified for the school/community.

    c. List possible activities to meet the stated objectives for each grade level or school division.

STAGE II: Implementation

---

    a. Plan specific activities to meet the stated objectives for identified learners (time, place, key individuals, etc.)

    b. Provide experiences for learners to meet the stated objectives.

STAGE III: Evaluation

---

    a. Debriefing sessions should incorporate feedback from all concerned groups (teachers, students, parents).

    b. Further organization or continued implementation would be the result of these sessions.

Some activities generated by using the model are as follows:

1. Every Tuesday and Thursday Mrs. Stevens' first graders visited the residents of the J-H home for senior citizens to read books to each other and share stories and poems they had written. The objective was to learn to show concern for the well-being and dignity of others.

2. To teach children respect for others who are different from them, a kindergarten teacher and Mrs. Yakimoto, a parent, arranged that groups of six kindergarteners at a time would visit Mrs. Yakimoto's home and help her prepare an authentic Japanese meal. As they were preparing the meal, she shared many family traditions with them.

3. To help children learn to approach civic decisions rationally, Mr. Esteban's third graders organized to take a survey of the community regarding the installation of traffic lights at an intersection near the school. The class designed the survey and teams of students and adults went out to collect the data.

David Armstrong and Tom Savage propose another model for the use of community resources, a model based on the recognition that children have many stimulating and educational experiences simply by living in their community. "A successful community-focused social studies program for the middle grades depends on (1) a careful identification and categorization of *stimulus experiences* and (2) a clear explication of categories of *anticipated pupil learnings.*" [12] Armstrong and Savage identify three broad categories of stimulus experiences: (a) historical residues, (b) present interactional processes, and (c) likely future patterns. Likewise they divide anticipated pupil learnings into three areas of ability: (a) to make grounded generalizations, (b) to examine values (community and personal), and (c) to make decisions.

Armstrong and Savage advise that a teacher wanting to use the community to provide social learnings should first match appropriate stimulus experiences with anticipated pupil outcomes: "When a relationship between a specific stimulus experience and an anticipated pupil learning is made clear, planning for instruction is facilitated." [13] Stimulus experiences matched with pupil learning and augmented by appropriate questions are the basic elements of potentially successful instruction. Possible combinations of these three elements are given in table form on the next page.

Note that both the Buggey and Armstrong-Savage models begin with the determination of specific objectives. This step prevents the misusing of community resources simply to entertain or to pass the time.

A third approach to the effective use of community resources is presented in a series of articles that Arthur Ellis solicited and edited (published in *Social Education*) on the use of research techniques to obtain information about human beings. In one article, Ronald Wheeler and Kevin Kelly present the instructional implications of historical research:

> When the students start to consider family size at different intervals of time, they are beginning to grapple with precisely the same kinds of questions that professional historians are interested in. Questions like: Does family size change through generations? If so, why? What variables might affect change? An historian might go directly to published U.S. census reports in attempting to answer some of these questions, but in the classroom a more appropriate procedure would be for the teacher to have the students generate their own data. Together the teacher and students can construct a questionnaire to be taken home and completed by the students' parents and other members of their family. [14]

In another article Alan Hoffman reports that a group of children, wanting to find out what attitudes people hold today about women, constructed a survey. [15] On the left side of a sheet of paper were listed activities (cooking, teaching, making decisions, etc.) and traits (practical, intelligent, open-minded, etc.); on the right side were three columns in which respondents were to check whether each activity or trait was characteristic of men, or of women, or of both. The survey was then admin-

A Framework for Focus Questions in Community-Centered Middle-Grades Social Studies *

	Historical Residues	As Stimulus Materials Pupils Look at Present Interactional Processes	Likely Future Patterns
Make Grounded Generalizations	What has been left? What do residues tell us about what life used to be here? How could we check on the accuracy of the conclusions?	What is made here and sent out? What is brought into the community? What is your evidence? Where do people live and where do they work in the community? How do they get back and forth? How do you know? How do you account for any changes you see? How might we check on the accuracy of your explanation?	What is life in the community going to be like in 10 years? In 50 years? What specific things are happening now that lead you to predict what life will be like in the future? What changes that have not yet been observed must take place before your predicted future for the community can occur?
Examine Values	*Community Values:* What values of people who lived in this community in the past are suggested by remaining residues? *Personal Values:* How do you feel about life in the past in this community as it is suggested by remaining residues?	*Community Values:* What values, priorities are associated with present ways of life in this community? *Personal Values:* How do you feel about values, priorities reflected in present ways of life in this community?	*Community Values:* What values are reflected in the likely future of this community? *Personal Values:* How do you feel about values reflected in the likely future of this community?
Make Decisions	What do you think life in the community was really like in the past? Why did you reach that conclusion? What features of life deriving from this community's past should continue to be emphasized? Why? Were there some things that happened in the past that set undesirable precedents for the present and the future? Which ones and why?	What aspects of present life in this community most appeal to you? Why? What aspects of present life in this community do you find most distressing? Why? What aspects of life in this community are most in need of change? Why? How might you begin working with others to bring about changes you desire?	What kind of community would you like to live in? Why? What are the differences between the kind of community you would like to live in and this community? How might you begin to work with others to bring about the type of community here you would most like to live in?

* David E. Armstrong and Tom V. Savage, Jr., "A Framework for Utilizing the Community for Social Learning in Grades 4–6," *Social Education*, 40 (March 1976), 167. Reprinted with permission of N.C.S.S., David G. Armstrong, and Tom V. Savage, Jr.

istered in class and was sent home with the children to obtain the responses of parents, relatives, and friends.

In still another article Ellis and David Johnson describe how experimental research methods can be used to yield knowledge of a locality.[16] Finally, the late John Lee used descriptive research procedures to obtain information from the children's immediate environment.[17]

Planning a Field Trip

A section on community resources would not be complete without some suggestions on planning and carrying out field trips. (It should be emphasized, however, that undertaking expensive and difficult field trips is only one way to use community resources; there is a variety of potentially instructional community experiences that children can have on their own or with parents.) A successful class field trip involves many details demanding attention, which can be classified in three categories:

A. Planning the trip
   1. Visit the place alone, and study available literature.
   2. Find out who the guide is and discuss the objectives of the trip.
   3. Discuss the trip with the class and make sure they understand the purpose of the trip.
   4. Secure permission from school authorities.
   5. Arrange for transportation.
   6. Prepare permission slips and secure parents' signatures.
   7. Discuss the questions the trip may answer.
   8. Discuss and clarify standards of behavior while on the trip.
B. While on the trip
   1. Always keep the objectives of the trip in mind.
   2. Give the children some time to wander around.
   3. Answer their questions.
   4. Advise children to keep notes.
   5. Check to make sure you have all children when you arrive and before leaving.
C. Following the trip
   1. Have a discussion to find out whether the trip helped to achieve the objectives.
   2. Discuss other things the children have seen that were of interest.
   3. Send a letter of appreciation.
   4. Organize the children to prepare reports.
   5. Refer to the experiences and the reports whenever they appear to be relevant in the course of teaching.
   6. Help the children relate what they experienced with what they read.

For further information consult Edgar Bye's practical guide prepared for the "How to Do It Series" of the National Council for the Social Studies.[18]

CURRENT EVENTS

"Current events," "contemporary events," "current affairs," "contemporary affairs" are all used as synonyms in this book. They apply to what is happening in the community or what is happening elsewhere that influences conditions in the community. In this sense, current events are a form of community resources. The terms "world affairs" and "world events," also occasionally used to mean current events, are not advisable substitutes because they imply events with a worldwide scope that may be remote from the children's everyday experiences and thus may lack appeal. Of course, world affairs should not be ignored, especially if they in some way affect the local community.

The Value of Current Events

Current events are valuable for the same reasons that community resources are valuable: They make learning relevant and therefore easier; they bring the children closer to the community and provide opportunities for social action; they facilitate the development of a variety of citizenship skills and dispositions; and they make the following specific contributions:

1. They are a source for meaningful issues.
2. They bring textbook materials up to date.
3. They convey the changing nature of society as well as the persistence of some issues.
4. They enhance the children's ability to judge and distinguish between fact and opinion.
5. They help children become knowledgeable about their world—a valuable characteristic of citizenship.

The first contribution listed above is a significant one in view of the dynamic nature of contemporary social studies and its emphasis on treatment of issues. Although the new social studies does not ignore the past, it also, unlike traditional social studies, deals with the present and attempts to make the children aware of the problems and controversies of today's society. There is no reason, for example, why the children should study past changes in the family structure but ignore its present problems and strains, which will determine the family's future structure.

Although contemporary textbook writers try to present the issues, such are the logistics of publishing that ordinarily textbooks are about two years behind the times. Attention to current events helps close that gap and enables children to deal with the most current and most relevant issues. Another problem with textbooks can be overcome by studying current events. As already noted, textbook publishers tend to submit to pressure groups and avoid controversial issues. Study of current events can thus include issues that are alive in a community but omitted from textbooks.

What may be considered old today was current yesterday, and what is current today will be old tomorrow. When children study current events they may compare today's newspapers or news magazines with older issues to note differences and discover trends toward change. They may also note that some issues persist—such as coping with crime, caring for the elderly, or dealing with poverty and world conflict. Social change and the persistence of some issues are basic characteristics of our society, as students should learn.

Moreover, the newspaper, among the major sources of information on current events, is composed of both facts and opinions. When used properly, it can be the best means for developing the essential skill of distinguishing between these two types of communication.

Finally, it is generally thought that current events contribute in the development of knowledgeable citizens. Quite often I quiz university students and practicing elementary school teachers to see how much they know about society and the world in general. Too often the findings are disappointing. How much their partial or complete ignorance impairs the quality of their citizenship I cannot precisely say, but we know that participatory democracy requires knowledgeable and active citizenry. Yet party precinct caucuses are usually attended by the same few people who dominate the decision-making process. This and the poor voting record of the young make one wonder what went wrong in the schools and in the teaching of social studies in particular. Can emphasis on current events make a difference? It appears that it could.

Current Events and the Social Studies Program

Current events are being used in the classroom in a variety of ways. Some appear to be sound within the total context of the social studies program, whereas others go contrary to it. We now examine some of the ways of presenting current events and take note as to which seems most in harmony with the social studies program as presented in this book.

CURRENT EVENTS AS A SEPARATE ENTITY   In some schools current events are taught apart from the social studies program. A period is set aside during which the youngsters discuss or report on current events, or read from a special current events magazine or the local paper. Once a week children are usually tested on what happened during that week.

The validity of this method can be challenged on several grounds. First, the elementary school curriculum is crowded; if new elements could be incorporated in the present program without adding new periods, they would be more easily accommodated. Moreover, current events are so much a part of social studies that it seems illogical to teach them separately, and observation of separate current events classes most often reveals a routine, dry presentation that children dislike. For many children, the current events lesson consists of reading the weekly current events magazine and being tested on it. Furthermore, themes or items of current events may be unrelated to each other and when taught separately from social studies are often difficult to unify in meaningful ways.

CURRENT EVENTS IN THE FORM OF CONTROVERSIAL ISSUES   Controversial issues are now as much a part of the social studies program as are concepts and generalizations. As we have seen, this was not so in the past, when teachers dealt with issues only in connection with current events. Issues were thus treated only occasionally, and current events were less useful than they can be when conjoined with concepts and generalizations or used to initiate new topics. For example, a reported recent interracial conflict in a local school can be used not only to introduce the issue of how to reduce interracial tensions, but also to teach the composition of the community's population, the differences among cultural groups, and many other facts and concepts. Finally, some issues persist and need systematic treatment rather than an occasional discussion.

CURRENT EVENTS AS THE BASIS FOR SOCIAL STUDIES   Some schools base the structure of their social studies program entirely on current events, or on the study of one relevant theme such as personal relationships. This method seems inadequate, because it neglects all other forms of human relationships. A child needs to know not only how to get along with others in the immediate environment but also how to deal with and influence the institutions that affect our lives, such as the government.

Moreover, a social studies program based entirely on current events lacks a fundamental contemporary prerequisite: a sound structure based on the major generalizations and issues of the social sciences. Few teachers have the competence to build a sound program on their own.

CURRENT EVENTS AS A RESOURCE   The most reasonable use of current events is as a vital resource, as an aid in developing predetermined concepts, generalizations, and issues. Say, for instance, a teacher wants to teach the concept of change in society. For the children to develop this concept through inquiry, the teacher must expose them to as many specific instances of social change as possible. Because social change is most often manifested in social institutions, the teacher might direct the children to books, films, and other resources to learn about such changes in the past. But they could also be directed to current changes in social institutions, such as the overthrow of a democratic regime and the establishment of a dictatorship, or the establishment of an independent nation.

This recommendation—that current events be a resource in the teaching of a preplanned substantive program—does not mean that current events are unimportant or should be dealt with casually. It is hoped that teachers will make every effort to relate all important current issues and events to the regular program. If a suddenly important issue or event cannot be integrated with the regular program, the teacher should deal with it separately and later try to integrate it. This use obviously is completely different from the practice of allocating a daily period during which the class searches for current events to fulfill the demands of a routine.

Also, the lack of a regularly scheduled current events period should not mean that the teacher refrain from a constant effort to indirectly alert the youngsters to current events. The classroom environment should be properly arranged, through the use of news, maps, and other materials, to stimulate the children toward attention to current happenings. News magazines and newspapers should be constantly available for browsing. Products of current events activities, undertaken in class in relation to the regular social studies program, should be displayed. The teacher's example can be the best inspiration for children. Parents should be encouraged to discuss current events and allow the children to participate; to have news magazines and newspapers around the house; and, at least once a day, to watch or listen to a major TV or radio news broadcast.

EXAMPLES OF COMBINING CURRENT EVENTS WITH A STRUCTURED SOCIAL STUDIES PROGRAM   In the structured social studies program recommended in this book, kindergarten is devoted to the study of the individual. Current events that might be useful could include: the birth of a baby brother or sister; someone from the class or a relative having an operation; a wedding; or any observable or reportable event that could be related to the development of the individual.

The recommended area of study for the first grade is the family. Examples of relevant current events are: the arrival of a new family in town; the birth of twins; a report on a runaway child; reports on crimes against older people; visits from grandparents; the arrival of a family from another country; dramatic rise of food prices; or any event that affects the family.

The area of study for the second grade is the community. Examples of current events include: the opening of a shopping center; election of a new mayor; a new cultural center; a new community swimming pool or park; a new business.

The third grade usually deals with the city. Events could include: cultural events; racial conflicts; crime; pollution alerts; urban renewal; new facilities; traffic jams.

"People Need the Earth" is the area of fourth grade study. Current events could include reports of: a drought; a new sale of grain abroad; food shortages in various parts of the world; the building of a dam; a new housing development; dispute over the proper use of a piece of land or wilderness area.

The area of study for the fifth grade is "The Making of Our Nation." Current events of national import could include: passage of new laws by Congress; disputes between the president and Congress; Supreme Court decisions; new agreements with other nations; elections; inflation; inter-racial conflicts that gain national attention; energy programs or problems; environmental pollution.

The recommended area of study for the sixth grade is the world in general—a rich quarry of current events, which could include: debates in the United Nations and meetings of the various international alliances, which could serve to teach about forces that unite or divide the world; international conflicts, from which could be traced the cultural and national differences; food and energy crises, which could be used to show the unequal distribution of resources and the close interdependence of peoples.

Using Commercial Programs for Current Events

The most common commercial programs used to bring current events into the classroom are those developed by local (mainly metropolitan) or nationally circulated newspapers. Teachers should check with the local paper(s) to find out whether it has a program. One of the most extensive newspaper programs is that of the *New York Times*. It includes a component for the fifth and sixth grades of the elementary school entitled "A Year's Growth Through the *New York Times*." As the New York Times College and School Service department advertised recently, "Developed by a former elementary teacher, principal and supervisor of student teachers, the program develops self-awareness, skills, values. . . . It helps improve communication skills, too." [19] Usually the program is divided into the months of the school year with a theme—leisure time, for instance—for each month.

A class using the *New York Times* program receives the following:

1. The *New York Times* every school day, delivered for half the regular newsstand price . . . just 10 cents a day.
2. Every week, the *New York Times School Weekly*, a special tabloid-size newspaper that adds to the ideas one gets from the *Times.*
3. Every month, a special Background Report to round out the children's understanding of what is going on around them.

4. Also, a free booklet, "What's in It for You," that makes reading the
   Times easier. It even tells how to read the weekly issue of the *Times*
   in just 15 minutes.

For more information write to New York Times College and School Service, 229 W. 43rd Street, New York, New York 10036.

Another nationally available program is the Newsweek Educational Program, more appropriate for high school but usable with the upper elementary school grades. The program includes (1) Map-of-the-Month and Work Sheet, 35" × 45" wall display maps illustrating key places and topics in the news with current and historical facts, graphs, and charts; (2) Current Affairs Case Studies, 30-page units on key social studies topics with duplicating masters, related visuals, and detailed teacher's guides; (3) News Pointer, published four times a year, providing eight duplicating masters with current news and background on timely subjects like "Africa: The New Powder Keg"; (4) News Focus, 16-page studies of specific topics with maps, charts, pictures, cartoons, and diagrams; (5) Monthly News Quiz and Current News Test, available three times each semester in duplicating masters. For more information write to Newsweek Educational Division, 444 Madison Avenue, New York, New York 10022.

One of the most appropriate programs for general coverage of current events in the elementary school is the *World News of the Week*, published weekly by News Map of the Week, a division of Printway Incorporated, 100 Subscription Processing Center, South Milwaukee, Wisconsin 53172. Each week this poster-type publication deals with the topics of the week, ranging from people and issues to careers; arts, sciences, travel and recreation, social issues, and many other such areas are also included.

In addition to these programs of general coverage, some programs direct materials to each grade. The most popular ones for the elementary school are from Scholastic Magazines, Inc., 902 Sylvan Avenue, Englewood Cliffs, New Jersey 07632; and Xerox Education Publications, Education Center, Columbus, Ohio 43216. The chart below shows the available titles for each grade:

Graded Weekly Publications on Current Events

Grade Level	Scholastic	Xerox
First	News Pilot	My Weekly Reader 1
Second	News Ranger	My Weekly Reader 2
Third	News Trails	My Weekly Reader 3
Fourth	News Explorer	My Weekly Reader 4
Fifth	Young Citizen	My Weekly Reader 5
Sixth	Newstime	My Weekly Reader 6

Monthly filmstrips are also available to help the teacher deal with current events. For information on some of the most important ones write to: (a) Current Affairs Films, 527 Madison Avenue, New York, New York 10022; (b) The New York Times Company, Office of Educational Activities, Times Square, New York, New York 10036; and (c) VEC Newsprogram, Visual Education Consultants, Inc., P.O. Box 52, Madison, Wisconsin 53701.

Using Programs Developed by the Teachers

A teacher who does not want to invest in commercial programs can develop a program in a variety of ways, the most common approaches being:

1. *News bulletin board:* The class may be divided into small groups and each group is responsible for displaying one type of news—sports, for instance—on the bulletin board. How it should be displayed is left to the resourcefulness of each group. One popular way is to place a world map on the board and arrange the news items around the map. Strings are used to connect each story with its appropriate location. For details, refer to *How to Use a Bulletin Board.*[20]

2. *Weekly discussion:* The children usually collect the news from the local newspaper and from other sources and once a week have a discussion on what took place during the week. Discussion has been called "A Democratic Force," [21] and is useful for developing a number of important skills—among them expressing oneself before a group and critical evaluation of points of view.

3. *News broadcast:* Some teachers organize their class into a news studio with reporters, editors, pupil-made toy cameras, camera operators, etc. Each day or every other day the class broadcasts the news. Usually the children alternate roles to be able to develop different skills.

4. *News notebook or clipping file:* Each child could have a notebook in which to record the major current events. Still better might be to have each child develop a file of clippings from local newspapers and other sources. However, both the notebook and the clipping file can be difficult for children to undertake individually. In such a case the class as a whole can jointly develop one notebook or clipping file. The children may be divided into committees to look for different types of news items. For example, one committee may report on world news, one on national news, one on state news, and so on.

Keep in mind that the above approaches are not complete by themselves. Current events, again, should not be perceived as a separate entity, but as part of the children's continuum of experiences. They should be used as resources to make concepts, relationships, and issues better understood.

Government Publications as Sources of Current Events

As mentioned in the previous chapter, government publications are good sources for free or inexpensive materials. They are also good as background information for the analysis of current events. Say, for example, that the most talked-about news in one metropolitan area is the layoffs from a large factory and the consequent rise in local unemployment. The teacher relates this news to a series of lessons on career education and what observable present trends appear to forecast about future occupational patterns. The *Occupational Outlook Handbook* or the *Occupational Outlook Quarterly,* published by the Bureau of Labor Statistics of the Department of Labor, could be useful in developing these lessons.

Government publications may sometimes be obtained free by writing directly to the issuing department or to one's representative in Congress. Materials can be purchased directly from the Superintendent of Documents, U.S. Government Printing Office, Washington, D.C. 20402. To find out what is available consult the *United States Government Publications Catalog.* The catalog is inexpensive, but those who do not wish to pay a subscription may use the less extensive but nevertheless useful free semimonthly publication, *Selected United States Government Publications* (see the list of free and inexpensive materials in Chapter 8).

Though it is written mainly for the high school teacher, elementary school teachers can also find useful information on how to locate government publications and those published by world affairs organizations in *How to Locate Useful Government Publications*, by Stanley Wronski.[22]

SUMMARY

Community resources and current events are elements in the children's immediate environment that can be used to illustrate concepts, generalizations, values, or human conflicts. Whether they be things, processes, persons, or events, they can be effective instructional aids because they are closely related to the children's everyday experiences. They provide a more direct approach to the achievement of educational objectives than does a textbook, and bring the school and the community closer together.

There is a great variety of community resources. Some professionals think of the local community as the best laboratory for teaching just about anything in social studies. Specific resources and activities for the area of study in each grade are recommended in this chapter. In view of the value of the community resources, the teacher must get to know the local community. A number of ways of doing so are suggested. In addition, three models are provided for systematically using community resources to achieve both content and process objectives. Finally, specific procedures for conducting effective field trips are outlined.

Current events are, in a sense, a community resource. It is recommended that they be treated as instructional resources to support an ongoing structured social studies program. Two approaches are to be discouraged: In one, current events constitute the entire social studies program; in the second, they are treated separately from social studies, usually once a week or whenever convenient.

Many commercial programs for current events are available, but teachers may also develop their own programs, the commonest approaches being the news bulletin board, the weekly discussion, the news broadcast, and the news notebook or clipping file.

Government publications also provide background information for the analysis of current events. The chapter closes with suggestions on how to locate government publications.

ACTIVITIES

1. Observe classroom instruction in the local area to determine whether textbooks or the children's experiences are more relied upon to reach social studies objectives.

2. Using the scope and sequence developed in Chapter 3, survey the local community to identify and list community resources that could be helpful in the teaching of the various topics.

3. Select the community resources and activities suggested for a particular grade and indicate which concepts, generalizations, or issues could be taught through them.

4. Using the focus questions developed by Armstrong and Savage, identify in the local community the stimulus materials that could help children make grounded generalizations, examine values, and make decisions.

5. Plan a class field trip using the procedure suggested in the chapter.

6. Select a unit from the scope and sequence in Chapter 3. Then follow a newspaper for a week and indicate how you would use the current events covered in the paper to teach that unit.

7. Make a thorough examination of a commercial program on current events.

8. As a class or individually, organize a news bulletin board or a news broadcast.

9. Start a news notebook of your own to habituate yourself to being alert for current events, to familiarize yourself with what is going on around you, and to become able to understand events in the future as they occur.

NOTES

1. Theodore Kaltsounis, "The Community: Laboratory for Social Learnings: Introduction," *Social Education,* 40 (March 1976), 158.

2. Miller R. Collings, *How to Vitalize Community Resources,* How to Do It Series—No. 13 (Washington, D.C.: National Council for the Social Studies, 1967), p. 1.

3. Ibid., pp. 6–7. Reprinted with permission of the National Council for the Social Studies.

4. Adapted from unpublished work by Linda Roose and Rich Lindstrom, teachers in the Puget Sound area in the state of Washington.

5. Collings, *How to Vitalize Community Resources,* p. 3.

6. Alberta P. Sebolt, *Field-Study Guide to Community* (Sturbridge, Mass.: Resource Learning Lab., 1970).

7. William E. Whitehill, Jr., et al., *A Directory of Primary and Community Resources in the Probe Area* (Oneonta, N.Y.: Catskill Area School Study Council, 1968).

8. Charles R. Duvall and Donald W. Truex, *Computerized Community Resources Handbook* (South Bend, Ind.: Community School Corporation, 1970).

9. J. Pope Dwyer, "Modernizing Social Studies Instruction," *The Social Studies,* 62 (January 1971), 23, 26; Joel W. Eastman, "Putting Life into the Study of the Past: Local History Materials in the Classroom," *New England Social Studies Bulletin,* 29 (Winter 1972), 5–6; Bernard Kravitz, "Teaching Primary Children the Location of Neighborhood Services," *Journal of Geography,* 70 (October 1971), 411–14; George C. Lindemer, "Historical Museums for Educational Enrichment," *The Social Studies,* 62 (November 1971), 258–62; Ralph W. Cordier, "The Study of History Through State and Local Resources," *The Social Studies,* 60 (March 1969), 99–105.

10. JoAnn Buggey, "Citizenship and Community Involvement: The Primary Grades," *Social Education,* 40 (March 1976), 161.

11. Ibid.

12. David G. Armstrong and Tom V. Savage, Jr., "A Framework for Utilizing the Community for Social Learning in Grades 4–6," *Social Education,* 40 (March 1976), 164.

13. Ibid., p. 167.

14. Ronald Wheeler and Kevin P. Kelly, "Instructional Implications of Historical Research for the Elementary Grades," *Social Education,* 39 (November–December 1975), 485–86.

15. Alan J. Hoffman, "A Case for Using Survey Techniques with Children (With Some Reservations)," *Social Education,* 39 (November–December 1975), 489–92.

16. Arthur K. Ellis and David W. Johnson, "The Utilization of Experimental Methods by Teachers and Students," *Social Education,* 34 (November–December 1975), 493–96.

17. John R. Lee, "Some Thoughts on Descriptive Research Procedures for Children," *Social Education,* 39 (November–December 1975), 487–88.

18. Edgar C. Bye, *How to Conduct a Field Trip,* How to Do It Series—No. 12 (Washington, D.C.: National Council for the Social Studies, 1967).

19. From a brochure distributed at the 1976 annual meeting of the National Council for the Social Studies, held in Washington, D.C.

20. Marion R. Grubola, *How to Use a Bulletin Board,* How to Do It Series—No. 4 (Washington, D.C.: National Council for the Social Studies, 1965).

21. Ruth E. Litchen, *How to Use Group Discussion,* How to Do It Series—No. 6 (Washington, D.C.: National Council for the Social Studies, 1965), p. 1.

22. Stanley P. Wronski, *How to Locate Useful Government Publications,* How to Do It Series—No. 11 (Washington, D.C.: National Council for the Social Studies, 1968).

OBJECTIVES

Studying this chapter will enable the reader to:

1. become familiar with map and globe skills and understandings, and sequence them logically.
2. from research, justify the teaching of map and globe skills and understandings in the primary grades.
3. identify the main approaches used in the teaching of map and globe skills and understandings.
4. become familiar with specific activities for the teaching of particular skills and understandings.
5. identify commercially available programs for the teaching of map and globe skills and understandings.
6. classify maps and globes in different categories and explain the use of each category.
7. list the various types of audiovisual aids other than maps and globes.
8. locate the sources for the various types of audiovisual aids and the specific materials distributed by each.
9. list and use some of the journals that introduce new audiovisual aids.
10. validate the educational potential of nonnarrative student-made films.
11. explain why audiovisual aids are means for the development of concepts, generalizations, and issues.
12. realize the value of charts, graphs, and tables in organizing and using information.

10

MAPS, GLOBES, AND OTHER AUDIOVISUAL AIDS

Reading materials, community resources, and current events are major resources for enriching social studies. Other resources long and closely associated with the teaching of social studies are maps and globes and audiovisual aids, all three of which this chapter treats. What are they and how can they be used most effectively?

MAPS AND GLOBES

The ability to read maps and globes is crucial both in learning and in everyday life. Yet, schools are not very successful in developing this ability, as June Chapin and Richard Gross declare:

> Evidence increasingly indicates that many students are not learning much about either geography or map interpretation. Tests of elementary and secondary school students as well as adults show that map-reading skills are not well developed, and that many have erroneous and inadequate understanding of such relatively simple concepts as directions and cannot read road maps.[1]

Gertrude Whipple and Martha Palmer suggest that "we will succeed with children only if the necessary skills are identified, taught in proper sequence, presented slowly enough for the child to acquire them, and maintained in higher grades."[2] In this section we shall do just that: identify, in a logical sequence, the basic map and globe skills and the necessary understandings; recommend procedures and techniques for their development; list commercial maps and their sources; and, finally, show how maps and globes can be used to develop concepts and generalizations and to contribute to resolving issues.

Map and Globe Skills and Understandings in a Sequence

The skills and understandings recommended by Whipple and Palmer are organized under sequential headings: [3]

GRADES I AND II: Providing a Wide Acquaintance with Landscape Features

1. Familiarize children with common landscape features in their neighborhood such as rivers, valleys, and hills.
2. Acquaint them with landscape features in other environments.

GRADE III: Developing Readiness to Undertake Map Reading

1. Teach children the cardinal directions by reference to the position of the sun.
2. Familiarize children with the types of landscapes shown on the maps they will use (e.g., mountainous, hilly, and level lands; lake, river, and ocean scenes).
3. Acquaint children with simple map terms (e.g., island, mountain range, plain).
4. Develop the concept that the earth is a huge sphere or globe and that half of the earth is called a hemisphere.

GRADES III AND IV: Introducing Flat Maps

1. Teach that the globe is the only true map because it shows the roundness of the earth.
2. Lead the children to understand that a map represents an area on the earth and shows certain facts about that area—not all facts, but selected facts such as surface or growing things.
3. Show the children that any part of the globe may be transferred to a flat map.

GRADE IV: Developing Initial Concepts in the Use of the Globe and More Complex Map Symbolization

1. Introduce the directions northeast, northwest, southeast, and southwest.
2. Show the children that the globe may be divided into hemispheres in many different ways; distinguish the eastern, western, northern, and southern hemispheres.
3. Present the rotation of the earth on its axis from west to east as the reason for day and night.
4. Give as much explanation of the reason for seasonal changes as the children can comprehend; make clear that the northern and southern hemispheres have different seasons and that the seasons at the poles are different from those at the equator.
5. Discuss the different types of map symbols.

GRADE V: Developing Fundamental Skills in the Use of Maps

1. Establish the habit of interpreting the key before trying to read the map.
2. Review directions on maps, avoiding the idea that north is always on the top of the map—where north is depends on the location of the north pole, which may even be in the center of the map.

3. Develop the use of east-west lines in determining direction. Teach the word *latitude*, but not *degrees of latitude*, which is too difficult a scale of measurement for children of this age.

4. At the same time that the concept of latitude is introduced, the teacher should also introduce the concept of longitude.

5. Stress the idea that the map is a method of recording the positions of natural and cultural features which can be *seen*, such as a national park that a child in the class has visited.

6. Teach the necessary symbols and terms used on maps, such as rivers, cities, capital cities, railroads, highways, deltas, peninsulas, isthmuses, gulfs, and bays.

7. Introduce the children to the scale of miles; lead them to use it in measuring distances which they want to know.

8. Encourage the children to realize that maps are drawn to different scales and that the larger the scale used, the larger any specific feature appears on the map. Lead them to compare the size of the regions shown on the same map or on maps drawn to the same scale.

GRADE VI: Developing Advanced Map-Reading Skills

1. Explain the key of a population map showing the number of people to a square mile of land; explain a dot map.

2. Introduce the measurement of latitude and the influence of latitude upon climate; teach the location of the low latitudes (a third of the distance from the equator to either pole), the higher latitudes (a third of the distance from each pole to the equator), and the middle latitudes (between the low and high latitudes).

3. Teach the abbreviations commonly found on maps.

4. Acquaint the children with the meaning of additional map terms (e.g., port, harbor, ocean current, fiord, cape, coral reef, and belt, as in corn belt or hay and dairy belt).

5. Train the children to choose the right map for a particular purpose.

6. Lead the children to gain information by comparing maps which give different facts about the same area.

7. Lead the children to an understanding of longitude and time zones.

This sequential list, only one of many available, is valid in general terms but may not be appropriate for every child or class in a given grade. Teachers must adapt the nationally circulated sequences to their students' learning characteristics and to classroom conditions. At times the lists will have to be broken down to more specific objectives—especially in the primary grades. The following sequential list of objectives, developed by a group of primary teachers in the Northwest, is suggested as a supplement to the Whipple and Palmer list. Under my supervision, the project used consultants who are specialists in the field of maps and globes. The objectives, covering kindergarten through grade three, are classified into understandings and skills: [4]

KINDERGARTEN:

The student knows:

the directions of left and right; up and down

the Earth is the place in which we live

the globe is a representation of the Earth

The student is able to:

identify a map as being a special flat drawing of a location

identify a globe as a small model of the Earth

identify land and water (by color) on the map or globe

FIRST GRADE:

The student knows:

map symbols are special combinations of colors, shapes and lines on maps

map symbols stand for real objects or information

map symbols and maps are much smaller than the objects they represent

the names of the four main geographic directions are North, South, East, West

the letter symbols N., S., E., W., stand for the words North, South, East, and West

the opposites of each of the four cardinal directions

maps and globes provide information about names of places, what they are and where they are located

oceans are the largest bodies of water and continents are the largest land areas

North America is the name of our continent and it is surrounded by three oceans

North America is divided into countries and the United States of America is the name of our country

the United States of America is divided into 50 areas called states, and (the name of the state) is the name of our state

his/her city or local community is within the state

day and night are caused by the sun and the spinning earth

The student is able to:

identify water and land by color

draw a simple room map using symbols

name the four cardinal directions

match the cardinal directions with the symbols N., S., E., W.

refer to maps and globes for geographic information

locate and identify North America and its surrounding oceans (Pacific, Atlantic, Arctic)

locate his/her country (USA) on a map or globe

locate his/her state on a map or globe

SECOND GRADE:

The student knows:

the meaning of several commonly used map symbols; rivers, mountains, cities

the meaning of both the terms "key" and "legend"

the importance of the key or legend as the first reference to use in order to discuss the meanings of map symbols

the names of the four main directions and their opposites

that directions are used to find the locations of places on maps and globes

that the word "sphere" is used to describe the round shape of the earth

that the globe is very small and the earth is very large (scale)

that the globe is the most accurate representation of the earth because it has the same shape

that maps provide more detail than globes

an atlas contains many different kinds of maps

The student is able to:

locate the key or legend on a map

use the key on a map to explain the various symbols found on a map

locate West, North, and South when given the direction East (where the sun rises)

use directions to locate places on a map

find and identify some oceans, continents, countries, states and cities on globes and maps

THIRD GRADE:

The student knows:

the names and locations of the seven continents and four oceans

the difference between the terms continents, oceans, countries, states and cities

that the equator is an imaginary line that divides the earth in half, midway between the North and South poles

that the word "hemisphere" describes half of a sphere and that the earth can be divided into any number of hemispheres

that all of the earth north of the equator is the northern hemisphere and that all the earth south of the equator is the southern hemisphere

that winter, spring, summer and autumn are the names of the four seasons and that the tilt of the earth and its movement around the sun is the cause of seasonal changes

the term "distortion" and that a globe is a more accurate representation of the earth than a flat world map

that world maps can be more detailed and convenient to use than globes and that they are valuable references as long as the observer is aware of the distortion

that the key and/or legend is used to interpret symbols on a map

that maps show both manmade and natural features on earth (bridges, dams, roads, cities, mountains, lakes, rivers, islands)

the difference between map symbols for an international boundary and a national boundary, cities of different sizes and capital cities on a United States map

The student is able to:

locate the equator on maps and globes

locate the northern and southern hemispheres on a globe

indicate how the climatic conditions of an area would change with the changes of the angles of the sun's rays upon the earth

use the term "distort(ed, ion)" to explain why the globe is a more accurate representation of the earth than a flat world map

give reasons why world maps are sometimes more useful than globes

label the seven continents and four oceans on either a nameless slate, globe or a world map

give examples of a continent, ocean, country, state and city on a globe

use a key and/or legend to interpret map symbols shown on a map

identify the natural and manmade features shown on a map

show examples of an international boundary, a national boundary, a city of over one million and a capital city on a United States map.

Although the grade allocation of these objectives should be considered tentative, their sequencing is carefully structured and should be observed. If, for example, a group of children reaches the second grade without any systematic development of map and globe skills, it makes no sense to try to teach the understandings and skills allocated for the second grade. The teacher should conduct diagnostic evaluation to review the children's understandings and abilities and then proceed accordingly, to prevent gaps that might prove detrimental to their progress.

Other recommended lists of sequenced objectives are that of Paul Hanna, Rose Sabaroff, Gordon Davies, and Charles Farrar and that of Eunice Askov and Karlyn Kamm.[5]

Teaching Map and Globe Understandings and Skills

A teacher sequencing map and globe understandings and skills and preparing to teach them must be aware of certain factors and limitations noted by researchers:

1. When properly taught, children can develop map skills rather early— even before school age. Studies by J. M. Blaunt and David Stea show that children can construct maps using concrete objects beginning at the age of three.[6]

2. Some of the skills children are expected to develop are too difficult even for older youth. For example, Lawrence Sorohan found that his

criteria for mastery of certain skills were not met for scale of miles and map projection by any group tested up to and beyond the mental age of 15 years, 11 months.[7]

3. Studies by Jack Miller and by Russell Cobb and Joseph Stoltman show that perspective ability is basic to map conceptualization, especially as it relates to scale.[8] Perspective should therefore be systematically dealt with before scale is taught.

4. Map skills were once not introduced until about the third grade. After studies like Haig Rushdoony's in the early '60s the trend has been to start them earlier.[9]

5. Judith Meyer found that map skills are most effectively introduced through maps of small and familiar locations such as the classroom and the neighborhood.[10] As David Satterly also verifies, highly generalized small-scale maps of large areas are not the best to begin with.[11]

6. Effective teaching of map and globe skills requires individualization of instruction where activities are tailored to suit the student's past experiences and ability and intelligence. William Murdock's research has shown what appears to be obvious: Map-reading ability is correlated with the above factors and especially with intelligence.[12]

BASIC APPROACHES TO MAP AND GLOBE SKILLS   There are two basic approaches to map and globe skills: One is to teach these skills as needed while working toward content objectives (this approach accords with the skills-development approach recommended in this book); the other approach is more systematic, on the assumption that map and globe skills are complicated and demand several prerequisite understandings. For example, a globe cannot be used to explain the seasons unless the child knows that the earth revolves around the sun.

Newly published textbooks favor the systematic approach; for each grade there is usually a separate unit with accompanying aids for teaching map-related understandings and skills. Probably the best approach is a compromise: the teaching of maps and globes as they are needed in the development of content objectives with frequent periods of instruction on specific understandings. This approach is especially more appropriate in the primary grades.

SOME COMMON ACTIVITIES   The detailed objectives listed earlier give an idea of what some of the activities will be. In the following list, the commonest activities range from those intended to develop simple objectives to those intended to develop more complicated objectives.

1. Take walks around the neighborhood and talk about various cityscapes the children encounter.

2. Encourage children to talk about trips they take to forests, mountains, beaches, lakes, rivers, parks, and the like.

3. Have a discussion about astronauts and about their trip (1969) to the moon.

4. Show a globe and tell the children that if they go to the moon some day the earth will look like the globe.

5. Show color pictures with bodies of water and ask children to determine the color of the water. Immediately show a globe and ask them to hypothesize what parts of the globe might be covered with water.

6. Take the children outside on a clear day and teach the cardinal directions by reference to the position of the sun.

Figure 10–1
(a) Semipictorial Map

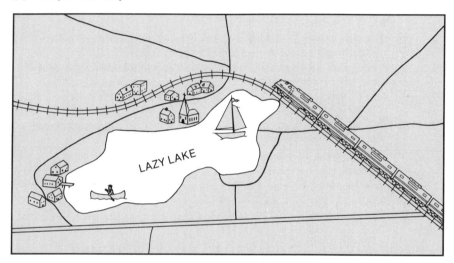

(b) The Semipictorial Map Above Made More Abstract

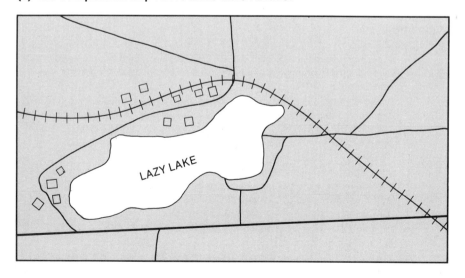

7. Display a globe on a table. Darken the room, point a flashlight toward the globe, and indicate that the flashlight represents the sun. Explain the concept of day and night. Rotate the globe slowly and ask the children to observe what happens.

8. Children make a map of the room using various objects (various sizes and colors of blocks or specifically prepared objects) to represent the things in the room.

9. Children make a map of the neighborhood in the same way.

10. Make a key, or legend, to show what each object on the map represents.

11. Give the children pictorial or semipictorial maps and ask them to reduce to more abstract forms as shown in Figure 10-1. Ask them to make a key to represent every symbol they use.

12. Give the children outline maps of the community and ask them to trace the routes to their homes and other familiar places.

13. The teacher displays a variety of maps and explains why different maps are used for different purposes. The class concentrates on a physical map to locate land features and on a political map to locate states and countries.

14. Children identify things that were made in different countries and place pins on a wall map identifying those places.

15. Children make their own globes using balloons and strips of paper.

16. Cut oranges in halves to illustrate the concept of "hemisphere."

17. Have children collect or draw pictures depicting the four seasons.

18. Show aerial photographs to illustrate that the larger the area in a photograph, the smaller the features shown. Relate this to maps.

COMMERCIAL PROGRAMS   In addition to the activities above, the teacher may use a variety of commercial programs to teach map and globe concepts and skills, especially difficult ones like scale, longitude and latitude, and distortion. The understandings or skills developed through the program determine the grade for which they are appropriate. Among the commercial programs available are:

1. *Where and Why*, Dale Brown and Phillip Bacon. A complete map and globe program presented in cassette form. Chicago: A.J. Nystrom and Company, 1974.

2. *Using Maps and Globes,* John W. Kelly. Eight mini-systems with tapes, teacher's guides, and activities sheets emphasizing orientation, identification, location, and interpretation of map and globe data. Designed for individualized instruction. New York: Globe Book Company.

3. *First Book of Maps.* 12 transparencies and 14 duplicating masters that include lessons on making a map of the classroom, using a map key, and directions on a map. Available through Social Studies School Service, 10000 Culver Blvd., Culver City, California 90230.

4. *Making Inferences from Maps.* 12 color transparencies and 14 spirit duplicating masters. St. Louis: Milliken Publishing Company.

5. *Map and Globe Skills.* 10 charts, 8 duplicating masters, and a teacher's guide. Dansville, N.Y.: Instructor Publications.

6. *Map and Globe Skills Kit.* Deals with the basic understanding and skills. Chicago: Science Research Associates.

7. *Map Reading Skills.* 12 color transparencies and 14 spirit duplicating masters. St. Louis: Milliken Publishing Company.

8. *Map Skills Project Book 1.* Includes map skills and activities such as mapping a bedroom, the classroom, and the community. New York: Scholastic Book Services, 1974.

9. *Mapping Games.* A book of 39 mapping games. Washington, D.C.: Educational Development Center, 1971.

10. *Teaching About Maps Grade by Grade,* Susan Marsh. Teacher's Publishing Corporation, 1965.

11. *Teacher's Manual for Mapping,* Harold E. Tannenbaum and Beulah Tannenbaum. Contains lessons on map scales and grids. New York: McGraw-Hill, 1967.

In addition, the *Education Index* refers to several articles reporting techniques for developing specific understandings and skills (interestingly, most were published in the 1960s, very few in the '70s). And recent textbook series contain sections with activities for developing those understandings and skills.

Variety and Sources of Maps and Globes

Maps and globes can be classified as either two-dimensional or three-dimensional. Two-dimensional, or smooth-surfaced, maps and globes are more abstract than raised-relief maps and globes. Relief maps and globes are good for showing the physical characteristics of an area, but being more difficult to make, they are more expensive.

The two-dimensional maps and globes (more commonly the maps) are classified as slated, physical, political, and special-purpose. Examples of such maps are shown in Figure 10-2. Slated maps and globes simply outline the major land areas and political borders. Physical maps and globes use different colors to outline land and water areas and to show varied land elevations and sea depths. (Cartographers appear to be moving away from the conventional identifying colors toward natural colors combined with a clear legend. It is better to teach youngsters how to read the legend than to make them memorize the conventional colors.) Political maps and globes show national boundaries by use of different colors; they usually also show major cities, rivers, and transportation routes.

Special-purpose maps most commonly found in schools include those that identify climate, economic activities, population densities, historical events or trends, world geography, and literature. Many special-purpose maps come in sets, such as "Our America" history maps, "World History" maps, "World Geography" maps, "Environmental and World Cultures" maps, and "Literature and Music Maps," all published by Denoyer-Geppert Company.

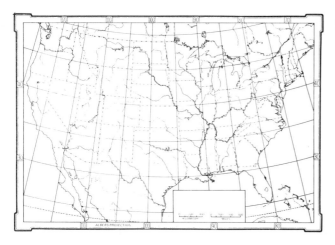

A Slated Desk Activity Map of the United States. Reprinted in Reduced Form with the Permission of Denoyer-Geppert Co.

A Raised Relief Map of Africa. Reprinted with the Permission of NYSTROM, Division of Carnation Company.

A Special Purpose Map of the World Showing the International Flow of Petroleum. From *Petroleum in the Marine Environment*, 1975, Data from the U.S. Department of the Interior, Office of Oil and Gas.

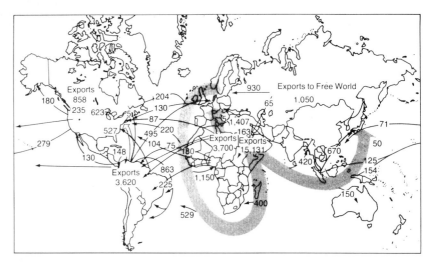

Figure 10-2.

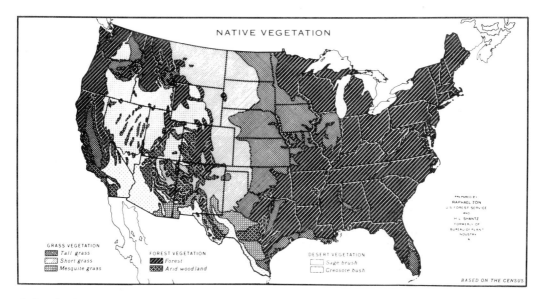

NATIVE VEGETATION

GRASS VEGETATION
Tall grass
Short grass
Mesquite grass

FOREST VEGETATION
Forest
Arid woodland

DESERT VEGETATION
Sage brush
Creosote bush

PREPARED BY
RAPHAEL ZON
U.S. FOREST SERVICE
AND
H. L. SHANTZ
FORMERLY OF
BUREAU OF PLANT
INDUSTRY

BASED ON THE CENSUS

A Special Purpose Map of the United States Showing the Native Vegetation. From USDA.

A Political Map of the United States. Reprinted with the Permission of NYSTROM, Division of Carnation Company.

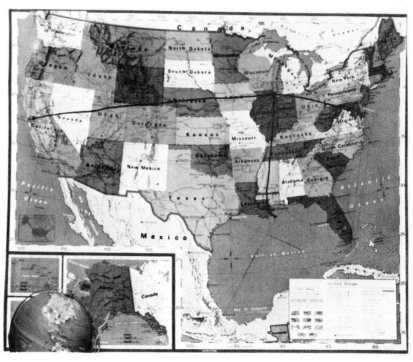

Maps and globes can also be classified by their difficulty. Some are simple, without too much information, so that they can be used with young children to learn such basic information as land and water masses, major rivers, the shape and location of various countries and states, and the location of major cities. The maps and globes used in the upper grades contain too much information for the young child to grasp without becoming confused.

Teachers familiar with the great variety of available maps and globes can find teaching social studies much easier and more meaningful. Among the map companies that publish catalogs of their stock are:

1. American Map Company, 11 West 46th Street, New York, New York.
2. Aero-Service Corporation, 236 East Courtland Street, Philadelphia, Pennsylvania. (A good source of relief maps and globes.)
3. Cenco Educational Aids, 2600 S. Konster Avenue, Chicago, Illinois.
4. George F. Cram Company, Inc., 730 East Washington Street, Indianapolis, Indiana.
5. Denoyer-Geppert Company, 5235 Ravenswood Avenue, Chicago, Illinois.
6. A. J. Nystrom and Company, 333 Elston Avenue, Chicago, Illinois.
7. Rand McNally and Company, P.O. Box 7800, Chicago, Illinois.
8. Replogle Globes, 315 Hoyne Avenue, Chicago, Illinois.
9. Universal Map Company, Inc., 22 Park Place, New York, New York.
10. Webster Costello Company, Chicago Heights, Illinois.
11. World Map Company, Box 336, Tarrytown, New York.

Maps and Globes Should Be Used as Means

Learning how to read maps and globes is not an easy task—which is why textbook publishers now, as mentioned, specifically deal with them. Yet maps and globes should not be thought of as ends in themselves, but rather as means for conducting inquiry, solving problems, and reaching conclusions. Again, the objectives of social studies are achieved by the study and development of concepts, generalizations, and issues. Maps and globes should be used to facilitate the understanding of these and their application in making decisions. As soon as a skill is learned, the teacher should design activities to put it to use. In the paragraphs that follow are activities using maps to help students understand generalizations.

One primary grade teacher devoted much time helping the children develop some understanding of the generalization "Life on earth is influenced by the earth's (global) shape, its size, and its set of motions." He planned many lessons and used many instructional materials. A specific objective related to the generalization was the understanding that the earth's rotation on its axis causes day and night and influences people's activities. To reach this objective the teacher used an activity mentioned earlier in the chapter. In a semidark room he shined a flashlight, representing the sun, on a globe. The children could clearly see that half the globe was bright, half dark. They were asked to determine if the United States was on the dark or the bright side. They were also asked to separately list night activities and day activities, and then were asked to explain the differences.

Another teacher, whose class was studying Japan, wanted to illustrate the generalization "Geographical features influence the way people live." The teacher displayed a relief map of Japan so that the children could see that the mountainous terrain did not lend itself to large-scale agriculture. After a short discussion the children concluded that this was a likely major reason why the Japanese turned to industry.

A third teacher was developing the generalization "People constantly seek to satisfy their need for food, clothing, shelter, and their other wants; in so doing, they attempt to adapt and exploit the earth." To demonstrate the relationship inherent in this generalization, the teacher used a series of maps to show how the local community had developed in the last hundred years. She pointed out that the town was very small at first and occupied only the present downtown area. Some of the present outlying neighborhoods now occupy what was a huge forest, cut down to make room for housing as well as to provide lumber. The children learned that small hills were leveled to make room for shopping plazas as well as to facilitate transportation.

Finally, a first grade teacher was developing a number of lessons on the generalization "Interdependence has been a constant factor in human relationships everywhere." Placing a world map before the children, he pointed out the places around the world from which we obtain natural resources and indicated how important is our mutual friendship with these peoples.

Maps and globes can also be used to study issues and plan social action. One class decided to clean up their community. They made a map of it in which they identified their homes. With these as the central points they divided the community into small sections. Children were asked to survey the section around their homes and report the exact locations where they found litter. From this information the class prepared another map on which they identified all the litter spots. They organized a cleaning operation by forming committees, and from the map each committee knew exactly where to go and what it had to do.

OTHER AUDIOVISUAL AIDS

American social studies teachers have at their disposal an unprecedented and unrivaled variety and quality of audiovisual aids. Indeed there appear to be more such materials available for social studies than for any other subject. What Stephen Johnson says about film perhaps applies to all teaching media: "The vast majority of the titles in film libraries has always been social studies films. Because of the wide variety of topics and disciplines, social studies films have always represented the richest source of films for any film user." [13] Each year there is an American film festival, sponsored by the Educational Film Library Association, to recommend educational films: "In each of the years since 1970 more than one third of the categories in which new films were entered was dedicated to social studies films. In those same years, the best-of-show prizes went to social studies films half of the time." [14]

Films are only one audiovisual aid. Others are:

Filmstrips	Videotapes
Film loops on specific single concepts	Realia of all kinds
Slides	Records
Study prints	Tape recordings
Photographs	Display boards
Illustrations	Radio
Charts	Television
Transparencies	Models

Sources of Audiovisual Aids

Teachers (especially in the primary grades) using a textbook series can obtain accompanying audiovisual aids from the publisher, as seen in Chapter 8. Some publishers provide more aids than others. The most common are filmstrips (silent and sound), audiotapes, large pictures or posters, transparencies, records, and spirit masters.

Silver Burdett, for example, provides a large picture book for kindergarten dealing with the earth as human habitat. For each grade level there is a book of about 20 spirit masters to involve the children in activities related to the areas of study in the texts. The fourth and fifth grade programs include four sound/color filmstrips, each with cassettes, records, and a teacher's guide; the sixth grade materials contain six filmstrips. In addition, Silver Burdett produces several related large (19" × 23") picture packets on general topics: The Earth: Home of People; Families Around the World; Holidays and Special Occasions; and the American Revolution.

Acknowledging reading difficulty in the lower grades, most programs have an extensive audiovisual program. The Houghton Mifflin program, for example, offers eight overhead visuals, five 20-frame filmstrips, and a 64-sheet pad of activities. In addition to their media packages corresponding to their textbook series, Science Research Associates has developed several others—for example, a series of filmstrips on American life, the Constitution, world issues, controversial issues, and families around the world.

Teachers should consult publishers' representatives to find out what kinds of audiovisual aids are available. In fact, I recommend that teachers, especially in the lower grades, purchase two or three different media kits of particular programs instead of a book for each child. Coordinating several media kits yields a more stimulating and creative program than any one textbook can provide.

A review of the exhibits in a recent annual meeting of the National Council for the Social Studies revealed the following audiovisual sources among exhibitors:

COMPANY AND ADDRESS	MATERIAL AVAILABLE
1. Academic Paperbacks Saw Mill Road West Haven, CT 06516	An audiovisual package on ecology with filmstrips, records, and cassettes.
2. African-American Institute 833 United Nations Plaza New York, NY 10017	Resource packages on aspects of life in Africa.
3. Anti-Defamation League of B'nai B'rith 315 Lexington Avenue New York, NY 10016	Films, filmstrips, slides, recordings, tapes, and simulations on ethnic studies, civil rights, prejudice, women and other minorities.
4. Current Affairs–Young World 24 Danbury Road Wilton, CT 06897	Sound/color filmstrips on immigration, urbanization, family relations, aspects of American culture, and world cultures.
5. Denoyer-Geppert Audio-Visuals 5235 Ravenswood Avenue Chicago, IL 60640	Sound filmstrips on most elementary school areas of study, including world cultures.
6. EMI Teaching Aids Box 4272-H Madison, WI 53711	Simulations, cards, games, filmstrips, records, and cassettes on all topics studied in the elementary school. Comprehensive catalogs available upon request.
7. Globe Book Company, Inc. 175 Fifth Avenue New York, NY 10010	Minisystems for individualized instruction on Famous Black Americans; on Northeast: Megalopolis in the Making; and on the Living Constitution.
8. InterCultural Associates, Inc. Box 277 Thompson, CT 06277	Multimedia learning kits, filmstrips, slides, sound recordings, films, drama programs, and textiles that tell a story.
9. International Film Bureau, Inc. 332 S. Michigan Avenue Chicago, IL 60604	Films and filmstrips on American history and American problems; also, world history on a rather advanced level.
10. Learning Corporation 1350 Avenue of the Americas New York, NY 10019	Animated and regular 16mm films for the young on several elementary school topics. Also, American history, world cultures, values, ecology and future studies, and ethnic studies.

COMPANY AND ADDRESS	MATERIAL AVAILABLE
11. McGraw-Hill Films 1221 Avenue of the Americas New York, NY 10020	Series of films to match the traditional scope and sequence of the elementary school, beginning with the family and the school and ending with various cultural regions around the world. Also, films on value clarification.
12. Multi-Media Productions, Inc. P.O. Box 5097 Stanford, CA 94305	Series of sound filmstrips to supplement the most popular curriculum publications. Includes filmstrips on the home, school, neighborhood, the world of work, holidays, ethnic studies, and others.
13. NOVO Educational Toys and Equipment Corporation 124 W. 24th Street New York, NY 10011	Games and sets of other types of materials like flannel board aids to teach about the family, the community, history, geography, and other aspects of social studies.
14. Picture Films Distribution Corporation 111-8th Avenue New York, NY 10011	Films on history, American studies, ethnic studies, human relations, and ecology. Good coverage of twentieth-century America
15. Prentice-Hall Media 150 White Plains Road Tarrytown, NY 10591	Complete sound filmstrip programs on American history, the American Indian and other minorities, career awareness, and values. All materials are for K–8.
16. Schloat Productions, Inc. 150 White Plains Road Tarrytown, NY 10591	Filmstrip programs on minorities, the city, contemporary issues, American history, world cultures and other topics.
17. Scholastic Social Studies Center 904 Sylvan Avenue Englewood Cliffs, NJ 07632	A multimedia program on American adventures. Includes paperbacks, filmstrips, and ditto masters.
18. Society and Mankind, Inc. 2 Holland Avenue White Plains, NY 10603	Sound-slide programs on American values and on moral dilemmas.
19. Teaching Resources Films The New York Times New York, NY 10036	Filmstrips on citizenship, area studies, and current affairs. Also multimedia kits on various parts of the world.
20. Xerox Educational Publications 1250 Fairwood Avenue P.O. Box 444 Columbus, OH 43216	Cassettes, records, and filmstrips on drugs, career education, and various aspects of American life.

One of the most useful sources for audiovisual aids, available free to social studies teachers, is the annual catalog of Social Studies School Service (10000 Culver Blvd., Culver City, California 90230), which lists one of the widest varieties of audiovisual aids classified under such topics as American problems, Asia, black studies, the Civil War, United States government, elections, the energy crisis, and many others. Several "mini-catalogs" are also available from the same source, including: "Law and Youth Catalog," "Consumer Education Catalog," "Religion/Philosophy Values Catalog," and the most important one for elementary teachers, "Grades 4–8 Catalog."

The 1977 "Grades 4–8 Catalog," for example, begins with a listing of paperback teacher resource materials—such as *Role-Play in the Elementary School, Use the News, Learning for Tomorrow, Mask-Making with Pantomime and Stories from American History, Learning Centers in the Open Classroom, Social Studies in the Open Classroom*, and many others. Also included are a list of specific simulations and games; a list of materials on values, learning centers, multi-ethnic studies, women's studies, and law in action; lists of aids on skills development, on pictorial charts and maps, documentary photo aids, posters, jackdaw kits, models and artifacts, study prints, teaching pictures (more appropriate for K–3), activity cards, duplicating masters, transparencies, outline maps, filmstrips on practically all elementary school areas of study, records, cassettes, and 8mm single-concept filmloops. All these materials can be ordered through Social Studies School Service.

Locating Audiovisual Aids

It is difficult for a teacher to keep up with all the producers and distributors of audiovisual aids. The busy teacher usually needs a quick general guide to what is available on a topic and how to obtain it. There are many such references; among those usually found in school libraries, media centers, and faculty rooms are:

1. *Educators Guide for Free Films.* Educators Progress Service, Randolph, Wisconsin 53956.
2. *Educators Guide to Free Filmstrips.* Educators Progress Service, Randolph, Wisconsin 53956.
3. *Educators Guide to Free Tapes, Scripts and Transcriptions.* Educators Progress Service, Randolph, Wisconsin 53956.
4. *Films—Too Good for Words: A Directory of Non-narrated 16mm Films,* by Salvatore Parlato. New York: R. R. Bowker, 1972.
5. *Films for Children: A Selected List,* by Children's and Young Adults Section of the New York Library Association. Carol Cox Book Co., 20 Booker Street, Westwood, New Jersey 07675.
6. *Folk Recordings, Selected from the Archive of Folk Song.* The Library of Congress, Music Division, Washington, D.C. 20540.
7. *Free Loan Educational Films: School Catalog.* Modern Talking Picture Service, 1212 Avenue of the Americas, New York, NY 10036.
8. *Guide to Educational Media: Films, Filmstrips, Kinescope, Phonodiscs, Phonotapes, Programmed Instruction Materials, Slides, Transparencies*

and Video-Tapes, by Margaret Rufsvold and Carolyn Guss, 1971. American Library Association, 50 East Huron Street, Chicago, Illinois 60611

9. National Achives and Records Service, General Services Administration, 18th and F Streets, N.W., Washington, D.C. 20405. The following titles are available:

   a. *Select Audio-Visual Records: Pictures of the Civil War,* 1972.

   b. *Select List of Sound Recordings: Voices of World War II: 1937–1945,* 1971.

   c. *Select Picture List: Indians in the United States,* 1971.

   d. *Select Picture List: Negro Art from the Harmon Collection,* 1971.

   e. *Documents from America's Past: Reproductions of Historical Documents in the National Archives,* 1972.

   f. *Select Audiovisual Records: Contemporary African Art from the Harmon Collection,* 1972.

   g. *Select Audiovisual Records: Pictures of the Revolutionary War,* 1971.

10. *Recordings for Children: A Selected Listing of Records and Cassettes,* by Children's and Young Adults Section of New York Library Association. Carol Cox Book Co., 20 Booker Street, Westwood, New Jersey 07675.

11. *The Seed Catalog: A Guide to Teaching/Learning Materials,* by Jeffrey Schrank, 1974. The Beacon Press, 25 Beacon Street, Boston, Massachusetts 02108.

One very important source of current information concerning social studies audiovisual aids is *Social Education,* the official journal of the National Council for the Social Studies. This journal often reviews new audiovisual aids either as a separate feature or in connection with specific themes. In the March 1976 issue, for example, media available for teaching about the American culture are described; in the October 1976 issue instructional media dealing with "Consequences of Scientific and Technological Development for the American People" are cataloged. In addition, *Social Education* carries advertisements for most new social studies audiovisual aids. Teachers ought to become familiar with this journal and make sure it is available in their school.

An equally important source is *Media & Methods,* 401 N. Broad Street, Philadelphia, Pennsylvania 19108. Published September through June, it carries articles both on media for specific purposes and on how to use media. A monthly feature is "Media-bag," in which new media are introduced. *The Instructor, Teacher,* and *Learning* also keep elementary school teachers (to whom they are solely directed) apprised of new audiovisual aids. They cover all subjects taught in the elementary school, but each issue describes or advertises a considerable number of audiovisual aids suitable for social studies.

Other references help locate instructional media for specific disciplines, areas of study, and topics. Reviews of media related to geography, for example, often appear in the *Journal of Geography,* the official publication of the National Council for Geographic Education, Department of

Geography, University of Houston, Houston, Texas 77004. Media related to historical topics are usually found in *The History Teacher*, the official journal of the Society for History Education, California State University at Long Beach, Long Beach, California 90804.

Specific agencies or projects issue special publications listing and reviewing media on specific fields. For example, in 1976 the University of California at Los Angeles Committee on Comparative and International Studies published a *Teacher's Resource Handbook for Asian Studies* developed by John N. Hawkins. The same author published in 1975 a *Teacher's Resource Handbook for Latin American Studies* in connection with his work at the Latin American Center at the University of California at Los Angeles. Similar handbooks are available in Near Eastern Studies and East European Studies. All of the above handbooks include annotated bibliographies of curriculum materials from preschool through grade twelve. The materials, classified by grade, include multimedia packages, filmstrips and slides, posters, tapes, records, pictures, maps, and transparencies.

In 1973 the American Bar Association published a catalog of *Films and Filmstrips on Legal and Law-Related Subjects* listing and describing over 800 films. It can be obtained from the Division of Communications of the American Bar Association, 1155 East 16th Street, Chicago, Illinois 60616. In 1972 *Films of a Changing World*, by Jean Marie Ackermann, was published by the Society for International Development, 1346 Connecticut Avenue, Washington, D.C. 20036. Also in 1972 Brigham Young University Print Service, Provo, Utah, issued a *Bibliography of Nonprint Instructional Materials on the American Indian*, compiled by Irwin R. Goodman.

From Expository to Student-Made Audiovisual Aids

Experience has brought about a change in the type of audiovisual aids used in schools. In the beginning, audiovisual aids were expository, with a clear message to the learner. Films, for example, dealt systematically with the past and conveyed well-established historical generalizations. More recent films, however, deal with topics in the behavioral sciences and with social issues. Moreover, their content, like that of other recent audiovisual aids, is more reality-oriented; they depict social situations realistically for children to analyze and reach their own conclusions. Stephen Johnson says that the more recent popular films "differ from earlier most popular social studies films in that most of these films were produced as television programs and later released as films and that they are more behaviorally oriented in topics and documentary in treatment." [15]

But educational films do not simply depict reality. Increasingly more educators see the value of nonnarrative films. Leonard Ingraham says: "In my experiences of using, observing, evaluating, researching and establishing learning centers in a variety of educational settings, the non-narrative film has demonstrated its efficacy for social studies instruction." [16] In-

graham elaborates on the benefits of nonverbal films to students: "They were offered opportunities for critical thinking and creativity. They developed new concepts; new moods were set; they expressed their ideas and views in a wide variety of ways." [17]

The most recent trend in audiovisual aids is for children, working as a class, in small groups, or independently, to make their own. Learning activities, remember, should accommodate the children's individual differences and, as we saw in Chapter 6, allow them to engage in activities related to organization and self-expression. Their producing their own instructional aids facilitates both practices. Viola Woodruff Opdahl lists these observations of a class following the use of student productions: [18]

1. A stimulation of interest among a majority of the students in discovering unique approaches to their own research.
2. Appreciation and pride in student productions often identified in student-to-student and student-to-teacher dialogues.
3. Good overall comprehension of problems related to themes of production. . . .
4. Student enjoyment in being able to participate in an evaluation program of student-made films.

Illustrations of the Use of Audiovisual Aids

Again, remember that concepts, generalizations, and issues derived from the social and behavioral sciences and the social realities are the backbone of the social studies program and the basis of its instructional objectives. Audiovisual aids have no other function than to enhance these objectives; they are not meant simply to entertain or fill the time. Before using an audiovisual aid, the teacher must preview it and ascertain what specific objective(s) can be reached through its use, as can be seen in the next several paragraphs.

A first grade teacher was trying to convey to children the meaning of the generalization "Societies have customary but different ways of treating distant family members such as grandparents, uncles, aunts, cousins, and others." He showed the film *Two Families: African and American* (Learning Corporation), which shows two contemporary family structures: an interdependent African tribal family and an independent space-age family in New York City. Awareness of the differences referred to in the generalization led to the consideration of the issue: "Which life style is better?"

A second grade teacher based several lessons on the generalization "Communities cooperate to solve common problems or to meet common needs." The implicit concept is "interdependence." The teacher used the delightful film *Why We Need Each Other: The Animals' Picnic Day* (Learning Corporation) to emphasize the importance of cooperation between different groups.

A third grade class was studying a unit that included the generalization "The proportion of lower status groups decreases as one moves from the center of the city to the periphery; people move to the suburbs for prestige." The teacher wanted the children first to understand that housing differs in different parts of the metropolitan area, so he used the film *Cities and Geography: Where People Live* (McGraw-Hill).

Another teacher, to develop the basic generalization "The world is shrinking in distance and time," wanted to expose the children to all the modern means of communication and make them aware of how they in effect make the world smaller. She directed the children to popular magazines and advertisement catalogs to cut out pictures of modern communication devices. The clippings were then arranged on the bulletin board with their names and dates of invention. The bulletin board served as a reference and starting point for many discussions and other activities.

To give his students information to be later used to develop the generalization "Life on earth is influenced by the earth's shape, its size, and its set of motions," a kindergarten teacher divided the bulletin board into four sections labeled SPRING, SUMMER, FALL, WINTER. Given a collection of pictures, each depicting a scene from the lives of people during the various seasons, the children were asked to place each picture on the appropriate section of the bulletin board. The discussion during this lesson was lively and the whole lesson was fascinating to the children.

Finally, a first grade teacher used a model of a farm to explain to the students the role that each family member plays in maintaining and operating the farm. This activity was directed toward the students' eventual understanding of the generalization "The work of society is performed through organized groups. Group membership requires that individuals undertake varied roles involving differing responsibilities, rights, and opportunities.''

Charts, Graphs, and Tables

Now that the skills of analyzing, interpreting, integrating, and forming generalizations are central to social studies, graphic materials such as charts, graphs, and tables have become very important. Charts are a key element, for example, in Hilda Taba's strategies for teaching and learning social studies.[19]

For instance, Taba suggests that a class studying about South America be organized in committees, each with responsibility to collect information on a particular country in terms of the following topics: people, education, language, area, family structure, centers of population, work of people, chief exports and buyers, and imports and importers. All these data are then put on a single chart that Taba calls a data retrieval chart, as shown below.

	Brazil	*Argentina*	*Etc.*
People	European—62% Mestizo—26% Negro—11% Others—1%	European—97% Indian and others—3%	
Education	Pop.—78,000,000 Literacy—62% Etc.	Pop.—22,000,000 Literacy—92% Etc.	
Etc.			

With the help of appropriate questions, the children contrast and compare the information about the various countries, to make inferences about relationships.

Although charts, graphs, and tables are among the most useful ways of organizing information for purposes of comparison, they are highly abstract devices. In the past, graphic materials were not considered appropriate for children in the lower grades, but they now appear in published materials intended for all elementary grades. Young children are able to grasp their usefulness when properly taught through actual experiences.

As Figure 10–3 shows, charts may be introduced in the primary grades by making a list of the types of food we eat and then distinguishing through discussion those produced locally and those not. On another occasion the children classified themselves among those born in town and those born elsewhere. Other types of charts can tabulate items, record group standards and experiences, show the sequence of events diagrammatically, and the like.

Graphs can record a variety of information. Bar graphs can show, for instance, the enrollment in each grade or any school in the last 10 years. Readymade bar graphs can also be used to bring important information to the attention of the children—for example, the bar graphs in Figure 10-3 showing the educational attainment by gender in 1950 and 1975. Circle graphs, pictorial graphs, and line graphs are also used to show relationships.

Figure 10–3
Student Produced Charts

Types of food	Produced locally	Produced elsewhere	Children in class	Born here	Born elsewhere
Bread			George		
Chocolate			Andreas		
Meat			Marla		
Bananas			Mark		
Milk			Morgan		
Etc.			Etc.		

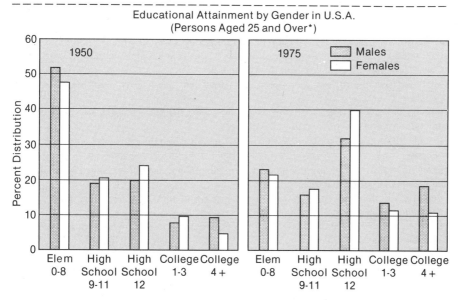

Educational Attainment by Gender in U.S.A.
(Persons Aged 25 and Over*)

*Population Reference Bureau, Inc. "Status of Women in the United States, 1950 and 1975." Reprinted by permission of the Population Reference Bureau, Inc., Washington, D.C.

Tables are another convenient way of organizing information.[20] For example, the steel-producing countries may be listed in one column and the amount they produce in another. The industrial status of these countries can be inferred from such tables.

SUMMARY

No conscientious teacher today would try to teach social studies without using maps and globes and other audiovisual aids—films, filmstrips, pictures, models, transparencies, tapes, and the like—to enhance the development of concepts, generalizations, and issues. This chapter assists the teacher in locating and using aids effectively.

First, teachers are urged to familiarize themselves with the wide variety of maps, globes, and other aids. Current sources are listed.

Second, the use of any and all audiovisual aids requires teacher and students alike to develop specific skills. Relevant sources and activities for helping the development of these skills and concepts are listed.

Finally, the teacher should use audiovisual aids only when educational objectives require them. The chapter provides several illustrations of such uses.

ACTIVITIES

1. Locate another set of sequenced objectives for maps and globes (those in a current textbook series could be used) and compare it with one or both of the sets provided in the book. What similarities and what differences do you notice? Is there an explanation for the differences?

2. Carefully and fully review any studies related to teaching map and globe skills and understandings.

3. There are the casual and the systematic approaches to teaching maps and globes. Each student in class interview one teacher to determine which method is used. Collate findings to determine which method is prevalent.

4. Interview teachers to find out what special activities they use to teach maps and globes.

5. Whenever possible, try with children some of the activities collected in activity number 4 or any of those listed in the chapter.

6. Examine thoroughly any of the commercial map and globe programs listed in this chapter.

7. Examine the catalog of any well-known map and globe company and make a list of all the special-purpose maps.

8. Select any generalization or issue from Chapter 3 and show how maps and globes can be used to facilitate its teaching.

9. Examine any one company's social studies program to find out the types of audiovisual aids it has available.

10. From the list of 20 companies that produce audiovisual aids, each student select one and make a complete list of all the materials it has available for social studies. Distribute these lists among yourselves and use them as references.

11. Examine the latest Social Studies School Service catalog or the latest issues of appropriate journals to make a list of the latest audiovisual aids. Key these aids to the topics of the scope and sequence your class developed or the one provided in Chapter 3.

12. Select any of the generalizations or issues in Chapter 3 and show how audiovisual aids can be used to facilitate its teaching.

NOTES

1. June R. Chapin and Richard E. Gross, *Teaching Social Studies Skills* (Boston: Little, Brown, 1973), p. 107.

2. Gertrude Whipple and Martha E. Palmer, *How to Introduce Maps and Globes: Grades One Through Six,* How to Do It Series, No. 15. (Washington, D.C.: National Council for the Social Studies, 1967), p. 1.

3. Gertrude Whipple and Martha E. Palmer, *How to Introduce Maps and Globes: Grades One Through Six,* How to Do It Series, No. 15. (Washington, D.C.: National Council for the Social Studies, 1967), pp. 2–7 (adapted). Reprinted with permission of N.C.S.S.

4. *Small Schools Social Studies Curriculum, K–3* (Working copy, Olympia, Wash.: State Superintendent of Public Instruction), pp. 70, 185, 252, 316.

5. Paul R. Hanna et al., *Geography in the Teaching of Social Studies—Concepts and Skills* (Boston: Houghton Mifflin, 1966), p. 12; Eunice H. Askov and Karlyn Kamm, "Map Skills in the Elementary School," *Elementary School Journal,* 75 (November 1974), 112–21.

6. J. B. Blaunt and David Stea, "Mapping at the Age of Three," *The Journal of Geography,* 73 (October 1974), 5–9.

7. Lawrence J. Sorohan, "The Grade Placement of Map Skills According to the Mental Ages of Elementary School Children," *Dissertation Abstracts,* 23 (1962), 2452.

8. Jack W. Miller, "Measuring Perspective Ability," *Journal of Geography,* 66 (April 1967), 167–71; Russell L. Cobb and Joseph P. Stoltman, "Perspective Ability and Map Conceptualization in Elementary School Children" (paper presented at the Annual Meeting of the National Council for Geographic Education, Washington, D.C., November 1973. ERIC #ED 086 615).

9. Haig A. Rushdoony, "Achievement in Map Reading: An Experimental Study," *Elementary School Journal,* 64 (November 1963), 70–75.

10. Judith M. W. Meyer, "Map Skills Instruction and the Child's Developing Cognitive Abilities," *Journal of Geography,* 72 (September 1973), 27–35.

11. David J. Satterly, "Skills and Concepts Involved in Map Drawing and Interpretation," *The New Era,* 45 (November 1964), 260–63.

12. William J. Murdock, "A Study of the Relationship Between Factors of Intelligence and Map Inferring Ability in Seventh Grade Pupils," *Dissertation Abstracts,* 33 (1972), 6746.

13. Stephen C. Johnson, "Films for the Social Studies: Pedagogical Tools and Works of Art," *Social Education,* 40 (May 1976), 264.

14. Ibid., p. 272.

15. Ibid., p. 271.

16. Leonard W. Ingraham, "Non-Narrative Film: A Social Studies Resource for K–College," *Social Education,* 40 (May 1976), 265.

17. Ibid., p. 268.

18. Viola Woodruff Opdahl, "Student-Made Audiovisual Productions," *Social Education,* 40 (May 1976), 279.

19. Hilda Taba, *Teachers' Handbook for Elementary Social Studies* (Reading, Mass.: Addison-Wesley, 1967), 63–72.

20. John U. Michaelis, *Social Studies for Children in a Democracy,* 5th ed. (Englewood Cliffs, N.J.: Prentice-Hall, 1972), p. 496.

Studying this chapter will enable the reader to:

1. distinguish among dramatic play, games, and simulations.
2. identify and define the various forms of dramatic play, including: informal dramatic play, formal dramatization, role-play, sociodrama, puppetry, and pantomime.
3. distinguish among games, simulations games, and simulations.
4. explain the value of dramatic play, games, and simulations in achieving social studies objectives and especially in helping children to develop their ability to make decisions.
5. identify those contributions toward the learning process made by simulation exercises that are supported by research.
6. become familiar with the games and simulation exercises available for the elementary school on a grade-by-grade basis.
7. develop simulation exercises for achieving specific educational objectives.

DRAMATIC PLAY, GAMES, AND SIMULATIONS

Our society requires that we know how to cope with conflicts and make sound decisions. Success in adult life is based on how well we have developed our personal powers to face our problems and control our destiny within the complexity of human relationships. Hence this book has stressed the dynamic character of social studies. The more opportunities children have to deal with their everyday problems and decision-making situations, the more they will develop the qualities necessary to succeed later in life. To this end, dramatic exercises, games, and simulations have been found most useful devices in the elementary school. Fannie and George Shaftel identify three concerns that are always present in simulations, games, and role playing:

1. conflict of interest, personal or interpersonal or intergroup, in which players
2. face alternatives from which to choose, and
3. must make individual decisions.[1]

This sequence of concerns corresponds closely to the steps of decision making as outlined in previous chapters.

In this chapter dramatic play, games, and simulations are defined and their specific contributions described. Classroom examples are given, as are ways for teachers to develop their own games and simulations. Finally, commercial games and simulations are listed and briefly described.

FORMS OF DRAMATIC PLAY

Dramatic play is natural with young children, who long before they enter elementary school voluntarily engage in it—playing house, mom and dad, the storekeeper or many other persons in their lives. Recent experiences or particular toys help to stimulate children to organize and spend much time—many hours sometimes—dramatizing specific life situations. Informal dramatic play continues in kindergarten and in the primary grades.

As the children grow, dramatic play becomes more deliberate under the direction of the teacher, and is directed toward achieving specific objectives closely related to those of social studies. The Shaftels state:

In the classroom today, dramatic play differs from the casual play of yard and field and the earlier practices in the primary grades in that the teacher feeds it with developmental experiences until it assumes a sequencing that leads children to ever-expanding understandings and skills. Not only is it used to help young children explore and experiment with the social relations of their own immediate environment under teacher guidance, but it is also used as a social studies technique to help children acquire concepts in and identify themselves with cultures and events that may be at a remove in time and space.[2]

Several terms are used in the literature to represent the various forms of dramatic play: informal dramatic play, formal dramatization, role playing, sociodrama, puppetry, and pantomime.

Informal Dramatic Play

Informal dramatic play is spontaneous. It enables children to identify with particular characters, portraying their roles and behavior as they understand them and with no outside constraints. Informal dramatic play is not necessarily limited to the primary grades: Intermediate grade children, and even older ones, play war games, for instance, that last for days.

Formal Dramatizations

Formal dramatization is guided more by the real life situation that is being reenacted. For example, in organizing a Mexican fiesta, children read relevant books and watch films, noting the costumes, music, dances, and food, and then prepare themselves to appear as nearly authentic as possible. Authenticity is the key to formal dramatization; it motivates the children to study and acquire much information, enabling them at the same time to work together and enhance their social skills.

Role Playing

I once participated in a foreign travel leadership workshop in which each participant was asked to play the role of an American tourist defending the United States and its way of life against criticisms from someone' who played a citizen of a foreign country. There was no script and no preparation. In the beginning the whole experience appeared artificial and somewhat humorous. It did not take very long, however, for some participants to become angry, and even for some to cry. They forgot the actual circumstances and became fully involved in the role of harassed American tourists. After each role-playing incident there was a discussion to analyze what had been said and consider alternative ways that the "American tourist" could have handled the situation.

It can be seen, then, that role playing differs from formal dramatization in that the role player is allowed to individually interpret the assigned role. A child playing a police officer, for example, may present the police officer either as someone to be feared or as someone helpful, according to the child's experiences with the police. Hence a class of children playing a police officer will yield a variety of interpretations. A discussion of the various interpretations will bring out the actual role of the police officer as an essential agent of the community who, like everyone else, can make mistakes in the performance of sometimes difficult duties.

The two examples above show how role playing can be used to examine alternative solutions to conflicts and to acquire knowledge. Other closely related objectives can be reached through role playing. H. A. Altman and K. M. Firnesz suggest that an individual having low self-esteem and inadequate self-evaluation skills may benefit by modeling the behavior and decision making of a competent and assured individual.[3] That is, they assume that learning how a competent individual deals with insults, failures, and anxieties, resolves ambiguities, and makes decisions gives a person behavioral alternatives that will influence self-esteem.

Leslie Zeleny and Richard Gross claim that role playing significant issues has a balancing effect on the cognitive and affective counterparts of social studies, because the student not only will know life but will feel it, too.[4] Hence, those who role play issues should find transition from school life to real life easier. Zeleny and Gross caution, however, that success depends upon careful presentation of an issue of interest and proper identification of opposing roles. They believe that having students assume reverse roles with respect to an issue improves critical thinking and appreciation of others' points of view.

Role playing, like decision making, also serves to modify values. As the Shaftels write:

> Through role-playing of typical conflict situations, children and young people can be helped to articulate the ways in which they tend to solve their problems. In the enactments, the consequences (social and personal) of the choices they make become more explicit. Analyses of these choices can lay bare the values underlying each line of action. Young people can thus learn that they act (make decisions) on the basis of the values they hold, which may be consciously, but most often unconsciously, held. Once aware of their own valuing, they are in a position to modify their values.[5]

(It is difficult to discuss the importance of role playing in social studies without referring to Fannie and George Shaftel's *Role-Playing for Social Values,* a book both theoretically astute and practical. Those wishing to use role playing extensively should examine it closely.)

Sociodrama

Sociodrama is difficult to define because in the literature it is not clearly distinguished from role playing on the one hand and formal dramatic play on the other. The Shaftels consider sociodrama an extension of dramatic play: "*dramatic play* is a spontaneity experience focused on exploring roles and acquiring content. Sociodrama is a group learning procedure focused on providing practice in solving problems of human relations." [6] Zeleny defines sociodrama as an extension of role playing: "The *sociodrama* is an easy transition from role-playing. 'Volunteers' from the class may role-play a problem in social relations before the class in the form of a 'drama'—a *sociodrama*." [7]

For example, in connection with the study of World War II, a teacher and his class were discussing the evolution of the Iron Curtain and how it affected people living near the Curtain. The following true story was related to the children by a postwar immigrant: Soon after Albania fell under the domination of the communist faction of the anti-Nazi underground, the adult members of a particular family living in southern Albania (populated mainly by Greek nationals) were considered reactionaries and were marked for execution or for exile in northern Albania. As soon as this became evident, the family decided to escape into Greece, on the other side of the Iron Curtain.

One night the family walked through the mountains and as they were approaching the border they heard voices in the distance. Fearing it might be an Albanian border patrol, they sat down and kept very quiet. At that moment, the five-month-old baby of the family began to cry. The whole family was in great danger—so much so that the father thought of throwing the baby off a nearby cliff to save the rest of the family. Quickly he communicated his thoughts to his wife, who wept quietly, fell into her husband's arms, and pleaded: "I'd rather see us all die together than do something like that."

At that point the teacher stopped the visitor's narration and asked the children for volunteers to assume the roles of the family members and dramatize the conflict. They had to find a solution to the problem. Following the sociodrama the class discussed the resolution and evaluated its implied consequences. (By the way, the baby was not thrown off the cliff after all; and the distant voices turned out to be another escaping family.)

Although sociodrama resembles formal dramatization, the actors or role players do not follow a script. As in role play, they are free to interpret their roles within the given context of the story.

Puppetry

Puppetry is not another form of dramatic play but rather a different way of involving children in informal and formal dramatization, in role playing, and in sociodrama. It is less expensive in terms of costumes and stage settings and allows even the shy child to participate and learn. Puppetry provides the children with opportunities to demonstrate their creativity and develop many social skills as they cooperate to prepare for a puppet show.

Pantomime

Pantomime—the silent imitation of action or telling a story by bodily movement alone—is another way to involve the children in the various forms of dramatic play. Youngsters are good mimics and enjoy pantomime, which stimulates reflection and discussion of situations. It is a guessing, or hypothesizing, game in which the whole class participates. A second grade teacher discussing with her class various types of career occupations listed about a dozen on the blackboard. Individual children were then asked to come before the class and pantomime one of the occupations without telling which one it was. The class was supposed to guess the occupation. If the children had difficulty the performer gave them an oral clue.

GAMES

In the literature are articles that refer to "games," "simulation games," and "simulations" interchangeably as if all meant the same thing. Hence the three must be distinguished one from another, as well as from role playing, before being discussed in detail.

Samuel Livingston and Clarice Stoll make the following distinction among the three terms: "A *simulation* is a working model of an object or situation. . . . *Games* are activities with goals and rules. A *simulation game* is a game that is also a simulation—that is, a game that is intended to represent some other situation." [8] The same authors also distinguish between simulation games and role playing:

> The main difference between a simulation game and a role-playing exercise is in the incentives used to motivate the player. In a simulation game, the scoring system provides rewards which depend on the results of the players' decisions. The results and the accompanying rewards are made to correspond as closely as possible to those in the real situation. In a role-playing exercise the player is simply instructed to act as he thinks the person whose role he is playing would act. [9]

Pointing out that "no two 'experts' can agree on what simulation and related terms mean," Gary Shirts differentiates them as follows: "The essence of simulation is the creation of an experience which models a process or condition in the real world. If the simulation is a model of a process that is gamelike, such as the stock market, a political contest, or a war, then the simulation takes on gamelike characteristics." [10] Shirts also distinguishes between role playing and simulations—although he considers role playing one form of simulation in which a person simulates being in the position of another person. . . . The difference is that in role-playing the forces to which the participant reacts largely come from the initial description of the situation, the person's imagination, or from the other people in the role-playing exercise, whereas in a simulation, the participant is also bound by reality as it is represented in the rules and structure of the simulation. In other words, the participant in role-playing has greater freedom.[11]

Games and simulation games differ both in theory and in practice, just as do informal dramatization and role playing.

Games

Games are more informal and cover a wide range of experiences, while simulation games reflecting a real-life situation are more structured, and are addressed to specific educational objectives. Games have long been an important instructional medium in the elementary school. Any activity book for teachers, any teacher's guide or any teacher's edition of a social studies textbook series will verify this. There are spelling games, arithmetic games, social studies games, and so on. They usually take the form of a contest. For example, a teacher divides the class into two teams, each of which tries to win by, say, spelling more words correctly. Another teacher uses the team approach in studying geography; children on both teams take turns naming, say, the continent in which a particular country is located and finding it on the globe. The team that locates more countries correctly is the winner.

Some long-established games have had an educational purpose; others only amuse. Monopoly, for example, is a game played for amusement. Most games in the past were pupil-made or teacher-made and were viewed as less formal than simulation games are viewed today.

Games for amusement and educational games are not easily distinguishable. A game that has no educational value for one teacher can have it for another teacher under different circumstances. On the other hand, all games have *some* educational value because all require interpersonal relations and enhance development of social skills. Hence, rather than try to categorize games, it is probably better to place them in a continuum and allow each teacher to decide which are for amusement and which are educational. Some games, like the one below, fall in both categories.

While teaching a fifth grade unit on the Constitution, three teachers working together under my supervision believed that the children still lacked a clear notion of the human effort that went into formulating the document. The teachers asked the class to develop a game within the following framework: "(1) The game had to be new. It could use some elements from familiar games; but overall it had to be different. (2) The equipment had to be available in the classroom or school building. (3) All class members had to be able to participate." [12]

After many suggestions and much discussion, the children used the ballot to decide which game to adopt. The game was a relay race designed for two teams and was to be played as follows:

> The two teams form separate lines at a given starting point. One member from each team is stationed at a relay point about 25 feet beyond. The first person in each line has a jump rope. Each of the two team members at the relay point has a ball.
>
> To start the race, the player at the head of each line jumps rope to the relay point. When he arrives, the teammate with the ball bounces it back to the line. Then the next player in the line bounces the ball to the relay point. The teammate waiting there then jumps rope to the line. The next player in the line then jumps rope to the relay point—and so forth. The race continues in this fashion until all members on one team have had two turns. This team is declared the winner.[13]

As the children started playing the game, they discovered some problems. For example, they had not defined what constituted "bouncing the ball" and as a result there were some questions as to whether some children were bouncing the ball fairly. The same was true of jumping the rope. It was obvious that more discussion was needed before they could produce a good clean game.

From the children's questions, the teachers related the game to the formation of the Constitution, and the children were able to see the parallel between the two apparently different processes of creation. A comparison chart emerged:[14]

CONSTITUTION	GAME
Designing laws	Making rules
Problems in designing laws	Problems in designing games
Constitution in effect—more problems	Playing the game—more problems
Amendments	"New, improved version"

Simulation Games

Simulation games are not very different from informal games played to achieve an educational objective. Simulation games simulate a real-life process or condition; the only other noticeable difference might be the tendency to think of simulation games as only those which are available commercially, come in a box with a variety of materials, and require that the teacher become familiar with them before use. James Coleman defines the characteristics of simulation games:

> A "simulation game" combines the properties of games in general. The essential properties of a game . . . are these: (1) Its basic elements are players or actors, each striving to achieve his goal; (2) it is limited to a small,

fixed set of players; (3) its rules limit the range and define the nature of legitimate actions of the players; (4) again, through the rules, it establishes the basic order, sequence, and structure within which the actions take place; (5) it is delimited in time as well as extensivity, with an end defined by the rules; and (6) its rules constitute a temporary suspension of some of the ordinary activities of life and rules of behavior by substituting for them these special time-and-space delimited ones.[15]

The relay game described earlier meets these criteria to an extent; another simulation game for the elementary school, *The Road Game,* meets the criteria exactly: [16]

1. The players are the children in a classroom divided into four teams. Each team stands around a large piece of paper divided into four parts. The purpose of the game is for each team to draw as many roads as possible that would begin from its section of the paper and go through other areas to the edge of the paper.
2. The children must play the game by themselves; the teacher is not supposed to assist in any way after the game starts.
3. The game begins with the teacher reading a set of fifteen rules the children must follow. In addition to the purpose of the game, the children are told that neatness counts, and other similar rules. Each team is given a different color of paint and one brush. The leader of the team cannot paint.
4. The children are to follow the rules in painting the roads, but no clarification of the rules is allowed.
5. The game stops when the teacher decides and the winning team is the one with the greatest number of roads.
6. The teams are asked to evaluate the performance of others and question any roads that might have been constructed without following the rules. Disputes between two different teams are settled by a majority vote of the members of the other two teams. A discussion under the direction of the teacher follows after the winner is declared.

The value of the game lies in this postgame discussion. By proper questioning, the teacher brings out instances of questionable behavior, when the rules were ignored or violated. Children are asked to examine the reasons for such behavior. This experience can eventually motivate a study of similar behavior in society. Life can easily be perceived as a series of games in which there are winners and losers—the "moral" being that life can become unbearable if the players in real life—people in general—do not follow a set of rules.

SIMULATIONS

As defined earlier, simulation is an abstraction or reduction of a real object, process, or situation to a model. Simulations of forms and processes of human interaction are sometimes called social simulations. All dramatic play and educational games—especially simulation games—are to some extent simulations: All try to model some aspect of reality. Simulations, however, are those well-structured representations of real-life situations that do not involve the element of competition and the other gamelike characteristics. Nor do they allow the freedom of role interpretation that role playing does.

An example of a simulation is the following sixth grade activity developed and implemented in an inner-city school by Lynn Hoff under my supervision.[17] The children had to make decisions to solve a problem reflecting the conditions and constraints of real life: A school board was reviewing a busing program meant to achieve integration; it had to decide whether busing should be continued as is, changed in some way, expanded, or dropped.

In preparation for the simulation the teacher specified the roles and defined them on 5" × 7" cards. Among the characters were not only school board members but also parents—some against busing, some for it—a businessman, a PTA officer, a young militant, the school district attorney, the school system's testing director, the finance officer, and other staff members. The children chose the characters they wanted to portray and studied the appropriate cards. They were obligated to play the chosen role as it was described on the card. Also, a card distributed to all children described the conditions that segregation produced—particularly the variety of educational problems.

As the children organized to start the meeting, they reviewed parliamentary procedure (which they had studied earlier) and the school board chairman reviewed the purpose of the meeting—to hear from those concerned before making a decision. Following the hearings (which took three social studies class periods), the school board members had a discussion and voted on the various options before them.

They voted to discontinue the plan. But that is not the important outcome of the activity. The most important outcome was the children's realization that some problems are difficult to solve. What appears to be the right solution for one person might be the wrong solution for another. Although they decided to discontinue busing, the children were convinced that no matter what the board does, someone is not going to be satisfied.

The above is a well-organized short-term simulation activity; often teachers organize their classes in ways that simulate long-term real-life situations—for the whole school year sometimes. I remember visiting a fifth grade class that was organized to facimilate the organization of the federal government, although the children were unaware of the similarity. At the beginning of the year the teacher simply suggested that the class should elect a committee (the legislature) to draw up some rules (the laws) for

the class. Next the class was guided to elect another committee (the executive) to make sure that the members of the class were observing the rules. What if the executive committee and a member of the class differed in interpreting and implementing a rule? A third committee (the judiciary) was elected to resolve any differences. Time was regularly set aside to resolve such differences.

The class had a library corner and one rule was that "no books should be left on the desks during recess." The intent of the rule was to keep the books in the library corner as much as possible to make them available to everyone in the class. One day the time came for recess and George ran for his soccer game, dropping a library book in his seat. Upon returning from recess, George was brought to trial for breaking the rule. George observed, however, that the book was not left on his desk, as the rule specifies, but in his seat. The teacher took advantage of this opportunity and taught the class the concept of "loopholes" in laws. This is a difficult concept, but because of their immediate experience the class had no difficulty understanding it.

By simulating the federal government as a class, the children were not only learning the facts about the nature of our government, but were also developing an empathy about how it operates and the kinds of problems it must confront.

311

THE VALUE OF DRAMATIC PLAY, GAMES, AND SIMULATIONS

As was said earlier, all simulation activities resemble the decision making process. As such, they provide stimulating experiences for practice in the skills of decision making. Donald Wentworth and Darrell Lewis state: "Games and simulations have been identified as valuable learning experiences because they provide a setting in which students are allowed to try out behavior, to learn from experience, to predict consequences and to use feedback to achieve goals." [18]

Everett Keach approaches the value of simulation games from a much broader perspective: They play a continuous, significant role in human affairs. For example, children's play often "is a simulation of the regulations and roles acted out by the adults of the society. In some instances, simulation is essential for learning one's future role in his society." [19] In addition, simulation has been much used to advance technology and, more importantly, to help people understand and solve many of their problems, as well as to understand "the processes involved in man-man and man-land interactions." [20] Furthermore, Keach points out, games have a motivational value and involve children in the learning process.

After reviewing the literature and testing several simulation exercises, one teacher concluded that simulations: [21]

1. are extremely Interesting to the participants, which makes them good vehicles for learning as well as motivating further learning in the same area of study;
2. enable the players to discover system interrelationships;
3. enable the players to identify with diverse roles which facilitates attitude change;
4. allow students with different levels of academic skills to participate fully in group activities;
5. improve students' decision making abilities by allowing them to practice in risk-free situations.

Beginning in the late '60s many studies have been conducted to assess the value of dramatic play, games, and simulations with particular respect to certain questions:

1. Are simulation exercises more effective than conventional classroom techniques in promoting acquisition and retention of knowledge?
2. Do simulation exercises enhance the development of intellectual skills and critical thinking?
3. Do simulation exercises change the students' attitudes toward those aspects of the real world about which they study?
4. Do simulation exercises have any effect on students' attitudes toward social studies as a subject and the learning process in general? Do they increase student interest, motivation, and enjoyment?

5. Do such variables as age, sex, and academic ability have any effect on the children's ability to benefit from simulation exercises?

The answers to some questions are clearer than others, but in all cases more research is needed. Wentworth and Lewis summarize the research:

First, they [simulation exercises] do not appear to have any clear advantage in teaching content to students. If content learning is the major instructional goal, then it appears that other activities and techniques such as lectures, programmed learning, reading or intensive group practice in information gathering and recall may be equally or even more effective.

Second, games and simulations appear to have positive influence on student attitudes. However, this may be due more to the novelty and quality of each exercise than any other factor. A boring game is just as educationally useless as a boring book or lecture.

Third, games and simulations appear to be influential in encouraging students to become more actively involved in the learning process. A teacher trying to involve students in learning can receive considerable aid from the available simulations and games.[22]

Of much interest to elementary school teachers is the variable of age: Can younger children benefit from simulation exercises? Most researchers found that elementary school children do just as well with simulations as older children. M. L. Pippenger compared teaching with simulations to a traditional approach in the sixth grade geography and observed a trend in favor of teaching with simulations, but the difference was not significant.[23] R. I. Wing, using two computer simulations with sixth grade students, found one produced significantly better learning than a traditional approach.[24] G. Fennessey et al., comparing simulations to other methods in third, fourth, and eighth grade classes, found no significant differences.[25]

In regard to other variables, J. L. Fletcher noted that boys showed a more favorable attitude toward the game *Caribou Hunt* than girls, but traces this difference to the sexual bias of the game.[26] Both Fletcher and K. J. Edwards found separately that student ability correlates with the ability to generalize from the results of simulations.[27]

AVAILABLE SIMULATION EXERCISES
FOR THE ELEMENTARY SCHOOL

Everett Keach says: "there has been little productivity among simulation game developers in terms of games for the elementary school."[28] In fact, for the primary grades nearly none exist. Following is a list of simulation games recommended for each grade on the basis of their relevance to that grade's area of study. A game might sometimes prove difficult for students in the grade assigned, so teachers must use their judgment—especially on those recommended for the primary grades. Following this list of titles is a separate one giving addresses of sources.

Game and Source	Purpose
Grade K: Me and Others	
Can of Squirms EMI Teaching Aids	*"Can of Squirms* is a simplified role-playing game conceived in a fun-format to make it easy for players to say what they feel and feel what they say." Available at all levels.
First Grade: My Family and Other Families	

Seal Hunting
  Educational Development
  Center
	To familiarize the children with the concept of cooperative family hunting for seals in the Alaskan Eskimo culture. Actually designed for intermediate grades.

Second Grade: My Community and Other Communities	
Help Abt Associates	Presents the children with crisis situations and familiarizes them with community emergency services.
Micro-Community Classroom Dynamics	Through the use of micro-money young people experience the free enterprise system. It is recommended for fourth grade and should be adapted for second grade.
Neighborhood Abt Associates	Members of teams work to build an ideal community. The advantages of the various components of community are weighted and decisions are made.
People in Action Abt Associates	Enables children to understand the nature of social problems and involves them in solving them.
Post Office Abt Associates	Teaches the workings of the post office and such skills as letter writing and addressing.
Transportation Abt Associates	Helps children plan, arrange, and "take" trips using various means of transportation.
Third Grade: Movement Toward and Around the Cities	
City Council Simile II	The children play the roles of resident, police officer, or city council member on issues of law enforcement, pollution, and other proposed ordinances.
Gomston: A Polluted City Social Studies School Service	Children (the entire class) assume the roles of city officials, environmentalists, reporters, industry representatives, farmers, and other interested parties in a project to clean up an industrial city. Must be adapted for third grade.
River City Social Studies School Service	Involves students in democratic decision making as their town faces the possibility of having its nearby forest become a national park.

Game and Source	Purpose
Fourth Grade: People Need the Earth	
Climate and Land EMI Teaching Aids	A memory game in which students match physical characteristics with climatic factors included in a unit consisting mainly of study prints.
Dirty Water Damen Education Company	A game showing the effects of water pollution.
Ecopolis Interact	The children try to solve ecological problems in a simulated large city.
Ecology Damen Education Company	A game dealing with the relationships between human beings and nature. Shows the need for humans to control their impact on environment.
Githaka CBS Learning Center	Simulates the system of land use by the Kikuyu tribe of East Africa.
Pollution Abt Associates	Children are asked to make choices between the high cost of pollution control and the disastrous effects of increasing pollution.
The Sumarian Game BOCES-Westchester County	A computer-based game in which the player makes decisions to improve the lot of poor people in an agricultural economy.
Where Do We Live Scott, Foresman	To help children recognize geographic reasons for settlements.
Fifth Grade: The Development of Our Society	
Americard Social Studies School Service	Games designed to familiarize children with the size of the United States and the location of its cities and other landmarks.
American Revolution Game Social Studies School Service	An inexpensive game to show the actions and strategies from which the revolutionary leaders had to choose.
Democracy Academic Games Associates	To show how Congress and other legislative bodies work. Children learn parliamentary procedure.
Discovery Interact	The children make decisions in the role of trapper, trader, banker, settler, and others during colonial times. Wise use of resources is emphasized.
Election Educational Games Company	Teaches children government and political science concepts.
Equality Interact	Gives the children an opportunity to experience social discrimination.
Explorers I and II Simile II	Familiarizes children with Early American history and the problems of the early settlers.

Game and Source	Purpose
Gold Miners and Merchants Georgia Environmental Curriculum Studies	Teaches such concepts as goods, supply and demand, profit, loss, surplus, scarcity, savings, etc.
Hat in the Ring Changing Times Education Service	A game showing how presidential candidates are nominated. Children plan and enact strategies to win the nomination.
Homesteaders Simile II	Another game on American history providing children with opportunities to experience the westward movement.
Mr. President Social Studies School Service	Six games to familiarize the students with U.S. presidents and some of their actions.
Panic Interact	Students play the roles of members of economic pressure groups in the United States between 1920 and 1940.
Poor People's Choice Academic Games Associates	Students experience the plight of people in a poor neighborhood as they try to improve their situation.
Powderhorn EMI Teaching Aids	Teaches about the early settlers, abuses of power, the meaning of democracy, and the importance of checks and balances.
Spirit of America EMI Teaching Aids	Three games on the birth of a revolution, the years of crisis, and the War of Independence.
Sixth Grade: The Interaction of World Cultures	
Baldicer John Knox Press	Teaches about hunger in the world and related world affairs.
Culture Contact Abt Associates	Teaches a number of anthropological and sociological concepts.
Dig Interact	Teams create hypothetical civilizations, bury them, and then excavate and restore them.
Euro-Card Games EMI Teaching Aids	Games that teach many details about various European nations. They also provide opportunities to practice the use of almanacs, atlases, and other reference materials.
Import Simile II	Children play the role of trustees of large import companies that are buying goods from different countries. They learn about the world and practice decision making.
Phoenix EMI Teaching Aids	The game simulates a world catastrophe and introduces such concepts as sharing, fear and danger, loneliness, future, survivor, epidemic.
Sailing Around the World Georgia Environmental Curriculum Studies	Simulates exploration of the oceans of the world by the seafarers of the sixteenth century.
Sierra Leone BOCES-Westchester County	A computer-based game in which the student assumes the role of an economic adviser attempting to improve the U.S. economy.

Game and Source	Purpose
Trade and Develop Academic Games Project	The children experience the processes of international trade and economic development.
Worldbeater EMI Teaching Aids	Using a combination of auto-race and rally tactics, children travel through and learn about different parts of the world.

For sources of games listed above the addresses are:

1. Abt Associates Inc., 55 Wheeler Street, Cambridge, Massachusetts 02138.
2. Academic Games Associates, Inc., 430 East 33rd Street, Baltimore, Maryland 21218.
3. BOCES, Westchester County, Yorktown Heights, New York 10598.
4. CBS Learning Center, 12 Station Drive, Princeton Junction, New Jersey 18550.
5. Changing Times Education Service, 1729 H. Street N.W., Washington, D.C. 08550.
6. Classroom Dynamics, 231 O'Connor Drive, San Jose, California 95128.
7. Education Development Center, Inc., 15 Mifflin Place, Cambridge, Massachusetts 02138.
8. Damen Education Co., 80 Wilson Way, Westwood, Massachusetts 02090.
9. Educational Games Co., Box 363, Peekskill, New York 10021.
10. EMI Teaching Aids, P.O. Box 4272-H, Madison, Wisconsin 53711.
11. Georgia Environmental Curriculum Studies Project, 128 Fain Hall, University of Georgia, Athens, Georgia 30602.
12. Holt, Rinehart & Winston, Inc., Media Department, Box 3670, Grand Central Station, New York, New York 10017.
13. Instructional Development Corporation, 7708 O'Neil North, Salem, Oregon 97305.
14. Interact, P.O. Box 262, Lakeside, California 92040.
15. John Knox Press, Box 1176, Richmond, Virginia 23209.
16. Scott, Foresman and Co., 1900 E. Lake Ave., Glenview, Illinois 60025.
17. Simile II, 1150 Silverado, La Jolla, California 92037.
18. Social Studies School Service, 10000 Culver Blvd., Culver City, California 90230.

DEVELOPING YOUR OWN SIMULATION EXERCISES

Because there are few commercial simulation exercises for the elementary school—especially the primary grades—and because many of the available exercises might be too advanced for some children at a given level, "teacher resourcefulness and creativity," says Joseph Stoltman, "are especially important in the selection and use of simulations."[29] Elementary school teachers often must adapt packaged simulations or develop their own. Stoltman differentiates among homemade, adapted, and prepackaged simulations:[30]

1. Homemade Simulations—the basic simulation idea is presented through educational sources, but the teacher and students must collect the necessary materials.
2. Adapted Simulations—the basic simulation is presented through educational sources, but at a level or for a purpose different from that envisioned by the teacher. The teacher adapts it to a level appropriate for the new classroom situation.
3. Prepackaged Simulations—all materials are neatly packaged (usually by a commercial source) for a designated student level(s).

Stoltman illustrates each of the three types. For the homemade variety he chooses a simulation activity from the SRA social studies program, *Our Working World: Families*.[31] In this activity the children establish two competing food stores, themselves collecting the materials and setting the rules under the teacher's guidance. To illustrate the adapted variety he chooses *The Shopping Game*.[32] To illustrate the packaged variety he chooses a simulation game from the Holt Databank System, designed to show the advantages and disadvantages of the assembly line.[33]

Simulation exercises in the elementary grades must be simple, and the best guarantee of simplicity is to use homemade exercises, which many of the illustrations in this chapter are. Whether the exercise is to involve the entire class or only a few children, its design should follow these basic steps:[34]

1. Decide what you want your game to teach.
2. Select the real-life situation you want your game to simulate.
3. Design the general structure of your game.
4. Design the materials for your game.
5. Write the rules.
6. Test and revise the game.

Teachers wishing to develop their own simulation exercises will find the following sources very helpful:

1. Robert Maidment and Russell H. Bronstein, *Simulation Games—Design and Implementation.* Columbus, Ohio: Charles E. Merrill, 1973.
2. Glenn S. Pate and Hugh A. Parker, Jr., *Designing Classroom Simulations.* Belmont, Calif.: Fearon, 1973.
3. Craig Pearson and Joseph Marfuggi, *Creating and Using Learning Games.* Palo Alto, Calif.: Education Today, 1975.

SUMMARY

Whereas dramatic play and informal games have always been used in the elementary school as instructional devices, simulation games and simulations are rather new. In fact, most commercial games and simulations are designed for the secondary school and must be adapted for use in the elementary school.

Dramatic play consists of informal dramatic play, formal dramatization, role playing, and sociodrama. Informal dramatic play is spontaneous, while formal dramatization is meant to reproduce an actual situation. Role playing differs from formal dramatization in that the role player is allowed to personally interpret the assigned role. Sociodrama is group role playing of a social problem. Puppets and pantomime are often used to involve children in dramatic play.

Games are classified as either informal instructional games or those that are more structured and simulate a real-life situation. All games have goals and rules. The players are motivated by the rewards their decisions will produce. Simulations are well-structured representations of real-life situations that do not involve the element of competition and other gamelike characteristics.

Simulation exercises are valuable mainly because they can motivate students to become involved in the learning process. They appear to enhance the development of skills needed in conflict resolution and decision making. Yet with respect to overall achievement, simulation exercises produce no better results than other, more-traditional methods of teaching.

Commercial simulation exercises for the primary grades are practically nonexistent. A number of simulation exercises have been produced for the upper elementary school grades, and some secondary simulation exercises can be adapted for use in the elementary school. All are listed in this chapter (as are the addresses of their sources).

Nevertheless, in view of the inadequate supply of commercial simulation exercises for the elementary school, teachers are encouraged to develop their own. Many of the illustrations provided in this chapter are purposely of the homemade variety. The chapter closes with the necessary steps in developing simulation games.

ACTIVITIES

1. A proposal to eliminate social studies from the elementary school was recently submitted to the school board of the community in which you are teaching. You have been invited to testify before the board in favor of keeping social studies. What will you say and/or do?

2. Select a setting remote in time or place and develop a short script for formal dramatization. What will the children learn enacting your play?

3. Examine the issues in Chapter 5 or in your local community and identify social situations from which sociodrama(s) could be developed.

4. Select a commercial simulation exercise listed in the book and examine it thoroughly.

5. Design a game or a simulation game. What will be its educational significance?

319

6. Design a simulation of a social situation with all the materials needed to have it implemented by a class of children.
7. Select a simulation exercise and organize as a class to play it.

NOTES

1. Fannie R. Shaftel and George Shaftel, *Role-Playing for Social Values* (Englewood Cliffs, N.J.: Prentice-Hall, 1967), p. 12.
2. Ibid., p. 132.
3. H. A. Altman and K. M. Firnesz, "A Role-Playing Approach to Influencing Behavioral Change and Self-Esteem," *Elementary School Guidance and Counseling,* 7–8 (May 1973), 276–81.
4. Leslie Zeleny and Richard Gross, "Dyadic Role Playing of Controversial Issues," *Social Education,* 24 (December 1960), 354–64.
5. Shaftel and Shaftel, *Role-Playing,* p. 9.
6. Ibid., p. 148.
7. Leslie D. Zeleny, *How to Use Simulations,* How to Do It Series—No. 26 (Washington, D.C.: National Council for the Social Studies, 1973), p. 3.
8. Samuel A. Livingston and Clarice Stasz Stoll, *Simulation Games* (New York: Free Press, 1973), p. 1.
9. Ibid., p. 5.
10. R. Garry Shirts, "Simulations, Games, and Related Activities for Elementary Classrooms," *Social Education,* 35 (March 1971), 301.
11. Ibid.
12. Theodore Kaltsounis, contributing ed., "Using Action-Analogies: Games and Government," *Professional Growth for Teachers: Elementary School Edition, 4–6,* First Quarter Issue, 1969–1970 (New London, Conn.: Croft Educational Services), p. 2.
13. Ibid.
14. Ibid., p. 3.
15. James S. Coleman, "Academic Games and Learning," in *Educational Simulations and Games* (Johns Hopkins University. Mimeographed, n.d.), p. i.
16. *The Road Game* (New York: Harder and Harder).
17. Lynn Hoff, "Must Something Be Right or Wrong? Report in a Simulation Activity," *Professional Growth for Teachers: Elementary School Edition, 4–6,* 1969–1970 (New London, Conn.: Croft Educational Services), pp. 6–7.
18. Donald R. Wentworth and Darrell Lewis, "A Review of Research on Instructional Games and Simulations in Social Studies Education," *Social Education,* 37 (May 1973), 433.
19. Everett T. Keach, Jr., "Simulation Games and the Elementary School," *Social Education,* 38 (March 1974), 285.
20. Ibid.
21. Joe Reed, "Elementary Social Studies Simulation Games" (Unpublished paper submitted in fulfillment of requirements for a seminar in social studies education, 1975).
22. Wentworth and Lewis, "A Review of Research," p. 438.

23. M. L. Pippenger, "The Cognitive Learning and Attitudes of Sixth Grade Pupils Playing the Simulation Game *Remote Island*" (Unpublished doctoral thesis, University of Kansas, 1972).

24. R. I. Wing, "Two Computer-Based Economic Games for Sixth Graders," in S. S. Boocock and E. O. Schild, eds., *Simulation Games in Learning* (Beverly Hills, Calif.: Sage Publications, 1968).

25. G. Fennessey et al., *Simulation, Gaming, and Conventional Instruction: An Experimental Comparison* (Baltimore: Johns Hopkins University, 1972), ERIC No. ED 062 303.

26. J. L. Fletcher, "Evaluation of Learning in Two Social Studies Simulation Games," *Simulation Games,* 2 (March 1971), 259–86.

27. K. J. Edwards, *The Effects of Ability, Achievement, and Number of Plays on Learning in a Simulation Game* (Baltimore: Johns Hopkins University, 1971), ERIC No. ED 955 309.

28. Keach, "Simulation Games," p. 284.

29. Joseph P. Stoltman, "Simulation Activities at the Early Elementary Levels," *Social Education,* 38 (March 1974), 287.

30. Ibid.

31. Lawrence Senesh, *Families: Teacher Resource Game* (Chicago: Science Research Associates, 1973), p. 155.

32. R. Walford, *Games in Geography* (London: Longmans, 1969).

33. W. Fiedler and G. Feeney, *Inquiring About Cities* (New York: Holt, Rinehart & Winston, 1972).

34. Livingston and Stoll, *Simulation Games,* p. 30.

Special Considerations
in Social Studies

Studying this chapter will enable the reader to:

1. identify the variety of alternative schools and special programs that have been designed to overcome the deficiencies of the traditional graded school.
2. explain the similarity between the objectives of the open school and the social studies program as presented in this book.
3. apply the principles of open education in designing teaching units that can be implemented in a traditional classroom setting.
4. recognize the multi-ethnic character of our society.
5. identify resources that can help in identifying the most common stereotypes, distortions, and omissions in social studies textbooks.
6. identify criteria for evaluating social studies programs to determine how well they reflect the multi-ethnic character of society.
7. justify the need for some minorities to develop transitional ethnocentric programs that can help them develop their identity and social power.
8. design ethnocentric programs that do not neglect the overall objectives of social studies.
9. explain how social studies in early childhood education helps reach the objectives of autonomy and independence in young children.
10. identify ways in which gifted children can be challenged through social studies.
11. identify social studies objectives for physically and mentally handicapped children and locate materials for teaching toward these objectives.
12. identify and use situations during multiple-day excursions and camping trips to reach important social studies objectives.
13. identify the various special programs, such as environmental and career education, and determine how the objectives of these programs could be achieved within the regular social studies program.

SOCIAL STUDIES
FOR ALTERNATIVE SCHOOLS
AND SPECIAL PROGRAMS

This book is addressed mainly to those who teach or will teach in a typical K–6 elementary school that follows a traditional curriculum: reading and language arts, mathematics, social studies, science, the arts, and physical education. Most schools across the nation are organized this way. Also, most teacher education programs around the country prepare teachers for such schools. This book, then, deliberately follows a somewhat traditional approach, on the assumption that it is better to reach present teachers and help them to gradually become synchronized with new trends than to begin with an idealistic but impractical approach.

Yet there are, relatively speaking, widespread deviations from the common practice. Many alternative schools or programs have been organized to overcome some of the traditional school's deficiencies or to promote new ideas. Among such schools or programs are the nongraded and open schools, the multi-ethnic or multicultural or bicultural schools, the early childhood education schools or programs, and the programs for the gifted and the mentally and physically handicapped. Among alternative programs there are also multiple-day excursions, camping trips, and the like, organized for children in the so-called traditional schools. What kind of social studies program is appropriate for these alternative schools and special programs?

In this chapter we shall see that social studies as advocated throughout this book is adaptable to any of the alternative schools and programs mentioned. Its objectives, logical structure, and methodological approaches can be implemented within any organizational framework ranging from the most traditional to the most progressive. In fact, the objectives of the social studies program described in this book comport better with those of the alternative schools and programs than with those of even the best traditional schools.

SOCIAL STUDIES AND THE NONGRADED OR THE OPEN SCHOOL

The nongraded school emerged as a reaction to deficiencies of the standard approach to education. In the latter approach all children entering the first grade were assumed to be at the same level of proficiency, and each subsequent year were expected to meet a rigid set of grade standards. If they did not meet the standards, they were forced to repeat the grade. This approach was unfair to young children who came from backgrounds that did not prepare them for the school environment and its typical tasks. It ignored individual differences and expected the same performance from all children. Children made to repeat a grade tended to see themselves as failures and to be discouraged from doing their best.

The nongraded school was advanced to equalize educational opportunity. What is basic to the nongraded approach, however, is not simply the artificial elimination of grade levels, but an entirely different perspective on children and the instructional process. J. D. McAulay describes its principles:

> Nongrading is a method of organization by which children progress through school at their own rates. Each child covers as much of a social studies program as he can during the year, and then, at the beginning of the next school year, picks up where he left off and again works at his own speed; there are no promotions and there are no retentions. A slow child may take four years to cover the work the average child does in three, but he does not repeat work as he would if he were held back a year under the graded system. The academically talented individual may complete a social studies program faster than he would in a graded school but he does not "skip" material nor become bored and lazy waiting for less able children to catch up.[1]

The nongraded school is generally child-centered and adheres to the principles of continuous progress, flexible grouping, and individualization of instruction. These same principles also characterize open education, but open education appears to go much further than this, as is obvious in Susan Silverman Stodolsky's description of open educators' assumptions about the way children learn:

> They accept the developmental view that children learn through direct experience and are curious and motivated to learn. They accept the idea that children differ in the ways they learn and the times at which various aspects of development occur. Open educators believe that children have interests which are expressed in their activity and play and that these interests should generally be respected and nurtured in the school.[2]

Dan Reschly and Darrell Sabers ascribe several objectives for open education: [3]

1. Emphasis upon achievement process or problem-solving skills.
2. Gains in broader social and affective developmental areas.
3. Fostering of unique social skills such as personal space preferences, independence, curiosity and an ability to ask questions.
4. Influence on the quantity and the quality of adult/child interactions and peer interaction, on the frequency of signs of boredom, frequency of cooperative versus competitive behaviors and similar behaviors.

Susan Stillman and Barbara Jordan, two teachers in an open school, describe the open school and its objectives in more practical terms:

> Writers on the subject agree that the open school should guide the children in initiating their own activities and carrying them out with the drive of their interest in the subject. Rather than force students into a pre-ordained structure, the teachers tailor the program to fit the children's interests. The emphasis is on the child's ability to shape his/her own life from his/her strengths and creative potential. In the process he/she will take responsibility for his/her learning and learn to respect and care about himself/herself and other people. Often in carrying out their programs, open schools mix ages, avoid rigid time schedules, individualize, offer choices to students in all subject areas, and include a variety of books and manipulative materials in interest centers.[4]

The nongraded school, especially the open school, is theoretically appealing. Schools operating by the open education approach appear to have more respect and concern for the individual child than do schools operating by the traditional graded approach. As a result, they quickly became popular and widespread throughout the country. As Arthur Salz points out, "Today . . . we find open classrooms, open schools, and publicly and privately supported alternative schools in practically every major city and suburban school district across the country. Open plan school architecture has become *de rigeur* and it is the rare district that does not boast of its new facility without walls."[5]

If open education is indeed superior to the graded approach, and appears to be the trend of the future, why, one may ask, does this book present a social studies program that appears to be more attuned to the graded system than to the nongraded school and open school? This design was deliberate, for a variety of practical reasons.

1. Though open education appears to be spreading, it is still in its infancy, and the overwhelming majority of schools continue to follow the graded approach.

2. Most teachers are trained to operate in graded schols with self-contained classrooms.

3. The present emphasis on accountability and the "back to basics" movement could reverse the trend toward open education.

4. It is not always clear how the principles of open education should be implemented in practice. As Stillman and Jordan pointed out, "If a consensus of open education teachers were taken, their aims would probably agree, but their styles of teaching and the physical nature of their classrooms would vary considerably."[6] There can be tremendous differences between one open school and another—some practitioners believe in a totally unstructured program, whereas others prefer that the open school operate within a structured framework. "It would be easy," writes Stodolsky, "to get the impression that, with children following their own interests the best open classroom is one in which the teacher

intervenes the least. Some authorities take this position, but it seems to reflect a basic misunderstanding of informal principles." [7]

5. This book addresses the traditional classroom teacher without rejecting or overlooking the principles of open education. It is possible to implement the spirit of open education in a regular classroom and thus be able to influence more teachers in the right direction, as Arthur Salz indicates: "But more important than numbers is the enormous change that open education has wrought in classroom after classroom throughout the country. The relaxed, spontaneous, natural atmosphere found in these classes is enormously impressive. Children are active both physically and mentally. The classroom is enriched and beckons the child to inquire, to create, to learn." [8] A school building without separate rooms is not needed to implement open education. "What is important," say Stillman and Jordan, "is not how a school looks, but what it does." [9]

Thus, a program focused primarily on the nongraded or open school would have served only a few teachers and would possibly have alienated most others. Instead, the social studies program in this book is designed to reflect the basic principles of open education and to be easily adaptable for use in nongraded or open schools—provided only that the school operates within some kind of a structured framework. Stillman and Jordan make this quite clear:

Although most schools have social studies programs, there will never be complete agreement as to the purpose of these programs. Suffice it to say that social studies goals in the open school are not necessarily different from those in any school. In general social studies should help students become aware of the values they hold, interpret and understand the world in which they live and learn how to make rational individual and group decisions. These are the objectives students need to reach in order to satisfactorily cope with the changes in society. The open school accepts the traditional goal of social studies—the creation of a responsible, democratic citizen—and attempts to achieve it through the development of individuals who feel capable of interacting with their environment for the determination of their destiny.

With the individual as the primary target, social studies in the open school is a constant process of unfolding the child's potential. Avoiding the use of a text to direct the program, the teacher has unlimited possibilities. However, none of them will work without pupil interest. For this reason the initiation of a topic is critical. Students' questions arising out of a story they hear or a movie they see should not be brushed aside. They should be used as springboards to lead specific individuals or the whole class to sources of knowledge. The children and the teacher investigate together, often bringing in outside people, and sometimes leaving the school. It is expected that social studies will overlap heavily into other areas such as art, science, mathematics and literature.[10]

Everything Stillman and Jordan advocate for the open school is also appropriate to the unit plan described in Chapter 6. Within a logical overall structure, the selection of objectives and the selection and design of learning activities is flexible and diversified. Through investigation-oriented (inquiry) approaches children are challenged to pursue their own interests, even their own instructional objectives, to achieve overall common goals. Meaningful issues and social action are basic aspects of open education and of the proposed social studies program alike.

Though textbooks are the most commonly used method of teaching social studies, the best approach to the study of social phenomena and situations, as is practiced in open education and advocated throughout this book, is through the children's experiences and other instructional resources. The emphasis on diagnostic and formative evaluation clearly accords with continuous progress and individual differences and thus makes the proposed social studies program appropriate for nongraded and open schools.

Again, the overall structure of the school matters far less than what happens in the individual classroom. Whether in a nongraded, open school, or a conventional classroom, social studies should be taught in the same way, always directed to realizing the following characteristics, which, as it happens, are here prescribed for the open school classroom: [11]

1. An atmosphere of natural trust and respect among teachers and children.
2. The teacher acts as guide, adviser, observer, provisioner, and catalyst, constantly seeking ways to extend children in their learning. The teacher views himself as an active learner and typically works without a predetermined, set curriculum.
3. A wide assortment of materials for children to manipulate, construct, explore, etc., thus providing rich opportunities to learn from experience. Materials will have diversity and range with very little replication.
4. Learning through play, games, simulations, and other autotelic activities is legitimized. Childhood is respected.
5. Activities arise often from the interests children bring with them to school.
6. Children are able to pursue an interest deeply in a setting where there is frequently a variety of activities going on simultaneously.
7. There are few barriers between subject matter areas and a minimum of restrictions determined by the clock, thus providing a fluid schedule that permits more natural beginning and ending points for a child's learning activities.
8. Children's learning is frequently a cooperative enterprise marked by children's conversations with each other.
9. Older children frequently assist younger children in their learning.
10. Parents participate at a high level in the classroom sharing in children's learning. They also assist children outside the classroom where much of the children's learning takes place.
11. Emphasis is on communication, including the expressive and creative arts.

SOCIAL STUDIES, MULTI-ETHNIC EDUCATION, AND BICULTURAL SCHOOLS

In the 1973 yearbook of the National Council for the Social Studies it is stated that:

> Institutional racism is pervasive in America. It adversely affects its perpetuators and victims. Racism causes majority groups to develop a sense of false superiority and confused identities and ethnic minority groups to inculcate feelings of inferiority and deflated self-concepts. In a racist society, all groups are unable to develop positive attitudes toward self and others. Racism is a dehumanizing and destructive social phenomenon which must be critically analyzed in the classroom if we are to develop a more just society.[12]

Unfortunately, schools no less than individuals have been racist. Until very recently schools, like every other institution in our society, operated by the "melting pot" concept. Everyone in our society was to be melted down and remolded in the Anglo-American image (a notion that met with tough resistance from the American Indians, who found it, naturally, absurd and repellent). It has only recently been realized that the melting pot idea did not work. As I have pointed out elsewhere, "The melting pot idea did not work because in essence it was an effort on the part of a majority to suppress and dominate all others. The analogy used now to describe the nature of American society is that of a 'salad bowl,' in which the ingredients preserve their identity while at the same time they blend into a desirable unit." [13]

It was long assumed that only what was Anglo-American was American. Thus, the school curriculum was usually perceived as, in James Banks' term, "Anglo-American Centric." [14] It later became "ethnic additive"; that is, ethnic content was added to what remained an Anglo-American-oriented curriculum. Most schools today appear to be ethnic additive; American history, for example, continues to be taught from the traditional Anglo-American point of view, with an additional unit or course on black history, Indian history, or the history of whatever minority group happens to be most populous in a district.

Banks denounces the "Anglo-American Centric" and the ethnic additive models and recommends the multi-ethnic curriculum model, in which "the students study events and situations from several ethnic points of view. Anglo-American perspectives are only one group of several and are in no way superior or inferior to other ethnic perspectives." [15] Charlotte Crabtree echoes this advocacy: "What is now proposed for students of all ethnic backgrounds is fuller consideration of the multi-ethnic, multicultural heritage of this nation." [16]

There is no question that the civil rights movement of the '60s forced our schools to acknowledge the multi-ethnic and multicultural nature of our society. The program presented in this book clearly stresses the need for children to learn about society as it really is and to deal with the issues of human relationships. Moreover, textbook publishers now make sincere efforts to treat minorities and women realistically. Teacher education programs throughout the nation expose prospective teachers to the diversity of our population and the consequent richness of our national heritage. Children who speak another language, eat ethnic foods, or act from different values and traditions are no longer (not openly, at least) reprimanded for doing so—many teachers extoll their broader cultural background.

Nevertheless, American education has far to go before it is no longer an instrument of racism and injustice for minorities and women. The Council on Interracial Books for Children, systematically reviewing American history textbooks published in the 1970s, discovered that stereotypes, distortions, and omissions about Asian Americans, blacks, Chicanos, Native Americans, Puerto Ricans, and women still characterize some of the most widely used textbooks. Teachers and future teachers are urged to review *Stereotypes, Distortions and Omissions in U.S. History Textbooks.*[17] In it they will find: (1) important information that is still missing from the newer textbooks; (2) guides to racist and sexist stereotypes and distortions common in recent textbooks; (3) alternative ways of viewing past and present events; (4) rating instruments for evaluating any U.S. history text; and (5) a bibliography of resources for further study.

How can our schools, and especially our teachers, better promote multi-ethnic education? The National Council for the Social Studies proposes specific guidelines:[18]

1.0 Ethnic pluralism should permeate the total school environment.

2.0 School policies and procedures should foster positive multi-ethnic interactions and understandings among students, teachers, and the supportive staff.

3.0 The school staff should reflect the ethnic pluralism within American society.

4.0 Schools should have systematic, comprehensive, mandatory, and continuing staff development programs.

5.0 The curriculum should reflect the ethnic learning styles of the students within the school community.

6.0 The multi-ethnic curriculum should provide students with continuous opportunities to develop a better sense of self.

7.0 The curriculum should help students to understand the totality of the experiences of American ethnic groups.

8.0 The multi-ethnic curriculum should help students understand that there is always a conflict between ideals and realities in human societies.

9.0 The multi-ethnic curriculum should explore and clarify ethnic alternatives and options within American society.

10.0 The multi-ethnic curriculum should promote values, attitudes and behaviors which support ethnic pluralism.

11.0   The multi-ethnic curriculum should help students develop their decision-making abilities, social participation skills, and sense of political efficacy as necessary bases for effective citizenship in an ethnically pluralistic nation.

12.0   The multi-ethnic curriculum should help students develop the skills necessary for effective interpersonal and interethnic group interactions.

13.0   The multi-ethnic curriculum should be comprehensive in scope and sequence, should present holistic views of ethnic groups, and should be an integral part of the total school curriculum.

14.0   The multi-ethnic curriculum should include the continuous study of the cultures, historical experiences, social realities, and existential conditions of ethnic groups, including a variety of racial compositions.

15.0   Interdisciplinary and multidisciplinary approaches should be used in designing and implementing the multi-ethnic curriculum.

16.0   The curriculum should use comparative approaches in the study of ethnic groups and ethnicity.

17.0   The curriculum should help students to view and interpret events, situations, and conflict from diverse ethnic perspectives and points of view.

18.0   The curriculum should conceptualize and describe the development of the United States as a multidirectional society.

19.0   The school should provide opportunities for students to participate in the aesthetic experiences of various ethnic groups.

20.0   Schools should foster the study of ethnic group languages as legitimate communication systems.

21.0   The curriculum should make maximum use of local community resources.

22.0   The assessment procedures used with students should reflect their ethnic cultures.

23.0   Schools should conduct ongoing, systematic evaluations of the goals, methods and instructional materials used in teaching about ethnicity.

The reader is advised to refer to the original publication and study the detailed treatment of each numbered guideline item. Included in the publication is an extensive checklist by which to evaluate any school program to determine how well it realizes the goals of multi-ethnic education.

The Western Education Department of the Anti-Defamation League of B'nai B'rith distributes another list of guidelines for multi-ethnic education. They recommend that the personnel of each school respond to the following questions: [19]

1.   What is the ethnic composition of your school?

2.   Do your school's bulletin boards reflect the multi-ethnic character of your school? How do you define multi-ethnic?

3.   How much multi-ethnic material is available in your school library? In the teachers' professional library?

4.   Does the composition of your school staff reflect an appreciation of a multi-ethnic society? How about the PTA and other parent-advisory groups?

5. Is there a place in your school course of study and/or school activities to draw on the multi-ethnic cultural heritage? Do *you* do this?

6. Is there a place in your school course of study and/or school activities to discuss current social problems of minorities? Do *you* do this?

7. Do students' extra-curricular activities encourage nonsegregated patterns? (Take a look at your playground, your cafeteria, your student government and honor roll, for example.)

8. Is there any structure or organization—for teachers or for students— where honest discussion of difference takes place and where stereotypes can be dispelled?

9. Are the expectations of school and parent groups the same for all students in your school?

10. Which of the following statements would come closest to describing the overall impression your school might give an outside visitor:

    a. "Life is fun in a blue-eyed, fair-skinned smiling world."

    b. Our minority students prefer to stay by themselves.

    c. America is a melting pot; our students are treated exactly alike.

    d. We try to make creative use of differences.

All schools throughout the nation regardless of their racial or ethnic composition should implement multi-ethnic education. Some schools, however, are attended mainly by minority groups—they might be called *de facto* segregated schools. They are found on Indian reservations, in farming areas with large Chicano populations, and in the centers of most large cities. Designing a social studies program for these schools is made difficult by conflicting points of view among the students' parents: Some wish to reject traditional social studies entirely and teach only the history and culture of their ethnic group; others wish their children to learn not only their ethnic history and culture but also the knowledge and the skills required for success in our pluralistic society.

I was confronted with such a dilemma while director of the social studies curriculum development project for the Navajo school system. From such experience I make the following suggestions:

1. Do not rely on "paternalistic" advice from self-styled advocates of the cause of minorities or only on vocal minorities within the community.

2. Organize parent groups with broad representation and listen to their views and opinions concerning the present program. Involve the leadership of the community.

3. Study the existing program.

4. Prepare an outline of a program that would reflect a compromise between the existing program and the parents' views.

5. Organize parent-teacher meetings to present the program outline and seek approval.

6. Develop the program in parts and present each part to groups of parents and teachers for feedback.

7. Incorporate feedback.
8. Familiarize volunteer teachers with the program and implement it experimentally.
9. Use feedback from experimental implementation to develop a final version of the program.
10. Familiarize all teachers with the program and implement it systemwide.

By use of the above procedure a program was developed for the Navajos with the following characteristics:

1. The program was a compromise between a sound social studies program and the community's specific interests.
2. The overall objectives of the program were no different from any sound social studies program, but the development of pride in the Navajo culture and the strengthening of the children's self-concept were given equal importance.
3. The study of major social science concepts and generalizations began with illustrations from the children's own environment and expanded to other societies.
4. Each topic was approached first from the Navajo perspective. In studying about the family, for instance, the Navajo family was studied first. The Navajo tribal government was studied to introduce youngsters to political science concepts. They continued to study the state governments of Arizona and New Mexico and the federal government mainly as they relate to tribal affairs.
5. American history and Indian history were combined to provide a realistic understanding of the development of our present society.
6. In studying about the world, those countries were selected that had to cope in the past with economic and social problems similar to those of the Navajos today.

Following is the scope and sequence of the Navajo social studies program: [20]

Grade:	Beginners (equivalent to kindergarten)
Area of Study:	The School
Unit Topics:	Safety in the School
	Learning About My School

Grade:	One
Area of Study:	When I Am at Home
Unit Topics:	The Family Group
	The Hopi Family
	The Family in Mexico

Grade:	Two
Area of Study:	The Neighborhood
Unit Topics:	The School Neighborhood
	The Rural Neighborhood
	The Urban Neighborhood

Grade:	Three
Area of Study:	The Community
Unit Topics:	The Economics of Community Life
	The Eskimo
	The Nomadic Community
	Community Life in the Netherlands

Grade:	Four
Area of Study:	Cultural Geography
Unit Topics:	The Navajo and His Land
	The Plains Indian and His Land
	The Southern California Indian and His Land
	The Kibbutz in Israel

Grade:	Five
Area of Study:	The Contributions of Indian Societies to the American Heritage
Unit Topics:	The Navajo Heritage
	The Pueblo Heritage
	The Iroquois Heritage
	The Pacific Northwest Indian Heritage

Grade:	Six
Area of Study:	Changing Cultures and People Between Two Cultures
Unit Topics:	The Modernization of Mexico
	Unity and Diversity in Brazil
	The Industrialization of Japan
	Changing Village Life in India

Grade:	Seven
Area of Study:	The Navajo Tribe in American History
Unit Topics:	American Indian and Anglo-American Conflict in the Western United States, 1830–1880
	The Southwestern United States
	The Immigrant in United States History

Grade:	Eight
Area of Study:	Governments of the Western Hemisphere
Unit Topics:	The Navajo Tribal Council
	State Government in Arizona, New Mexico, or Utah
	The Navajo Tribe and the United States Government
	American Indians and the Government of Canada

Some believe that such programs as the one described are divisive for our society—that they put too much stress on ethnic differences among people. This may be true to some extent, but let us not forget that the ethnic qualities of minorities—who make up much of our population—were so neglected in the past that many such groups felt alienated and rejected. They need to overcome this feeling. The present is a time of transition during which minority groups demand the right and the opportunity to emphasize their history and culture to develop self-awareness and self-pride. Only in this way can they increase their power of self-determination. The government encourages this approach through the Ethnic Heritage Studies Program.[21] We must recognize the legitimacy of ethnic studies and the contributions of ethnic groups. When ethnic minority groups no longer feel alienated and the dominant group or groups no longer feel as self-righteous as they have in the past, a truly uniform and balanced multi-ethnic and multicultural program will be possible.

SOCIAL STUDIES IN EARLY CHILDHOOD EDUCATION

Dale Brubaker, Lawrence Simon, and Jo Watts Williams propose that the teaching of social studies usually fits one of five models.[22] The first model teaches about the past and uses it as a guide to good citizenship. The second model implements a student-centered social studies program. The third model is process oriented and emphasizes reflection through inquiry. The fourth model stresses the importance of the structure of the disciplines. The fifth model is based on sociopolitical involvement.

The approach in this book reflects no one of the above five models exclusively but is a composite of all. Each makes a distinct contribution to a well-rounded program. But for early childhood education the student-centered model appears to be the most compatible with the overall objective: the development of autonomy and independence in young children.[23]

As Brubaker, Simon, and Williams claim, at the center of the child-centered approach is the student

> who should be nurtured in his natural growth. He or she is viewed as the source of all content in the social studies program, with curriculum and instruction based on his or her nature, needs and interests. The content of the student-focused social studies curriculum begins with the personal experiences of the student in his or her total environment. . . . The good teacher is one who teaches the whole child. . . . This teacher can work with the student in order to integrate the various learnings that emerge from new experiences into the everyday living of the student. Accordingly, evaluation of the student should be shared, subjective assessment of pupil progress in light of the total development of the person.[24]

Alan Hoffman and Thomas Ryan make the objectives of student-centered social studies more explicit. They see four operations, or cross-currents as they call them, as present in each stage of the individual's development: awareness of one's self and environment; awareness of the consequences of one's behavior; awareness of the means to achieve a variety of ends; and choice. "Choice," say Hoffman and Ryan, "represents the highest level of operation." [25] Because Hoffman and Ryan's operations underlie the individual's entire educational development, they should underlie every early childhood education program.

Unfortunately, however, early childhood education appears not to have a clear direction. "The sponsorship of an early childhood program," says Bernard Spodek, "may determine the emphases in the program." [26] To put it more bluntly, early childhood education suffers from being "freewheeling" and "ad hoc," lacking a unified approach. Programs are usually tied too much to the traditional concept of education, and the textbooks often have such chapter titles as: "Science in Early Childhood Education," "Mathematics in Early Childhood Education," "Social Studies in Early Childhood Education," and so on, covering each of the traditional elementary school subjects.

The goals of early childhood education should be, as Spodek and Winick point out, developing children's autonomy and independence—goals best achieved in a child-centered social studies program that, through awareness of self, the environment, and the consequences of behavior, leads to the ability to make choices. Social studies is therefore basic in early childhood education, moreso possibly than reading readiness, for example, or the raising of scores in any of the traditional tests (through rewards that are probably more beneficial to candy stores than to children). If one other area should compete in preschools with the child-centered social studies it is physical movement. But as Lolas Halverson, Mary Ann Roberton, and Christina Harper point out, even this area is not dealt with systematically.[27]

More specifically, social studies in early childhood education should deal with the child's experiences: Children should be made aware of their abilities, how they resemble or differ from each other, and how they relate with others and with the things around them. More importantly, children should be guided to make choices. "Initially," say Hoffman and Ryan, "choices reflect the individual's concerns with his own needs. Ultimately, his choices affect those who share his environment." [28] It is important at this level that children experience successes and feel proud of their abilities, knowledge, and accomplishments. Such experiences strengthen the child's self-concept, an important prerequisite to independence and autonomy.

SOCIAL STUDIES AND SPECIAL EDUCATION

The term "special education" usually brings to mind physically and mentally handicapped children. Gifted children, who ordinarily are bored by traditional teaching and therefore cannot benefit from it, are too seldom thought of. Unfortunately, social studies education has paid little attention to social studies for either the gifted or the handicapped. This is a serious omission because of this nation's children an estimated 10 percent are handicapped and another 1 or 2 percent are gifted.[29] As James Gallagher wrote, "All educators, both general and special, bear the burden of meeting the needs of the different child with quality programs—and we still have a long path to travel." [30]

The Gifted

In 1972 the School Board of the Houston (Texas) Independent School District authorized a special elementary school for the gifted. "Any parent in the city who wished to have his child attend this specialized school, which will attempt to provide a highly enriched curriculum for gifted children, could make an application to the District and his child would be considered for placement in this special school." [31] The school was available for students in grades three–six. Is this the best approach to challenge the gifted? Many will disagree.

For those schools that do not wish to isolate the gifted children, contemporary social studies could be a source of challenge to them. In Chapter 6, individualization of instruction was advocated through a variety of learning activities. Gifted children could be assigned stimulating learning activities; they could be directed, for example, to analyze social situations, to evaluate existing social systems, and to create new and more workable systems. They could be guided to assess important values and determine their validity in the light of present conditions. Gifted children could be given opportunities to discuss a topic or an area of study and be allowed to determine their own projects within it. What gifted children need is more freedom to pursue their interests. But such pursuits can be of great value for the entire class.

Physically and Mentally Handicapped

Herbert Goldstein, an experienced teacher and researcher of special education, designed a program for special education classes entitled *The Social Learning Curriculum*.[32] As described in a publication announcement,

> The emphasis of *The Social Learning Curriculum* is basic to social adaptation. Activities such as listening, discussion, role playing, motor involvement, music, art, games, and other student-teacher interactions are carefully selected to develop the student's potential for critical thought and independence. *The Social Learning Curriculum* aids the special student in assuming responsibility, both personally and socially, and in making decisions and acting upon them within the broad limits society describes as social adaptation.

The program comes in packaged form and is divided into 16 phases; 1–10 are the primary phases, and 11–16 the intermediate. Following are the titles and objectives of each phase:

Phase 1: *Perceiving Individuality.* The student should be able to identify himself by stating his name, sex, address, and telephone number.

Phase 2: *Recognizing the Environment.* The student should be able to identify and locate objects, rooms and areas that make up his school environment.

Phase 3: *Recognizing Interdependence.* The student should be able to demonstrate his interdependence with the people, rules, and objects in his environment by telling when he needs help; who or what could best help him; and how people, rules, and objects could help fulfill his particular needs.

Phase 4: *Recognizing the Body.* The student should be able to locate and identify specified body parts; state what they do; and state whether he is taller, shorter, heavier, or lighter than another student in his class.

Phase 5: *Recognizing and Reacting to Emotions.* The student should be able to identify specific emotions; causes of the changes in emotions; consequences of emotional reactions; degrees of emotions; and moods created by emotions.

Phase 6: *Recognizing What the Senses Do.* The student should be able to identify his five sense organs, use them to interpret his sensory environment, and describe their functions.

Phase 7: *Communicating with Others.* The student should be able to state why communication is necessary; to categorize communications as oral, gestural or written; and to use each form of communication properly.

Phase 8: *Getting Along with Others.* The student should be able to demonstrate that he can use appropriate social skills in everyday interpersonal relationships and that he understands the possible consequences of not following social customs.

Phase 9: *Identifying Helpers.* The student should be able to demonstrate his awareness of interdependence by identifying various helpers and describing their duties; by distinguishing between activities he can perform alone and those with which he needs help; by explaining how he can be helpful; and by telling how he can get help when it is needed.

Phase 10: *Maintaining Body Functions.* The student should be able to name and locate parts of four body systems; explain how each system functions; and tell how to care for his body.

Phase 11: *Identifying Family and Home.* The student should be able to identify his family and describe characteristics of his family members; identify homes and describe characteristics of his own home; and identify home furnishings and household objects.

Phase 12: *Recognizing Basic Physical Needs.* The student should be able to tell what constitutes adequate nourishment, rest, and exercise, and to explain how he can keep himself healthy and safe.

Phase 13: *Recognizing Personal Needs.* The student should be able to explain how shelter, clothing, people, and objects can protect him; how he can provide protection for others; and how he can fulfill his individual psychological needs.

Phase 14: *Acting on Interdependence.* The student should be able to describe situations in which he is dependent on others; name people on whom he depends; request assistance appropriately; and how he can be independent and helpful.

Phase 15: *Maintaining Self and Environment.* The student should be able to identify grooming aids and tell how they help him stay neat and clean; recognize family and professional appearance helpers; tell what he can do to improve the quality of his environment; and demonstrate ways of maintaining his physical comfort.

Phase 16: *Communicating Effectively.* The student should be able to tell when communication is taking place; identify the sender, message, medium, and receiver in the communication chain; communicate accurately through speech, writing, or gestures; and use communication media appropriately.

Both the primary and the intermediate packages include a variety of materials: a book for each phase, a set of stimulus pictures, spirit duplicating masters, transparencies, slides with sound cassettes, teacher's guides, a scope and sequence chart, and assessment record charts.

Note that the Goldstein program does not deviate much from any regular contemporary social studies program. Any teacher familiar with the latter can identify elements that can be addressed to the limitations of special education children. However, the abilities of special education children vary, and some children probably will not profit at all from the Goldstein program. More work in this area is needed, as are more programs.

SOCIAL STUDIES AND MULTIPLE-DAY EXCURSIONS OR CAMPING TRIPS

Many schools across the country have programs that take the children away from the classroom for anywhere from two days to two weeks. Some school districts maintain their own rural camping facilities to give the children an opportunity for intimacy with nature. These programs have always been thought good opportunities to teach science and other subjects, but social studies has always been neglected. Even a 1971 article in *Social Education* presented such camping programs as more valuable for studying the environment than for the variety of human relationships that multiple-day camping trips or excursions can afford.[33] In addition to excellent opportunities for studying human behavior, such trips constitute a valuable laboratory for practicing many intellectual, social, and value-

clarification skills. Two teachers, Michael Jacobson and Stuart Palousky, demonstrated this through some of the activities they undertook with their children to achieve social studies objectives: [34]

1. The children were involved in consumer education by deciding what to purchase for the camp, how to finance the program, and where to get the best deal. They checked prices in different stores and collectively made decisions based on the information they gathered.

2. The children observed and discussed in class how they were received by the store owners. Why did some receive them with suspicion and even hostility?

3. To improve their map skills, the children practiced "orienteering": a new concept borrowed from Sweden. "It is designed," the authors say, "as a competitive exercise in which participants find their way along a predetermined course using a map, compass, and perhaps a series of teacher-supplied clues. The objective was to find the shortest route around a series of control points." [35]

4. The children explored a cemetery to gather such information as the age of the tombstones, evidence of infant mortality rates and life expectancy and indications of epidemics. "After their day in the field," the teachers write, "the students offer hypotheses concerning the lives of the early settlers, major causes of death, patterns of family living, etc. Students are asked to test these hypotheses using library research when they return to the classroom." [36]

5. Another major activity was a litter census. Children were asked to hypothesize as to the types of litter they would find and the season during which they would find the most. Then they collected the litter, classified it, and reached conclusions.

342

In addition to these activities, the teachers indicated another boon: They were able to relate better with their students and the students were able "to gain new self-understanding and additional insight into the problems of living with other people." [37]

Teachers are encouraged to follow the example above. A structured contemporary social studies program makes it possible to use long excursions or camping trips to achieve basic social learnings.

SOCIAL STUDIES AND SPECIAL PROGRAMS

In recent years several special programs have emerged to demand a place in the curriculum, among them: (1) environmental education, (2) career education, (3) sex education, (4) consumer education, (5) law-focused education, and, more recently, (6) future studies and (7) energy education. Interest groups all over the country promote these programs, and the government and private organizations have variously allocated money to develop curriculum guides and teaching materials for these special fields. Teachers are pressured from many directions and often do not know what to do.

As was argued in an earlier chapter, all of these special programs are important areas for study, but they should be integrated into the regular social studies program as special dimensions in the areas of study and topics. Career education, for example, can easily be incorporated into the study of the family and how families meet their needs. All grades are conducive to the study of the environment, energy, and the future. Sex education also comports with the family or any other area of study. Sex education, however, should not be confined to the reproductive process. Often a teacher preparing to teach sex education runs to the resource center to find a film or a filmstrip on how babies are born. But the relationships between men and women constitute a wide field of study and children need to learn many things before learning how a woman becomes pregnant or how babies are born.

In some classrooms, and even entire schools, a special program has usurped the social studies program. Whatever the school or the excitement of a special program, a structured program should not be sacrificed. Special programs should enrich social studies, not replace it.

SUMMARY

Though the social studies program presented throughout this book is directed mainly to the graded elementary school, it can be adapted to all alternative school settings. The nongraded or the open school have objectives compatible with those of social studies, and share the inquiry approach and the method of conflict resolution advocated throughout this book.

Schools should become instrumental in eliminating racism and sexism from our society. The social studies curriculum should abandon the "melting pot" concept for a program that accurately reflects our multi-ethnic and multicultural society. Although all schools should ultimately become multi-ethnic, some schools are now attended predominantly by one ethnic minority. The social studies program in these schools should reflect that minority's history and culture and concentrate on its members' peculiar social problems. This should be done, of course, without abandoning the objectives and framework of a sound social studies program.

Early childhood education suffers from a lack of direction, which could be provided by a child-centered social studies program with the ultimate objective of developing decision-making ability. Preschool children need to develop autonomy, independence, and a healthy self-concept before they need to know the alphabet or how to count; social studies can supply those needs.

The program presented in this book is structured but flexible. As such it can be adjusted to be challenging to the gifted as well as hospitable to physically and mentally handicapped children. A program available for special education is described in this chapter.

In this chapter it is also demonstrated that multiple-day excursions or camping trips can be excellent laboratories for teaching many social studies objectives, heretofore neglected on such trips.

Finally, the regular social studies program should incorporate such special programs as environmental education, career education, sex education, consumer education, law-focused education, future studies, and energy education. However, these special programs should enrich the regular program, not replace it.

ACTIVITIES

1. Interview someone in the headquarters of your school district to find out what types of alternative schools and special programs operate in the district. Organize in groups and visit each of them to find out what kind of social studies programs they have. Discuss the findings in class.

2. From the 11 characteristics of the open school classroom presented in this chapter, design an observation checklist and each one of you visit different regular classrooms to determine the extent to which these characteristics are present. Collate the findings and discuss them. Can these characteristics be present in regular classrooms?

3. Analyze one school's social studies program or one publisher's program to determine whether it is "Anglo-American Centric," ethnic additive, or multi-ethnic.

4. Secure a copy of the multi-ethnic guidelines checklist of the National Council for the Social Studies and use it to evaluate a particular social studies program. Use the questions distributed by the Anti-Defamation League of B'nai B'rith to evaluate the multi-ethnic character of a particular school.

5. Develop a scope and sequence for a social studies program to be used in a school that enrolls many children from a specific ethnic group, one well represented in

your area. Make sure the program meets the needs of the ethnic group without neglecting the overall purposes of social studies.

6. Each member of the class design a social studies learning activity that would assist very young children to develop autonomy and independence.

7. Examine the program of a special education school to determine the extent to which they attempt to reach objectives similar to those advocated in this book for social studies.

8. Plan a specific multiple-day excursion or trip and indicate the specific social learnings that could result from it.

9. Select one of the six special programs mentioned in this chapter and find an appropriate resource to identify its objectives. Refer to the scope and sequence in Chapter 3: Through what units might it be possible to achieve these objectives?

NOTES

1. J. D. McAulay, "Social Studies for the Nongraded School," *Social Education,* 36 (April 1972), 452.

2. Susan Silverman Stodolsky, "Identifying and Evaluating Open Education," *Phi Delta Kappan,* 57 (October 1975), 113.

3. Adopted from Dan Reschley and Darrell Saber, "Open Education: Have We Been There Before?" *Phi Delta Kappan,* 55 (June 1974), 677.

4. Susan Stillman and Barbara Jordan, "Open Schools and Citizenship Education Through Involvement in the Community," *Social Education,* 40 (March 1976), 168.

5. Arthur E. Salz, "The Truly Open Classroom," *Phi Delta Kappan,* 55 (February 1974), 388.

6. Stillman and Jordan, "Open Schools," p. 168.

7. Stodolsky, "Identifying and Evaluating," p. 113.

8. Salz, "Truly Open Classroom," p. 388.

9. Stillman and Jordan, "Open Schools," p. 168.

10. Ibid., pp. 168–69.

11. Vito Perrone and Lowell Thompson, "Social Studies in the Open Classroom," *Social Education,* 36 (April 1972), 461. Reprinted with permission of the National Council for the Social Studies.

12. James A. Banks, ed., *Teaching Ethnic Studies,* 43rd Yearbook of the National Council for the Social Studies (Washington, D.C.: National Council for the Social Studies, 1973), p. 1.

13. Theodore Kaltsounis, "The Need to Indianize Indian Schools," *Phi Delta Kappan,* 53 (January 1972), 291.

14. James A. Banks, "Ethnicity: Implications for Curriculum Development and Teaching" (Paper presented at the symposium "New Perspectives in Education: Trans-Cultural Issues in Curriculum," Los Angeles, California, May 7–8, 1976), pp. 19–22.

15. Ibid., p. 21.

16. Charlotte Crabtree, "Fostering Trans-Cultural Learnings in the Social Studies: Perspectives and Practices" (Paper presented at the symposium "New Perspectives in Education: Trans-Cultural Issues in Curriculum," Los Angeles, California, May 7–8, 1976), p. 5.

17. The Council on Interracial Books for Children, *Stereotypes, Distortions and Omissions in U.S. History Textbooks* (New York [841 Broadway, 10023]: Racism and Sexism Resource Center for Educators, 1977).

18. NCSS Task Force on Ethnic Studies Curriculum Guidelines, *Curriculum Guidelines for Multiethnic Education. Position Statement* (Washington, D.C.: National Council for the Social Studies, 1976), pp. 18–41. Reprinted with permission of the National Council for the Social Studies.

19. "Is Your School Making Use of the Multi-Ethnic Experience?" (Checklist distributed by the Western Education Department of the Anti-Defamation League of B'nai B'rith, 6505 Wilshire Blvd., Los Angeles, California 90048.) Mimeographed.

20. Theodore Kaltsounis, director, *Navajo Area Curriculum Development Project: Social Studies,* 2 vols. (Window Rock, Ariz.: Branch of Curriculum and Instruction, Navajo Area Office, Bureau of Indian Affairs, 1970).

21. *Ethnic Heritage Studies Program* (Washington, D.C.: National Education Association, 1977).

22. Dale L. Brubaker, Lawrence H. Simon, and Jo Watts Williams, "A Curriculum Framework for Social Studies Curriculum and Instruction," *Social Education,* 41 (March 1977), 201–5.

23. Bernard Spodek, *Teaching in the Early Years* (Englewood Cliffs, N.J.: Prentice-Hall, 1972), p. 51; Mariann P. Winick, *Before the 3 R's* (New York: David McKay, 1973), p. viii.

24. Brubaker, Simon, and Williams, "A Curriculum Framework," p. 203.

25. Alan J. Hoffman and Thomas F. Ryan, *Social Studies and the Child's Expanding Self* (New York: Intext Educational Publishers, 1973), p. 40.

26. Spodek, "Teaching in the Early Years," p. 14.

27. Lolas E. Halverson, Mary Ann Roberton, and Christina J. Harper, "Current Research in Motor Development," *Journal of Research and Development in Education,* 6 (Spring 1973), 56–70.

28. Hoffman and Ryan, *Social Studies,* p. 40.

29. James J. Gallagher, "Phenomenal Growth and New Problems Characterize Special Education," *Phi Delta Kappan,* 55 (April 1974), 516.

30. Ibid., p. 520.

31. Hunter O. Brooks and Paula R. Barber, "Alternative Schools in a Traditional Setting," *Social Education,* 37 (November 1973), 651.

32. Herbert Goldstein, *The Social Learning Curriculum* (Columbus, Ohio: Charles E. Merrill, 1976). Reprinted with the permission of Charles E. Merrill Publishing Co.

33. Robert I. Dwyer, "School Camping Programs: Ecology in the Outdoor Classroom," *Social Education,* 35 (January 1971), 74–77.

34. Michael Jacobson and Stuart Palousky, "School Camping and Elementary Social Studies," *Social Education,* 40 (January 1976), 44–46.

35. Ibid., p. 45.

36. Ibid.

37. Ibid.

Studying this chapter will enable the reader to:

1. explain the need for cooperation among teachers, administrators, and parents in implementing a sound social studies program.
2. define "goal displacement," and describe its effect on social studies in the elementary school.
3. identify some activities outside the classroom in which a teacher can become involved to develop commitment toward social studies.
4. identify several ways in which administrators can contribute toward the development and maintenance of a sound social studies program.
5. explain how the parents can be vital in the school context in implementing a strong social studies program.
6. identify ways in which the parents can help their children at home achieve social studies objectives.

GUIDELINES TO TEACHERS, ADMINISTRATORS, AND PARENTS

We saw in Chapter 1 that the "back to basics" movement has put elementary school social studies at a disadvantage. This is substantiated by a national survey on the status of social studies conducted under the direction of Richard Gross, who reports:

> An accurate breakdown in subject or time allotments in most elementary school systems just does not exist. Nevertheless, in both our state and district responses we were informed over and over again that elementary teachers are backing away from the social studies. Informal reports of district surveys in both Montana and California, for example, indicated that 70 percent or more of the K–4 teachers were doing little or nothing with social studies in the current "back to basics" mania. A survey of two Colorado districts was reported as revealing that elementary teachers are averaging but one hour per week devoted to social studies. State fundamental tests, which usually do not include evaluation of social studies learnings, have been launched in several states and these contribute further to the debacle.[1]

The arguments in favor of social studies for the elementary school were offered in Chapter 1 and will not be repeated here, but the phenomenon can possibly be briefly explained. As demonstrated in Chapter 1, there are three levels of educational objectives: (1) broad, state or district objectives; (2) overall objectives for the subject; and (3) specific instructional objectives. Dale Brubaker and Roland Nelson label these three levels purposes, goals, and objectives, respectively.[2] They point out that

> One of the problems in working with objectives is that they may become the total focus of the school to the point that those making decisions lose sight of the original goals of the organization. . . . This phenomenon of overly focusing on objectives is referred to by many social scientists as "goal displacement." [3]

Is it possible that elementary school administrators and teachers become so involved with the objectives of specific skills that they forget the broader goals of education? How else explain why states and districts issue goals that emphasize the development of the individual's ability to cope with the social and physical environment, while in the classroom the systematic pursuit of such goals is neglected? How else explain the substantial or total neglect of the study of society and the development of social skills? If most of the broad educational objectives sound like social studies objectives, why is social studies given little attention in the elementary school? Is this neglect the responsibility of the administrators, the teachers, or the parents? Indications are that all three are responsible.

This entire book has concentrated on what the teacher can do as the director of the teaching–learning process to assist children to understand and cope with their social environment. But whether teachers successfully implement the suggestions depends to a great extent on the support of administrators and the students' parents. The effective teaching of any subject, and more so the social studies, is a cooperative venture.

Administrative and parental support is rarely easy to come by. Usually teachers must aggressively seek it. Some are successful, while others become discouraged and give up. Persistence and effective rebuttal of arguments against a sound social studies program require a degree of commitment from the teacher. This commitment develops through personal involvement in a variety of ways other than classroom activities. This last chapter outlines several suggestions for such personal involvement.

The chapter includes also guidelines for administrators and parents— few of whom, it is true, will ever lay their hands on this book. But the guidelines are provided so that teachers know what to ask of them when seeking their support. (Also, most teachers are or will become parents, and some eventually will become administrators.)

GUIDELINES FOR TEACHERS

Note that not all suggestions for the teacher are cited here for the first time; some have been made earlier in the book. They are repeated here to provide a complete picture of how teachers may develop commitment in social studies and wide support for what they do.

1. *Be aggressive, but also be tactful when you deal with administrators and parents.* Administrators and parents usually hold their positions or opinions sincerely. Antagonizing them may erect a wall between them and you. You need their understanding; no drastic change can take place without first winning the support of the "establishment." Listen to them and reply to their positions with logical arguments.

2. *Try to develop a philosophical point of view as a social studies teacher.* To argue with administrators and parents you need a philosophical point of view. Do you teach social studies because you strongly believe in what you are trying to accomplish? Helping pupils function well in contemporary society should be your ultimate aim.

3. *Study to understand world events.* A deep personal desire to understand the course of world events is indispensable. Read as much as you can in all fields of social sciences and do not hesitate to venture into analy-

sis of what you read. In planning a master's program, or when you simply go back to college for refresher studies, take some social science courses—especially those that touch upon the major problems of our society, such as urban geography, minority groups in the United States, the labor movement, and the like. Do not limit yourself to education courses only.

When taking substantive courses, make sure you obtain from them what you need as a teacher. Identify generalizations and issues and ask the professor to verify their validity. Use these generalizations and issues to evaluate your program and determine whether it is accurate and up to date. Submit teaching units you have developed and ask the professor to evaluate their concepts, generalizations, and issues.

4. *Keep in mind that you are an expert in teaching.* When it comes to teaching, everyone knows how to do it best and is ready with advice for the teacher. People forget that the teacher has studied teaching for years and also has a wealth of firsthand experience. Stand up for your professional rights, but first be sure of your professional stature and know how to defend what you stand for intelligently.

5. *Travel as much as you can.* Traveling is one of the most enriching experiences. If you can afford to go to Europe or Latin America or any other part of the world, do so. But you can visit much closer places without much expense. If you are teaching in a rural area, visit the nearest large city and observe situations related to what you are teaching the youngsters. Visit ports, slum areas, suburbs, industrial areas, museums, and historical places. Just as artists are noted for perceiving from an artistic point of view, teachers should develop a teacher's viewpoint—in essence, intellectual curiosity.

6. *Open your classroom and even your house to foreign visitors or individuals from many subcultures.* Some visitors might not appear to have anything to offer directly to children. Get to know them anyway. Much can be learned in informal conversations with them.

7. *Join various professional organizations.* The most important organization for teachers interested in social studies is the National Council for the Social Studies. Many teachers do not even know that this organization exists. This advice is directed especially to teachers who majored in social sciences as undergraduate students. Find out about the state and local social studies organizations and participate in their activities. Make sure your school subscribes to *Social Education*, the official journal of the National Council for the Social Studies. The elementary supplement of this journal will keep you abreast of what is happening in social studies and provide you with practical ideas for teaching. Start a collection of professional materials in social studies. For this task consult a special article by John Haas, Sydney Meredith, and Karen Wiley.[4]

8. *Join civic and community organizations.* Ours is an age of groups. It is difficult for someone to understand and participate in society without

being a member of various groups. Within such groups the teacher can learn the dynamics of community life and the backgrounds of the children.

9. *Try new methods advocated in research articles.* The ferment in social studies has stimulated much research. Teachers should not only read research reports but also should try in their classrooms some of the new methods recommended. Do not hesitate to depart from routine. The most likely result is that the children will become excited about social studies.

10. *Listen to consultants and seriously consider their advice, but do not allow them to dictate what you should do.* This suggestion is concerned mainly with outside consultants, but it does not exclude regular social studies consultants. Consultants are good for answering questions and providing stimulation; they should work with the teachers in developing a general framework of operation. But the details within the classroom should be the duty of the teacher, who usually knows best how to work effectively with a particular group of children.

11. *Do not forget that you are a professional person.* Your ultimate responsibility is to the children. You do not work for the principal. Both of you should work together so that the children can learn. The principal has a responsibility to evaluate you, but you should demand that the evaluation be by clearly established criteria and well-defined method.

12. *Always talk about the children with respect.* Often teachers' rooms turn into gossip centers where it is not unusual to hear teachers refer to children as "brats," "monsters," and other colorful words. This is totally unprofessional.

13. *Do not isolate yourself from other teachers.* There is much to be learned from each other. Visit other rooms when possible and open your classroom to your colleagues. Discuss your plans with them and ask for suggestions.

GUIDELINES FOR ADMINISTRATORS

1. *Make sure you are not guilty of "goal displacement."* Each state or district usually has a set of goals for education. Examine them carefully and compare them with those of the teachers. Specify a month during which the teachers should record all the objectives they try to reach daily. Classify these objectives according to the district goals. Are there adequate objectives under each one of the goals? If not, you are guilty of goal displacement. Every time the school is about to invest large sums for new materials, make sure the materials considered reflect all the goals specified for your district or state. (If no such goals exist, they should be developed.) A program not based on broad goals is like a house built on sand or like starting on a long trip with no real destination.

2. *Direct your school forward to basics instead of back to basics.* Ben Brodinsky quoted one educator as saying: "Back to basics? Look, we're moving *forward* to basics. We're broadening the basics to teach children to think, analyze problems, make wise decisions, develop confidence in themselves. As for the three R's, why return when we've never left them? . . ." [5] If there is pressure in your community to define the "basics" narrowly as the three Rs, involve the school board and the entire community in discussing the implications. They are certain to favor the three Rs, but, given the chance to reflect, they would not want to relinquish certain advancements in education. Brodinsky reports:

> Although four-fifths of the nation's school boards believe their schools should put greater emphasis on reading, writing and arithmetic, according to a National School Boards Association survey, few boards have adopted policies to set into motion formal back-to-basics programs. . . . Why? . . . [Brodinsky quotes a school board member:] "Consider what it would mean to policy development to go all the way back to the basics as some partisans demand. . . . It would mean restructuring the board's policy statements on philosophy, goals, instructional program, discipline, homework, counseling, extra-curricular activities—to mention but a few topics. No board is about to do that." [6]

3. *Provide an atmosphere that allows the teachers to see the need for and take the initiative in curriculum improvement.* Pronouncements about

curriculum development and revision that come exclusively from the administration are not likely to produce the desired results. Teachers work best on curriculum not when they are told to do so but when they feel the need. If there is a need for curriculum improvement and the teachers do not see it, the administrator's job is to develop awareness of this need by indirect methods, not by edicts.

4. *Give teachers the flexibility to be creative.* Each classroom being a unique situation, the teachers should not be expected to follow a rigid approach. A teacher who is convinced that teaching can be better done without a textbook should be allowed to do so whatever the school board ruling may be. Scheduling should also be flexible: In planning the schedule, learning activities are of first priority—not lunch, routine health activities, announcements, and the like. Let us not forget that learning is the primary responsibility of the school. Everything else is designed to facilitate the learning process.

5. *See that the school builds a good library and keeps it open for the children at all times.* There is no excuse for any school not to have a good library. Getting a library is one thing, using it properly is another. Some libraries stay closed most of the time, each class being allowed access one hour a day or only twice a week. Many librarians tend to be overly protective of the books, and the children hesitate to borrow them because they are afraid that they might not be able to keep them in perfect condition. Books are to be used and worn out; and it should be expected that some will be lost.

6. *See that teachers also obtain other types of necessary materials.* Several chapters in this book describe the various types of materials and their importance in the teaching of social studies. Make sure the teachers obtain these materials. A film, for example, is of benefit only if it can be used at the proper time in the development of a particular unit.

7. *Support the teachers in the treatment of controversial issues.* Controversial issues have a place in the elementary school, but many teachers hesitate to address them for fear of causing conflict with some parents. Often such conflict has lost teachers their jobs. The administrator should protect the teacher and find ways of enlightening the public in regard to the treatment of controversial issues.

8. *Support the teachers in social action.* Dealing with issues provides opportunities for decision making, which in turn implies action. To engage in social action, the teacher and the children need moral and logistical support. Make it possible for the teachers to use the community as a laboratory for social learnings.

9. *Do not use faculty meetings to make announcements.* Announcements should be mimeographed and distributed; the meetings should be turned over to the teachers for professional matters. Social studies is a

continuously evolving subject and there is much to be brought to the teachers' attention for discussion and implementation.

10. *Be a colleague to the teachers.* Administrators who consistently assume an attitude of superiority or refer to the faculty as "my teachers" or to the school as "my school" are not apt to promote good morale. Educating children is a common responsibility of both teachers and administrators. Both groups are professionals. They should work in a spirit of cooperation, not of jeopardy and insecurity. The school should not be viewed as a factory or organized as management versus labor. The school is an educational institution and should be referred to as "our school."

11. *Evaluate the teachers in your school on the basis not of personal qualities but of progress toward achieving predetermined objectives.* Accountability has forced school administrators throughout the nation to take teacher evaluation seriously. The Executive Director and the Associate Director of the Education Commission of the States wrote: "The eagerness to evaluate is valid, but individual states and school districts need to first establish for themselves what they want to achieve, how they want to pursue their goals, and who they want to measure their performance." [7] If teachers show progress toward achieving the established objectives, they are succeeding; if they do not, administrators and teachers should work together to remedy the situation. Judging teachers and the entire school performance on the basis of objectives is called in the literature Management-by-Objectives (MBO). Says one administrator: "MBO does not want to know if a teacher (or an administrator) is 'energetic, healthy, personable, and cooperative.' MBO wants to know what he or she planned to do that semester and the result of the planning." [8]

12. *Administrators should keep abreast of new developments in social studies.* Few elementary schools subscribe to *Social Education*, the official journal of the National Council for the Social Studies. This is an excellent journal to keep administrators and teachers alike abreast of new developments. *Social Education* is usually perceived as a journal for secondary teachers, but this is not true. Every other month the journal publishes an extensive supplement directed to elementary teachers. Moreover, many general articles apply to both elementary and secondary teachers.

13. *Know the dynamics of the community and use them for the benefit of the teachers.* Teachers often become the victims of a small minority in the community with some narrow interest to protect. Most parents are willing to reason, to understand, and to accept sensible programs. Instead of yielding to the attacks of pressure groups, organize open meetings in which more than one side of an issue will be heard. Individuals or groups that oppose school policies and practices are well known to administrators, but do you know who your strong supporters are?

GUIDELINES FOR PARENTS

It is well established among educators that the school is only one of many educational agencies in the community. Among all the others, the family, and particularly the parents, are probably the most influential in the child's development. Parents can support a good program and make it work or they can destroy it. The school and the parents must therefore be in constant communication. To facilitate communication between parents and the social studies teachers from kindergarten through high school, Daniel Roselle, the editor of *Social Education*, wrote a guide. Roselle attempts to inform the parents by answering the following questions: [9]

1. What are the social studies?
2. How are the social studies taught?
3. Why do social studies educators say that knowing information is not enough?
4. Why are there so many social studies courses?
5. What is happening to the language of the social studies?
6. What issues are discussed in social studies classes?
7. How can parents help their children in the social studies?

The first six questions are answered throughout this book. The seventh question is answered in this section. Several guidelines are provided to enable parents to become helpful partners in the teaching of social studies. These guidelines reflect Roselle's but are adapted for the elementary school:

1. *Give the children opportunities to make free choices.* This does not mean that there will be no rules at home. Within the framework of the rules, however, there are quite often several options. For instance, the children must have cereal in the morning, but you can allow them to choose which kind to have.

2. *Encourage your children to express opinions.* For example, is park A or park B better? Where do you think we should spend this afternoon, George? Here are several books. Which one would you prefer to read? Why do you like that advertisement?

3. *Each time your children make a decision, ask whether other alternatives were considered. Encourage the children to do so.* A child may say, for example: "I am going to use the $10 grandfather gave me to buy a good knife." Find out how the knife was decided upon. Were other purchases thought of? Are other things needed that you could bring to the child's attention without biasing the decision?

4. *Encourage your children to pursue hobbies.* Hobbies are indicators of children's strong interests or values. The more they have, the better. Hobbies enable them to feel a sense of accomplishment and pride, and help them to develop independence and a stronger self-image.

357

5. *Take every opportunity to show that you trust your children.* Take them seriously and do not routinely doubt their word. Trust them with such things as cameras, safe power tools, and the like. Make them feel that they can handle them.

6. *If you have more than one child, treat them all equally and fairly.* Provide an atmosphere of harmony, cooperation, and concern for each other rather than competition and jealousy. Never play one child against another.

7. *Be a model citizen to your children.* Show an interest in what is happening in your community. Exercise your right to vote. Discuss candidates and election issues in the presence of your children and allow them to participate. Whenever possible, speak out against discrimination and in favor of human rights. Evaluate the government's actions and talk about such matters in the presence of your children. Participate in civic activities intended for the common good.

8. *Make sure your children have some basic information about our country.* However young your children are, make sure they at least know the names of our country and of its current president. If possible, they should know the names of your governor and your mayor as well as any historical information about your area's contributions to U.S. history.

9. *Discuss world, national, and local events as a family.* Watch at least one news broadcast daily and make sure to comment about the news at the dinner table or whenever the family is together.

10. *Have magazines and newspapers at home.* Such items will eventually attract the children's attention.

11. *Have a globe or a world map around the house.* Whenever a place is mentioned in the news or in a family conversation, locate it on the globe or map.

12. *Encourage your children to read books.* Spend some time with your children in the local library and encourage them to check out books. Let them decide what they want to read. If they ask for assistance make several suggestions from which they can choose.

13. *Have a good reference encyclopedia at home.* Refer to Chapter 8 of this book for specific encyclopedias.

14. *Encourage your children to take advantage of appropriate television programs.* Check the TV guide weekly and identify shows that help increase children's knowledge about people and the world.

15. *Join the PTA.* As a member of this organization encourage the discussion of educational issues. Do not allow its activities to deteriorate to raising money for the playground or having a couple of social events. Discuss the curriculum; examine the textbooks the children use. Invite outside speakers to give you their views on what is practiced in your school or what more can be done. Make the PTA a strong positive force. In each community there are groups that, though representing small segments of

the community, are vocal in opposing school policies and programs. Try to play a constructive role by reacting to their arguments.

16. *Make sure the schools have a rounded program.* Many schools have fallen victim to the pressures for accountability and concentrate only on objectives for which they can produce test scores. Such a practice displaces important educational goals and your children are shortchanged. Make sure social studies, art, music, and science are not eliminated or treated casually.

17. *Support your school's efforts to update the programs.* Do not expect things to be done exactly as they were when you were in elementary school. Social studies has changed considerably since the 1950s. Try to understand these changes and support your school in adopting new approaches.

18. *Notice significant holidays.* One school known for the quality of its multicultural program prepared a calendar in which national and important religious holidays from all over the world are identified. Do your children know the significance of Thanksgiving or of Martin Luther King Day? Do they know why the fifth of May is an important holiday for Chicanos?

19. *Visit historical places around your community or while traveling.* As was emphasized in Chapter 9, your community can be the best laboratory for the teaching of social studies. Use it as much as possible. Check with the local chamber of commerce or with the local historical society to identify historical places in your community. Be especially sure to take your children to the nearest museum.

20. *Eat in ethnic restaurants whenever possible or visit different churches.* Use restaurants and churches to teach your children about the various subcultures in our society.

21. *Invite foreign students and people from different cultural groups to your home.* Those living in university towns have an excellent opportunity to bring their children into close contact with people from other countries. However, local exchanges between various cultural groups can also be good learning experiences.

22. *Visit government offices and various service agencies.* Schools usually visit the fire station, the post office, or the local airport, but field trips are usually difficult for a school to plan. You can take your children to a court session, to a police station, a factory, a farm, and many other such places.

SUMMARY

Administrators, teachers, and parents are often at odds with each other. Much confusion is caused by attention to school details to the neglect of important educational goals—in other words, goal displacement has occurred. As a result, children are deprived of a rounded education. Administrators, teachers, and parents are advised to act as checks on each other to assure that their school is not guilty of goal displacement and that social studies is given adequate attention.

Also it is emphasized that administrators and teachers must see themselves as colleagues and work together for the common purpose of educating the children. Several suggestions are made as to how both groups can improve their professional stature. Their relationships and their behavior within the school context should serve as models for the children.

Parents are also recognized as partners in the teaching of social studies. A number of suggestions are given as to how parents can assist in the social development of their children.

It is hoped that with the close cooperation of administrators, teachers, and parents, a social studies program will emerge that develops each child's powers to live successfully in our society and to try to improve it. It is entirely possible that a strengthened social studies program will further understanding among people and help eliminate some of the major evils that plague our society. It is possible that more people will work toward the common good, guided by the rational process and the still-valid principles of our heritage.

ACTIVITIES

1. Using the guidelines for teachers, prepare a questionnaire to determine how many of the items suggested are practiced by teachers. Each student contact an elementary school teacher and use the questionnaire. Collate the data and have a discussion.

2. Repeat the above activity with administrators, using the appropriate guidelines.

3. Do the same with the parents, using the appropriate guidelines.

4. To one or more administrators, give a copy of the guidelines for administrators to study. Ask them to come give their reactions to the guidelines.

5. Repeat the above activity with a panel of parents.

6. As a class prepare a list of general trends in social studies education and interview teachers or school administrators to find out what types of individuals or groups may oppose or support certain trends.

7. Inquire with the local district whether there are any controversies concerning the teaching of social studies. What are they and what is being done about them?

NOTES

1. Richard E. Gross, "The Status of the Social Studies in the Public School of the United States: Fact and Impressions of a National Survey," *Social Education,* 41 (March 1977), 198.

2. Dale L. Brubaker and Roland H. Nelson, Jr., "The School as an Organization: A Determinant of Social Studies Curriculum and Instruction" (Publication #2 of the University of North Carolina—Greensboro, Humanistic Education Project, October 1973). Mimeographed.

3. Ibid., pp. 5–6.

4. John D. Haas, Sydney J. Meredith, and Karen B. Wiley, "A Social Studies Professional Library," *Social Education,* 40 (May 1976), 291–300.

5. Ben Brodinsky, "Back to the Basics: The Movement and Its Meaning," *Phi Delta Kappan,* 58 (March 1977), 523.

6. Ibid., p. 524.

7. Wendell Pierce and Ronald Smith, "Evaluation Should Be a Welcomed Experience," *Instructor,* 83 (April 1974), 34.

8. Robert R. Spillane, "Management by Objectives (or) I'll Try to Find Time to Observe More Teachers Next Year," *Phi Delta Kappan,* 58 (April 1977), 625.

9. Daniel Roselle, *A Parent's Guide to the Social Studies* (Washington, D.C.: National Council for the Social Studies, 1974).

INDEX

Evaluation (*cont.*)
and measurement (*see* Measurement)
placement diagnostic, 180
program (*see* Program evaluation)
remedial diagnostic, 180, 183
summative, 160, 176, 183, 228
techniques of, 160
types of, 183
Excursions, 324, 342
Expanding horizons, 228
Experiences, children's, 330
Exposition, 80, 93
definition of, 86
Expository teaching, 86

Facts, 82
Fair, Jean, 24, 108
Family of Man, 215
Farrar, Charles, 279
Feeney, G., 321
Fennessey, G, 313, 320
Fenton, Edwin, 88, 108
Festinger, Leo, 140
Fiedler, W., 321
Fieldtrip, 246, 260
Firnesz, K. M., 304, 320
Fleckenstein, John V., 108
Fletcher, J. L., 313, 321
Formal education. *See* Education
Formative evaluation. *See* Evaluation
Formative objectives, 32
Foster, Clifford, 86, 107
Fox, Robert, 221
Fraenkel, Jack R., 43, 140, 155, 174
Frazier, Alexander, 54, 79
Future studies, 343

Galbraith, Ronald, 20, 24
Gallagher, James, 97, 108, 339, 346
Games, 300, 302, 306–9
illustrations of, 307–8
value of, research evidence, 312–13
Generalizations, 46, 80, 215, 225, 272, 286, 352
classification of, 64
components of, 85
definition of, 50
development of, 63, 85
examples of, 39, 50, 68–76
and instructional objectives, 100

Generalizations (*cont.*)
reduction of, 84, 86
Geography
cultural, 228
urban, 352
Gifted children, 324, 338, 339
Globes. *See* Maps and globes
Goal displacement, 348, 350
Godbold, John V., 43
Goldstein, Herbert, 339, 346
Gordon, Ira J., 199, 210
Government publications, 246, 268
Graphs, 272, 296–97
Greater Cleveland Social Science Program, 55–57, 217, 218
Gronlund, Norman E., 179, 185, 191, 196, 209, 210
Gross, Richard, 237, 244, 274, 299, 304, 320, 350
Grouping, flexible, 327
Group work, 191
Grubola, Marion R., 271
Guilford, J. R., 42, 43, 108

Haas, John, 352, 361
Halverson, Lolas, 338, 346
Hamburg, Dennis, 157, 174
Hand, Harold, 132, 140
Handicapped children, 324
Hanna, Paul, 279, 299
Harmin, Merrill, 18, 24, 33, 113, 134, 140, 141
Harper, Christina, 338, 346
Harrison, Sylvia, 107
Hastings, Thomas J., 32, 42, 182, 209
Herber, Harold, 244
Hertzberg, Hazel, 51, 79
Hill, Wilhelmina, 155, 174
Hills, James, 108
Historical approach, 228
Historical research, 258
Historical residues, 258
Hodgson, Frank, 54, 79
Hoff, Lynn, 320
Hoffman, Alan, 258, 270, 337, 346
"How To Do It Series," 261
Hunkins, Francis P., 99, 109
Hypothesis, 88

Imperatives, cultural, 2, 21
Indian history, 331
Indians, American, 49, 249, 331
Individualization of instruction, 181, 193, 249, 327

Inductive reasoning, 87
Inductive thinking, 80
Information, basic, 358
Ingraham, Leonard W., 293, 299
Inner city, 310
Inner direction, 117
Inquiry, 15, 50, 80, 86, 93, 94, 96, 217, 228
definition of, 87
models of, 88, 94–95
process, 17
steps of, 88–89
Instructional objectives, 26, 77, 80, 100, 180, 330
definition of, 29
development of, 41
examples of, 30, 40, 102, 128
steps in determining, 36
types of, 33–34
value of, 30
Integration, 310
Intellectual skills, 34, 80, 93, 225, 296
categories of, 34
lists of, 90–93
Interaction, human, 310
Interaction skills, 6
Interactional process, 258
Interdisciplinary projects, 215, 225
Interest inventories, 198
Internalization, 112, 113
Interracial conflict, 263
Issues, 17, 46, 110, 112, 225, 272, 286, 331, 352
alternative solutions of, 121, 122
controversial, 65, 66, 355
criteria for, 66
dealing with, sample plan, 127
definition of, 65
examples of, 39, 68–76
and facts, 120–21
presentation of, 119
resolution of
and decision making, 120
steps in, 119

Jacobson, Michael, 342, 347
Jarolimek, John, 51, 79, 96, 107
Johnson, David W., 260, 270
Johnson, Stephen C., 287, 299
Johnston, Montgomery A., 67
Jones, Thomas, 20, 24
Jordan, Barbara, 328, 329, 345
Joyce, Bruce, 49, 79